Quandaries and Quests

Center for Archaeological Investigations

Southern Illinois University at Carbondale

Visiting Scholar Conference Volumes

Lithic Resource Procurement:
Proceedings from the Second Conference
on Prehistoric Chert Exploitation
(Occasional Paper No. 4)
edited by Susan C. Vehik

Foraging, Collecting, and Harvesting:
Archaic Period Subsistence and Settlement
in the Eastern Woodlands
(Occasional Paper No. 6)
edited by Sarah W. Neusius

Emergent Horticultural Economies
of the Eastern Woodlands
(Occasional Paper No. 7)
edited by William F. Keegan

Tracing Archaeology's Past:
The Historiography of Archaeology
(Southern Illinois University Press,
Publications in Archaeology)
edited by Andrew L. Christenson

Between Bands and States
(Occasional Paper No. 9)
edited by Susan A. Gregg

Processual and Postprocessual Archaeologies:
Multiple Ways of Knowing the Past
(Occasional Paper No. 10)
edited by Robert W. Preucel

Quandaries and Quests

Visions of Archaeology's Future

Edited by
LuAnn Wandsnider

Center for Archaeological Investigations
Southern Illinois University at Carbondale
Occasional Paper No. 20

CC
173
Q36
1992

Copyright © 1992 by the Board of Trustees, Southern Illinois University
All rights reserved
Printed in the United States of America
ISBN: 0-88104-075-4
Library of Congress Catalog Card Number: 91-75555

Edited by Ruth N. Kissell
Designed by Linda Jorgensen-Buhman
Production supervised by Donna Whitfield Butler
Word processing by Brenda Blythe Wells
Graphics layout by Thomas Gatlin

Contents

Figures and Tables   vii
Preface   ix

1. Quandaries and Quests
   LuAnn Wandsnider   1

I. Critical Archaeological Resources

2. Commerce or Service: Models of Practice in Archaeology
   Michael J. Shott   9

3. Managing America's Archaeological Resources
   Francis P. McManamon   25

4. Where the Money Goes: Current Trends in Archaeological Funding
   Miriam T. Stark   41

5. The Potential for Future Relationships Between Archaeologists and Native Americans
   Lynne Goldstein   59

6. Reflections on Critical Archaeological Resources
   LuAnn Wandsnider   72

II. Archaeological Paradigms and Concepts

7. Global Cultural Resource Archaeology in the Early Twenty-First Century
   Alan H. Simmons   79

8. A Feminist Program for Nonsexist Archaeology
   Suzanne M. Spencer-Wood   98

9. Archaeology in a Democratic Society: A Critical Theory Perspective
   Mark P. Leone and Robert W. Preucel   115

10. Conceptual Issues in Americanist Archaeology: A Commentary
    Linda S. Cordell — 136

III. Archaeological Tools and Analysis

11. Future Directions: Management of the Archaeological Data Base
    Anne I. Woosley — 147

12. Instrumentation and the Future of Archaeology
    Ronald L. Bishop — 160

13. Computer Technology, Paradigms, and Quantified Archaeological Analysis
    LuAnn Wandsnider and Timothy A. Kohler — 170

14. Ethnoarchaeology: Obnoxious Spectator, Trivial Pursuit, or the Keys to a Time Machine?
    Steven R. Simms — 186

15. Directions in Archaeological Analysis: A Commentary
    Nan A. Rothschild — 199

IV. Archaeological Programs and Goals

16. Archaeology and Evolutionary Science
    Robert C. Dunnell — 209

17. Archaeology and Behavioral Science: Manifesto for an Imperial Archaeology
    Michael Brian Schiffer — 225

18. The Role of Theory in Solving Enduring Archaeological Problems
    Alan P. Sullivan III — 239

19. Toward a Reconciliation of Processual and Postprocessual Archaeology
    Robert L. Kelly — 254

20. Visions of Archaeology's Future: Some Comments
    Jeremy A. Sabloff — 266

Contributors — 273

Figures and Tables

Figures

3-1.	Percentage of costs by activity for federal archaeology, 1987	33
4-1.	NSF predoctoral and postdoctoral funding for New World research	44
4-2.	NSF predoctoral funding by geographic area, past and present	44
4-3.	NSF funding by subject (predoctoral and postdoctoral combined): 1986–1989	47
4-4.	Proportion of academic versus nonacademic research reported in *American Antiquity*: 1970–1990	51
4-5.	Dissertation subjects by North Americanists across culture areas (1977–1989 sample)	54
4-6.	New analytic techniques and predoctoral funding	54
4-7.	Geographic areas of funding for ethnoarchaeological doctoral research	55
13-1.	Proportion of *American Antiquity* articles with different levels of quantification	172
18-1.	Map of Site AZ I:1:20(ASM) showing the distribution of artifact density classes and the spatial extent of subsite areas defined on the basis of artifact density clinal variation	242
18-2.	Cumulative percentage graph of debitage assemblage variation between the six subsite areas at Site AZ I:1:20 (ASM)	243
18-3.	Bar chart of plainware percentages for subsite Areas 2 and 3 at Site AZ I:1:20(ASM)	244

18-4. Profile illustrating architectural elements at Site AZ I:1:17 (ASM) ... 246

18-5. Bar chart of the lengths of 14 manos recovered from Site AZ I:1:17(ASM) ... 248

Tables

2-1. Artifact Recovery Rate per Inspection and by Density in Selected Studies ... 12

3-1. Federal Archaeological Activities: Identification and Evaluation; Research Activities and Costs, 1987 ... 27

3-2. Federal Archaeological Activities: Identification and Evaluation; Research Activities and Results, 1987 ... 29

3-3. Federal Archaeological Activities: Data Recovery Activities, 1987 ... 30

Preface

The chapters in this volume were first presented as papers at the Center for Archaeological Investigations' Seventh Annual Visiting Scholar Conference, *The Future of the Past: American Archaeology in A.D. 2001*, at Southern Illinois University at Carbondale in the spring of 1990. At the conference, contributors and other participants were invited to reflect on critical aspects of the current and future state of Americanist archaeology. The present volume developed from this deliberation.

Support for this volume and for the conference from which it sprang came from many people in many quarters. It is my pleasure to acknowledge them here. First, I thank George Gumerman and the staff at the Center for Archaeological Investigations—Brian Butler, Kim Smiley, and Patrice Teltser—for the opportunity to ponder the state and future of Americanist archaeology as a Visiting Scholar at the Center. Others there who aided the effort include Deanna Diel, Carolyn Taylor, Pat Harris, and Amy Speiss, and their assistance is much appreciated.

The conference was jointly sponsored by the Center and the SIUC Division of Continuing Education. Andy Marcec and his staff at Continuing Education ensured that the conference ran smoothly, for which I am most appreciative. Chancellor and Mrs. Lawrence Pettit graciously extended their hospitality to the conference attendees. I thank them and SIUC President and Mrs. John Guyon for hosting the congenial gathering and, for her organization of it, Joni Mecum. I am grateful likewise to Victoria Molfese, director of the SIUC Office of Research Development and Administration, and John Jackson, dean of the College of Liberal Arts, who provided financial assistance. I am also indebted to Department of Anthropology students, especially Lisa Renken and Jim Carucci, for innumerable services.

The volume itself reflects the careful regard of the Center's Director of Publications, Patrice Teltser, and her staff, Donna Butler, Brenda Wells, and Tom Gatlin. I thank them for that care and for their help at the conference. I also wish to acknowledge Ruth Kissell, whose editorial skills contributed greatly to the finished product. I expressly want to thank Patrice who, above and beyond the call of either duty or friendship, served as a conduit of information between me and the volume authors while I was in India. She also furnished critical feedback as well as hours of thought-provoking discussion.

Travel expenses to attend the conference were borne by the institutions with which the participants are affiliated and by the participants themselves. Without their personal sacrifices, the conference could not have happened. I appreciate greatly this contribution of the participants as well as that of their thoughts and words. I especially want to acknowledge Linda Cordell, Nan Rothschild, and Jerry Sabloff for their exceptional service in their roles of critical commentators. William A. Longacre II and Charles McGimsey III made important contributions to the conference that unfortunately could not be included here; I remain grateful to them for their stimulating conference participation.

Finally, at the University of Nebraska-Lincoln, Dorothy McEwen assisted in bringing this effort to fruition. I greatly appreciate her help and the support of the Department of Anthropology.

1. Quandaries and Quests

LuAnn Wandsnider

Americanist archaeology, that is, archaeology with an anthropological foundation commonly practiced by archaeologists schooled in North America, is in a quandary. In the vast amount of archaeological research conducted since the glory days of culture history, no one overarching paradigm can be recognized. Some view this chaos as a healthy diversity that enables the pursuit of an articulated hierarchy of goals (e.g., Schiffer 1988) and as evidence of a maturing discipline (Trigger 1989:xiii). Others (Hodder 1985, 1986; Tilley and Shanks 1987) see it as evidence of the inadequacies, sometimes considered fatal, of the new archaeology, the first research program to attract significant allegiance since the 1930s and 1940s. Still others lament this anarchic state, pointing to the deleterious effects it has on the conservation of a dwindling prehistoric archaeological record (Watson 1991) and on the cogent training of students (Binford 1989).

As a distressed and impatient archaeologist sympathizing with the sentiments of the latter, I seek to expedite consensus in the field through an examination of archaeological goals and practice. The selection of the contributing authors reflects my personal inclination that an archaeological science is a good and desirable thing. The chapters further reflect, I think, a maturation in our understanding of how an archaeological science should perform. That is, they acknowledge that the external world influences our notions about how archaeological variation may be explained but defer to the practice of science to evaluate those notions, recognizing also the arbitrary way in which the scientific method can be applied (McCormack 1982). Further, the volume affirms that to sort through good, bad, and ugly science, discourse among ourselves and with the empirical world is imperative (Hull 1988). Thus, this volume, with its exposé format, serves as the vehicle to convey these critical analyses to the marketplace of discussion.

Americanist archaeology today generates three main products, namely, representations of the archaeological record, the past, and processes of change through time. Rare agreement among archaeologists exists on the low or underdeveloped or unknown quality of these products. For example, Cowgill

Quandaries and Quests: Visions of Archaeology's Future, edited by LuAnn Wandsnider. Center for Archaeological Investigations, Occasional Paper No. 20. © 1992 by the Board of Trustees, Southern Illinois University. All rights reserved. ISBN 0-88104-075-4.

(1986, 1989) calls attention to the unknown accuracy and precision of survey data and the attendant lack of comparability of data between projects. Descriptive scenarios that allege knowledge about past states or conditions are likewise recognized as inadequate, resting as they often do on unwarranted assumptions about the meaning of particular configurations of archaeological material (Binford 1981; Dunnell 1982; Thomas 1986). In as much as understanding of evolutionary processes depends on exactly that knowledge, as well as on accommodative theory, the interpretive vacuum poses serious impediments to the discipline.

Unhappiness with current archaeological representations is pervasive (e.g., contributors to Meltzer et al. 1986), and debate continues on their appropriate form and the means of their production. Many prescriptions for fortifying the development of descriptive and interpretative scenarios have been offered, including more technology (Fagan 1989 and other contributors to *Archaeology* 1989:42[1]), conceptual revolution (Ebert 1989; Willey and Sabloff 1980:259), theoretical revolution (Dunnell 1989; O'Connell et al. 1982), and investment in method (Binford 1986; Thomas 1986). The proof of the pudding, however, is in the eating. So far, no one program has produced a descriptive or interpretive scenario that a majority of archaeologists acknowledge as contributing knowledge about the past that is nontrivial, well warranted, and, with respect to the informational content of the archaeological record, nonabusive. It may be that more time is required for the contending strategies to develop (Keegan 1987); it may be that other solutions are required.

Which brings us to the ultimate goal of this volume, attainment of an archaeological synthesis. *Archaeological synthesis* here refers to the appearance of consensus on the nature and scale of questions to be answered by the archaeological record, as well as agreement on methods by which those questions can be answered.[1] Consensus of that kind characterized the work of the culture historians of the 1930s and 1940s (Dunnell 1986:25–32). Agreement cannot be decreed, and a discipline cannot be rushed toward a new consensus; it matures in its own time (Kuhn 1970). Because of the imperiled nature of the archaeological record (Knudson 1989; Watson 1991), however, it is vital to expedite the maturation process. This exposé, then, juxtaposes statements by thoughtful and productive archaeologists on their vision of the goals and the practice of archaeology. It is hoped that the statements and the discussion they prompt may speed along a coherent archaeological science.

Volume chapters present assessments of the state of some aspect of archaeology. Some also offer programs for correcting or modifying that state. As a whole, the volume is structured along two independent dimensions. The first is the historian's and philosopher's artifice of the external and internal dialogue. The external dialogue centers on the relationship of archaeology with the rest of the social sciences and the social world, whereas the internal dialogue has to do with "the distinctive concerns of archaeology as a discipline" (Trigger 1989:2). The goals and practice of archaeology, as influenced by and responding to external and internal voices, are considered along this dimension.

The second dimension reflects the sentiments of the emergent history of technology in focusing attention on the instruments of the trade, which themselves are incapable of the prevarication that sometimes attends their manipulators (Rapp 1981). Thus, the latter dimension concerns archaeological tools, which reflect the practice and, to a lesser extent, the goals of archaeology. Both hardware and software (or tangible and intangible resources) along this dimension receive scrutiny.

Part I (commentary by LuAnn Wandsnider) appraises archaeology's interaction with the outside world and the critical resources, that is, funding and access to archaeological materials, that this world provides. Chapters by Michael Shott (the organization of cultural resource management archaeology), Frank McManamon (the federal commitment to archaeology), Miriam Stark (directions in research funding), and Lynne Goldstein (relations between Native Americans and archaeologists) contemplate the current state of Americanist archaeology in those areas. Measures for expanding and more effectively using limited resources are examined.

In Part II (commentary by Linda Cordell), the more intangible aspects of the external (and rapidly becoming internal) interaction are assessed, and the sociopolitical paradigm within which archaeological science is transacted is explored. The authors here discourse on restructuring the archaeological discipline on the basis of their experiences with the global archaeological community (Alan Simmons), feminist science (Suzanne Spencer-Wood), and a politicized democracy (Mark Leone and Robert Preucel).

Part III (commentary by Nan Rothschild) focuses on the hardware of the archaeological discipline, highlighting aspects of the internal dialogue. Anne Woosley considers the often neglected, but increasingly critical, state of museum collection management. Analytic tools that have not delivered in proportion to their promise are contemplated as well. The role and contribution to archaeology of quantitative methods (LuAnn Wandsnider and Timothy Kohler), high-technology applications (Ronald Bishop), and ethnoarchaeology (Steven Simms) are appraised.

Finally, internal dialogue on archaeological goals is considered in Part IV (commentary by Jeremy Sabloff). Included here are presentations by Robert Dunnell, on evolutionary archaeology; Michael Schiffer, on an imperial science of material culture; Alan Sullivan, on independent archaeological theory; and Robert Kelly, on archaeological contributions to understanding the world as a dynamic system. These chapters present programmatic statements that invite dialogue.

Several comments on the volume contents are appropriate. Some issues obviously critical to the present and future state of Americanist archaeology are omitted here. For example, philosophical perspectives are not explicitly presented, having been treated in depth elsewhere (e.g., Pinsky and Wylie 1989). Further, the topic of each chapter could in and of itself serve as a volume theme, and it is hoped that the analyses may serve as points of departure for other developed treatments of the same. While it is unlikely that a fully developed archaeological synthesis is emergent in this volume, others will find, it is hoped, this introspection useful to frame such a synthesis.

Finally, evident in several of the chapters, especially those by senior archaeologists, are notes of optimism, muted by weariness and wariness, about the present and the future of Americanist archaeology. As Dunnell (1982, 1986:41) has observed, the challenges posed by the new archaeology, to which the field is still responding, are very demanding. Given the relatively short time that has elapsed since those challenges were issued, really, much has been accomplished. But plenty remains to be done. The critiques offered here, especially those by Cordell and Sabloff, point to directions where our efforts may be best expended. At those and other points of entrée identified here, the potential for contribution by students of archaeology is tremendous. The framework provided by the elusive archaeological synthesis, however, would better channel and coordinate these efforts.

Almost 20 years ago, David Clarke (1973) wrote of archaeology's loss of innocence in its achievement of critical self-consciousness. As a result of the continuing self-evaluation, archaeologists command an extraordinary facility for the practice of archaeology in each of the several domains that Clarke distinguished as part of a general archaeological theory. In this volume, the authors continue to foresake innocence, identifying new quandaries requiring our attention and presenting their vision quests for a coherent archaeological science.

Acknowledgments

Linda Cordell, Nan Rothschild, Patrice Teltser, and an anonymous reviewer commented on earlier versions of this essay, for which I am most grateful.

Note

1. In a 1990 presentation at Southern Illinois University in Carbondale, Illinois, Michael Brian Schiffer used the term *archaeological synthesis* to describe an internally coherent archaeological science.

References

Binford, Lewis R.
   1981 *Bones: Ancient Men and Modern Myths*. Academic Press, New York.
   1986 In Pursuit of the Future. In *American Archaeology Past and Future: A Celebration of the Society for American Archaeology 1935–1985*, edited by David J. Meltzer, Don D. Fowler, and Jeremy A. Sabloff, pp. 459–479. Smithsonian Institution Press, Washington, D.C.
   1989 "Culture" and Social Roles in Archaeology. In *Debating Archaeology*, edited by Lewis R. Binford, pp. 3–11. Academic Press, New York.
Clarke, David L.
   1973 Archaeology: The Loss of Innocence. *Antiquity* 48:6–18.
Cowgill, George L.
   1986 Archaeological Applications of Mathematical and Formal Methods. In *American Archaeology Past and Future: A Celebration of the Society for American*

Archaeology 1935–1985, edited by David J. Meltzer, Don D. Fowler, and Jeremy A. Sabloff, pp. 369–394. Smithsonian Institution Press, Washington, D.C.

1989   Formal Approaches in Archaeology. In *Archaeological Thought in America,* edited by C. C. Lamberg-Karlovsky, pp. 74–88. Cambridge University Press, Cambridge.

Dunnell, Robert C.
1982   Science, Social Science, and Common Sense: The Agonizing Dilemma of Modern Archaeology. *Journal of Anthropological Research* 38:1–25.
1986   Five Decades of American Archaeology. In *American Archaeology Past and Future: A Celebration of the Society for American Archaeology 1935–1985,* edited by David J. Meltzer, Don D. Fowler, and Jeremy A. Sabloff, pp. 23–52. Smithsonian Institution Press, Washington, D.C.
1989   Aspects of the Application of Evolutionary Theory in Archaeology. In *Archaeological Thought in America,* edited by C. C. Lamberg-Karlovsky, pp. 35–49. Cambridge University Press, Cambridge.

Ebert, James I.
1989   Processual Archaeology: What We Will Know in the 21st Century, and How We Will Know It. Paper presented at the symposium, The Organization of Land and Space Use, Technology, and Activities in Past and Present Societies, University of New Mexico, Albuquerque.

Fagan, Brian
1989   A.D. 2050: The Science of Humankind Comes of Age. *Archaeology* 42(1):22–24.

Hodder, Ian
1985   Postprocessual Archaeology. In *Advances in Archaeological Method and Theory,* vol. 8, edited by Michael B. Schiffer, pp. 1–25. Academic Press, New York.
1986   *Reading the Past: Current Approaches to Interpretation in Archaeology.* Cambridge University Press, Cambridge.

Hull, David
1988   *The Process of Science.* University of Chicago Press, Chicago.

Keegan, William F.
1987   Comment on Processual Archaeology and the Radical Critique. *Current Anthropology* 28(4):518.

Knudson, Ruthann
1989   North America's Threatened Heritage. *Archaeology* 42(1):71–73, 106.

Kuhn, Thomas S.
1970   *The Structure of Scientific Revolutions.* 2d ed. University of Chicago Press, Chicago.

McCormack, Thelma
1982   Good Theory or Just Theory? Toward a Feminist Philosophy of Social Science. In *Women in Futures Research,* edited by Margrit Eichler and Hilda Scott, pp. 1–12. Pergamon Press, Oxford.

Meltzer, David J., Don D. Fowler, and Jeremy A. Sabloff (editors)
1986   *American Archaeology Past and Future: A Celebration of the Society for American Archaeology 1935–1985.* Smithsonian Institution Press, Washington, D.C.

O'Connell, James F., Kevin T. Jones, and Steven R. Simms
1982   Some Thoughts on Prehistoric Archaeology. In *Man and Environment in the Great Basin,* edited by David B. Madsen and James F. O'Connell, pp. 227–240. *Society for American Archaeology Papers,* vol. 2.

Pinsky, Valerie, and Alison Wylie (editors)
　1989　*Critical Traditions in Contemporary Archaeology.* Cambridge University Press, Cambridge.

Rapp, Friedrich
　1981　*Analytical Philosophy of Technology.* Boston Studies in the Philosophy of Science, vol. 63. D. Reidel, Dordrecht, Holland.

Schiffer, Michael B.
　1988　The Structure of Archaeological Theory. *American Antiquity* 53:461–485.

Thomas, David Hurst
　1986　Contemporary Hunter-Gatherer Archaeology in America. In *American Archaeology Past and Future: A Celebration of the Society for American Archaeology 1935–1985,* edited by David J. Meltzer, Don D. Fowler, and Jeremy A. Sabloff, pp. 237–276. Smithsonian Institution Press, Washington, D.C.

Tilley, Christopher, and Michael Shanks
　1987　*Social Theory and Archaeology.* Polity Press, Cambridge.

Trigger, Bruce G.
　1989　*A History of Archaeological Thought.* Cambridge University Press, Cambridge.

Watson, Patty Jo
　1991　A Parochial Primer: The New Dissonance As Seen from the Midcontinental United States. In *Processual and Postprocessual Archaeologies: Multiple Ways of Knowing the Past,* edited by Robert W. Preucel, pp. 265–274. Center for Archaeological Investigations, Occasional Paper No. 10. Southern Illinois University, Carbondale.

Willey, Gordon R., and Jeremy A. Sabloff
　1980　*A History of American Archaeology.* 2d ed. W. H. Freeman, San Francisco.

I. Critical Archaeological Resources

2. Commerce or Service: Models of Practice in Archaeology

Michael J. Shott

Abstract: Current professional practice in archaeology is predominantly commercial, and services are packaged as commodities. The shortcomings of this model for inventory survey, the critical first stage of archaeological research—small survey areas, single inspections, dense ground cover—can be eliminated only by changing practice from commerce to service and by reorganizing it programmatically. Answers to questions prompted by this new model of practice—acceptable survey intensity, number and methods of inspections—are unknown but knowable. The programmatic model will increase data for both research and planning, and we can also implement nonsite or distributional approaches on a systematic basis. Shifting from commodity to service will increase survey efficiency and effectiveness but will require rather extensive reorganization of the funding and administration of archaeological practice.

Introduction

Practice is professional activity that involves an acquired body of knowledge, analytical methods, and technical skills. Traditionally, archaeological practice has been scholarship, the accumulation and refinement of knowledge. Increasingly, as all archaeologists know, it is applied, sponsored by the federal government or private developers to secure compliance with federal preservation laws. In the course of this transformation, archaeological practice itself has increasingly become commercial activity, whether conducted by universities or private firms.

Most commercial activities satisfy the desires of individuals or commercial firms. Only commercial activities dealing with public works or public service (e.g., trash collection, arms production) meet broader public or social needs, real or imagined. Conflicts between private gain and public interest in those domains are well documented, to say the least. Commerce in those areas sometimes—by no means always—is the best way to meet social needs (Donahue 1989).

In current archaeological practice, professional services are commodities whose nature, quality, and cost are determined by market forces. Archaeological practice, however, is commercial not because it relates intrinsically to commerce but because the commercial model of professional practice is firmly entrenched in our entrepreneurial society. Significantly, the federal statute that revolutionized archaeological practice—the National Historic Preservation Act (NHPA) of 1966, as amended in 1980—established policy but said little about how to carry it out. Even NHPA's implementing regulations, 36CFR800, discuss agency responsibilities but do not specify precisely how to discharge them.

The commercial model of practice, then, is established in fact but not ordained by law. Although the model has served reasonably well to date, it has generated controversy over the possibly conflicting responsibilities of practitioners to the archaeological record and to sponsors (Fitting and Goodyear 1979), the influence of commercial practices like competitive bidding on the quality of archaeological work (Lacy and Hasenstab 1983; Macdonald 1976), and the respective roles and obligations of profit and nonprofit practitioners (Garrow 1982; Macdonald 1976; McGuire 1987). Because of those problems, it is time to examine the virtues of the commercial practice model and to consider alternatives.

The Organization of Archaeological Practice

Federal policy established by NHPA and other laws and regulations promotes archaeological preservation where possible and mitigates or minimizes destruction where unavoidable. Federal agencies must consider the effects on archaeological remains of actions they carry out or authorize. They must also allow the Advisory Council on Historic Preservation (ACHP) to comment on those actions and measures they take to avoid or mitigate damage to remains. Technically, ACHP has no authority to enforce compliance with NHPA or 36CFR800, but it possesses such authority as a practical matter. Few archaeologists would question the wisdom of overall federal policy as far as it goes, but it may not be sufficient or even desirable in the long run.

The Existing Organization of Practice

Archaeology in the United States is practiced largely in response to specific development projects and is confined to the areas affected by the projects. Practitioners must gear up for work in areas that are arbitrarily defined with respect to the distribution of archaeological remains and must conform to schedules that impose arbitrary constraints on their work. Existing practice, in effect, mandates project-specific actions executed in relatively short periods of time. It promotes the view that archaeological services—survey, evaluation, mitigation, the three-stage sequence of activities—are discrete and readily packaged for immediate and brief use. In short, the existing arrangement treats archaeological services as commodities.

But that arrangement has several serious drawbacks that reduce efficiency and impair the effectiveness of archaeological efforts. Archaeological services are not commodities to be purchased or leased for brief use. They do not meet the needs of individuals or private firms but a social need codified in federal law and policy, and the commercial model of practice is not necessarily the best way to meet such needs (Donahue 1989). Accordingly, we must identify the most desirable arrangements under which to perform archaeological services. Survey to identify archaeological remains is no more important than evaluation and mitigation. It is, however, the first stage in the three-stage sequence and therefore the logical stage to consider first. As the following arguments will show, the existing organization of practice is far from ideal at this critical first stage.

Survey efficiency is maximized when relatively large areas are covered. Any survey, no matter the size, has certain fixed costs. The larger the survey area, the lower the percentage of total costs composed of fixed costs. Although much project-specific archaeological research involves large tracts of land, much—probably most in fact—does not (Hasenstab and Lacy 1984; Powell and Rice 1981; Wobst 1983).

What is more, the most favorable and efficient survey conditions (at least in the eastern United States) obtain where large expanses of the ground surface—and the remains lying on them—are exposed. In practical terms, those conditions are found in cultivated fields in contrast to forested or abandoned areas. In current practice, many tracts are surveyed under those conditions. At least in the eastern United States, however, many are not, having been abandoned by farming or actually removed from cultivation by land developers and speculators. In these cases, archaeological remains at risk of destruction are covered by dense brush, seriously complicating survey efforts.

Whatever the survey area size and ground cover conditions, surveys conducted in compliance with existing preservation authority typically are carried out in a single episode, less often in a two-stage reconnaissance and intensive survey sequence (Plog et al. 1978). Surfaces, however, whether desert pavements or cultivated fields, are complex sampling universes. Even the theoretically most intensive survey of cultivated surfaces will recover only what is exposed, not what is temporarily buried in the plow zone. Rarely will a tract present the same appearance in the character and distribution of artifacts on successive visits. Surface survey, then, is inherently a sampling process with its own biases and shortcomings. To minimize the biases, it is simply imperative that surfaces be sampled more than once, perhaps substantially more than once. Exposure on cultivated surfaces is governed by factors that include the nature and extent of tillage, soil properties, and degree of surface weathering. Based on controlled experiments, density appears to vary more than distribution or assemblage composition (Table 2-1). Density

Table 2-1. Artifact Recovery Rate per Inspection and by Density in Selected Studies

Source	Number of Collections	Recovery Rate (%)	Artifact Frequency[a] Mean	SD	Area (m^2)
Ammerman 1985	4[b]	5.5	25.0	7.1	
Ammerman and Feldman 1978	3		146.3	52.8	21000
Ammerman and Feldman 1978	2		897.0	25.4	2448
Ammerman and Feldman 1978	2		416.5	68.6	1152
Dunnell 1988	3		313.7	410.6	323887
Frink 1984	3	6.5[c]	47.7	7.0	
Frink 1984	3	6.5[c]	40.0	7.0	
Jermann 1981	3		466.0	321.7	37500
Hirth 1978	3		282163.3	199090.2	70000
Lewarch and O'Brien 1981	2	6.8	146.5	16.3	
Lewarch and O'Brien 1981	2	6.7	19.0	1.4	
Lewarch and O'Brien 1981	2	6.2	27.0	5.6	
Odell and Cowan 1987	12	5.6	55.6	16.5	232
Reynolds 1982	6	16.6[d]			
Riordan 1982	2		2194.5	1067.0	4320
Tingle 1987	3	2.8	92.3	77.6	220000
Trubowitz 1978	3	3.7	336.3	66.4	9294

[a]Combined total of all artifact classes reported, except for Tingle 1987 (flakes only) and Hirth 1978 (sherds only).
[b]Four collections reported, but data presented on only two.
[c]Estimate only.
[d]Number of collections and recovery rate only; no other data reported.

variation can produce interpretive dilemmas (Dunnell 1988:35–36) that only repeated surface collections can resolve. What appears as an isolated artifact in a single inspection may form part of a sparse cultural deposit after several collections, and a sparse deposit may emerge gradually as a surprisingly dense one after repeated collection. Valid interpretations of the archaeological properties of survey tracts must await a sufficient number of inspections to distinguish among these possibilities. As one brief example, Paleoindian bifaces sometimes are found as "isolated" discoveries, but it is rare for investigators to return repeatedly to the same location in search of other remains. Such "isolated" finds, typically interpreted as chance losses in hunting, may register patterns of land use and forms of cultural behavior not otherwise observed if they are followed by repeated visits.

Practitioners, in sum, often survey relatively small areas formerly cultivated but overgrown at the time of survey. They are forced to use methods that are labor-intensive and inadequate for discovering artifact concentrations (Krakker et al. 1983; Shott 1985; Wobst 1983); they cannot exploit the scale economies inherent in large survey areas; and, typically, they inspect survey tracts one time only. All of this is part and parcel of the commercial model of practice. Under these circumstances, archaeologists are working harder than they need to and accomplishing less than they can.

Reorganizing Practice

To remedy this situation, it is necessary to abolish the strictures of project-specific compliance and to elevate archaeological practice for compliance to a higher, programmatic level of planning. Archaeological organizations, be they government or nonprofit institutions, or even private firms, should be engaged to survey relatively extensive areas—perhaps on the order of thousands of square kilometers—preferably characterized by high surface visibility. The survey areas would not necessarily be threatened with imminent destruction but would be selected on the basis of planning studies that identify long-term spatial trends in development. In the short term, most such areas probably will remain in cultivation, offering the optimal survey conditions required for adequate documentation. Large areas could be surveyed efficiently in this manner, at least more efficiently than is the case now. Comparisons between different sections of the larger regions would be more reliable than they are now, because data would be consistent, having been collected using a set of uniform practices. Repeated inspections of the same tract will correct the deficiencies of one-pass practices and ensure that survey results do not incorporate or magnify the inherent variation of cultivated surfaces.

This reorganized model of practice has the foregoing advantages, but it raises a set of questions in its own right. What survey intensity is optimal or even minimally adequate? Exactly how many inspections of survey tracts are necessary? What is to be done in tracts where surface inspection is impossible or impractical?

Survey Intensity

Survey intensity is the amount of archaeological effort invested per unit of surveyed land. Intensity effects have been documented in several surveys (Judge 1981; Plog et al. 1978; Schiffer and Wells 1982; Syms 1982; Thoms 1979; Wandsnider and Ebert 1984) in which the number of sites found varies directly with intensity of effort. That is, the harder you look, the more you find. This fact hardly requires belaboring, but it has an important and neglected implication: minimum technical standards governing survey intensity must be established. But there are few, if any, rigorous standards that specify minimum survey intensity, a situation ripe for abuse in commercial practice, where market forces constantly act to depress effort as a way of reducing costs and winning competitive bids (Donahue 1989:79–80; Lacy and Hasenstab 1983; Macdonald 1976). Some state and federal guidelines speak of adequate amounts of effort but rarely specify precise terms. We need clear, measurable standards for survey intensity, expressed probably in areas covered per unit time, holding constant at some close interval the spacing between adjacent surveyors. Alternatively, standards simultaneously measuring spacing and coverage rate could be developed (e.g., Schiffer and Wells 1982:351). In their absence, there is nothing to guarantee at least a degree of consistency between different results, and differences between survey tracts are hopelessly compounded as the joint product of the record itself and how it is documented.

There is much to learn yet about the precise effects of survey intensity, and no arbitrary value will suffice in all cases. Following a well-designed series of experiments, however, we should be able to estimate the optimal intensity for a range of field conditions. Data returns must decline at some point on the intensity scale (Judge 1981) beyond which increasing intensity yields little gain. But that point may be higher than often imagined (Ebert et al. 1986:237–238). At least in the eastern United States, survey rates in exposed tracts of roughly 8 ha per person-day, sometimes higher, are common. The rates required, however, in at least one intensive western study were less than 2 ha per person-day (Wandsnider and Larralde 1986:154), and even then approximately 20% of exposed material may not have been recovered.

Number of Inspections

Exactly how many inspections are adequate is a difficult question to answer, although the answer is not yet urgent. We know that at least several are required. Available experimental data on recovery rate per inspection are remarkably consistent (Table 2-1). Excluding estimated figures, a rate of approximately 7% seems reasonable if not generous. If so, 10 collections are needed to recover approximately half of the archaeological remains in survey tracts (Bradley 1987:39).

Moreover, recovery rate varies directly with mean artifact density in Table 2-1 ($r = .98$, df = 2, $p = .11$). Inherent differences in results between collection episodes, measured by the coefficient of variation, vary inversely with both recovery rate ($r = -.81$, df = 8, $p = .01$) and mean density ($r = -.56$, df = 9, $p = .09$). Thus, survey intensity must be greater or more collections must be made in tracts with lower densities of remains than in more "productive" ones to secure comparability in results at some acceptably low level of variation.

Subsurface Inspection

Because the surface of some survey tracts in the eastern United States is not exposed, methods other than simple surface inspection are required to adequately document the distribution of archaeological remains there. Shovel-test sampling was the first systematic method used for that purpose (e.g., Lovis 1976). Debate over the method has become rancorous, to put it mildly (Lightfoot 1989; Nance and Ball 1989), but its severe limitations are documented at length (Shott 1985, 1989; Wobst 1983). Ironically, shovel-test sampling is a perfectly reasonable measure for limited characterization of distributions, a point stressed repeatedly (Nance 1983; Shott 1985:466, 1989; Wobst 1983), but its extreme labor requirements make it prohibitive in all but the smallest survey tracts.

Under such circumstances, there is no alternative to some sort of efficient, large-scale surface exposure (Shott 1989). If surface growth is not too dense, formerly cultivated areas can simply be plowed again, but other measures are needed where plowing is impractical. Surface survey of clear-cut forest tracts, for instance, has produced results far superior to prior shovel-test sampling of the same tracts (Fish and Gresham 1990; Shott 1989:402). Other studies (DeBloois et al. 1975; Gallagher 1978) document a modest but significant degree of disturbance to remains from land-clearing activities. Since most remains in overgrown areas lie below a dense surface mat, it may be possible to devise efficient but low-impact exposure methods that minimize damage. It is easy to question the efficacy of such measures before devoting serious attention to them, a luxury that archaeology can ill afford.

Evaluation Stage

Attention to the technical requirements of and the organizational model appropriate to survey by no means implies that subsequent stages of practice are unimportant. But it is justified because survey and documentation logically precede evaluation and mitigation and because surveys are more common than later-stage research. In reality, of course, all three stages of research and practice are important. Therefore, attention must also be devoted to the optimal organization of second-stage evaluation, which again may be programmatic and not project-specific, and to the efficient design of sampling strategies in evaluation, where at present some classes of remains are sampled redundantly and others poorly or not at all (Shott 1987).

Advantages of Reorganized Practice

Planning Benefits

The programmatic model frees practitioners from the exigencies of project-specific conditions with all of their inherent disadvantages, yet still secures compliance with federal law. In fact, the large-scale regional data generated can further promote preservation by integrating archaeological data into long-term land use planning, ultimately at considerable savings (Ferguson 1986).

Eventually, reasonably accurate and consistent data on the abundance of distribution of archaeological remains will be produced for many areas. As specific developments are proposed in those areas, planners may simply consult the data base and quickly determine if sites or other remains will be endangered by the development. In all likelihood, many projects would be cleared immediately at no cost or delay to the developer. Others that threaten important remains can be redesigned to avoid impact at an earlier stage of planning than is customary now, or the developers would need to fund the expense of partial mitigation of the remains involved. In the first case, developers and the archaeologists they retain would have sufficient time to plan and carry out necessary work without delaying project schedules. In both cases, project-specific archaeological costs probably would be far less on average than they are now.

In a transitional period, perhaps a decade or so, project-specific measures will remain necessary. Gradually, however, project-specific compliance will decline, since many areas will have been cleared for development through programmatic means, or development plans will be modified in light of documented remains. At no point, however, will the need for at least some project-specific measures vanish. There will remain instances of direct conflict between archaeological remains and development plans that can only be resolved through mitigation or salvage.

Substantive Archaeological Benefits

The scale effects of reorganized practice can produce other benefits as well. Planting control populations—of poker chips, tiles, whatever—whose size and distribution are known (but not to the surveyors) can determine the efficiency and effectiveness of survey crews. Only in this way can the results of different surveys, even those with identical research designs, be calibrated and strict comparability between survey areas secured (Wandsnider and Ebert 1984). Control populations also can be used in replicate studies of item dispersal in plow zones and the effects of item size, shape, and color on recovery rate (Ammerman 1985; Ammerman and Feldman 1978; Lewarch and O'Brien 1981; Odell and Cowan 1987; Tingle 1987; Trubowitz 1978; Yorston et al. 1990).

Reorganized practice could have a second pleasant side effect: discarding the concept of "site" as an observational unit at the survey stage (though not necessarily an analytical unit at subsequent stages of research). In its place, long-term survey could determine the archaeological properties—density and distribution of various classes of artifacts and features—of large areas of the landscape. An emerging body of theory in archaeology has raised serious doubts about the validity of sites as traditionally conceived (Dunnell and Dancey 1983; Ebert 1986; Foley 1981; Thomas 1973; Wobst 1979, 1983). Although that issue is not yet settled, the value of the "site" concept must be demonstrated, not assumed.

Data collection free of notions of "site" would have several practical advantages. First, it would eliminate the need to make difficult, almost impossible, decisions regarding the status of observed clusters of artifacts. A great deal of effort is expended in needless agonizing over the status of particular clusters, effort put to better use in fieldwork and analysis. And negative decisions, of course, frequently have drastic and irreversible consequences for some areas of the landscape. Second, methods of nonsite observation and analysis are well developed and hold great promise for the explication of complex archaeological distributions at the regional scale (Ebert 1986:302–358). Third, sites can be defined and studied as distinct analytical units with data produced using a nonsite research design, but regional data cannot be produced from site-oriented survey. Archaeologists, in effect, risk nothing by adopting a regional, nonsite perspective and stand to gain a great deal from it. Fourth, the distributional approach can be extended to the eastern United States to somewhat counterbalance the strong western cast of existing applications (Ebert 1986:368; but see Hickson and Katz 1989).

A distributional approach may have theoretical advantages as well over site-centered views, at least in the archaeological study of nonsedentary societies. Documenting archaeological distributions away from the density modes we call sites can provide a clearer view of the material correlates of prehistoric behavior, free of the complicating and obscuring effects of overlaying occupations (Wobst 1979:62–63). Types of behavior at the margins of cultural norms may also be revealed because they occur at the margins of spatial norms as well (Root 1980; Wobst 1979). Better understanding of innovation, an important set of culture processes, may be gained in this way. As Wobst (1978; 1979:63) argues, much archaeological interpretation reproduces the ethnographic record, but that record is incomplete in ways that a distributional approach to the archaeological record can rectify. Ebert (1986) has documented at length the daunting but informative complexity of archaeological distributions and the patterns of prehistoric cultural behavior they reflect. Instead of forcing data into site types, his data collection and surprisingly straightforward analytical methods reveal considerable variability in the form and scale of patterning in empirical distributions that enriches interpretations of prehistoric cultures and their dynamics.

Implementing the Programmatic Model

The programmatic approach requires a semipermanent institutional framework to be successful. Large areas would be assigned to specific institutions that would then survey them gradually over a period of years. Long-term contracts—on the order of 10 years or more, conditional upon satisfactory performance in shorter probationary periods—would be awarded to contracting archaeological organizations. Payments would be made at regular intervals upon completion of interim goals. Contractors who, for whatever reason (e.g., seeking more lucrative work elsewhere), abandon their efforts before the contract expires would forfeit all funds received, not merely those yet to be disbursed. That would penalize contractors who do not live up to the contract terms and probably would act to confine interest to those having genuine, permanent commitments to research in the region.

Obviously, funding for this arrangement and its administration by federal or state governments would have to be distributed over a fairly broad base. Since impacts would be from a combination of many public and private developments, no single sponsor would be liable for all costs. Currently, however, private developers probably pass on their costs for archaeological services to others in the form of higher prices for their goods and services. Thus, archaeological costs are distributed across the economy as a whole. For that reason, economywide levies at the federal level are justifiable since they would have the same effect as the current arrangement. At any rate, the distinction between federal and private actions disappears in the longer view. Many federal actions stimulate private development, as they are designed to do, yet current authority and practice extend only to actions directly funded or licensed by the federal government. Extending authority and practice to all actions recognizes the aggregate effect of federal actions and is consistent with federal policy, if not the relatively narrow strictures of existing law. And because efficiency will be increased at the first, critical stage of inventory survey, the real costs of archaeological preservation are apt to decline. Lower archaeological costs distributed across a broad base would be less burdensome than the current arrangement, and they would have the pleasant side effect of promoting public support for the entire effort.

Objections to the programmatic approach are easily imagined. Who will administer the programs? How will the survey areas be identified? How will programmatic contractors be selected for the necessary work? How intensive must survey be? How many visits, under what range of conditions, will be necessary to adequately gauge the archaeological properties of any area? How will survey be conducted in areas subject to unforeseen and unplanned development pressures? All are legitimate questions, and few answers can be provided at this point. However, they are questions to take into account, not obstacles impossible to overcome. Taking the latter view will only preserve the status quo.

A final objection to the programmatic model to preservation and archaeological practice may involve the conflict between survey needs and private property rights. After all, much, if not most, land surveyed under this arrangement would be in private hands. Although the great majority of landowners probably would be agreeable, if not actually receptive, to archaeological survey on their property, others almost surely would object. How could they be compelled to permit survey crews access to their property? Alternatively, could the property of resistant landowners be omitted in the regional surveys engendered by the programmatic approach? Denial of access by any considerable fraction of landowners would seriously hinder, if not fatally flaw, the regional character of the programmatic approach. Crews must be permitted to survey all parts of any area likely to witness development in the foreseeable future. The conflict with private property rights, however, is more illusory than real. Even in this nation, which probably places greater value on such rights than any other, they are not absolute. For legitimate reasons, government officials and their agents— including archaeologists in this context—may enter private property without owner consent. Moreover, it is a widely recognized social principle that private property rights must conform, at least broadly, to community standards of use and public policy. That is why zoning laws exist. No one enjoys complete freedom, for instance, to convert his or her backyard into a toxic waste dump or an artillery range. A degree of archaeological preservation, and the measures needed to secure it, can and should legitimately be included among the public policy goals that govern or at least modify private property rights. Such measures would include the right of access to private property for survey purposes and the recovery of archaeological remains from them for curation and public benefit.

Expanding the Scope of Preservation Policy

Obviously, many development projects involve federal funds or licensing but, equally as obvious, many do not. Until systematic measures of the sort described here are enacted, state- or local-authority preservation measures are all that protect threatened archaeological remains in the latter case. Fortunately, a number of major cities have implemented such measures (Yuskavitch 1986). Subjectively, however, they appear to protect historic archaeological remains far more often than prehistoric ones. Obviously, historic remains deserve protection, but so do prehistoric ones. Effective local-authority preservation plans that engage prehistoric remains are rarer, but they exist in Ann Arbor, Michigan (Shott and O'Shea 1985), Durango, Colorado (Duke and Matlock 1985) and Pensacola, Florida (Bense 1987). At the state level, a highly detailed plan has been proposed in Virginia (MacCord 1987), involving a network of archaeologists at the local level. New Mexico has drafted a model preservation ordinance for local governments there (Piper et al. 1985). Those efforts deserve greater recognition and emulation than they have yet received, and archaeologists elsewhere may find in them the inspiration for similar measures in their own communities.

Discussion

The fate of a proposal as far-reaching as this one is problematic. But we must consider the way in which practice *should* be organized, not merely what is possible politically in the short term. There is nothing immutable about the current organization of practice. Project-specific management and conservation was the most sensible and politically attainable approach when federal requirements were established. But we are more aware now of the strengths and weaknesses of some of our field methods, especially concerning survey, and that awareness casts doubt on the efficacy of methods currently in use. It would be a serious failure if we ignored the problem or refused to take steps to correct it.

Even in the best of archaeological worlds, however, reorganized practice remains a partial preservation measure. In fact, the most far-reaching preservation efforts imaginable will come not from anything that we do as archaeologists but from reforming social norms. Consumerism in advanced societies fosters an ethic, trivially, of consumption. Although we ordinarily identify consumption with things like pizza and new cars, it is in fact a lifestyle that embraces a wide range of services and commodities. These include the sorts of living arrangements—large houses in the suburbs—that we are encouraged to seek and that we can link directly to destruction of archaeological remains. In a less direct but no less consequential manner, other remains are destroyed in the sprawling commercial development that follows those residential patterns, and many Appalachian and western sites have been strip-mined for fuel to power the appliances and amenities that we have grown to regard as necessities.

Consumerism alone, however, does not impel those desires or determine how we act on them. The maintenance of race and class distinctions has been a strong impetus to the consumer cast of our society, or at least its residential land-use practices. In turn, the practices foster commercial sprawl, further accelerating archaeological destruction. In fact, the dynamics of race and class distinctions are played out on an ever-spiraling geographic scale. We are witnessing today the appearance of second- and third-generation suburbs, suburbs of suburbs in a sense, created to preserve racially or economically homogeneous enclaves established in earlier suburbs and "threatened" by more recent diversity.

Conclusion

The commercial model of professional practice treats archaeological services as commodities and encourages the project-specific measures that are traditionally identified with contract practice. However well that model may have served in the past, it compares poorly to a programmatic model that frees practice from project-specific constraints, improves technical performance standards, and best promotes archaeological preservation.

Acknowledgments

Thanks are due to LuAnn Wandsnider of the University of Nebraska for her invitation to participate in the conference and for her able editing of this essay. Robert Dunnell of the University of Washington, James Ebert of Ebert & Associates, and Charles McGimsey of the University of Arkansas also provided useful comments. Responsibility for any errors or omissions is mine alone.

References

Ammerman, A. J.
   1985   Plowzone Experiments in Calabria: Some Results. *Journal of Field Archaeology* 12:33–40.
Ammerman, A. J., and M. Feldman
   1978   Replicated Collection of Site Surfaces. *American Antiquity* 43:734–740.

Bense, J. A.
   1987   Development of a Management System for Archaeological Resources in Pensacola, Florida. In *Living in Cities: Current Research in Urban Archaeology*, edited by E. Staski, pp. 83–91. Society for Historical Archaeology, Special Publication Series No. 5.
Bradley, R.
   1987   A Field Method for Investigating the Spatial Structure of Lithic Scatters. In *Lithic Analysis and Later British Prehistory: Some Problems and Applications*, edited by A. Brown and M. Edmonds, pp. 39–47. British Archaeological Reports, B.S. No. 162. Oxford.
DeBloois, E., D. Green, and H. Wylie
   1975   A Test of the Impact of Pinyon-Juniper Chaining on Archaeological Sites. In *The Pinyon-Juniper Ecosystem: A Symposium*, pp. 153–161. Utah State University, Logan.
Donahue, J. D.
   1989   *The Privatization Decision: Public Ends, Private Means*. Basic Books, New York.
Duke, P. G., and G. Matlock
   1985 An Archaeological Policy for the City of Durango. *Southwestern Lore* 51:12–15.
Dunnell, R. C.
   1988   Low-Density Archaeological Records from Plowed Surfaces: Some Preliminary Considerations. *American Archaeology* 7(1):29–38.
Dunnell, R. C., and W. Dancey
   1983   The Siteless Survey: A Regional Scale Data Collection Strategy. *Advances in Archaeological Method and Theory*, vol. 5, edited by Michael B. Schiffer, pp. 267–287. Academic Press, New York.
Ebert, J. I.
   1986   *Distributional Archaeology: Nonsite Discovery, Recording and Analytical Methods for Application to the Surface Archaeological Record*. Unpublished Ph.D. dissertation, University of New Mexico, Albuquerque.
Ebert, J. I., S. Larralde, and L. Wandsnider
   1986   Distribution Archeology: Survey, Mapping and Analysis of Surface Archeological Materials in the Green River Basin, Wyoming. In *The Seedskadee Project: Remote Sensing in Non-Site Archeology*, edited by D. Drager and A. Ireland, pp. 227–242. Bureau of Reclamation, Salt Lake City.
Ferguson, J.
   1986   Spend Now to Save Later: Baseline Cultural Resources as an Essential Planning Tool. Ms. on file, U.S. Army Engineer District, Philadelphia.
Fish, P. R., and T. Gresham
   1990   Insights from Full-Coverage Survey in the Georgia Piedmont. In *The Archaeology of Regions: A Case for Full-Coverage Survey*, edited by S. Fish and S. Kowalewski, pp. 147–172. Smithsonian Institution Press, Washington.
Fitting, J. E., and A. C. Goodyear
   1979   Client-Oriented Archaeology: An Exchange of Views. *Journal of Field Archaeology* 6:352–360.
Foley, R.
   1981   A Model of Regional Archaeological Structure. *Proceedings of the Prehistoric Society* 47:1–17.
Frink, D. S.
   1984   Artifact Behavior within the Plow Zone. *Journal of Field Archaeology* 11:356–363.

Gallagher, J. G.
   1978   Scarification and Cultural Resources: An Experiment to Evaluate Serotinous Lodgepole Pine Forest Regeneration Techniques. *Plains Anthropologist* 23:289–299.

Garrow, P.
   1982   Response to: "The 'Small Business Act' and Archaeological Research." *Southeastern Archaeology* 1:171.

Hasenstab, R. J., and D. M. Lacy
   1984   The Reporting of Small-Scale Survey Results for Research Purposes: Suggestions for Improvement. *American Archaeology* 4:43–49.

Hickson, R., and S. Katz
   1989   Abstract of "A Distributional Approach to the Archaeology of the Interior Uplands, West-Central Illinois." *Midcontinental Journal of Archaeology* 14:94.

Hirth, K.
   1978   Problems in Data Recovery and Measurement in Settlement Archaeology. *Journal of Field Archaeology* 5:125–131.

Jermann, J. V.
   1981   Surface Collection and Analysis of Spatial Pattern: An Archaeological Example from the Lower Columbia River Valley. In *Plowzone Archaeology: Contributions to Theory and Technique*, edited by M. J. O'Brien and D. Lewarch, pp. 71–118. Publications in Anthropology No. 27. Vanderbilt University, Nashville.

Judge, W.
   1981   Transect Sampling in Chaco Canyon: Evaluation of a Survey Technique. In *Archaeological Surveys of Chaco Canyon*, edited by A. Hayes, D. Brugge, and W. Judge, pp. 107–137. National Park Service, Washington, D.C.

Krakker, J., M. Shott, and P. Welch
   1983   Design and Evaluation of Shovel-Test Sampling in Regional Archaeological Survey. *Journal of Field Archaeology* 10:469–480.

Lacy, D., and R. Hasenstab
   1983   The Development of Least Effort Strategies in Cultural Resource Management: Competition for Scarce Resources in Massachusetts. In *The Socio-Politics of Archaeology*, edited by J. Gero, D. Lacy, and M. Blakey, pp. 31–50. Department of Anthropology Research Report No. 23. University of Massachusetts, Amherst.

Lewarch, D., and M. J. O'Brien
   1981   Effects of Short Term Tillage on Aggregate Provenience Surface Pattern. In *Plowzone Archaeology: Contributions to Theory and Technique*, edited by M. J. O'Brien and D. Lewarch, pp. 7–49. Publications in Anthropology No. 27. Vanderbilt University, Nashville.

Lightfoot, K. L.
   1989   A Defense of Shovel-Test Sampling: A Reply to Shott. *American Antiquity* 54:413–416.

Lovis, W. A.
   1976   Quarter Sections and Forests: An Example of Probability Sampling in the Northeastern Woodlands. *American Antiquity* 41:364–372.

MacCord, H. A.
   1987   The Virginia Plan: Archaeology by Echelons. *Southeastern Archaeological Conference Newsletter* 29(2):28–32.

Macdonald, W.
   1976   Introduction: Archaeology and the Profits of Research. In *Digging for Gold*:

Papers on Archaeology for Profit, edited by W. Macdonald, pp. vii–xiii. Museum of Anthropology Technical Report No. 5. University of Michigan, Ann Arbor.

McGuire, D. J.
    1987   The Business of Archaeology: A Perspective from Private Consulting. In *Perspectives on Archaeological Resource Management on the "Great Plains,"* edited by A. Osborn and R. Hassler, pp. 71–79. I & O, Omaha.

Nance, J. D.
    1983   Regional Sampling in Archaeological Survey: The Statistical Perspective. In *Advances in Archaeological Method and Theory*, vol. 6, edited by Michael B. Schiffer, pp. 289–356. Academic Press, New York.

Nance, J. D., and B. F. Ball
    1989   A Shot in the Dark: Shott's Comments on Nance and Ball. *American Antiquity* 54:405–412.

Odell, G. H., and F. Cowan
    1987   Estimating Tillage Effects on Artifact Distributions. *American Antiquity* 52:456–484.

Piper, J., M. F. Schmader, and R. C. Chapman
    1985   Model Archaeological Ordinance for Local Governments in New Mexico. Office of Contract Archaeology, University of New Mexico, Albuquerque.

Plog, S., F. Plog, and W. Wait
    1978   Decision Making in Modern Surveys. In *Advances in Archaeological Method and Theory*, vol. 1, edited by Michael B. Schiffer, pp. 383–421. Academic Press, New York.

Powell, S., and G. E. Rice
    1981   The Incorporation of Small Contract Projects into a Regional Sampling Design. *American Antiquity* 46:602–610.

Reynolds, P. J.
    1982   The Ploughzone. In *Festschrift zum 100 jahrigen Bestehen der Abteilung für Vorgeschichte*, pp. 315–340. Naturhistorische Gesellschaft, Nuremberg.

Riordan, R.
    1982   The Controlled Surface Collection of a Multicomponent Site in Southwestern Ohio: A Replication Experiment. *Midcontinental Journal of Archaeology* 7:45–59.

Root, D.
    1980   Tracking the Archaeological Record: Interpretations of the Archaic Period in Southern New England. Paper presented at the 45th Annual Meeting of the Society for American Archaeology, Philadelphia.

Schiffer, M., and S. Wells
    1982   Archaeological Surveys: Past and Future. In *Hohokam and Patayan: Prehistory of Southwestern Arizona*, edited by R. McGuire and M. Schiffer, pp. 345–355. Academic Press, New York.

Shott, M. J.
    1985   Shovel-Test Sampling as a Site Discovery Technique: A Case Study from Michigan. *Journal of Field Archaeology* 12:457–468.
    1987   Feature Discovery and the Sampling Requirements of Archaeological Evaluations. *Journal of Field Archaeology* 14:359–371.
    1989   Shovel-Test Sampling in Archaeological Survey: Comments on Nance and Ball, and Lightfoot. *American Antiquity* 54:396–404.

Shott, M. J., and J. M. O'Shea
    1985   Archaeology in the Planning Process: The Ann Arbor Plan. Ms. on file, University of Northern Iowa, Cedar Falls.

Syms, E. L.
   1982   Survey Sampling: Is Anyone Getting an Adequate Record? In *Directions in Archaeology: A Question of Goals*, edited by P. Francis and E. Poplin, pp. 115–144. Archaeological Association of Calgary, Alberta.

Thomas, D. H.
   1973   An Empirical Test for Steward's Model of Great Basin Settlement Patterns. *American Antiquity* 38:155–176.

Thoms, A.
   1979   Survey Error: A Result of Intensive Archaeological Surveys. In *Scholars as Contractors*, edited by W. Mayer-Oakes and A. Portnoy, pp. 95–105. Department of the Interior, Heritage Conservation and Recreation Service, Washington, D.C.

Tingle, M.
   1987   Inferential Limits and Surface Scatters: The Case of the Maddle Farm and Vale of the White Horse Fieldwalking Survey. In *Lithic Analysis and Later British Prehistory: Some Problems and Approaches*, edited by A. Brown and M. Edmonds, pp. 87–99. British Archaeological Reports, B.S. 162. Oxford.

Trubowitz, N. L.
   1978   The Persistence of Settlement Pattern in a Cultivated Field. In *Essays in Northeastern Archaeology in Memory of Marian E. White*, edited by W. Englebrecht and D. Grayson, pp. 41–66. Occasional Publications in Northeastern Archaeology No. 5. Franklin Pierce College, Rindge, N.H.

Wandsnider, L., and J. Ebert
   1984   Accuracy in Archaeological Survey in the Seedskadee Project Area, Southwestern Wyoming. *Haliksa'i* 3:9–21.

Wandsnider, L., and S. Larralde
   1986   Seedskadee Cultural Resource Assessment Project: Report to the Branch of Remote Sensing, National Park Service. In *The Seedskadee Project: Remote Sensing in Non-Site Archeology*, edited by D. Drager and A. Ireland, pp. 151–209. Bureau of Reclamation, Salt Lake City.

Wobst, H. M.
   1978   The Archaeo-Ethnology of Hunter-Gatherers or the Tyranny of the Ethnographic Record in Archaeology. *American Antiquity* 43:303–309.
   1979   Computers and Coordinates: Strategies for the Analysis of Paleolithic Stratigraphy. In *Computer Graphics in Archaeology: Statistical Cartographic Applications to Spatial Analysis in Archaeological Contexts*, edited by S. Upham, pp. 61–67. Anthropological Research Papers No. 15. Arizona State University, Tempe.
   1983   We Can't See the Forest for the Trees: Sampling and the Shapes of Archaeological Distributions. In *Archaeological Hammers and Theories*, edited by J. Moore and A. Keene, pp. 37–85. Academic Press, New York.

Yorston, R. M., V. L. Gaffney, and P. J. Reynolds
   1990   Simulation of Artefact Movement Due to Cultivation. *Journal of Archaeological Science* 17:67–83.

Yuskavitch, J.
   1986   Buried Treasure. *Planning* 52(10):18–22.

3. Managing America's Archaeological Resources

Francis P. McManamon

Abstract: The last 25 years have witnessed the development of national systems for management of the archaeological resources in the United States. Federal agencies, which control a total of about one-third of the land in the United States, have developed archaeological resource management programs. State historic preservation programs in each state have begun to function as the managers of much of the archaeological record that is not on public land. That expansion of public archaeology has had profound effects upon the discipline of archaeology in the United States. Archaeologists in public agencies increasingly are charged with the preservation of the in situ archaeological record. More recently the importance of preservation of archaeological collections, records, and reports has become recognized. In order to better preserve America's archaeological heritage effectively, new initiatives in those areas are needed. They include more and better public education, improvements in the availability of archaeological information, better preservation of the in situ record, more progress in the inventory of in situ resources, and improvements in the curation of archaeological collections and records. Archaeologists in academic positions need to support and engage in these initiatives if preservation of the archaeological record is to be successful.

Introduction

Organized concern for the preservation of archaeological resources in the United States is at least a century old. Initial preservation efforts led to the passage in 1906 of the Antiquities Act. That statute made it illegal to remove archaeological remains from federal and Indian lands without a permit (Lee 1970). In some areas the Act halted hasty excavations of archaeological sites, but it could not be enforced effectively because there was

Quandaries and Quests: Visions of Archaeology's Future, edited by LuAnn Wandsnider. Center for Archaeological Investigations, Occasional Paper No. 20. © 1992 by the Board of Trustees, Southern Illinois University. All rights reserved. ISBN 0-88104-075-4.

neither an organization nor a sufficient work force to do so (Lister and Lister 1981:2–62; Rothman 1989); also, it did not protect sites on state, local, or private land. Since the beginning of the twentieth century, the legal basis, organizational structure, and work force have expanded to provide better preservation of the archaeological record in the United States. However, much remains to be done.

The Structure of Current Management

Many federal, state, tribal, and, increasingly, local organizations have responsibilities for the consideration of archaeological resources that are on land they administer or are affected by their actions. That multiplicity of responsibilities makes it quite easy to devise a very confusing description of public archaeology in the United States. Wouldn't it be easier if fewer agencies, or even a single one, were primarily responsible for doing public archaeology here? It might be easier to describe, but it probably would not be as effective in preserving the resources, and we almost certainly would not see the same level of archaeological activity associated with public projects that currently exists.

There are roughly a dozen major federal land-managing agencies, that is, agencies that are responsible for managing from one million acres to hundreds of millions of acres of federal land and the archaeological resources in it. There are about half a dozen federal agencies that either fund or issue permits for substantial development actions and regularly require archaeological investigations as part of the developments. These federal development and regulatory agencies typically have state-level counterparts that usually are responsible for conducting or contracting for the archaeology required by the federal agencies. There are also state agencies that manage archaeological resources on state land and, with increasing frequency, there are municipal, county, and tribal agencies that are taking on some archaeological preservation responsibility.

To simplify somewhat, we can say that in the United States the management of archaeological resources is conducted in two ways: by federal agencies on the land that they administer, and by State Historic Preservation Offices in cases that do not involve federal land. By management, I mean the collection and analysis of information about archaeological resources and the use of that information to make decisions about the preservation, use, or destruction of archaeological resources within the context of land use or development activities.

Management on Federal Land

Federal agencies administer about one-third of the land area in the United States. Most of this land management is undertaken by a dozen federal agencies (Table 3-1). The Archaeological Resources Protection Act and the National Historic Preservation Act require those agencies to care for the

Table 3-1. *Federal Archaeological Activities: Identification and Evaluation; Research Activities and Costs, 1987*

Department	Agency	Number of Id./Eval. Studies	Costs in Thousands of Dollars				
			Agency Personnel	Agency Support	Agency Contract	Land Use Applicant	Total Expended
Land Management							
Agriculture	Forest Service	5123	4105	410	159	33	4707
Defense	Air Force	110	72	87	1012	44	1215
	Army	28	ND	ND	2000	ND	2000
	Marines	3	1	0	15	0	16
	Navy	66	ND	ND	207	ND	207
Energy		181	77	17	652	0	746
Interior	BIA	1921	109	54	1086	20	1269
	BLM	6245	ND	ND	150	ND	150
	Reclamation	146	450	49	718	ND	1217
	FWS	135	39	50	330	ND	428
	NPS	257	1803	741	637	40	3221
TVA		17	23	ND	58	ND	81
		14232					15257
Development							
Agriculture	FmHA	301	8	3	5	23	39
	SCS	96	0	0	177	0	177
Defense	COE	729	2260	741	4797	354	8152
EPA		95	49	9	ND	292	350
GSA		2	NA	NA	12	0	12
HUD		NA	NA	NA	NA	NA	0
Interior	OTIA	33	1	0	1	1	3
DOT	FHwA	NA	NA	NA	NA	NA	0
		1256					8733
Regulatory							
Commerce	EcDev	NA	NA	NA	NA	NA	0
FERC		NA	NA	NA	NA	NA	0
Interior	MMS	179	40	NA	NA	NA	40
		179					40

Note: Department/agency abbreviations

BIA – Bureau of Indian Affairs
BLM – Bureau of Land Management
COE – Army Corps of Engineers
DOT – Department of Transportation
EcDev – Economic Development Administration
EPA – Environmental Protection Agency
FERC – Federal Energy Regulatory Commission
FHwA – Federal Highway Administration
FmHA – Farmers Home Administration
FSW – Fish and Wildlife Service
GSA – General Services Administration
HUD – Department of Housing & Urban Development
MMS – Minerals Management Service
NPS – National Park Service
OTIA – Office of Territorial & International Affairs
SCS – Soil Conservation Service
TVA – Tennessee Valley Authority

NA – Agency reported that this category was not applicable to its program.
ND – Agency reported that it had no data for this category.

archaeological resources, and other kinds of cultural resources, on the lands within the context of the agencies' missions. Since the early 1970s, most of those land management agencies have hired and developed professional staffs to oversee their archaeological programs. Some, such as the Forest Service (FS), the Bureau of Land Management (BLM), and the National Park Service (NPS), have relatively large archaeological staffs. Others have smaller staffs and accomplish the work necessary for their archaeological programs through contracts with private firms or universities.

Each of the agencies has begun to assemble an inventory of the archaeological sites that it administers. The degree of completeness of the inventories varies widely (Keel et al. 1989:26–28). Before the 1980s, several agencies had programs to advance the inventories, but, with one exception, those programs were eliminated during the Reagan years. Most current inventory efforts come from archaeological investigations associated with development projects on agency land. Many of the agencies also have developed written overviews of the archaeology and history relevant to the lands that they manage. The overviews are designed to assist in the assessment of sites that have been or will be discovered on the land as well as to help in the prediction of where sites are likely to be found. Most of the land-managing agencies have incorporated archaeological considerations into their agency-specific guidelines for managers, and many provide training in cultural resources topics for the managers who are responsible for overseeing lands and resources administered by the agency.

Many of the land units, such as BLM districts, national forests, and units of the NPS, have management plans that include options or actions to be taken to protect or develop the resources within the unit. These plans contain directions on how archaeological resources within the land unit are to be treated.

Land-managing agencies conduct or pay for thousands of archaeological investigations each year (Keel et al. 1989:13–22). Most of the investigations are basic records, map checks, or identification and evaluation studies. Federal land-managing agencies reported nearly 15,000 identification and evaluation studies during 1987 (Table 3-1). Identification and evaluation studies usually involve fieldwork and analysis to provide a basis for determinations of eligibility for the National Register of Historic Places. One of the results of the work was the physical inspection of nearly 2.5 million acres of land and the discovery of more than 20,000 new archaeological sites (Table 3-2).

Land-managing agencies also undertake or require data recovery activities (Table 3-3). The activities typically involve excavation, extensive collection, analysis, reporting, and, increasingly we hope, curation of recovered remains and records. Land-managing agencies reported just over 800 such data recovery investigations during 1987, a small fraction of the identification and evaluation studies that they reported.

Managing Archaeological Resources on Nonfederal Land

Federal agencies also fund, through development projects, or require, as part of applications for regulatory permits, additional thousands of

Table 3-2. *Federal Archaeological Activities: Identification and Evaluation; Research Activities and Results, 1987*

Department	Agency	Number of Id./Eval. Studies	Costs (in 000s)	Thousands of Acres Inspected	New Sites Found	Sites Determined Eligible for NRHP
Land Management						
Agriculture	Forest Service	5123	4707	1600	7479	1129
Defense	Air Force	110	1215	95	421	44
	Army	28	2000	15	1100	50
	Marines	8	16	1	15	0
	Navy	66	207	66	151	16
Energy		181	746	24	540	51
Interior	BIA	1921	1269	93	1173	494
	BLM	6245	150	422	6531	1786
	Reclamation	146	1217	21	487	264
	FWS	135	428	20	325	39
	NPS	257	3221	61	1834	105
TVA		17	81	8	135	1
		14232	15257	2426	20191	3979
Development						
Agriculture	FmHA	301	39	9	18	4
	SCS	96	177	2394	173	25
Defense	COE	729	8152	720	3766	430
EPA		95	350	1	759	58
GSA		2	12	NA	0	0
HUD		NA	0	NA	NA	NA
Interior	OTIA	33	3	1	26	17
DOT	FHwA	NA	0	NA	NA	NA
		1256	8733	3126	4742	534
Regulatory						
Commerce	EcDev	NA	0	NA	NA	NA
FERC		NA	0	NA	NA	NA
Interior	MMS	179	40	980	0	0
		179	40	980	0	0

Note: Department/agency abbreviations

BIA – Bureau of Indian Affairs
BLM – Bureau of Land Management
COE – Army Corps of Engineers
DOT – Department of Transportation
EcDev – Economic Development Administration
EPA – Environmental Protection Agency
FERC – Federal Energy Regulatory Commission
FHwA – Federal Highway Administration
FmHA – Farmers Home Administration

FSW – Fish and Wildlife Service
GSA – General Services Administration
HUD – Department of Housing & Urban Development
MMS – Minerals Management Service
NPS – National Park Service
OTIA – Office of Territorial & International Affairs
SCS – Soil Conservation Service
TVA – Tennessee Valley Authority

NA – Agency reported that this category was not applicable to its program.

Table 3-3. *Federal Archaeological Activities: Data Recovery Activities, 1987*

Department	Agency	Number of Data Recovery Projects	Costs in Thousands of Dollars				
			Agency Personnel	Agency Support	Agency Contract	Land Use Applicant	Total Expended
Land Management							
Agriculture	Forest Service	504	460	82	310	24	876
Defense	Air Force	2	0	0	220	49	269
	Army	13	ND	ND	ND	ND	0
	Marines	0	0	0	0	0	0
	Navy	7	ND	ND	221	ND	221
Energy		7	15	3	166	0	184
Interior	BIA	38	56	5	924	0	985
	BLM	154	210	45	216	ND	471
	Reclamation	22	275	4	2509	ND	2788
	FWS	10	21	19	49	ND	89
	NPS	36	509	151	424	0	1084
TVA		8	25	5	6	ND	36
		801					7003
Development							
Agriculture	FmHA	105	3	2	0	1	6
	SCS	2	1	1	27	0	29
Defense	COE	96	660	163	2259	485	3567
EPA		36	86	11	ND	810	907
GSA		1	4	7	36	0	47
HUD		NA	NA	NA	NA	NA	0
Interior	OTIA	3	0	0	0	13	13
DOT	FHwA	NA	NA	NA	NA	NA	0
		243					4569
Regulatory							
Commerce	EcDev	NA	NA	NA	NA	NA	0
	FERC	NA	NA	NA	NA	NA	0
Interior	MMS	NA	NA	NA	NA	NA	0
		0					0

Note: Department/agency abbreviations

BIA – Bureau of Indian Affairs
BLM – Bureau of Land Management
COE – Army Corps of Engineers
DOT – Department of Transportation
EcDev – Economic Development Administration
EPA – Environmental Protection Agency
FERC – Federal Energy Regulatory Commission
FHwA – Federal Highway Administration
FmHA – Farmers Home Administration
FSW – Fish and Wildlife Service
GSA – General Services Administration
HUD – Department of Housing & Urban Development
MMS – Minerals Management Service
NPS – National Park Service
OTIA – Office of Territorial & International Affairs
SCS – Soil Conservation Service
TVA – Tennessee Valley Authority

NA – Agency reported that this category was not applicable to its program.
ND – Agency reported that it had no data for this category.

archaeological investigations. Most of these actions take place on nonfederal lands. The agencies that fund or require the investigations have functions such as the creation and maintenance of transportation, housing, communications, or energy systems, the improvement or maintenance of clean water and air, and the stimulation of economic development. We know from experience that some of the agencies, such as the Corps of Engineers (COE), the Federal Highway Administration (FHWA), the Environmental Protection Agency (EPA), and the Federal Energy Regulatory Commission (FERC), regularly fund or require archaeological investigations.

A number of important state-level archaeological programs, for example, were established to conduct the highway archaeology funded by the FHWA. With a few notable exceptions, such as the COE, the FERC, and the Soil Conservation Service (SCS), the agencies have not developed their own internal archaeological programs to oversee their archaeological activities. Nor do several of these agencies track the extent of the archaeological activities for which they are responsible; note the many "NDs" and "NAs" under the categories in Tables 3-1, 3-2, and 3-3. Among the development and regulatory agencies, for example, the EPA reported only 95 identification and evaluation investigations nationally during 1987. In addition, the lack of reporting by FHWA and FERC is evident in Tables 3-1, 3-2, and 3-3.

By and large, those agencies approach their archaeological responsibilities quite differently from the land-managing agencies. They do not administer the archaeological sites that their actions affect and, except for concurring with whatever preservation provisions might be in Memoranda of Agreement that are developed for specific projects, they eschew any management responsibilities for the long-term care of resources. Can we say, then, that there is any effective management of the archaeological resources that are not on federal or some other public land? There is, although it differs legally from the direct responsibility that federal land-managing agencies have for sites on the land they administer.

The management of archaeological sites not on public land is undertaken in many states by the State Historic Preservation Officers (SHPO). The national network of SHPOs developed during the 1960s and 1970s as a result of the National Historic Preservation Act. For the most part, these officials do not have the authority to manage archaeological sites as owners of the sites, but they are responsible for developing statewide inventories of archaeological resources, as well as other kinds of cultural resources. They also develop resource overviews, studies, or plans, sometimes referred to as historic contexts, to provide background and a framework for the evaluation of resources. Finally, and importantly, SHPOs consult with federal, and frequently also state, agencies when the actions of the latter will affect archaeological resources.

The SHPOs provide essential management elements: an inventory of resources, a framework for evaluating those resources, and a procedure for making decisions about the treatment of resources, although they lack the power of ownership and cannot dictate the treatment that resources will receive. We might quarrel with the decisions made by those officials or with the amount or kind of attention they afford to archaeological resource preservation, but they do constitute the nationwide system for managing archaeological resources not on federal land. Of course, in their function of working with federal agencies on their actions that affect archaeological resources, SHPOs also influence the preservation of resources on federal lands. They are an especially important factor in archaeological preservation in the eastern two-thirds of the country where federal land is scarce. The SHPOs constitute a group with which archaeologists interested in preserving America's archaeological heritage must work closely, with effective persuasion and cooperation.

Archaeological Management: The Big Picture

The management of America's archaeological resources, at present, is carried out by federal agencies that manage public lands and a network of state agencies responsible for managing cultural resources within individual states. The national information that has been collected recently (Keel et al. 1989) provides a general approximation of the level of effort in archaeology by federal agencies.

Federal agencies conduct, contract for, or require a very large portion of the archaeological work that is done in the United States. In 1986 the funding for archaeological activities reported by federal agencies totaled about $75 million, which we know from some of the items pointed out above is a minimum estimate. The reported data indicate a strong focus on inventory and evaluation activities with nearly half the reported costs going toward field surveys and nearly a quarter for literature and map research (Figure 3-1). For 1987, about 15,000 of those investigations were reported compared to about 1,000 data recovery actions (Table 3-3). We can hope this difference means that, in most cases, sites identified during project planning were avoided and preserved during the subsequent land modification or development activities.

The focus on survey and inventory might partially answer one of the often-heard criticisms of federal archaeology, that it has not produced advances in our understanding of the past equivalent to the funds expended. The kinds of research results from identification and evaluation activities, that is, records and map checking, survey, and limited testing, usually do not lead to the advances in knowledge that come from a similar amount of attention to excavation and the analysis of excavation data. Survey data require different kinds of analysis than excavation data. With so much federal activity in the survey area, greater standardization in the recording of the data and improvements in the methods and techniques for their analysis are needed.

The structure that has developed for the management of archaeological resources in the United States during the past 20 years is unlikely to change in the near future. This means that what pieces of the archaeological record are saved and how they are saved depends on the effectiveness of archaeologists in working with federal agencies and SHPOs. The changes in management

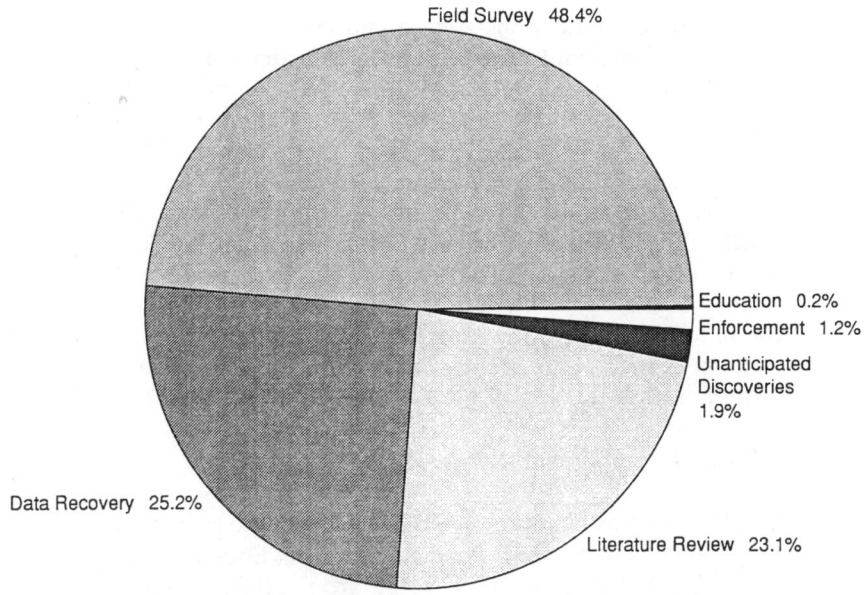

Figure 3-1. *Percentage of costs by activity for federal archaeology, 1987.*

called for by Shott (this volume) are unlikely to occur; however, some of the research that he recommends, such as research to develop better understanding of the physical characteristics of archaeological sites, could be conducted currently through SHPO programs using planning grants and projects. The kinds of archaeological investigations that are conducted by federal agencies, that is, identification and evaluation studies, are unlikely to change, but archaeologists should be able to improve the understanding of the results from those studies by focusing greater attention on the collection and analysis of survey data.

The preceding has been a description of the current management of archaeological resources in the United States. Although there have been many successes, we are not in a position to sit back and relax. Additional resources, if available, could be put to use profitably even within the framework of current activities. However, there are additional areas in which progress must be made.

Expanding Archaeological Resource Management

We all can do better at archaeological resource management. Looking back 20 years, one is staggered by the improvements that have occurred. Is it possible to make similar progress in the next decade or two? There certainly are areas that need additional emphasis; and, it is encouraging that progress has begun in each of them, but more attention to each is needed. They are areas where we need *more effort* and *more resources,* not just effort shifted from other duties, but new initiatives to match the progress that we have seen during the last two decades in the areas of project review during the planning stages of development actions. There are five areas for attention: (1) public education and participation; (2) better preservation of the in situ archaeological record; (3) improvement in the availability of information; (4) improvement in resource inventories; and (5) improvement in curation of archaeological collections and records. At the national level, Secretary of the Interior Manuel Lujan has recognized those needs. In a recent memorandum to the leadership of the Department of the Interior, he has called for a national strategy for federal archaeology and has directed bureaus to emphasize activities in those areas as part of their cultural resource management, public affairs, interpretation, and resource protection programs (Lujan 1990).

Public Education and Participation

Calls for efforts to open up archaeology to the public have become widespread. At recent annual meetings of the Society for American Archaeology (SAA), the calls have come from such differently placed advocates as Ian Hodder, leading theorist of postprocessual archaeology, and Jean Auel, best-selling author of Paleolithic romances. The calls are completely accurate; there is a real need for *more* public education efforts, and there are significant activities under way. The SAA is backing strongly both a new Committee on Public Education and the recently incorporated Foundation for American Archaeology, which will have a variety of public education functions. Other professional societies, federal agencies, state agencies, and individual archaeologists are becoming more involved in public education efforts.

Federal agencies seem to have the support of the political leaders in the current administration to emphasize public education and participation efforts. Both President Bush and Secretary Lujan have named education as an important goal. They have even backed up their statements with modest funding increases, but it remains to be seen whether the initiatives will continue.

Public education and participation encompass a wide variety of activities indeed; with a variety of individuals and groups involved, it is essential that efforts be well coordinated. One aspect of coordination is compiling and distributing information about existing activities and programs. The Archeological Assistance Program, NPS, is attempting to do this through the LEAP (Listing of Education in Archeological Programs) Clearinghouse (Knoll 1990). Also needed is information about the general public and special publics that we want to reach: we need to know about their perceptions of the past and what they would like to learn about it (Stone 1989). We need to identify specific audiences that should be the focus of attention, such as educators and students, Native Americans, planners and developers, legislators, and managers in public agencies (Gelburd 1989; McManamon 1991).

Reaching the general public also will require techniques, activities, and messages that archaeologists have not used widely to date. Most people have at best a modest interest in archaeology, but they seem to be positively inclined toward it. Popular magazines regularly include stories about archaeology. Clearly, there is a foundation of public interest in archaeology and archaeological sites to build upon. Our task in reaching the general public is to maintain that positive inclination and to strengthen the interest, understanding, and level of support.

The public education and participation topic includes a wide variety of activities. Success in this area will require a coherent plan, much cooperation, and an understanding that the effort has both long- and short-range goals. This area should become a more important part of the management of America's archaeological resources.

Preserving the In Situ Record

The destruction of archaeological sites by modern development and land-use practices, looting, and natural processes, such as erosion, is a worldwide phenomenon that America has not escaped. The last decade has seen the growth of activity in fighting the destruction. The success of the Archaeological Conservancy in purchasing archaeological sites for preservation is one of the best examples. While modest by the scale of the Nature Conservancy, the Archaeological Conservancy has grown and seems to have developed a solid base to support further growth. The more recent "Save the Past" initiative by the Society for American Archaeology (1990) and a variety of public agencies and private organizations was another important project that successfully focused attention on the dangerously rapid loss of our archaeological heritage. Within the discipline the same message needs to be picked up and action taken.

In the fight against looting on public lands, agency archaeologists have been gratified by the support, interest, and actions of law enforcement personnel. Both the BLM and the NPS have made budget increases specifically to fight archaeological looting.

The hints of progress in that area, however, should not make us overconfident. Another example illustrates the darker side of the topic. In December 1989, the superintendent of Bandelier National Monument, about 50 miles northwest of Santa Fe, New Mexico, stopped public access to the Tsankawi unit of the monument. In a press release concerning the closing, the superintendent noted that some people took advantage of the remote location of the unit to steal potsherds, knock over ruin walls, and scratch graffiti on the rocks. He cited examples of surveillance cameras in the area having recorded people filling shopping bags with artifacts. This in a national monument set aside for archaeological preservation!

Clearly, attention to looting is still needed. Yet attention to the preservation of the in situ record should be extended. Modern development and land use also are destroying the in situ record. Some have forecast the demise of the record in the not-too-distant future (Knudson 1989). These threats also must be met and means found to preserve more of the record in situ even in the face of modern land modification.

Making Information Available

The large number of archaeological investigations reported each year by federal agencies (Tables 3-1, 3-2, and 3-3) provides a graphic example of the growth of the primary literature on archaeological investigations in the United States. The figures reported indicate almost 20,000 investigations per year, the majority of which require a written report of some kind. Almost all of the reports are produced in very limited numbers and distributed to relatively few individuals and repositories. There are two primary needs in this area. First, more syntheses of these primary sources of information about the archaeological record are needed. The syntheses will have to be the products of experts in certain geographical, temporal, or topical subjects. The public agencies responsible for the management of archaeological resources have an obligation, as well as a need, to support the production of the reports but will need additional resources to do so.

The second primary need is for an easier means of access to the reports or specific information about sites themselves. The NPS has been laboring for many years on the National Archeological Database (NADB). This data base is one outgrowth of the 1981 report *Are Agencies Doing Enough or Too Much for Archeological Preservation?* (General Accounting Office 1981). One of the recommendations in the report that Congress acted upon provided for the creation of a national data base on federal archaeological activities in order to share information more rapidly and reduce redundancy.

Summary records have been collected for 100,000 archaeological reports so far; a software package has been developed to facilitate data entry, updates, and reporting. Each record includes standard bibliographic citation information about the report, as well as information about the general kind of archaeological investigation that it reports on, the geographic location of the investigation, where a copy of the report can be found, and a series of keywords that describe the topics covered in the report. We estimated the initial mass of reports in the "grey literature" to be about 200,000; our estimate of yearly increase in this area is 10,000–20,000 reports.

Current efforts are focused upon the creation of a national network of NADB users and contributors who will help to build the data base and provide initial access to the information. The SHPOs and some federal agency offices will compose the initial nodes of the network. However, more generally available "on line" versions of the data base are being investigated. Additional data collection will be needed to include the large number of existing reports in the data base.

Other NPS offices are working with SHPOs on data standards for site inventories and other computerized systems to help in the management of cultural resources. If America's archaeological resource managers are to have a well-coordinated system of information flow, more effort will be necessary during this decade.

Improving Resource Inventories

On average, federal agencies that manage land have conducted archaeological inventories on less than 10% of their land (Keel et al. 1989:26–28). In the Four Corners states it is estimated that only 6% of the FS, BLM, and NPS land has been surveyed (General Accounting Office 1987:39). The lack of information about the location of archaeological resources has been identified by many as one of the problems confronting agencies in protecting sites from looters. As mentioned above, during the 1980s most of those agencies that earlier had funded archaeological resource inventories dropped the programs for lack of funds. With the relative loosening of purse strings, agency archaeologists must again work within their offices to fund such investigations. In addition to assisting management in the preservation of sites, the data from the surveys can be used to improve the evaluation of inventory data from development and land-use projects.

Better inventories of archaeological resources on federal land will provide for better management and protection; they also are called for by recent amendments to the Archaeological Resources Protection Act and have been a part of the requirements of the National Historic Preservation Act since the 1980 amendments to that statute.

In this area we must renew and reinvigorate a commitment to activities that will lead over the long term to a fuller inventory of America's archaeological heritage. One improvement would be inventories that provide comparable data. It is unfortunately true that much of the existing inventory data are difficult, if not impossible, to compare on a large scale. One means of overcoming this would be to focus on more explicit physical descriptions of the archaeological record. For example, the use of density measures to characterize sites rather than only anthropological terms such as "camp" or "lithic reduction station" would be helpful (e.g., McManamon 1984:278, 1986). Use of density measures or other physical characteristics does not preclude use of anthropological or behavioral terms for interpretive purposes, but with only the latter, comparisons of such relevant topics as the intensity of prehistoric land use between or among areas or projects is impossible.

Improving Curation of Archaeological Collections

Federal agencies also are responsible for the curation of vast numbers of artifacts, other remains, and records of investigations from sites on the land they manage or from sites that their activities have disturbed. For sites that have been destroyed, those remains and records are all the heritage left to future generations about the archaeological record (also see Woosley, this volume). The percentage of the archaeological record that is in a collection rather than in situ grows daily; at least this is true for the prehistoric portion of the archaeological record.

Artifacts removed from public lands are considered the property, and therefore the responsibility, of the public agency that administers the land. Millions of dollars have been used to collect the artifacts and other remains.

With proper study that material can provide further information about important aspects of the past. Research on collections will be successful only if the remains and the records about their original archaeological context are linked, both can be found, and both are in usable condition. Adequate curation of remains and records is essential for those conditions to be met. A recent investigation by the General Accounting Office (General Accounting Office 1987:69–95) found that federal agencies were not doing a good job in caring for their archaeological collections. At the eight local agency offices that were visited, General Accounting Office investigators found no adequate systems to account for the location or composition of the archaeological collections from their lands. Also, the agencies did not have guidelines for determining the adequacy of facilities to curate collections and did not systematically inspect facilities either before they deposited collections with them or afterward (General Accounting Office 1987:78).

The NPS, which has the most detailed estimate of the size of this curatorial challenge, projects that decades of time and millions of dollars will be needed to overcome the curation challenge presented by the mountain of archaeological data already in its collection. Other federal agencies are beginning systematic programs in archaeological curation as well. The recent publication of regulations on the curation of federal archaeological collections (36 *CFR* 79) should stir archaeological and management interest in making progress on this topic.

The focus here has been on the need to improve accountability and management for federal and other public archaeological collections. As noted by Goldstein and by Leone and Preucel (this volume), there also is a need to address the question of the rightful ownership of archaeological materials. Increasingly, Indian groups are claiming for themselves all or parts of archaeological collections. They often have legitimate claims and understandable gripes about the way the archaeological heritage of their tribes has been kept from them. However, some balance must be achieved so that all Americans can have the benefit of the prehistoric and early historic past of the country.

Summary

The present structure for management of America's archaeological heritage is complex. It involves public agencies at the federal, state, tribal, and local levels of government. Both direct and indirect management responsibilities exist. The strength of the arrangement is that many agencies are responsible legally for preserving or at least considering the preservation of archaeological resources as part of their function. The potential weakness of the system is that leadership and coordination must be exercised effectively to keep all the components from flying apart.

The coming decade and the next century pose new challenges along with the ones that have confronted those concerned about archaeological preservation during the last 20 years. The areas currently addressed must continue to be addressed. For the most part we cannot afford to shift precious resources away from these activities to meet additional challenges, although some shifting may be necessary.

More and better public education and participation, better preservation of the in situ record, improvements in information availability, more progress in resource inventories, and improvements in the curation of collections and records require new efforts. Progress in all of these areas has the potential for substantial benefits if we can manage to address them effectively.

In order to continue and to improve the system of archaeological resource management as it has developed in the United States during the past 25 years, archaeologists from each of the major areas of employment—public agencies, academic departments, private firms, and museums—must work cooperatively. There is much to do, but it is necessary if our archaeological heritage is to have a useful future.

References

Gelburd, Diane E.
    1989   Improving the Public's Perception of Archaeology. In *Cultural Resource Management in the 1990s*, edited by Peter S. Miller, Diane E. Gelburd, and Glen Ellen Alderton, pp. 3–8. American Society for Conservation Archaeology.

General Accounting Office
    1981   *Are Agencies Doing Enough or Too Much for Archeological Preservation? Guidance Needed*. Report CED–81–61. General Accounting Office, Washington, D.C.
    1987   *Problems Protecting and Preserving Federal Archeological Resources*. GAO/RCED–83–3. General Accounting Office, Washington, D.C.

Keel, Bennie C., Francis P. McManamon, and George S. Smith
    1989   *Federal Archeology: The Current Program*. National Park Service, U.S. Department of the Interior, Washington, D.C.

Knoll, Patricia C.
    1990   *Listing of Education in Archeological Programs: The LEAP Clearinghouse 1987–1989 Summary Report*. National Park Service, U.S. Department of the Interior, Washington, D.C.

Knudson, Ruthann
    1989   North America's Threatened Heritage. *Archaeology* 42(1):67.

Lee, Ronald F.
    1970   *The Antiquities Act of 1906*. National Park Service, Washington, D.C.

Lister, Robert H., and Florence G. Lister
    1981   *Chaco Canyon: Archaeology and Archaeologists*. University of New Mexico Press, Albuquerque.

Lujan, Manuel, Jr.
    1990   A National Strategy for Federal Archeology. Memorandum, March 20, 1990. On file, Office of the Secretary, U.S. Department of the Interior, Washington, D.C.

McManamon, Francis P.
    1984   Discovering Sites Unseen. In *Advances in Archaeological Method and Theory*, vol. 7, edited by Michael B. Schiffer, pp. 223–292. Academic Press, New York.

1986 Units of Analysis and Prehistoric Land Use on Outer Cape Cod. In *Man in the Northeast* 31:151–172.
1991 The Many Publics for Archeology. *American Antiquity* 56:121–130.

Rothman, Hal
1989 *Preserving Different Pasts: The American National Monuments.* University of Illinois Press, Urbana.

Society for American Archaeology
1990 *Save the Past for the Future: Actions for the 1990s.* Office of Government Relations, Society for American Archaeology, Washington, D.C.

Stone, Peter G.
1989 Interpretations and Uses of the Past in Modern Britain and Europe. Why are People Interested in the Past? Do the Experts Know or Care? A Plea for Further Study. In *Who Needs the Past?: Indigenous Values and Archaeology*, edited by Robert Layton, pp. 195–206. Unwin Hyman, London.

4. Where the Money Goes: Current Trends in Archaeological Funding

Miriam T. Stark

Abstract: Socioeconomic forces shape the face of archaeological research, and funding availability affects how archaeological knowledge is produced. This study presents data on funding patterns by examining selected academic and nonacademic funding sources for North Americanist archaeologists. Two trends characterize the current situation: (1) nonacademic sources support the majority of research conducted in North America, and (2) an increasing number of projects merge academic and nonacademic funding sources. Evaluating where the money goes, who receives the funding, and how much of it is available provides an index of the state of North Americanist archaeology.

Introduction

During Sir Flinders Petrie's era, experience and brains, rather than money, were necessary for the practice of archaeology (1904:3). Nearly a century later, Petrie's dictum is but a half-truth. The availability of funding influences the types of research that archaeologists pursue. Examining the economic environment in which archaeological research is conducted is a starting point for understanding the state of our field. North American archaeology forms the focus of this funding study because of its relative importance and the accessibility of data regarding its funding. North American archaeology is first examined within a wider geographical framework. Evaluating where the money goes, who receives the funding, and how much of it is available provides some index of the state of North Americanist archaeology.

This study explores traditional sources of academic (or institutional) funding and of nonacademic funding alternatives. First, the relationship between archaeological research and archaeological funding is introduced.

Quandaries and Quests: Visions of Archaeology's Future, edited by LuAnn Wandsnider. Center for Archaeological Investigations, Occasional Paper No. 20. © 1992 by the Board of Trustees, Southern Illinois University. All rights reserved. ISBN 0-88104-075-4.

Academic funding is then examined at a general level: by geographic area, by gender, and by research emphasis. Nonacademic funding, by necessity, is largely restricted to federal archaeological programs. The changing importance of academic versus nonacademic funding for North Americanist research is addressed to lay the groundwork for future research on the impact of funding sources on directions in archaeological research.

Archaeological Funding in Historical Perspective

The relationship between archaeological research and the times in which it is practiced has only begun to be investigated (e.g., Patterson 1986; Trigger 1990). Until the 1930s, North Americanist archaeology was conducted under the sponsorship of wealthy patrons or institutions (Patterson 1986:13). With the advent of New Deal programs in the 1930s came the development of government-sponsored archaeology. The year 1934 saw governmental, academic, and museum archaeologists joining forces to create the Society for American Archaeology (Griffin 1985). The sustained economic growth following the end of World War II helped to fuel archaeological research, which continued until the late 1960s (Griffin 1985:17).

Several pieces of key cultural resource management (CRM) legislation were enacted in the late 1960s and early 1970s (see also Klinger 1975). The demand for archaeologists in both the public and the private sectors escalated, particularly in the realm of CRM (Fowler 1982; Schiffer 1979; Schiffer and Gumerman 1977). Concomitantly, funding from major agencies, such as the National Science Foundation (NSF) declined sharply across all subfields of anthropology (Plattner and McIntyre 1990). Smaller agencies, such as the National Geographic Society, or NGS, (Patterson 1986:18) and private funding agencies for area studies, emerged as significant funding sources for academic or institutional research.

This study examines key aspects of funding in North American archaeology from the mid-1970s to the present within academic and nonacademic spheres. Beginning in the 1970s, North Americanist archaeology has been intimately linked to CRM, as prospects for employment, research, and publication have ballooned in the contract sector (Fowler 1982; Schiffer 1979). Funding is increasingly available beyond the academy's walls through federal and private sources. However, the scale of the funding is difficult to characterize since data on those sources are highly variable.

Academic Funding Sources

Academic funding sources considered in this section comprise the largest contributors to anthropological archaeological research today. Sources include the National Science Foundation, the National Endowment for the Humanities (NEH), the Wenner-Gren Foundation for Anthropological

Research (Wenner-Gren), and the National Geographic Society. This list of funding sources is by no means complete and in part reflects the accessibility of funding from those foundations. However, patterns derived from those funding sources should be representative for the academic realm of archaeology.

Published data and periodic reviews that have been made public by NSF form the data base of this study (Plattner et al. 1987; Plattner and McIntyre 1990; Yellen 1991; Yellen and Greene 1985). NSF provides approximately 95% of the federal monies available for university-sponsored anthropological research (Greene 1985) and is thus a major source of funding for academically based North American archaeologists. Supplementing NSF data is information from public reports provided by Wenner-Gren, NEH, and NGS. Funding agencies vary widely in the average size of grants given. NSF postdoctoral grants between 1986 and 1989, for example, averaged almost $54,000 per award, while contemporary Wenner-Gren grants hovered around $5,000 (Wenner-Gren 1986). The adjusted average NSF award (i.e., adjusted for inflation) has decreased during the last 20 years (Casteel 1980; Watson 1989), yet the average NSF award size still dwarfs the size of awards given by Wenner-Gren, NGS, or NEH.

The focus in this section lies in where the money goes rather than in how much money goes where. Accordingly, the number of grants given is used as an index instead of the size of particular grants awarded. Surveying a range of academic funding sources produces a homogeneous finding: that funding for North American research is on the decline. Earlier research indicated that over 60% of NSF postdoctoral archaeology funding went to New World research between 1954 and 1983 (Yellen and Greene 1985). In 1989, over 50% of projects funded involved North American research. Nearly 65% of the predoctoral funding since 1965 has been allotted to New World research (Plattner and McIntyre 1990). This study extends that trend to 1989 in Figure 4-1, which illustrates the proportion of New World projects funded by NSF at the predoctoral and postdoctoral levels.

Traditionally, NSF has funded more archaeological research in North America (Yellen and Greene 1985) than in any other geographic area of the world. The amount of North American research that is funded has decreased (Casteel 1980; Yellen and Greene 1985), beginning around 1962 (Yellen and Greene 1985:339). Between 1983 and 1989, funding dropped from 26% to 18% of the total; concurrently, funding for Near Eastern and Pacific research increased by 11%. Moreover, NSF grants for North American research are shrinking in average size, relative to research in other parts of the world. Postdoctoral North American grants between 1986 and 1989 averaged $47,500, in contrast to an average award size of $60,000 for Near Eastern grants.

Changes are also evident in recent NSF predoctoral funding to particular geographic regions with respect to overall funding patterns from the inception of the NSF predoctoral program in 1965 (Figure 4-2). Relatively less research has been funded in North America (now 30% of research funded), while research in Mesoamerica has increased. That pattern is echoed in combined NGS and NEH funding between 1976 and 1985. From those

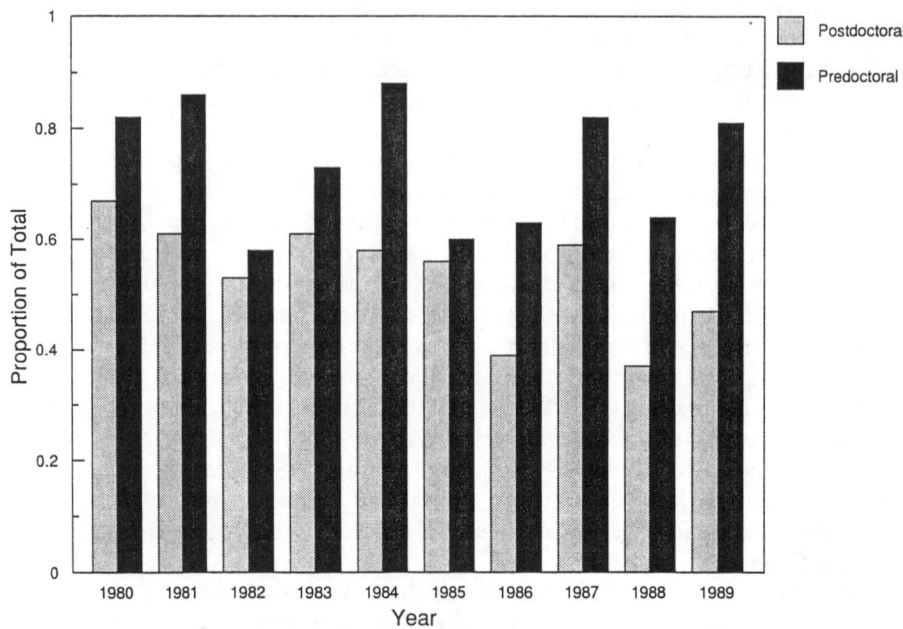

Figure 4-1. *NSF predoctoral and postdoctoral funding for New World research.*

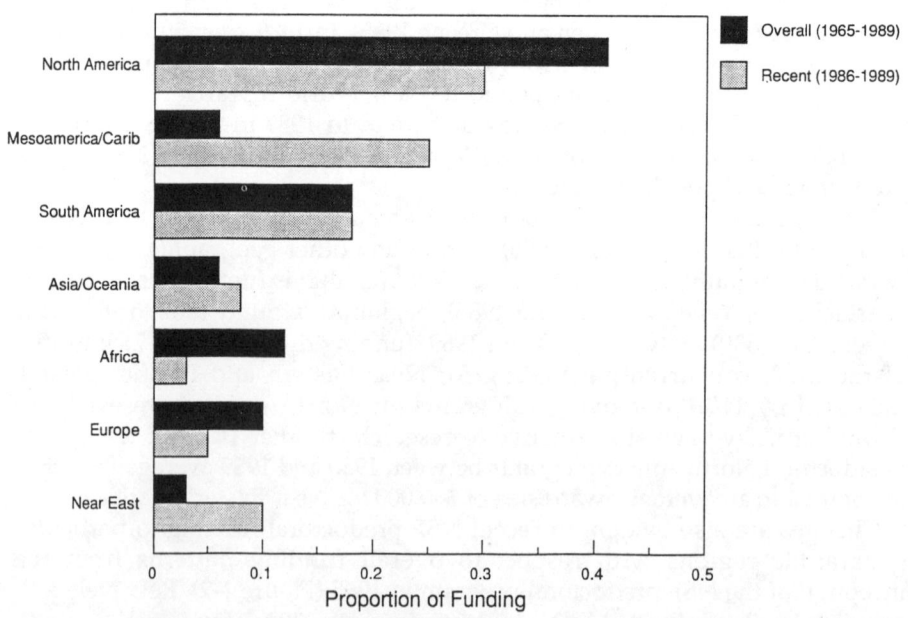

Figure 4-2. *NSF predoctoral funding by geographic area, past and present (1965–1989 data from Plattner and McIntyre [1990]).*

agencies, funding for North American research peaked at 50% in 1976 and 1979 and dropped to 20% of all areas funded by 1985.

Data from Wenner-Gren (Wenner-Gren 1986) exhibit less concentration on North American research than do NSF patterns. The geographical emphasis of Wenner-Gren funding in the 1980s (i.e., 1980–1985 and 1989) was nearly equally distributed across North America (20%), Mesoamerica (23%), and Europe (18%), with slightly less funding to African research (15%) and projects in South America (14%). A smaller proportion of Wenner-Gren funds is allotted for North American research, and that proportion is dropping (e.g., about 17.9% in 1991).

Gender and Funding

Gender-related differences in funding were examined in previous research that covered the period from 1980 to 1986 and relied upon data from NSF, NGS, and NEH (Kramer and Stark 1988). Gender inequities are decreasing in the domain of funding, a pattern also identified in NSF funding to cultural anthropologists (Plattner et al. 1987:857) and across subfields for predoctoral grants awarded between 1965 and 1989 (Plattner and McIntyre 1990). Recent analyses of NSF data suggest a trend away from gender bias in funding at the predoctoral and doctoral levels (Plattner and McIntyre 1990; Yellen, personal communication 1990). Gender parity across four fields of dissertation improvement grants was reached in the early 1980s (Plattner and McIntyre 1990:6). Within archaeology, younger females proved more successful than their female seniors and equally successful as their male peers during fiscal years 1989 and 1991 (Yellen, personal communication 1990).

No comparable data were accessible on success rates across other funding agencies considered in this study (i.e., Wenner-Gren, NGS, NEH). However, data are available on gender and funding to Canadian women archaeologists (Kelley and Hill 1991). Funding patterns in Canadian archaeology suggest that gender-based differences in success rates were not statistically significant. Canadian women archaeologists, underrepresented in academia, tended to request and receive slightly more money and to enjoy a slightly higher success rate than did their peers (Hill and Kelley 1991).

In conclusion, funding agencies are more responsive to gender issues than is the academy. Women remain grossly underrepresented in academic departments across the United States relative to the number of female graduate students and dissertations produced (Kramer and Stark 1988). Outside academia, in the public and private archaeological sectors, gender differences are less pronounced (Stark 1991).

Funding by Research Subject

Patterns in funding by research subjects, while gross in nature, are informative. To compensate for the weaknesses in information sources on funded research subjects, gross categories were devised that encompassed all but a small number of grants given in each year. The NSF data are analyzed through seven gross categories that provide only a general indicator of research subjects, with the Wenner-Gren information supplementing information derived from NSF.

The first subject identified was baseline research. Culture history, regional survey and excavation, the reconstruction of the culture history of particular geographic areas, and site-specific research were classed together as approaches that address fundamental research questions and are applied to virtually every given area of study. Several strategies—subsistence, mortuary, chronology, and modeling—were considered separately from baseline research because those approaches gained prominence during the new archaeology period and are not consistently conducted across geographic areas. Archaeological analysis was divided into traditional (i.e., standard analytic techniques) and nontraditional (i.e., new analytic techniques) approaches. Standard analytic techniques are regular components of most archaeological projects, including ceramic and lithic analysis, ethnobotany, geomorphology, osteology, and zooarchaeology. New analytic strategies (or instrumental techniques) were lumped: bone chemistry studies, compositional analysis, and residue analysis. Historical archaeology and ethnohistory were grouped together as nonprehistoric research. Ethnoarchaeology and experimental archaeology were classed together as actualistic studies. Method and theory included formation processes research and cross-cultural theoretical studies that were considered to be of general applicability.

Figure 4-3 presents data that illustrate the nature of archaeological research that NSF now funds, with predoctoral and postdoctoral funding combined. Of the subjects that receive funding in North American archaeology, baseline research forms the bulk of grants funded. Second, grants awarded to perform standard analytical techniques dropped from 45% of the grants awarded in 1986 to only 8% of those awarded in 1989, while nearly three times as many grants involving new analytical techniques were funded. Ceramic compositional studies exemplify the trend, where increasing numbers of characterization studies are being funded in lieu of more traditional ceramic analyses. A trend toward increased reliance on new analytic techniques is evident, and the ramifications of that trend are discussed by Bishop elsewhere in this volume.

Nonacademic Funding Sources

That nonacademic funding for research in the United States is increasingly common is no surprise to Americanist archaeologists. Knudson's (1985:339) prediction for the next fifty years—that funding for most archaeological research worldwide will come from federal agencies and cultural resource management firms carrying out legislative mandates—has already been borne out in the United States and abroad (see Simmons, this volume). Shrinking fiscal resources from traditional funding agencies, an ever-expanding archaeological community, and a growing public concern in

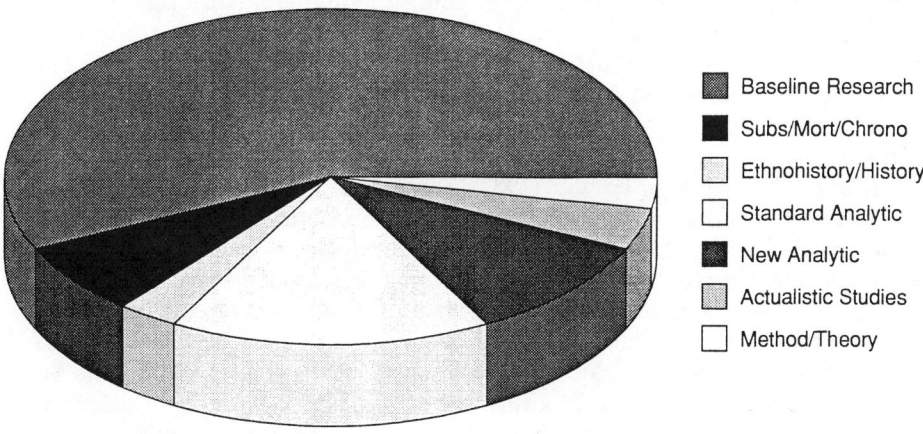

Figure 4-3. *NSF funding by subject (predoctoral and postdoctoral combined): 1986–1989.*

preserving cultural remains have all encouraged the trend toward public and private funding of archaeological projects. Most archaeological research in the United States has been supported by public funds for the last two decades (Fowler 1982:3). This study focuses on CRM within the United States. However, the trend toward global CRM is growing, as discussed by Simmons in this volume and elsewhere (e.g., Cleere 1988; Goodland and Webb 1987; Keatinge 1980).

The development of nonacademic archaeology began with the inception of the River Basin surveys during the Roosevelt administration, exemplified by the Tennessee Valley Authority project (Jennings 1985:282). Great strides were made during the 1960s that encouraged the development of federal archaeology. Legislation included the Historic Sites Preservation Act (1966) and the National Environmental Policy Act (1969). By 1971, approximately one million dollars of public money on the state and federal level was spent to recover or preserve archaeological resources (McGimsey 1985:330). The passage of Executive Order 11593 in 1971 and the Moss-Bennett Act in 1974 further encouraged government support of archaeological programs throughout the United States. The biggest, single, direct employers of archaeologists today are federal agencies and engineering firms (Fowler 1982:35).

A wealth of nonacademic funding sources is now available to interested archaeologists, from federally supported or state-supported projects to private corporate sponsorship (also see Simmons, this volume) and private foundations or volunteer-based research programs and amateur archaeological societies. Cultural resource management has become an influential force in shaping contemporary archaeology, whether in the public or the private sector (Jennings 1985:281). Funding for academic research is traditionally investigator-instigated and is characterized by a high degree of autonomy. At the opposite extreme is CRM research, which brought with it a boom in nonacademic "agency archaeologists" and "corporate archaeologists" (Fowler 1982:35).

Nearly a decade ago, Fowler (1982:36) remarked that archaeology was in the midst of a rapid transition from a strictly academic profession to one in which consulting and implementing are major areas of enterprise. In certain parts of the United States, the trend toward nonacademic funding has intensified. New and improved road systems, larger water sources such as reservoirs and dams, and even newly established state archaeology parks have emerged in the last decade with migration into states within the Sun Belt. The sustained demand for CRM—at a time when academic positions are scarce—has encouraged highly trained and motivated archaeologists to enter the contract world. While CRM archaeology is constrained by compliance specifications, the quality of research done outside the academic context has risen considerably. CRM agencies affiliated with universities have been awarded substantial contracts, and many of the management personnel have doctorates. Innovation, combined with clarity in research design, characterizes a sizable amount of CRM research today.

Up to this point, the study has focused on where the money goes, rather than in how much money goes where. Only a small portion of nonacademic funding can be examined in this study. CRM archaeology that is financed by nongovernment sources cannot be addressed here. One market analysis of contract projects in the state of Michigan was undertaken in the mid-1970s and briefly discussed in Fitting (1979). Such reports are rarely conducted, and even less available, at the state or the national scale.

State-supported funding is one important but elusive funding source, since policies and budgets vary by state. The only incontrovertible, quantified information derives from the early to mid-1970s (Klinger 1975). In 1970, state appropriations for archaeological research totaled nearly 1.1 million dollars, excluding salaries (Klinger 1975:97). That figure increased to 1.5 million dollars by 1973. More recent information is anecdotal in nature. For example, Missouri state archaeological funding is derived through a sales tax that gets channeled through the Department of Natural Resources (Klinger, personal communication 1991), but no annual figures are available.

Because detailed, quantitative data are accessible for federally funded archaeological research, federal archaeology is used as a nonacademic funding source to contrast with academic archaeology. Federal archaeology is an important component of nonacademic funding in the United States (McManamon, this volume). Federal archaeology funding has outdistanced academic funding for decades, and possibly since the inception of federal archaeology. The Missouri River Basin survey, begun in 1946, had a total budget of $60,000 and covered 500,000 square miles (Jennings 1985:285). More than 40 years later, the successful proposal for Bureau of Reclamation–sponsored Lake Roosevelt Project in central Arizona garnered a nearly 12-million-dollar contract, to be distributed among three contract archaeology organizations.

Budget figures from NSF and the federal archaeology program illustrate how nonacademic sources of funding dwarf traditional, academic funding sources. A single federal contracting office in the late 1970s was responsible for $1,244,000 in 23 states (Keel 1979:170). In contrast, for the 1978 fiscal year, NSF expended $480,800 on archaeological funding (Casteel 1980). More recent data look no different. In fiscal years 1989 and 1991, NSF and Wenner-Gren combined allotted approximately $2.88 and $3.4 million in archaeology funding, respectively (Watson 1989; Yellen, personal communication 1990).

The latest reliable estimates for federal archaeology expenditures are from fiscal year 1986, when $78.4 million dollars were spent on literature review, field survey, data recovery, and unanticipated recoveries (Keel et al. 1989:24). The 1987 budget looks to be quite similar (F. McManamon, personal communication 1990). Federal expenditures on enforcement ($959,508) and on education ($151,000) have been excluded to ensure comparability with the academic total. Since salaries (included within the federal archaeology budget) are generally excluded from academic grants, the two figures are not entirely comparable. Still, the difference in the scale of funding is remarkable.

The sampled funding agencies suggest that over 20 times as much money is allotted to CRM as is given to academic or institutional research. The relative importance of academic funding sources (compared to nonacademic sources) in North American archaeology is evidently minor. However, presenting data on academic funding patterns is important for two primary reasons. First, academic funding is peer-reviewed by active scholars in the archaeological community. In a sense, then, academic funding reflects a consensus regarding trends in North Americanist research. Second, academic-funded research has been prominent and continues to maintain prominence in eminent journals that focus on North Americanist research. The second point is addressed in the following section.

Reflections of Changing Funding Patterns in the Literature

The most direct method for exploring changes in where the money goes—and how much of it goes where—lies in describing funding patterns at the projects' starting points. To that end, data have been presented from various agencies in previous sections. Biases in the selection of funding sources that make their business public can be avoided by examining funding at projects' end points: publications resulting from funded research. This second approach complements the first in identifying broader patterns in funding, although details (e.g., the size of grants) are lost.

Because funding for academic archaeology has been on the decline for some years (see Casteel 1980:173 and others), nontraditional sources of funding have become increasingly important in supporting academic archaeological research. One reflection of the changing trends in academic funding sources lies in the acknowledgments section of *American Antiquity* articles. This journal and its parent organization (the Society for American Archaeology) have previously been upheld as representative of North American archaeology (cf. Casteel 1980:175–176; Sterud 1978).

Only articles in all four issues were examined between 1970 and 1990 in five-year increments (i.e., 1970, 1975, and so on).[1] Acknowledgments in 175 articles were inspected. About 69% (120) of those articles yielded data on academic versus nonacademic funding sources (Figure 4-4). Throughout the 20-year period, 46.7% of those articles for which funding information was provided cited academic sources analyzed in this study (i.e., NSF, Wenner-Gren, NEH, and NGS). Almost one-third (32.5%) of the projects reported were conducted under university sponsorship. CRM-funded projects represent 10% of all articles published, and approximately 13% of the articles acknowledged federal sources of funding.

A review of the last two decades of *American Antiquity* suggests several strategies now used to augment the meager resources for academic archaeological research. First is an increase in jointly sponsored research expeditions, some of which are multidisciplinary in focus. Multiresearcher projects consolidate meager resources and spread the responsibility for obtaining funding among a wider researcher pool. In addition, there exists a slight increase in range of funds listed for each study, as well as the number of coauthors listed (from 1.1 in 1971 to 1.7 in 1991). This may reflect a diversification strategy to capture multiple, smaller-sized grants now available. The need to "piggyback" several small grants for one project has also been discussed by Simmons (this volume).

Private sponsorship of archaeological research is becoming increasingly common as an alternative, or as a supplement, to traditional sources of academic funding. Some evidence exists for corporate sponsorship of field research and for support through private foundations. Additionally, there is an increase in the amount of research supported by private, volunteer-fueled, research organizations. Examples of such organizations include Earthwatch, University Research Expeditions, and in the American Southwest, Crow Canyon Research Center.

How are nonacademic funding patterns reflected in *American Antiquity* patterning? By focusing on that journal, some might argue that much of the "grey literature" (Brose 1985) of nonacademic archaeology is overlooked. A review of acknowledgments indicates that nonacademic archaeology is increasing its visibility in refereed publications. Nonacademic archaeology here combines federally sponsored and privately sponsored CRM. Collectively, the percentage of nonacademic research has increased between 1971 and 1991, while the proportion of academically funded research has held relatively steady. If *American Antiquity's* contents are indeed more progressive than other North American publications (cf. Cribb 1980:353), then the patterns described here are indicative of future trends.

The wall that separates academic and nonacademic archaeology (whether funded through federal or private sources) has indeed begun to crumble.

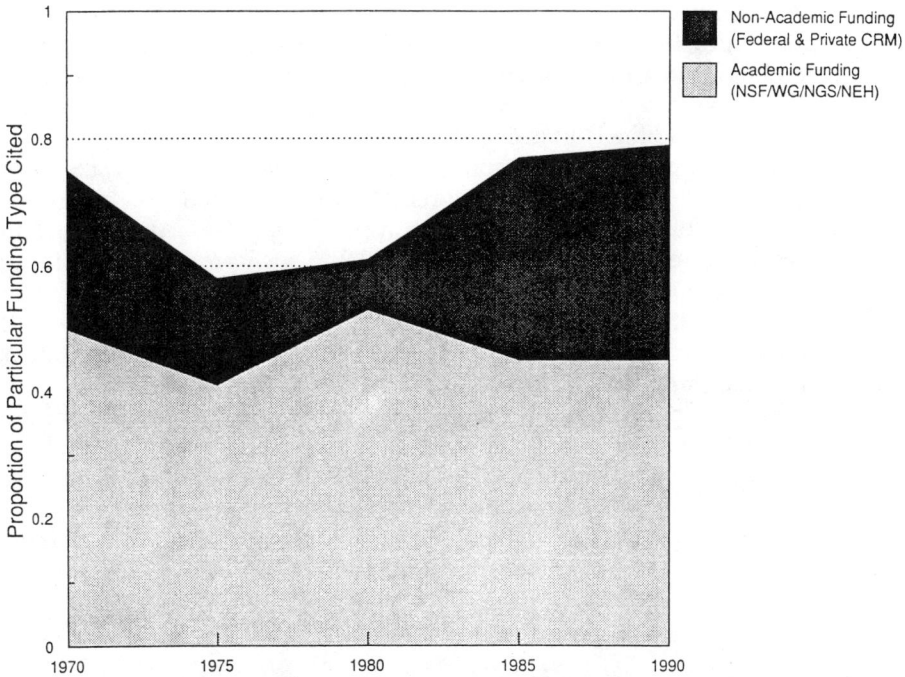

Figure 4-4. *Proportion of academic versus nonacademic research reported in* American Antiquity: *1970–1990.*

Cultural resource management projects have entered the research arena with increasing force. On the international level, Simmons (this volume) discusses the merging of both traditional and private funds in CRM research. At the national level, numerous federal and state agencies have begun to implement similar programs. Matching grants have gained popularity in federal and state agencies that now offer modest funding and logistical support to academic- and museum-sponsored field programs throughout the United States. Challenge Grant/Cost Share programs facilitate pilot studies, surveys, and long-term research projects and have been implemented in a number of federal archaeology agencies (e.g., Amme 1991; Clark and Smith 1991; Schneider and Braddock 1990). As executed by the Bureau of Land Management (BLM), the programs "contribute matching funds to private institutions of individuals where it can be demonstrated that there is a return benefit to the BLM towards public awareness and conscientious management of cultural resources" (Amme 1991:2).

BLM examples from Nevada, North Dakota, and Montana illustrate the utility of the program. The Nevada office of the BLM provided seed money to Brigham Young University that enabled it to test sites in the Ely District (eastern Nevada). That particular project culminated in the establishment of a field school (Amme 1991). Cooperative agreements between the BLM and academic institutions were instigated in 1984 in Montana and North Dakota (Clark and Smith 1991). Since that time, twelve research projects have been completed, and two more projects are in progress. Participating institutions include the University of Montana, Montana State University, the University of North Dakota, and the University of Maine.

A similar program began in the southern region of the USDA Forest Service in the mid-1980s. Forest Service–sponsored "Challenge Cost Share" programs in that region involved five CRM projects in fiscal year 1990. Approximately $14,000 was invested (to their partners' $24,000) in such programs, including excavations in conjunction with the University of Tennessee and with Penn State University (Schneider and Braddock 1990). Matching federal- and private-sector dollars in that region has also facilitated summer field schools, interpretive programs, and historic restoration.

The scale of support offered through such cost-sharing programs is minor, relative to the federal archaeology budget. However, increasing amounts of funding are available for academic researchers through that outlet. Schneider and Braddock (1990) note that no upper limit regarding the number of those programs currently exists for the Forest Service. Moreover, the results of cost-sharing research have begun to appear in the mainstream archaeological literature.

Impact of Funding on Types of Research Conducted

The best evidence that funding availability influences the choice of North American research areas and topics is contract archaeology. Americanist archaeology's relationship with applied funding sources beyond academe continues to grow. In the American Southwest, for example, this is particularly true with respect to such governmental agencies as the Bureau of Land Management and the Bureau of Reclamation. This growing relationship necessarily entails closer linkages between specific project goals of various agencies and their clients (Casteel 1980:179) and profoundly influences the types of research questions that are addressed in applied archaeological projects.

But to what extent do funding sources influence research topics? The relationship between funding and research topics varies in intensity across the United States. At one end of the continuum are those who are least dependent upon sources of funding described in this study. They are low-budget researchers with institutional affiliations and those who run volunteer-based projects aided by private research organizations. In the middle are archaeologists who find funding by an institutional base or through joint research. At the other end of the continuum are archaeologists who rely extensively on funding sources described in this study. Shifts in funding patterns during the coming decades will affect each of the groups differentially.

Subjects chosen for doctoral research represent one avenue for evaluating the impact of funding trends. Academic funding sources inspected in this study often support doctoral field research. Where dissertation research is conducted without the benefit of such funding, subsequent fieldwork and analysis may then tap various funding sources. Data from *Dissertation Abstracts International* were used to identify temporal trends in topical research by North American archaeologists between 1977 and 1989 (Figure 4-5).[2] The dissertation pattern resembles the funding data, as New World—and more specifically, North American—dissertation subjects dominate the arena of doctoral study. The dissertations sampled for this study are from three, evenly spaced years: 1977, 1983, and 1989. The relative importance of seven types of doctoral research in archaeology were examined, relying on categories discussed previously in the section on NSF funding. Baseline research and standard analytic techniques constitute the most common types of doctoral research supported through academic and nonacademic sources. New archaeology concerns are reflected in a gradual increase in dissertations using the last four approaches from 1979 to the present (Figure 4-6).

Is there a correlation between each type of "new" research and a particular geographic area? More actualistic studies (i.e., ethnoarchaeology) in Africa were funded than elsewhere. New analytic techniques are used primarily in the New World, as nearly half of all awards given in this area went to research in North America (Figure 4-7). Just why New World archaeologists—and North Americanists in particular—have pioneered new analytic techniques warrants further examination.

Summary and Conclusion

This study has examined patterning in archaeological funding by geographical area, by gender, and in terms of the scale of support given. Understanding where the money goes in North Americanist archaeology requires a historical perspective and the identification of funding parameters. In this study, an analysis of academic funding sources provides a standard for comparison. Comparing academic and nonacademic funding data presented here makes clear that academic funding composes an infinitesimal piece of the funding pie. Differences in the importance of academic and nonacademic funding agencies underscore the evergrowing importance of nonacademic research. How researchers respond to these shifts, with respect to research goals and choice of analytic techniques, will determine directions of North Americanist archaeology.

Archaeology is shaped by social and economic forces that affect every aspect of research, and we must understand the nature of these factors that affect the production of archaeological knowledge. As Fitting (1979:230) comments, archaeology is no longer the exclusive domain of the scholar. Decisions made by bureaucrats and business people, as well as those made by patrons of volunteer-sponsored field research, affect the nature of our research programs today. How funding sources affect the types of archaeology pursued is a complex issue that can only be superficially addressed in this study. Data presented here provide empirical footings for

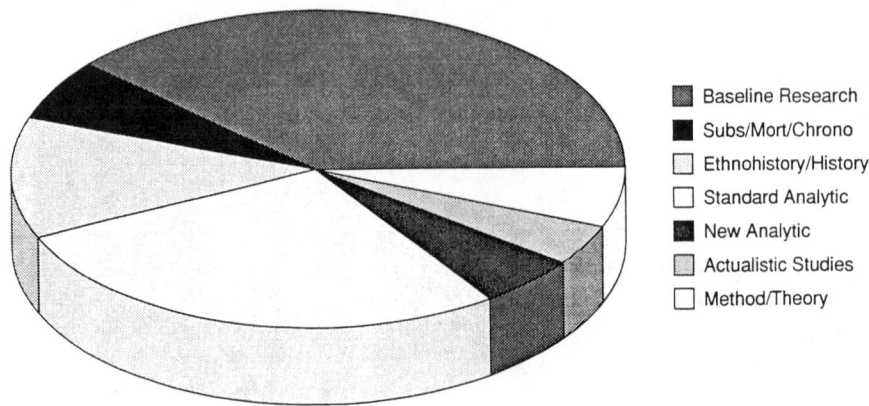

Figure 4-5. *Dissertation subjects by North Americanists across culture areas (1977–1989 sample).*

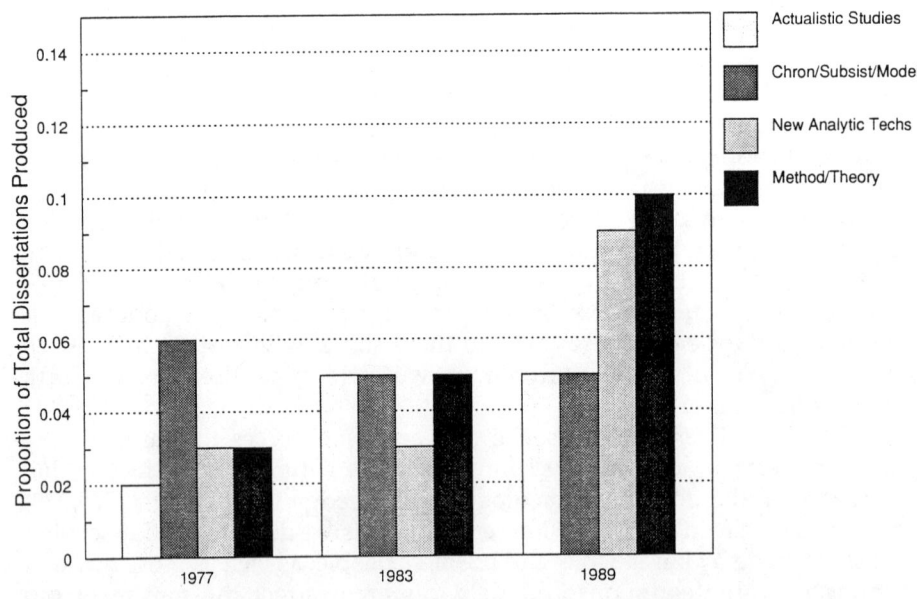

Figure 4-6. *New analytic techniques and predoctoral funding.*

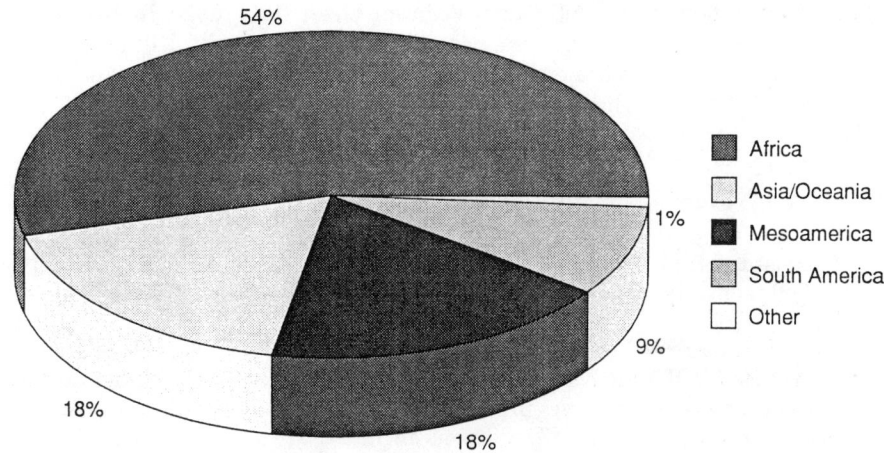

accounts for 10% of all grants awarded

Figure 4-7. *Geographic areas of funding for ethnoarchaeological doctoral research.*

critiques of the field, in terms of analytic questions to be pursued under different forms of funding. The current trend is one of merging academic and nonacademic funding and joint research. If the trend continues into the future, we can expect differences in the research objectives of academic and nonacademic archaeologists to diminish.

Studies of funding patterns in archaeology serve an important role in characterizing the state of our field in the early 1990s. Recent histories of our field have articulated historically based relationships between funding and broader national trends (cf. Patterson 1986; Schiffer 1979; Trigger 1990). This study sets the foundation for viewing funding emphases across different agencies and raises the issue of the relationship involving archaeological research and funding. How do trends in research affect funding, and vice versa? Understanding how we do science and the kinds of science we do requires a more thorough knowledge of how funding patterns influence archaeological research.

Acknowledgments

This study was begun during a research assistantship with Carol Kramer, who was the 1986 NSF Visiting Professor at the University of

Arizona. I gratefully acknowledge Carol Kramer for involving me in the funding research. Thanks are also extended to John Yellen and to Mark Mahoney for supplying NSF and Wenner-Gren data used in this study. Comments and information were also provided by Timothy Klinger, Francis McManamon, Teresita Majewski, Michael B. Schiffer, LuAnn Wandsnider, and Patty Jo Watson, whose generosity and time are deeply appreciated.

Notes

1. Only issue 2 from volume 50 (1985) was excluded from consideration, as it is the SAA fiftieth-anniversary volume and consists of solicited, rather than peer-reviewed, articles.

2. Only dissertations produced through American (i.e., United States) departments were considered in this analysis. *Dissertation Abstracts International* includes doctoral dissertations and masters' theses produced in Europe, Oceania, and North America (although the bulk of those dissertations included are from the United States) universities; only those abstracts from U.S. institutions were under consideration.

References

Amme, Brian C.
   1991   Promoting and Funding Research Proposals on Public Lands: An Example from Eastern Nevada. Paper presented at the 56th Annual Meeting of the Society for American Archaeology, New Orleans.

Brose, David S.
   1985   Good Enough for Government Work? A Study in "Grey Archeology." *American Anthropologist* 87(2):370–377.

Casteel, Richard W.
   1980   National Science Foundation Funding of Domestic Archaeology in the United States: Where the Money Ain't. *American Antiquity* 45:170–180.

Clark, Gerald R., and Gary P. Smith
   1991   The Cooperative Agreement as an Instrument for Archaeological Research and Resource Management: Cultural Resource Management in the Bureau of Land Management, Montana and North Dakota. Paper presented at the 56th Annual Meeting of the Society for American Archaeology, New Orleans.

Cleere, H. F. (editor)
   1988   *Archaeological Heritage Management in the Modern World*. Unwin Hyman, Winchester, Massachusetts.

Cribb, Roger L. D.
   1980   A Comment on Eugene L. Sterud's "Changing Aims in Americanist Archaeology: A Citation Analysis of American Antiquity"—1946–1975. *American Antiquity* 45:352–353.

Fitting, James E.
   1979   The Role of Market Analysis in Archaeological Planning. *Journal of Field Archaeology* 6(2):229–235.

Flinders Petrie, W. M.
   1904   *Methods and Aims in Archaeology*. Benjamin Blom, New York.

Fowler, Don D.
    1982   Cultural Resources Management. In *Advances in Archaeological Method and Theory*, vol. 5, edited by Michael B. Schiffer, pp. 1–50. Academic Press, New York.
Goodland, R., and M. Webb
    1987   *The Management of Cultural Property in World-Bank Assisted Projects*. World Bank Technical Paper No. 62. Washington, D.C.
Greene, Mary W.
    1985   The Support of Anthropology at the National Science Foundation. *Anthropology Newsletter* 26(3):1, 12–13.
Griffin, James
    1985   The Formation of the Society for American Archaeology. *American Antiquity* 50:261–271.
Jennings, Jesse D.
    1985   River Basin Surveys: Origins, Operations and Results, 1945–1969. *American Antiquity* 50:281–296.
Keatinge, Richard W.
    1980   Archaeology and Development: The Tembladera Sites of the Peruvian North Coast. *Journal of Field Archaeology* 7(4):467–475.
Keel, Bennie C.
    1979   A View from the Inside. *American Antiquity* 44:164–170.
Keel, Bennie C., Francis P. McManamon, and George S. Smith
    1989   *Federal Archaeology: The Current Program*. U.S. Department of the Interior, Washington, D.C.
Kelley, Jane, and Warren Hill
    1991   Relationships Between Graduate Training and Placement in Canadian Archaeology. In *The Archaeology of Gender: Proceedings of the 22nd Annual Chacmool Conference*, edited by Dale Walde and Noreen D. Willows, pp. 195–200. University of Calgary Archaeological Association, Calgary.
Klinger, Timothy
    1975   State Support for Archaeological Research Programs in the Early 1970s. *American Antiquity* 40:94–97.
Knudson, Ruthann
    1985   Contemporary Cultural Resource Management. In *American Archaeology Past and Future: A Celebration of the Society for American Archaeology 1935–1985*, edited by David J. Meltzer, Don D. Fowler, and Jeremy Sabloff, pp. 395–414. Smithsonian Institution Press, Washington, D.C.
Kramer, Carol, and Miriam T. Stark
    1988   The Status of Women in Archaeology. *Anthropology Newsletter* 29(9): 1, 11-12.
McGimsey, Charles R., III
    1985   "This, Too, Will Pass": Moss-Bennett in Perspective. *American Antiquity* 50:326–331.
Patterson, Thomas C.
    1986   The Last Sixty Years: Toward a Social History of Americanist Archaeology in the United States. *American Anthropologist* 88(1):7–26.
Plattner, Stuart, and Christopher McIntyre
    1990   The Funding of Dissertation Research in Anthropology at the National Science Foundation. Ms. on file, National Science Foundation, Washington, D.C.

Plattner, Stuart, Linda Hamilton, and Marilyn Madden
   1987   The Funding of Research in Social-Cultural Anthropology at the National Science Foundation. *American Anthropologist* 89:853–866.
Schiffer, Michael B.
   1979   Some Impacts of Cultural Resource Management on American Archaeology. In *Archaeological Resource Management in Australia and Oceania*, edited by J. R. McKinlay and K. L. Jones, pp. 1–11. New Zealand Historic Places Trust, Wellington, New Zealand.
Schiffer, Michael B. and George J. Gumerman (editors)
   1977   *Conservation Archaeology: A Guide for Cultural Resource Management Studies*. Academic Press, New York.
Schneider, Kent, and L. W. Braddock
   1990   Cost-Share: Treasure Chest or Pandora's Box? Paper delivered at the 55th Annual Meeting of the Society for American Archaeology, Las Vegas.
Stark, Miriam T.
   1991   A Perspective on Women's Status in American Archaeology. In *The Archaeology of Gender: Proceedings of the 22nd Annual Chacmool Conference*, edited by Dale Walde and Noreen D. Willows, pp. 187–194. University of Calgary Archaeological Association, Calgary.
Sterud, Eugene
   1978   Changing Aims of Americanist Archaeology: A Citation Analysis of American Antiquity—1946–1975. *American Antiquity* 43:294–302.
Trigger, Bruce G.
   1990   *A History of Archaeological Thought*. Cambridge University Press, Cambridge.
Watson, Patty Jo
   1989   Anthropology and the National Science Foundation. Paper presented at the 88th Annual Meeting of the American Anthropological Association, Washington, D.C.
Wenner-Gren Foundation for Anthropological Research
   1986   *Forty-fifth Anniversary Report*, vol. 1. Wenner-Gren Foundation for Anthropological Research, New York.
Yellen, John E.
   1991   Women, Archaeology and the National Science Foundation: An Analysis of Fiscal Year 1989 Data. In *The Archaeology of Gender: Proceedings of the 22nd Annual Chacmool Conference*, edited by Dale Walde and Noreen D. Willows, pp. 201–210. University of Calgary Archaeological Association, Calgary.
Yellen, John E., and Mary W. Greene
   1985   Archaeology and the National Science Foundation. *American Antiquity* 50:332–341.

5. The Potential for Future Relationships Between Archaeologists and Native Americans

Lynne Goldstein

Abstract: This chapter identifies five areas that must be considered in any plan for future interactions between archaeologists and Native Americans: (1) the nature of cultural conflict and its resolution, (2) the racism inherent in archaeological and Native American perspectives, (3) the benefits and burdens of education, (4) the nature of assistance, and (5) responsibilities for the future and the past. For each area, problems and possibilities are outlined, and a course of future action is suggested. The essay concludes with an agenda for action that includes the participation of national professional organizations, departments of anthropology, museums, and individuals. The thrust of the plan is that archaeologists must help forge a new series of relationships with Native Americans; those relationships will result in new interpretations of the past and, it is hoped, a joint stewardship of the past.

Introduction

In preparing this essay, I asked a number of colleagues what they thought the future would be for archaeological-Native American relationships. The majority provided the identical response: they groaned and said "Who knows?" or "Who knows—it frightens me to think about it." The more optimistic folks went so far as to commit themselves to "it depends." I admit to having had all of the same feelings at various times, but I will try to focus my remarks here on what I think *should* be the future of such relationships and what we should try to learn from the present. While I will of necessity discuss the reburial-repatriation controversy, that controversy is not the major

Quandaries and Quests: Visions of Archaeology's Future, edited by LuAnn Wandsnider. Center for Archaeological Investigations, Occasional Paper No. 20. © 1992 by the Board of Trustees, Southern Illinois University. All rights reserved. ISBN 0-88104-075-4.

focus of this presentation. Instead, I will try to outline the nature of the *potential* of future Native American-archaeological relationships. In a very real sense, this essay represents a call for action.

Given my informal survey cited above, one can propose a number of scenarios that might face archaeologists of the future: (1) native peoples are given an absolute right to determine who, how, where, and when their past is interpreted and examined; (2) the pan-Indian perspective that archaeology should be outlawed is implemented nationwide; or (3) the status quo is maintained. I would argue that none of those scenarios represents an optimistic or a healthy future for archaeology, but changing the tide will take effort, promotion, and determination.

There are several areas that any such change in Native American-archaeological relationships must address:

1. The nature of cultural conflict and its resolution
2. The racism inherent in archaeological and Native American perspectives
3. The benefits and burdens of education
4. The nature of assistance
5. Responsibilities for the future and the past

The Nature of Cultural Conflict and Its Resolution

In another paper (Goldstein and Kintigh 1990), Kintigh and I argue that the basis of the current problems between archaeologists and Native Americans is cultural conflict, where different systems of ethics collide. Ethics in this context represents a coherent system of values that specifies a code of conduct. A discussion of ethics is therefore a discussion of moral principles, with underlying definitions of Right and Wrong. That perspective on ethics implies that ethics is a cultural construction and that there can be more than one such system of ethics. Except to adherents of the particular culture, no particular system of ethics can be said to be absolutely right or wrong.

As anthropologists, we know and appreciate the differences in and between cultures and the differences in systems of ethics; anthropology promotes the notion of cultural relativism.[1] Although we know that ethics is a cultural construction, our problem in terms of Native American issues has often been the fact that our system of ethics is in conflict with the system of ethics of some of the descendants of the people we study and to whom we have certain obligations.

Although we may be quick to see that we have certain obligations to those we study, we are often less comfortable with our equally strong obligations to archaeology and anthropology generally. The anthropological or scientific worldview can also be seen as a cultural construction in which the excavation and curation of human skeletal remains is both proper and necessary. To put it simply, anthropology has a system of ethics beyond the notion that we have certain obligations to those we study. Eliminating sites or portions of sites from excavation or analysis because of the kind of items they contain is not an ethical stance for an archaeologist. Further, we must publicly state and defend our position; it is not easy to be attacked by the people you consider your natural constituents, but we should not be practicing anthropology if we cannot defend our research.[2] We have a mandate to preserve and protect the past for the future—an obligation to past cultures to tell their story and to future generations to preserve the past for their benefit. It is part of the culture of archaeology that we, as archaeologists, view ourselves as the stewards of the past. That point is addressed in several sections of this essay because our stewardship figures prominently in the future of archaeology.

From the perspective of those Native Americans who advocate reburial of all collections, the issue is often cast as a human rights concern—the deceased individuals, known elders or not, are ancestors and must be treated according to modern Native American wishes. Native Americans argue that the bones of their ancestors are being treated differently from those of others, and because the dead never gave their permission to be studied, they should be handed over to people who are at least their spiritual relatives. Excavation and analysis can only be done with the explicit permission of modern Native Americans. For the Native Americans who hold such views, their demands represent nothing more than righting a wrong.

How can we go about resolving such conflicts of ethics and cultures? A number of anthropologists would argue that because we are supposed to understand other cultures and because we have an obligation to the cultures we study, we should adjust our stance to align ourselves with modern Native American wishes and concerns. However, is that ethical for an anthropologist to do? Can we really shift our ethics based on the wishes of those we study? What about the ethics of our own discipline?

How do we, as archaeologists, balance our ethical concerns for knowledge and the archaeological record with our professional ethic of a belief in cultural relativism? I would argue that the only reasonable answer is compromise and mutual respect.

The development of a good or reasonable compromise is easiest when trust and mutual respect prevail between the parties. The trust is obviously enhanced through good faith interactions, but it is also enhanced by the perception of a "level playing field." The notion of a level playing field is very important to many Native Americans (Walter Echo-Hawk, personal communication 1989), and in my opinion, it is perhaps the key concept to acceptable resolution of the issues. Leone and Preucel (this volume) argue much the same point from the perspective of Habermas's theory of communicative action.

As professionals, we know the limits of our data; we know what we can and cannot say about a particular class of material or a particular data set. It is obvious to us, but we often overlook the fact that it is not obvious to others. Since Native Americans often have little idea of what we do, they may invent our culture for us, based on the limited information they have on hand. If both sides honestly presented what they know and the basis for that knowledge, it seems likely that reasonable compromise would be the outcome, and both sides would learn a great deal from each other.

This section, in part, represents a summary of the arguments developed and presented by Goldstein and Kintigh (1990) and is based on the notion that only if we treat others and other cultures with respect, sensitivity, and tolerance can we expect and demand the same in return. That paper closes with an enumeration of some basic principles for ethical conduct, and it is worth summarizing those points here:

> 1. Collections policies should conform to the institution's mission statement. Institutions whose mission does not require the preservation, study, and interpretation of human remains, funerary objects, and sacred objects should not collect or retain such items.
> 2. Where possible and appropriate, institutions should consult with relevant living cultural groups before undertaking projects that will result in the collection of human remains, funerary objects, and sacred objects, whether or not consultation is legally mandated. Research questions relevant to the group—even if they are somewhat outside the investigator's interests—should be considered seriously.
> 3. Institutions must interpret materials with accuracy, sensitivity, and respect, including consultation with appropriate groups whenever possible. Interpretation includes publication and dissemination of information to the general public, as well as to archaeologists and those who happen to visit museums. Interpretations must change as we learn more; we must also indicate the basis for such changes. There is not one and only one interpretation, and efforts should be made to be sensitive to and to include alternative interpretations.
> 4. Although financial considerations may be a major factor, institutions should take the initiative in compiling inventories and, in any case, should communicate with relevant native groups. Taking this initiative is the critical first step toward creation of a level playing field.
> 5. Institutions should promptly answer questions and requests for information. Even if the information they have is limited and minimal, they should share that information and explain the nature of the limitations.

The above items can be viewed as the first portion or basis of a call for action. Whether the institution is a museum, a university, a college, or some other kind of organization with collections, the above steps apply. Following those steps will lead to a series of case-by-case negotiations, involving descendants, archaeologists, and other interested parties. If the process of negotiation is open and fair, the parties can often reach a satisfactory resolution because such negotiations promote an atmosphere of good faith.

A significant number of archaeologists and cultural anthropologists argue that because of our obligations to the people we study, we should simply give materials to the people requesting them. I would argue that although it might be easiest to give the bones or whatever else is being requested to the group asking for them, what's easiest is not necessarily what is ethical or right. Once again, we have to be willing and able to defend our positions and our research. We have to address our natural constituencies, educate all of the publics about the past, and make certain that we don't alienate or disenfranchise past, present, or future generations. Even if we think we may lose, we cannot ethically fail to make the effort.

The next question becomes, What if we do all of this? What if we are indeed successful and fortunate and none of our original three scenarios come about?

The Racism Inherent in Archaeological and Native American Perspectives

Unlike many other countries in the world, Americans divide their country's history into two parts—Indian history and European history. Traditionally, Indian history has not been considered the more prestigious of the two. Tell someone that you are an archaeologist working in the United States and are interested in pre-European contact sites. The most likely response is: "Oh, you study Indian stuff." A number of authors, including Fowler (1986), Knudson (1986), and Trigger (1986), have raised the point, commenting on the fact that archaeological resources in the United States lack clear legal definition of ownership because there is no genetic continuity between the dominant political community and the prehistoric Americans. It is a point also raised by Goldstein and Kintigh (1990).

While public policies and laws may have changed some of our legal perspectives on the non-European past (cf. Knudson 1986: 397), the public perception has not changed. The public divides the United States into "us" and "them," and in many instances the view is "us versus them." However, until we treat all of this country's past as an integral part of the whole, racism in this area and others will continue. When newspapers and pollsters interview the public, they often record a general support for reburial. While it may or may not be surprising, the most telling point is that the individual interviewed will often indicate that since the bones are "theirs," the Indians should probably get them. We categorize "our" past according to ethnic identities rather than in terms of the heritage of the country as a whole. The categorization of heritage tends to happen in those countries where people are marginalized and racism is prevalent: it seems no coincidence that the United States, Australia, South Africa, and Israel come to mind. Changing the ethic will be difficult, but until the history and the prehistory of the United States are made the heritage of all Americans, Indian prehistory and history will never be treated with equal validity.

Return now to the notion that *we* are the stewards of the past—if there is the ingrained notion that the past divides into "we" versus "they," then who are we to be the stewards of *their* past? The underlying racism outlined above and inherent in the previous sentence must be eliminated from archaeology. Specific methods to achieve this are discussed in the next section.

What about racism in the Native American perspective? There are at least two positions that can be attributed to a kind of racism. First, Native Americans are as guilty as the rest of the country in maintaining the "us versus them" approach to the past, although their position may be more understandable. Nonetheless, isn't it racist to maintain that only Native

Americans can discuss Native American culture, display Native American exhibits, or provide appropriate interpretations? While the Native American perspective must be considered in exhibits, it is not the only view or the only information available on the past. Further, shouldn't the public be able to be educated where the bulk of the public lives? Should it be necessary to visit each Indian museum to learn about the country's past? Second, Native Americans fall victim to the kind of racism that comes out of ignorance. They often know little about archaeology and they know few archaeologists so they fall into the trap of stereotyping and generalizing. If you read the statements made by some Native American activists (e.g., Echo-Hawk, cited in Lichtenstein 1991:112), archaeologists are often portrayed as looters who regularly dig up the graves of known Indians without permission and display human bones in their museums for the public's gory interest. The reality, of course, is that there are few named individuals in the collections of the country's museums, and most archaeologists do not excavate burials. The archaeologists that do conduct burial excavations are required in most states to get permits and to gain the consent of a variety of relevant groups; the remains recovered are often reburied after analysis. Finally, for many years, museums have operated under some fairly strict guidelines regarding the display of human bone. Some Native Americans may be aware of those facts but find the extreme and outdated positions easier to use in their presentations. Nonetheless, those kinds of statements do nothing to further the stewardship of the past, and they ensure that Indians and archaeologists maintain their distance from one another.

The Benefits and Burdens of Education

Archaeologists often state that if we can educate the public and Indian communities about what we do, people would begin to understand our work and everything would be fine. People don't disagree with us: they just don't know what we actually study and what we actually do. While it is difficult to argue with the importance of education, it is naïve to think that education alone will solve our problems. Education is critical in this instance and others, and there is no question that we have been remiss in informing some of our most important constituencies about our work and what we have learned about the past. Nonetheless, while education is important and critical, it alone will not solve this or any other problem. We sometimes (consciously or not) assume that educating others will result in their agreeing with our perspective, but education does not mean changing someone's mind. Well-educated people can and do respectfully disagree.

Even if all of our public education efforts came to fruition, we still would not have done our job. Public education is but one part of the education task that faces us. And it is for the other area of education that I am most concerned—and most afraid that we address too late.

We have to do more than make certain that Native Americans learn about archaeology; we must make a concerted effort to encourage Native Americans to become archaeologists, physical anthropologists, and museum professionals. We may instill a desire to know about the past as well as a desire to build more tribal museums, but who is going to staff such museums? Who is going to have the expertise? The law profession guaranteed that there would be Indian lawyers by developing a nationwide, law school–sponsored, scholarship fund. Where there were almost no Indian lawyers 15 or 20 years ago, there are now about 1,000 (Paul Bender, personal communication 1989). Similarly, Indian students have been encouraged to pursue careers in medicine and engineering, areas where the payoff is tangible and obvious.

Anthropology and other social sciences have a very different nature from law, medicine, and engineering. What is the payoff to an Indian student who follows a career in social sciences? Traditionally, no one has encouraged such efforts because those areas have always been considered soft: they are less desirable from the standpoint of personal careers—can you get a job, and if you do, will it pay as much as a beginning job in law or medicine? More significantly, how might a career in anthropology help you and the tribe? Any Indian who sees the use of law in everyday life can understand why being a lawyer can help Indian nations. The number of treaty resolution cases alone makes a law career relevant for any Native American student. Similarly, the lack of adequate medical care on reservations and in urban Indian settings makes a career in any aspect of medicine—from physician to nurse to counselor to physical therapist—seem worthwhile. If federal, state, and other programs are going to pay for Indians to study for advanced degrees, the argument is that they should be pursuing something that is worthwhile financially and also benefits the tribe or nation. As social scientists, we haven't fought this pattern, and in fact we have bought into it. If *we* don't think our work meets the requirement of financial and tribal benefits, why should Indians think so? If we don't promote archaeology (or anthropology) as important and relevant for Indians, who will?

Why should a Native American student study anthropology or, more specifically, archaeology, physical anthropology, or museology? At my own university, the College of Letters and Sciences decided to prepare a brochure to encourage minority students (especially blacks and Native Americans) to follow careers in the social sciences. The decision was based on the knowledge that all programs, from the Bureau of Indian Affairs on down, encouraged students only in the "hard" sciences and law. To gather relevant information for the booklet, they sent a questionnaire to every social science department, asking it to outline why minority students would benefit from a degree in its field. Every department responded, but no department (including my own) really addressed the question. The answers indicated what one could do with a degree in a particular field, but not why an Indian or a black student should want to study in that field. The question we must begin to address is why anthropology or any part of it is relevant or helpful for a Native American. It's great to say that archaeology will allow you to learn about your past, but it is not sufficient.

Indians need to become anthropologists for the same reasons that they are attacking anthropologists—they want to gain control over their past, and the best way to do it is to discover and understand it, rather than asserting it and creating it. The activism focused on archaeology and physical anthropology is often characterized as a debate over who owns the past. Why do we care about who owns the past, and what does owning the past mean? In the present situation, owning the past means controlling it and access to it. People in power feel little need to control their past—they control the present and are not marginalized. Indians, however, are increasingly marginalized and isolated. Many were not raised in situations where they were taught either their language or culture. They now find that they want that sense of culture and history. One apparently simple approach to the problem is to obtain control of that past. Everything else has been taken away; surely someone can't take that too? In exploring this issue, Anne-Marie Cantwell (1989) develops the notion of the metaphor of the body (human bone) for the body politic. She documents the power of human bone and how, in a society's political development, human bones (whether of actual ancestors or not) are often used to establish a "timelessness" for an emerging body politic.

There are compelling reasons why Indians need to become archaeologists, physical anthropologists, and museum professionals. More and more tribes conduct building projects that require environmental impact statements, including archaeological surveys and mitigation. Why not have trained members of the tribe available for that work? Similarly, many tribes and Indian communities are developing their own museums to display their heritage. Museums are wonderful institutions that can instill pride and teach about the present and the past, but who will plan and administrate the museums? Where are the Indian museum professionals? How many non-Indians will rush to direct a museum on a reservation?

One might reasonably ask how anthropology can become a player in this game, let alone compete—we have a different structure and a different resource base than law schools or medical schools. How can we ever hope to develop a real training program that encourages Native Americans to become anthropologists? The Smithsonian Institution has developed an American Indian program to train and involve Native Americans as scholars and museum professionals, but if our public education efforts are successful, they will never be sufficient to meet the demand. No matter how good our intentions may be, a large effort is necessary. JoAllyn Archambault, director of the Smithsonian's American Indian program, has been gathering data on the number of American Indian scholars in the social sciences (personal communication 1990). She has found that there are fewer than two dozen Indian cultural anthropologists, not even a half-dozen Indian archaeologists, and even fewer Indian physical anthropologists in the United States. What does this say about our commitment to Native American cultures and the future?

How sincere are we about our education beliefs? How willing are we to have multiple points of view and multicultural perspectives expressed in anthropology? While we criticize Native Americans for wanting to own the past, how willing are any of us to share it?

Solving the problem will take a lot of effort on the part of a lot of people and institutions. It will take coordination of the country's anthropology departments and museums, and it will be necessary to find a number of ways to raise money for scholarships in anthropology and museum studies. Additionally, many of us will have to travel to actively recruit Indian grade school, high school, and college students to a career in anthropology. To do it, we must show that such a career will not only benefit them as individuals but as Indians. We have to become more active in creating a future for our profession.

This is how we address the racist partitioning of the past outlined in the preceding section. By actively recruiting Indian archaeologists, physical anthropologists, and museum professionals, we broaden the base of our discipline and make the perpetuation of such racism difficult, if not impossible.

The Nature of Assistance

Although many of the activists who bash archaeology would deny it, archaeologists have had a long history of providing assistance to Indian tribes and nations (some examples are presented in the 1991 Reburial Commission Report of the American Anthropological Association). The assistance has taken a number of different forms, from testimony in treaty rights cases and land claims to fighting looting of archaeological and historic sites to excavation and analysis of sites on Indian lands. Similarly, anthropologists who are museum professionals have assisted in the design and preparation of museum projects and exhibits, as well as grant proposals to create exhibits and to care for archives and photographs. That assistance has almost always been at the instigation of the Indian tribe, and it is both appropriate and correct. While such activity is laudable, the notion of assistance also raises some other points for discussion where the record is less impressive and the consequences more dire.

Most of us have no problem providing assistance to tribes and other Indian groups when it is requested, but we don't want to offer before we are asked. None of us wants to encourage or present an image of condescension or elitism—the idea that somehow we know what's good for you. At the same time, because of some of the education problems mentioned earlier, tribes may not know what we have to offer. Further, if we want to try and move toward being proactive rather than reactive, how do we balance between providing help that's wanted without presumption and assuming we know what's best? It seems to me that such actions are possible, as long as we approach the subject with great sensitivity and try to avoid the trap of condescension. Let me provide an example, beyond the previous discussion of the need to train Native American anthropologists.

With the increase in the number of Indian museums, tribes are discovering that while they want and need a museum, they cannot necessarily keep such a facility open at all times. Sometimes the museum will have to close because of economic difficulties, while in other instances the museum will close each year during the season(s) when visitors are fewer in number. Regardless of when such closings take place, the museums may discover that they have a real problem: the cost of insuring items and storing them continues (or sometimes even increases) and puts an equal or greater financial burden on the tribe. How can we help? Museums and other institutions can offer several different kinds of assistance: (1) when the museum is being planned, they can provide design assistance in how to close the building seasonally; (2) they can offer to store items for the museums during their off-season; or (3) they can arrange for long-term loans so that the individual museum avoids the problem of storage completely—they simply return items to the lender. Several museums have instituted such programs and both the tribal and nontribal institutions have benefitted. Some tribes have actually returned items they received for repatriation because they had no place to adequately care for the items.

In another chapter in this volume, Leone and Preucel argue that the reburial issue can be profitably viewed from the perspective of Habermas's (1979, 1984, 1989) theory of communicative action. Leone and Preucel discuss the four different speech acts outlined by Habermas for a communicative context in which every participant gets a fair chance to participate. While a critical analysis of the situation provides useful insights and potential directions for future interactions, I think that Leone and Preucel may have overstated their classification of the present situation. Their analysis includes a classification of the kinds of speech acts that archaeologists and Indians practice today, but I think the more significant point is that at present there is little communication.

It is presumptuous to talk about assistance and being proactive when so many archaeologists have never talked with an Indian. Over the past few years, I have conducted a number of informal surveys of American archaeologists and have discovered that talking about training Native American scholars may be premature since most of the archaeologists have been hiding in fear. Although the situation has improved dramatically over the last 10 years, it is probably still accurate to say that 10% or fewer of the archaeologists in this country have ever sat down and talked with an Indian, particularly about the archaeologist's research. I have no doubt that the number of physical anthropologists making such contacts is even less, since several physical anthropologists have told me that they pretend to be archaeologists when placed in a situation where Indians might be present so that they can avoid having physical anthropology be directly attacked. What kind of assistance can we offer or provide when we are afraid to talk or identify ourselves? Is this ethical? Perhaps the first proactive stance we must take is to determine our Native American constituencies and sit down and talk with them. It may be more difficult in a state like Ohio or Illinois where reservations and tribal councils are rare or absent, but it isn't impossible. Each archaeologist who talks with a Native American and gets him or her interested in archaeology will be taking a major step toward resolving many of the problems outlined here.

Finally, I'd like to comment on the ethics of working with Native American groups. I see the problem increasing in the present, and I fear that it may continue to increase in the future. An archaeologist working for a tribe recently told me that he would provide information and alternative views to the tribe when asked, but if the tribe told him to do something, he would do it. He thought that it was not up to him to question the tribe or its motives. Is that what we mean by respecting other views—agreeing with them no matter what? Do we agree even when that means doing something we don't believe is right? I don't think any tribe would sanction that or respect such a person for long.

The easiest approach may be to listen and to say that you respect the tribe's views and will go along with their wishes. You carefully and thoughtfully provide information when asked, but keep silent otherwise. It may make for a less stressful relationship, but it can be difficult in terms of ethics. If an Indian tribe is hiring you, presumably they want your expertise and opinion. You do no one a favor by blindly agreeing with their position. Once again, people can respectfully disagree.

That same archaeologist provides an excellent example of why his approach is wrong. The tribe's position on reburial is that no analysis should take place and reburial should occur on the spot. A burial was found eroding near tribal land, and another archaeologist was hired to excavate the grave and move it. The second archaeologist indicated that she could not and would not excavate the burial without analysis—after all, how could she even evaluate whether the individual belonged to that tribe? Her position was simply stated: here are my reasons, and either I do the analysis or you can hire someone else. The tribe considered the position and realized that they wanted to know who the individual was—they didn't want to rebury someone that might not belong to their tribe. After careful consideration they gave permission for full analysis, including destructive testing. What about our friend, the tribal archaeologist? He kept reminding everyone that the tribe didn't believe in analysis and that he couldn't recommend analysis because of that position.

Responsibilities for the Future and the Past

I have not completely outlined the future of Native American-archaeological relationships, but I think there are some very positive possibilities and some clear pitfalls. We will have to change the way we do business—we will have to incorporate the American Indian perspective and treat Native American claims equitably. An acceptance of the cultural conflict will need to be built into decision-making processes. The process will not be easy but will benefit all for the future.

This plan of action requires the input of individual archaeologists, institutions, and professional organizations. At all levels, we must try to create and maintain a level playing field. Some of the first steps can be outlined as follows:

1. Professional organizations—including the American Anthropological Association, the Society for American Archaeology, the American Association of Museums, and the American Association of Physical Anthropology—must coordinate efforts with each other and their members to develop a program to train Native American students in archaeology, physical anthropology, and museum studies. A comprehensive program must be developed, and funding sources must be located. The program might include a publication that clearly outlines why a career in anthropology would benefit Native Americans.

2. Departments of anthropology must find Native American students in their communities and encourage them to take courses. It is quite possible that waiting until students are in college is too late. Members of the department or graduate students in anthropology might develop a program to give presentations to grade schools and high schools and might travel to Indian reservations where practical. The focus must be on encouraging interest and outlining the direct benefits to the students, not on getting students to come to a particular school.

3. Museums and other institutions should include Native Americans in the development of exhibits and other materials and also should offer a variety of different forms of assistance in creating tribal museums and displays.

4. Archaeologists and anthropologists should make the effort to talk with Native Americans about their work. It might mean giving lectures or preparing special publications, but it can mean something as simple as talking with students or offering to serve as a mentor to a Native American student. The idea is to develop an interaction—the anthropologist learns about the concerns and issues of importance to the Native American, and the Native American learns why anthropology is relevant.

What might such changes mean? While we will have to adapt to the changing relationships between Indians and their heritage, we will also have to take an active part in creating some of the changes. By bringing Native Americans into the decision-making process, we will change the culture of archaeology and Indians: it will be a co-opting process. That process will result in changing interpretations of the past, and it will change the questions we ask about the past. The more involved Indian communities become, the less possible it becomes to support the notion of "us versus them." Unless this process happens, we can expect years of polarized conflict with no real winner or loser, except the past. We must co-opt Indians into a joint stewardship of the past in order to establish the notion that the past is neither yours nor mine, but ours.

Notes

1. For ease of reference, the term *we* will be used to refer specifically to Americanist archaeologists, although it could equally apply to any anthropologically trained archaeologist, physical anthropologist, or museum professional.

2. Anne Woosley, in another chapter in this volume, raises the issue in a different context. She notes that archaeologists will soon have to address the questions of why, what, and how we do archaeology not only from the perspective of social issues and interactions with others but also from the perspective of long-term museum curation.

References

Cantwell, Anne-Marie
    1989   The Body and the Body Politic: The Gift of the Dead to the Living. Paper presented at the World Archaeological Congress Meeting on Reburial and Repatriation, Vermillion, South Dakota.

Fowler, Don D.
    1986   Conserving American Archaeological Resources. In *American Archaeology Past and Future: A Celebration of the Society for American Archaeology 1935–1985*, edited by D. J. Meltzer, D. D. Fowler, and J. A. Sabloff, pp. 135–162. Smithsonian Institution Press, Washington, D.C.

Goldstein, Lynne, and Keith Kintigh
    1990   Ethics and the Reburial Controversy. *American Antiquity* 55:585–591.

Habermas, J.
    1979   *Communication and the Evolution of Society*. Beacon Press, Boston.
    1984   *The Theory of Communicative Action. Vol. 1, Reason and the Rationalization of Society*. Beacon Press, Boston.
    1989   *The Theory of Communicative Action. Vol. 2, System and Lifeworld*. Beacon Press, Boston.

Knudson, Ruthann
    1986   Contemporary Cultural Resource Management. In *American Archaeology Past and Future: A Celebration of the Society for American Archaeology 1935–1985*, edited by D. J. Meltzer, D. D. Fowler, and J. A. Sabloff, pp. 395–414. Smithsonian Institution Press, Washington, D.C.

Lichtenstein, Grace
    1991   Taking Back the Past. *Outside Magazine* 16(4):108–113, 168.

Reburial Commission
    1991   Reburial Commission Report. *Anthropology Newsletter* 32(3):1, 26-28.

Trigger, Bruce G.
    1986   Prehistoric Archaeology and American Society. In *American Archaeology Past and Future: A Celebration of the Society for American Archaeology 1935–1985*, edited by D. J. Meltzer, D. D. Fowler, and J. A. Sabloff, pp. 187–216. Smithsonian Institution Press, Washington, D.C.

6. Reflections on Critical Archaeological Resources

LuAnn Wandsnider

The analyses in the first section pertain to the status of those critical resources—time, money, and access—upon which the practice of Americanist archaeology is ultimately contingent. All contain statements about the current state of archaeology in light of those resources, and most attach a visionary program for action to either expand or make more effective use of them. Since they all deal with facts that are mostly unimpeachable, my comments will be directed toward drawing out further the consequences of the observed trends and remarking on the proposed programs. I comment as a recent Ph.D., who also happens to be a child of America's white suburbs, where African Americans, much less Native Americans, were rare visitors. My degree was paid for, indirectly, by the National Park Service, the Bureau of Reclamation, the Bureau of Land Management, and the U.S. Forest Service, and the comments presented here reflect those Cultural Resource Management (CRM) experiences.

The first contribution by Michael Shott, who also has a CRM pedigree, deals with the limited resources of time and money and our effective management of both in documenting the archaeological record. Most archaeologists would agree that, as currently practiced, cultural resource archaeology cannot guarantee conservation of cultural resources simply because, for reasons given by Shott, identification of the resources themselves is not assured. It is difficult to conserve the unknown. Shott's proposal, which undoubtedly will be seen as controversial by some, speaks directly to that basic issue. He argues that the current state of affairs is not owed to the quality of the archaeologists but to a commodity-based system that promotes the fixing of incomplete knowledge about the archaeological record. He advocates remodeling the system to one that is service-based. Projected benefits include increased efficiency and effectiveness in cultural resource inventory and conservation; an anticipated happy by-product is inventory comparability and atomic (i.e., artifact and feature descriptions and locations) results that may be synthesized

Quandaries and Quests: Visions of Archaeology's Future, edited by LuAnn Wandsnider. Center for Archaeological Investigations, Occasional Paper No. 20. © 1992 by the Board of Trustees, Southern Illinois University. All rights reserved. ISBN 0-88104-075-4.

according to need by managers and researchers. Because of the quality of the services and products it promises, I find the proposal appealing.

Shott anticipates several objections, to which I add two others. If implemented, the multi-pass inventory would find cultural resources virtually everywhere (Dunnell and Dancey 1983). This situation may be anathema to land managers and planners, whose blissful ignorance of the true depth of the cultural resource iceberg is ensured by the present commercial practice. I concur with Shott's estimate, however, that more often then not cultural resource clearance could be granted on the basis of the high-quality inventory results his reformed practice would yield.

Second, while the potential merit of Shott's proposal is obvious, cost-analysis that demonstrates its efficiency is required before those who employ archaeologists would agree to the proposed reorganization. But to make that analysis, two things are required. First, a measure of efficiency should be established. Should inventory practices strive to minimize acres surveyed or to maximize information (however that might be measured) per person-day? As Shott recognizes, there seems to be an unfortunate trade-off between the two.

A second requirement is better-defined technical standards, which I feel must already be in place rather than evolve from implementation of the model itself. Such standards follow directly from what we now know the character of the archaeological record to be and recognition of what it is we wish to learn from it (and, thus, conserve in it). Therefore, it may be prudent to decouple the development of technical standards from the model presented by Shott. In other economic domains, such critical instrumentation research is conducted by a variety of agents. Geology has the U.S. Geological Survey, private sources, and the academy. Agriculture has various U.S. Department of Agriculture offices, some attached to universities. Instrumentation in engineering is supported by venture capital, and there exist NSF instrumentation funds. Archaeology, of course, offers a benefit to the nation that is not easily assessed in monetary terms, unlike the benefits of geology, agriculture, and engineering. There are, however, possible funding sources in place. As noted by McManamon, State Historic Preservation Offices often promote archaeological investigation in those geographic areas otherwise not receiving attention. Perhaps the technical areas also merit their attention. Perhaps, also, alliances among government, academic, private-sector, and avocational archaeologists could share the costs of the investment.

In his presentation, Francis McManamon, who has worked in and published on a full range of CRM issues, provides an accounting of the commitment of federal dollars to cultural resource management, which receives the majority of the money spent on archaeology in the United States. Essentially, McManamon sees no change in, except perhaps increased support for, how cultural resources are currently inventoried and managed. He also targets specific areas where new efforts are desirable, and, most likely, all archaeologists would applaud his choices. My comments focus on current cultural resource inventory, a vital component of cultural resource conservation that, according to McManamon's figures, commands almost 50% of the total federal CRM expenditure.

In his essay, Shott expresses a variety of concerns with cultural resource inventory. An additional concern relates to the low-density archaeological record, about which we know increasingly more, but which is unsystematically inventoried, is not preserved, and for which no reporting system is in place. A historical overview (e.g., Willey and Sabloff 1980) of archaeological practice shows that archaeologists used to seek out and either excavate or preserve the rare archaeological Zs and Qs, the Pueblo Bonitos and Monk's Mounds of our world. More recently, archaeological practice has considered the slightly more common Ns and Hs, that is, relatively less spectacular architecture and artifact scatters. As of yet, few efforts have been made to *systematically* find and document the Es and Ts of the archaeological record, that is, the exceedingly common but unobtrusive isolated artifacts. Low-density distributions of artifacts may be the most intractable of the archaeological resources to systematically locate and document. But to understand prehistoric hunter-gatherer adaptations, as well as low-impact historic adaptations, such information is critical. Furthermore, information theory tells us that in order to decipher an unknown language, we must pay attention to the context of the common Es and Ts *as well as* the rare Zs and Qs. Our dialogue with an archaeological picture that is incomplete can only be less than satisfactory. In situ preservation of this portion of the record is not feasible, but measures for its conservation should be explored.

As far as I understand the present federal commitment to conservation archaeology, there exist no offices dedicated to the instrumentation research necessary to address the aforementioned and similar concerns. Such work (e.g., Osborn et al. 1987), however, may be conducted as part of other conservation agendas. Given the serious questions that remain about inventory completeness and validity of inventory results (Shott's concern), is it wise for cultural resources inventory to proceed apace? As mentioned above, other resource management disciplines have institutionalized support for research to facilitate better management of the resource. In addition to the crucial areas identified by McManamon, a heightened federal commitment (e.g., Tainter and Hamre 1988) to this critical aspect of cultural resource management may also be desirable.

In the second study focusing on monetary resources, Miriam Stark, who has tracked various sociological aspects of the discipline, presents a comprehensive study of recent funding trends in archaeological research. Several of her findings are of particular interest. First, that places outside of North America continue to receive increasing amounts of funding is intriguing. Does it represent the infilling of archaeological niches by determined North American archaeologists as some suggest? That notion invites other speculation. Can we anticipate geographic niche-packing followed by the dramatic cascading of research as seen in, for example, the American Southwest, where the archaeologist density is on par with that of surface scatters? Perhaps it would be in the interest of the discipline to encourage multiple archaeological investigations of the same phenomenon in the same areas to stimulate knowledge cascades as the National Science Foundation has recently done for research on global warming and from which the Southwestern Anthropological Research Group (e.g., Euler and Gumerman 1978) benefited.

Stark's observation that the gender gap is closing or has closed in the domain of funded research is likewise fascinating and also encouraging. As funded research features greatly in tenure decisions, we may expect the narrowing of the gap to have some repercussion in the tenured faculty domain, where females are still relatively underrepresented. It would be interesting to gauge the width of the gap in the area of publications, which also figures largely in tenure decisions.

Also of interest is her finding that recently relatively more dissertation effort is being devoted to methodological issues as compared with 13 and 7 years ago. Since funding for dissertation research is less heavily reviewed, the observed trend probably represents well the population of topics considered by doctoral students and, hence, the current interests of their advisors. If that is so, has it taken so many years for the mid-1970s' realization that, for example, formation process research is important to trickle down to doctoral research? Or is earlier research of that kind well disguised in the dissertation abstracts examined by Stark? Or, most likely, is it now permissible to submit a dissertation with a methodological, in contrast to a prehistoric, focus? Whatever the reason, the trend suggests that an arsenal of methodological tools is slowly accumulating and may be in place for grounding future descriptive and interpretative scenarios about the past.

Lynne Goldstein has worked with the Native American community for the Society of American Archaeology over the past several years. In her presentation, she considers current relations between Native Americans and archaeologists, touching on how that interaction affects future access to one critical resource, the archaeological record itself. It is clear from her analysis that for the discipline to take no action in this area is to court disaster, of which she offers several flavors. She also offers a broadly drawn prescription for averting the disasters that incorporates communication, education, and also recognition by society that archaeology has something unique and valuable to offer. The essay by Leone and Preucel (this volume) addresses in depth the issue of communication. On the issue of education, I leave it to the education experts and applied anthropologists to discuss the logistics of replicating the support system found at Dartmouth University, for example, to sustain those who venture from their culture to take the proffered archaeological scholarships and jobs. Without that support, Native American archaeologists will continue to number considerably less than legion, even after a decade of courting. The volume as a whole contemplates the contribution archaeology makes to a world bombarded by interpretations and sketches of the past from any number of vendors, including Native Americans. Working as anthropologists, archaeologists can help the public differentiate among the various offered pasts.

Together, the four analyses chart some established avenues, several points of interest currently without access, and the more extreme hazards to be found on the materializing map of resources critical to Americanist archaeology. Since we are the cartographers responsible for the final form of the map, consideration of its developing configuration is valuable. Assuredly, we want to avoid the perils described by Goldstein as well as those depicted by Shott. To sample the delights promised by them, an investment in infrastructure is necessary. Can we afford the investment? Can we afford not to invest? Do the broad avenues described by McManamon and Stark take us to a future we want? If so, are there more direct routes?

Acknowledgments

I thank Frank McManamon, Mike Shott, and Miriam Stark for their comments on an earlier version of this commentary. I remain responsible for the opinions expressed here.

References

Dunnell, Robert C., and William S. Dancey
    1983   The Siteless Survey: A Regional Scale Data Collection Strategy. *Advances in Archaeological Method and Theory*, vol. 5, edited by Michael B. Schiffer, pp. 267–287. Academic Press, New York.

Euler, Robert C., and George J. Gumerman
    1978   *Investigations of the Southwestern Anthropological Research Group*. Museum of Northern Arizona, Flagstaff.

Osborn, Alan, Susan Vetter, Ralph Hartley, Laurie Walsh, and Jesslyn Brown
    1987   *Impacts of Domestic Livestock Grazing on the Archaeological Resources of Capitol Reef National Park, Utah*. Occasional Studies in Anthropology No. 20. Midwest Archaeological Center, Lincoln, Nebraska.

Tainter, Joseph A., and R. H. Hamre (editors)
    1988   *Tools to Manage the Past: Research Priorities for Cultural Resources Management in the Southwest*. USDA Forest Service Technical Report RM-164, Fort Collins, Colorado.

Willey, Gordon R., and Jeremy A. Sabloff
    1980   *A History of American Archaeology*. 2d ed. W. H. Freeman, San Francisco.

II. Archaeological Paradigms and Concepts

7. Global Cultural Resource Archaeology in the Early Twenty-First Century

Alan H. Simmons

Abstract: It is inevitable that the twenty-first century will witness a shrinkage of barriers to scientific communication and interaction. American anthropological archaeologists need to adopt a more global view of how and why archaeology is conducted. We have for too long cultivated an anthropological "archaeocentric" perspective on the proper way to do archaeology. Several aspects of an "international archaeology" are addressed in this chapter. A major theme is the interface of archaeology with Third World development. It is argued that several aspects of the cultural resource management paradigm are appropriate in developing countries. Another theme involves the interaction of anthropologically trained archaeologists with professionals not schooled in that approach. The suggestion of developing more departments of archaeology is considered. Joint effort by the wide variety of scholars calling themselves archaeologists is a critical challenge in overcoming epistemological differences to achieve a common goal of conducting professionally defensible archaeology.

Introduction

This volume considers the state and future of various aspects of Americanist archaeology. In my contribution, I present some personal opinions about the conduct of archaeology for those working in developing countries, pointing out both problems and benefits that will be associated with what might be called international, or global, archaeology. I comment as one who has spent about 20 years doing archaeology in what we conveniently call the Third World.[1] Much of what I have to say might appear obvious, especially to those already working outside the United States, but sometimes

Quandaries and Quests: Visions of Archaeology's Future, edited by LuAnn Wandsnider. Center for Archaeological Investigations, Occasional Paper No. 20. © 1992 by the Board of Trustees, Southern Illinois University. All rights reserved. ISBN 0-88104-075-4.

the obvious bears repetition. I specifically direct this essay to North American researchers, primarily those with a background in anthropological archaeology.

Much of my discussion revolves around both the perception and the reality that American anthropological archaeology has been a major contributor to the discipline. Will it be true in the future? That question is examined from two related themes. The first and major theme is the relationship between archaeology and Third World development. American Cultural Resource Management (CRM) as a model for the relationship is considered. The second theme is the interaction of American anthropological archaeologists with both foreign archaeologists and American archaeologists who are not trained in our self-imposed paradigm of "anthropocentric" archaeology. This second focus is particularly important as barriers to global scientific communication shrink and Americans interact more frequently with foreign scholars.

Global Archaeology and the Third World—Is the CRM Model Appropriate?

There is no doubt that land-modifying development is proceeding on a global basis at an alarming pace and that cultural resources will be destroyed. There is, however, a benefit in this development to archaeology: as more and more international money is spent on disturbing the environment, those developed countries with a history of environmental concern (including that for cultural resources) will have the opportunity to impose environmental regulations on countries using their funding or sponsorship. That may sound patronizing and could give the impression that many developing countries have no regard for the environment, which is false. In many such countries there is a genuine concern with environmental issues; however, immediate life-supporting issues often take precedence (Black 1982:81).

Cultural Patrimony

It is impossible to discuss Third World archaeology without an examination of the concept of cultural patrimony and the context in which many developing countries view the discipline. As many countries assume a more self-confident posture in the world community, there comes an increased pride in national heritage. That heritage is often expressed archaeologically, and cultural resources can assume significance beyond their scientific importance. This, of course, is nothing new. Outside the Americas, in areas where direct or indirect historical antecedents can be demonstrated, archaeology has long been a political pawn, often being used as proof for nationalistic claims to disputed territory or for an imagined racial or cultural superiority (cf. Silberman 1982, 1989). Certainly in the United States today, archaeology also has become political, but for different reasons. While Anglo-Americans cannot claim a historic relationship with North American prehistory, Native Americans can, and they have seized upon the political significance of it.

While purists might denounce this political component to archaeology, it is undeniable. That does not mean that archaeologists have to actively participate in it, but we surely need to be aware of its existence. American archaeologists working in other countries must be careful not to become unwitting (or even worse, witting) protagonists in the political manipulations of archaeology.

Local Antiquities Infrastructures

Although rarely admitted in polite company, much less in print (but see such "classics" as Woolley 1952:34–44), many Westerners have long assumed a condescending and patronizing attitude toward Third World archaeologists. That is no longer morally or ethically defensible, if ever it was.

In contrast to the American system in which multiple state and federal agencies are responsible for cultural resources (McManamon, this volume), many countries have existing archaeological infrastructures in the form of departments of antiquity. Those services are composed of dedicated individuals who are poorly compensated for what often is perceived by higher government authorities as an unnecessary siphon of limited funds. Invariably, antiquities services are poorly funded and focus much of their attention on emergency or "salvage" projects or on restoration. Often archaeological management and conservation are not seen as immediate concerns.

Antiquities services also are responsible for issuing permits and for making certain that archaeological work is professionally conducted. Except for the language differences, obtaining a permit from a foreign antiquities service is little different than obtaining a federal or state permit in the United States and involves an application and the submittal of a research plan. Those are necessary parts of doing archaeology, and to successfully work in the Third World, one had better be prepared for bureaucracy at its best. The superior or arrogant attitudes sometimes displayed by Americans and other Westerners toward such bureaucracies will cause more problems than need to exist.

In addition to antiquities services, many Third World countries have their own cadre of university researchers, who often take a dim view of foreigners coming in to study what they consider their domain. Think, for an instant, how most North American archaeologists would react to a request from, say, an Iraqi university researcher wanting to excavate at Chaco Canyon. It behooves us to do some homework and communicate with local scholars beyond those who are in bureaucratic power.

The Role of American Researchers

Given the above, one might ask: "Is there a role for American archaeologists in doing archaeology outside the United States?" The answer is yes. Archaeology should not be nationalistically restricted. Americans (and others) may have research interests in areas where the data are best obtained from other countries. Within the mental template of American archaeology there are, after all, "Old" and "New" World archaeologists. But what is our role?

Many Third World archaeologists are oriented toward data recovery and descriptive analysis. There are several reasons for this, having to do primarily with training and low levels of funding. Americans, on the other hand, have had the benefit of abundant (relatively speaking) funding and of many of the most dramatic improvements in archaeological investigation, both from methodological and theoretical standpoints (cf. Kelley and Hanen 1988:142). We have become very sophisticated in the field of archaeology and should share our knowledge. Several specific contributions come to mind.

Analytic Strategy

There have been tremendous advances recently in the tools available for interpreting the past. They include, for example, remote sensing, digital imagery, microscopic artifact analysis, and chemical residue analysis—capabilities often not available in developing countries.

Ethnoarchaeology

Ethnoarchaeological research usually has been conducted in developing countries. The results of such research, however, have less often been shared with local researchers. There is a tremendous but shrinking potential for such studies, and by linking with local institutions, the ability to construct more realistic investigations will be enhanced. The concept of "native archaeologists" may be appropriate in some instances.

Training

North American universities are among the best in the world, and we should consider it an obligation to train Third World archaeologists to be more effective advocates and researchers. That can be accomplished by close interaction with such persons in the field, by working with local universities, and by sponsoring exchange programs where foreign nationals come to the United States either as students or for programs designed to supplement skills already possessed by professionals.

Research Design

Archaeology in many developing countries often focuses on impressive monuments or sites in imminent danger. Many American archaeologists have refined research design considerably, and we should be able to impart some of that knowledge to local researchers.

There is little question that North Americans indeed do have a role in Third World archaeology and that it can be a positive one benefiting not only archaeological resources but also the scientific structure of a country. In light of this, another topic, the concept of joint projects, needs to be considered here before addressing the role of CRM in the Third World.

Joint Projects

A joint project is one in which a foreign team is linked with a national team as *equal* partners. In some countries, such as Israel, joint projects are, I believe, required. That did not used to be the case, but it is easy to see why it has developed. As many countries have become more stable and sophisticated, they realize that foreign archaeologists have been taking a lot and giving little in return. A response to this has been: "If you want to work in my country, you will work with my countrymen."

Many North Americans' initial reaction to joint projects is a heavy sigh. In theory, such projects look great: they involve close cooperation with the local archaeologists; they train locals; publications are jointly produced; and so on. In practice, they can be more difficult. What are some of the benefits and liabilities of joint projects?

The benefits include the following: (1) logistics are greatly facilitated; (2) funding is often supplemented; (3) permitting is often facilitated; (4) the language barrier is lessened (most Americans are *not* fluent in languages other than English, but most foreign professionals *are*); (5) analysis is facilitated in that in many countries removal of artifacts is forbidden and analysis must be conducted in-country (curation also is facilitated by having an in-country base); and (6) the spirit of cooperation is achieved.

What about some of the liabilities? They include the following: (1) instead of dealing with two bureaucracies (your own university and a department of antiquities), there now is a third one—the joint sponsor's university; (2) philosophical differences between directors on how and why archaeology is done; (3) communication difficulties in areas of authority and responsibility; (4) publication rights and acknowledgments; and (5) cultural or religious differences among staff.

In short, the verdict is still out on the effectiveness of joint projects. It may be a moot topic in any case because joint projects probably will be required in most countries by the twenty-first century.

CRM Archaeology and the Third World

The concept of CRM is immensely complicated and fills much of the current American archaeological literature; considerable attention also has been devoted to it in the Third World (e.g., Cleere 1984, 1988; McCreery and Sauer 1983; National Park Service 1989; Wilson 1987; Wilson and Loyola 1982). My intent here is to indicate a few directions that CRM-based archaeological research in developing countries might take in the next century. A basic question to ask is: "Do we want to unleash a 'CRM Monster' in the Third World?" A few basic issues must be briefly examined here.

First, I admittedly am viewing CRM archaeology from the American perspective, fully aware that many other countries have equivalents. CRM archaeology in the United States, however, has become a highly structured entity, and many of the developments under what used to be called "salvage archaeology" have come from American sources.

Another issue involves exactly what CRM archaeology is. Most archaeologists who do CRM archaeology are not real cultural resource *managers*. They are technical "consultants" to the "real" cultural resource managers, who usually are persons within state or federal agencies having jurisdiction over landholdings. It might seem a small point, but it is not, especially when examining the CRM concept within a Third World context, where cultural resource managers will likely be associated with various host governments.

A third point is that the oft-cited, and unfortunate, dichotomy between "pure" research and "applied or CRM" research (cf. Fitting 1979; Goodyear 1979; King 1979; Lipe and Lindsay 1974; MacDonald 1976; Raab et al. 1980) has to be eliminated. In the United States, many of the more academically inclined archaeologists, usually associated with anthropology departments, often have looked down at CRM archaeology as an inherently inferior undertaking (Meighan 1986:6, 29–30). This action has led to an abundance of bitter acrimony, with accusations coming from both camps. There have been positive signs that the gap between "pure" and "applied" research is narrowing and, indeed, that the gap may be more of degree than of kind (cf. Kelley and Hanen 1988:143–149; Knudson 1986; Mayer-Oakes and Portnoy 1984; Piper 1990). In spite of that, however, personal experience suggests that the dichotomy still exists in the minds of some archaeologists, although it is rarely publicly acknowledged.

Regardless of such largely rhetorical issues, I have always maintained that it is not who is paying for the archaeology that makes it "real" research, but rather who is *doing* that archaeology, regardless of funding sources. There are, of course, constraints imposed by CRM archaeology, but that does not mean that it cannot be "real" research. That is a naïve assumption that has been disproven time and again. The point is that we have to be realistic about funding opportunities in archaeology, and the sources for "pure" research, like the National Science Foundation, will never be what they once were. Much of the funding is going to come from "applied" sources, and archaeologists need to be ready to deal with this fact.

The question initially posed at the beginning of this section has to be answered in the affirmative—"Yes, we do want to unleash the 'CRM monster'"—but it should not be regarded as such. The positive aspects of CRM archaeology, the beneficial things learned through years of mistakes and trial and error, need to be applied to a Third World context.

I now want to examine more specifically the role of CRM archaeology in the Third World. This discussion is by no means comprehensive; it points out some potential problems, although no ready answers are at hand.

The Archaeological Record

One issue that must be addressed involves the nature of the archaeological record. In simplest terms, the crux of the issue is a dichotomy between *prehistoric* and *classical* archaeology. In many countries, archaeology is viewed in terms of *monuments*. There should be no question that major monumental remains are significant. They will, and should, continue to receive a large degree of attention. Certainly many parts of the world contain the undeniably spectacular remains of classical (and other) antiquity. But what about that most common of all archaeological phenomena, the inglorious artifact scatter? Is it a site? Should it even be recorded, let alone excavated? Adding time depth complicates the issue even more. In much of the Third World, over a million years of human activity has occurred. That can produce a tremendous number of artifact scatters.

A lot has been learned in the United States over the past 20 years about the significance of low-visibility archaeological sites. Many anthropologically trained archaeologists would argue that they are important and cannot be neglected. Trying to make that same argument, however, to a director of antiquities who is faced with the destruction of sites that even the layman can recognize as significant is something else. It is an issue that increasingly will have to be addressed. The question is how to do so in a realistic manner. There needs to be an awareness that *small* also can be important. It is a delicate issue, for one aspect of CRM that I would hate to see imported wholesale is a bureaucratic obsession with claiming the significance of every single lithic scatter, for example. At some point, a degree of data redundancy is reached. I do not make this comment lightly, having spent a good deal of my professional career arguing *for* the importance of small, limited-visibility sites. We need, however, to have a realistic perspective on this issue, particularly in situations where funding is limited *and* researchers are faced with a complex cultural-historical record that includes monumental remains.

Universities, Government Agencies, and Private Firms

Another issue that researchers working in the Third World will soon have to grapple with is: Who actually will be doing the archaeology? Traditionally, archaeology in those areas has been conducted by university-affiliated researchers working closely, if not on an equal footing, with local government representatives who often have been viewed as a liability, as part of "the cost of doing business." That is changing substantially; *even if local representatives are not thoroughly trained*, we are working in their countries and need to consider them as equal professionals.

Understand that I am not minimizing the frequently frustrating problems of dealing with local officials. They can be outrageously bureaucratic and make it difficult to get even simple things done. That is not, however, a problem confined to developing countries. Furthermore, local government representatives are much better trained now than in the past. Many have professional degrees, often at the master's level and with increasing frequency at the doctorate level. In addition to government representatives, there also is an increasing cadre of professional archaeologists in local universities. They often are well-trained young professionals, and it is a mistake to circumvent them. Many of the people have been trained in the United States, although usually not within anthropology departments. Tapping that resource is an opportunity that anthropological archaeologists should not miss.

Finally, the role of the private sector in Third World CRM-oriented archaeology, a difficult and controversial issue, needs to be examined. As funding from nontraditional sources increases, as it surely must, there will be the opportunity for private firms to become involved in Third World CRM, with both good and bad results. If levels of professionalism can be maintained, and the results published in non-grey-literature formats, there should be few problems. If, however, the intense competition for funds that characterizes so much of American CRM archaeology enters the picture, only the resource will suffer. There are numerous problems here, including underbidding, substandard work, and unfamiliarity with local conditions and archaeology.

Funding

A final topic is funding. Over the next several years, essentially three sources of funding for American involvement in Third World archaeology can be identified: traditional sources, private corporations, and CRM-related funding.

The first, most traditional, source dispenses funding for so-called pure research and is exemplified by agencies such as the National Science Foundation. Other prominent traditional funding sources include the National Geographic Society, the Leakey Foundation, and the Wenner-Gren Foundation for Anthropological Research. A characteristic of all of those agencies, with the possible exception of the National Science Foundation, is that their grants usually are relatively small. The structure of most of those funding agencies assures that the majority of their support goes to university-based archaeologists. They also usually will not fund CRM-related studies. The National Science Foundation is one of the few agencies that will pay salaries for principal investigators (PIs), as well as institute indirect costs, or overhead. Sponsors such as the National Geographic Society simply disallow both PI salary and overhead; if salaries or overhead were included in their relatively small grants there would be pitiably few dollars for the actual research. Even the National Science Foundation has qualms about large overhead rates and salaries for PIs—usually they will pay only for "summer salary." Thus, private or "soft money" organizations are at a disadvantage vis-à-vis those funding sources, since such institutions usually find it difficult to absorb indirect or salary costs. In any event, such traditional sources of funding are becoming scarcer and, realistically, scholars wishing to work in developing countries are going to have to engage in "creative financing."

Other sources of funding are private sponsors or corporations. These opportunities, of course, are not new, but many traditional university-based archaeologists may be unaware of just how much money is available from such sources. Many corporations have operations in developing countries, and a grant is a small price to pay for the goodwill and public relations benefits that may accrue from supporting local archaeology. There also are a variety of private sponsors that fund archaeology. They generally require the recipient to be a nonprofit organization, something that most universities can easily arrange. As with the corporations, however, relatively small sums often are involved.

The merging of traditional and private funds will become more common in the future. A simple fact is that it is expensive to do proper archaeological research. With the relatively small sizes of available grants, it will be necessary to "piggyback" several sources for one project. That requires a certain degree of fiscal flexibility on the part of the recipient institutes, many of which may be ill-equipped to deal with a variety of small grants, each with different accountability requirements.

The final source of funding involves direct CRM-related archaeology and is perhaps the most promising, while simultaneously being the most potentially dangerous. It is likely that as developing countries continue to develop, there will be an increased awareness of the significance of cultural resources. It is a reasonable expectation that many of the First World-based funding sources for that development should incorporate a substantial funding for conservation of cultural resources. There are many precedents for development-related CRM, and the potential for greater support by development organizations is high. The World Bank, for example, has a strong commitment to cultural preservation (Goodland and Webb 1987). In addition, sources such as the U.S. Agency for International Development (USAID) and the United Nations Educational, Scientific, and Cultural Organization (UNESCO) have been tapped for archaeological investigations. Of course, researchers must be aware of political implications potentially associated with using funds from such sources (cf. Cordell, this volume).

The bottom line for archaeology today, be it conducted in the First or the Third World, is that scientifically defensible archaeology is expensive. Major world monetary and governmental agencies, with relatively large coffers and sensitive dispositions, will increasingly be relied upon to fund archaeological research. The potential for megafunding through those agencies is staggering, and this is where we have to be careful. The idea of actually having a sufficient amount of money available to do the kind of work necessary is an enticement, but we can learn some lessons from American CRM archaeology. There are at least two related issues. The first is whether or not archaeology as a discipline has matured enough to be able to handle megadollars. The second relates to why we do archaeology in the first place.

Many of my non-American colleagues are stunned when they find out how much money is available for CRM archaeology in the United States. In countries where a major project can cost $10,000, the very concept of having $100,000 or more is difficult to assimilate. What happens if all of a sudden huge amounts of money are available for Third World archaeology? It can get complicated here. On one hand, I am reluctant to see the proliferation of private American (or other) archaeological consulting firms in developing countries. On the other hand, such firms often have the pragmatic flexibility necessary for dealing with such countries. As most of us know, university business offices can be notoriously inefficient in terms of paying bills on time. That can be a big problem within a university's home state; take the project out of the country and it gets even more difficult. I recall an incident at a university with which I was affiliated where I required a $10,000 cash advance for a project in Egypt. Although the sponsor had already paid the money to the university, it simply did not have the mechanisms in place to advance me the funds. The university wanted to be billed. In the middle of the Sahara Desert, however, it is extremely difficult to even get a receipt, let alone a billing statement. Ultimately, the problem was resolved by a sort of perverse efficiency on the university's part: the funds were advanced to me from their flower fund! That points to the simple fact that many universities are not equipped or interested in dealing with the complex financial (and other) logistics involved in working in the Third World. Private companies, on the other hand, seem to be more adaptable.

It gets even more complicated, however. There are several issues involved relative to the second item mentioned above—why do we do archaeology in the first place? Is it to learn something about the past or to make a profit? Is Third World archaeology a service or a commodity (Shott, this volume)? Or is it a complex enterprise encompassing all of those different aspects? If the latter, then perhaps documentation and investigation of archaeological remains in the Third World demands a special hybrid organization that is accountable to scientific, conservation, management, development, and fiscal interests.[2]

In summary, put in basest terms, money largely determines how much and what kind of archaeology can be done. The person who controls the purse strings controls the research. In all likelihood, the future of archaeology, both in the United States and abroad, is going to see a much more eclectic funding base, and the discipline had best be ready to deal with this situation. One structural suggestion can be offered. Despite the undesirability of creating additional bureaucracy, perhaps some sort of "Cultural Property Clearinghouse"—a group composed of experts who could both channel projects to possible funding sources *and* evaluate the results of research—is needed. An international organization modeled after the Society of Professional Archaeologists (SOPA) might accomplish this.

Examples

To illustrate the type of archaeology that has been advocated here, I would like to provide two examples of projects that I have been involved with in what arguably might be called the Third World. They were not structured as CRM projects in the American sense of the word; however, if conducted in the United States, they probably would fall under that rubric. The first project is from Jordan, while the second is from Cyprus.

The concept of CRM is not alien to either country. In particular, Jordan has made a strong commitment to the approach (McCreery and Sauer 1983), even using the term *CRM*. The Jordanian CRM program is largely funded by USAID, is sponsored by the American Center of Oriental Research (ACOR) in Amman, and works closely with the Jordanian Department of Antiquities. The program conducts archaeological investigations in a CRM context and functions as a facilitating service. A major focus is on management-oriented issues and on apprising local government authorities of the significance of cultural resources. A point of interest is that, for its first phase, an American archaeologist *not* trained in either anthropological archaeology or CRM was hired by the program. He was extremely well-trained, but a true CRM orientation was not achieved. Having a person versed specifically in a CRM perspective might have facilitated the initial operation of what has become an ongoing and very successful program. The anthropological archaeology community may have missed an opportunity for placing "one of our own" in this important program. The Jordanian CRM program is one that we should watch carefully, for it has a tremendous potential.

Cyprus has a very well developed Department of Antiquities, as well as an American institute (the Cyprus American Archaeological Research Institute—CAARI) that facilitates many foreign (interestingly, not just American) projects. CAARI does not have a CRM program; "salvage" archaeology, however, is one function of the Department of Antiquities.

I should note the role of the American Schools of Oriental Research (ASOR) in promoting professional archaeology in the Near East. Both CAARI and ACOR are affiliates, and ASOR, which has a limited "anthropological" membership, has been a major positive force in structuring the nature of archaeological investigations in much of the Near East. I would strongly encourage a more active participation in the ASOR by members of the anthropological archaeology community who wish to work in the area.

Jordan

For the past several years, I have been codirector of a large, multidisciplinary project in Central Jordan that has focused primarily on one major site, 'Ain Ghazal, a huge Neolithic center on the outskirts of Amman, Jordan's capital. 'Ain Ghazal is one of the most significant Neolithic sites in the Near East, and research there has resulted in substantial modifications to what we know of the Levantine Neolithic (Simmons et al. 1988).

If 'Ain Ghazal were in the United States, there is little doubt that our investigations would be considered a CRM project. 'Ain Ghazal, located in a rapidly growing area of Amman, was initially exposed by road construction and is in severe danger of destruction by development. The Jordanian Department of Antiquities has been extremely helpful in our investigations, and we would not have had the success we have had without its active assistance. Why have we been so fortunate in our interactions with the department? This is not to say that the department is uncooperative with other projects; that is not the case. Jordan has probably one of the best-developed antiquities services in the Near East. But, overall, our project has gone very smoothly, I think, for the following reasons.

First of all, it is a joint project between San Diego State University, the Desert Research Institute, and Yarmouk University, which is a Jordanian university. The joint sponsorship has been critical for several reasons. First, when the project initially started, the primary director at that time was an American based at Yarmouk, so the project was conducted under the university's auspices. Second, even after the director moved, the project continued as a joint project, with active participation from Yarmouk. By this, I mean that one of the three codirectors is a professor at Yarmouk who shares full responsibility, that we use students from Yarmouk's program, that some of the graduate students have completed M.A. theses on the site, that some funding has come from Yarmouk, and that publication rights are shared. Third, Yarmouk University has a very well respected program housed within an Institute for Archaeology and Anthropology (I think the latter component is particularly interesting), whose researchers play an active role in the archaeology of their country.

A second reason for the success is that we have had an incredibly devoted professional staff. They have worked, in most cases, for little or no actual salary.

A third reason is that we have always worked closely and well with the Department of Antiquities. We have followed "the rules." We have turned in reports on time, we have actively involved departmental representatives in the project, and we have worked closely with the director.

Another reason for the project's success, I suspect, is political, a topic mentioned earlier in this essay. One of the most famous of all Neolithic sites is Jericho. Jericho is presently located in the West Bank and is under Israeli administration. 'Ain Ghazal in many ways exceeds the significance of Jericho, both in size (it is three times larger than Neolithic Jericho) and in information content. 'Ain Ghazal is also located in undisputed Jordanian territory. Thus, the site has been very visible and has enhanced Jordan's image as a country that cares about its past.

Funding has to be mentioned here. We have had a lot of money to work at 'Ain Ghazal, *by Near Eastern standards*. However, by American standards, and certainly by CRM comparisons, the budget has been pitiful. Much of our funding has come from the traditional sources—primarily the National Geographic Society and the National Endowment for the Humanities. We also have had substantial private support, as well as actual cash and in-kind contributions from the sponsoring universities.

These aspects of the project have conspired to its benefit. From the beginning, the importance of the site was recognized by all involved. Our initial excavations were concentrated on immediately endangered portions of the site—areas of "direct impact," using proper CRM terminology. As the project evolved, however, we expanded our efforts to less endangered portions of the site. We also conducted a survey around the site. One of the explicit goals of the survey was management oriented—we wanted to provide an inventory of sites in an area scheduled to undergo major development. The survey was unusual by local standards in that we even recorded small lithic scatters. We would like to think that it has contributed to a better understanding of Amman's past and will be used by planners as well as researchers.

Although we do not anticipate any more major excavation at 'Ain Ghazal, the project is far from finished. The site requires additional protection. Through the efforts of the codirectors, ACOR, and the Department of Antiquities, we have managed to convince the municipality of Amman to set aside a portion of the site for protection. That is no mean achievement, given the economic value of the land; however, it has worked (so far). Through a rational approach, everyone was convinced of the site's importance. Our final plans call for turning the protected part of the site into an open-air museum. At the moment, funding for this is problematic, but we are seeking support from a variety of agencies.

In short, the 'Ain Ghazal project may be seen as a model for the way that archaeology can be done in the Third World. It is a large and complex study, but it has progressed nearly ideally. From the beginning, we have had active involvement with local archaeologists, we have published the results rapidly, and we have been concerned with the protection of the site beyond just obtaining the scientific results that we wanted.

Cyprus

Now, let us briefly examine another, more modest, project located in the Republic of Cyprus that has only been ongoing since 1987. There is, again, a CRM element to the study in that the site is endangered, although the CRM nature is not as obvious as it is at 'Ain Ghazal. This time the danger is not so much from human agencies, but rather natural ones. The site is a collapsed rockshelter on the edge of a cliff overlooking the Mediterranean. Winters can be severe in Cyprus, and the site is rapidly eroding into the sea.

The site, Akrotiri-*Aetokremnos* (or Eagle Cliff; Simmons 1988a, 1988b, 1989, 1991a, 1991b), is unique to Cyprus in several ways, which has created complications in obtaining both necessary permits and funding. First of all, the site is prehistoric—it is the oldest well-documented site known in Cyprus and, indeed, on any of the Mediterranean islands. It dates to about 8500 B.C. and is probably early or pre-Neolithic. That is significant since no site predating the Neolithic has ever been firmly documented on Cyprus. In fact, there initially was some question as to whether or not Akrotiri-*Aetokremnos* even was an archaeological site. Second, the site is controversial because of its contents—it demonstrates an association of extinct Pleistocene fauna (primarily island-adapted pygmy hippopotamus and pygmy elephant) with cultural remains. That is intriguing because prior to our investigations such an association had never been demonstrated, and the implications for Pleistocene extinction studies are obvious. Third, the site is of a type—a limited-activity locale rather than a habitation—that has not been previously studied to any degree in Cypriot archaeology. Finally, the site is located on a British Royal Air Force base. That served as a complicating variable in terms of obtaining permits and deciding who had authority over the site.

Thus, Akrotiri-*Aetokremnos* is not a mainstream Cypriot site, which initially caused difficulties (Simmons 1991b). To understand why, it is necessary to know that most archaeology conducted in Cyprus dates to classical antiquity and its practitioners are not trained in anthropological archaeology. Convincing a conservative establishment of the significance of a site such as Akrotiri-*Aetokremnos* has, at times, been both frustrating and amusing. However, through close and persistent work, we were able to convince even skeptics of the site's importance. At first, obtaining a permit from the Department of Antiquities was delicate. The former director, a respected scholar, was rightfully cautious about a site that had the potential to generate a considerable amount of controversy. One requirement of my permit was that I have a "real" Paleolithic archaeologist on the staff. That came as a surprise to me since I have long considered myself as such. However, most of my recent Near Eastern work has been with the Neolithic; thus, the director was being careful in ensuring that someone with an intimate familiarity with pre-Neolithic materials would be associated with the site. In retrospect, this caution seems well-founded. Now, however, there is no question about the archaeological nature of the site and its significance, and the Department of Antiquities has been very cooperative in issuing the proper permits.

Summary

Both the Cypriot and the Jordanian projects represent diverse examples of successful Third World archaeology. The successes have been achieved by an often difficult series of compromises. The realization that we had to consider variables other than pure research interests has certainly facilitated the projects. Sincere and intentional cooperation with local authorities has been a critical element in the success of the projects.

The Nature of Archaeologists in the Twenty-First Century

I would like to conclude with a few observations on what archaeologists are and can be in the future. This was one of the hardest sections to write because I have had to change some of my own cherished notions as to what archaeology really is.

It is fair to say that most practitioners of North American archaeology were trained within what might be called the anthropological archaeology paradigm, resulting in an "anthropocentric" view of archaeology. Since we were undergraduates, we have been taught that "proper" archaeology has to have an anthropological perspective to it, or it is little more than dilettantism. Willey and Phillips's (1958:2) famous quote "Archaeology is anthropology or it is nothing" is something with which we have all been indoctrinated. That can no longer be the case, and, indeed, such a perspective is provincial.

It is, of course, easy to understand how and why archaeology developed in North America within the anthropological paradigm. Archaeology here grew hand in hand with anthropology, largely because of the presence of living Native American groups whose cultures were clearly distinctive from the dominant European culture. Archaeologists who work primarily in North America have come to believe that in order to be "real" archaeologists they have to be anthropologists first. One only need look at how many *archaeology* departments there are in North America: very few. Many American archaeologists are housed either in anthropology departments, anthropology museums, government agencies, or private companies. Most also have their backgrounds in anthropology, with specializations in archaeology.

There is nothing wrong with that, of course, and the anthropological perspective has contributed substantially to archaeology as a discipline, both in theory and in practice. There is, however, another world of archaeologists out there, both in the United States and elsewhere. Many of these professionals may never have opened an anthropology book, and, furthermore, many of them are excellent archaeologists. Archaeologists in the twenty-first century are going to have to be less concerned with labels and departmental affiliations, and more concerned with *archaeology*.

Let us examine a few of those "other" archaeologists. First, in North America there is a large community of "classical archaeologists." This is a broad and perhaps inappropriate rubric and includes both true classicists and biblical archaeologists. We American anthropological archaeologists have been, by and large, brought up to believe that those people do not "do" real archaeology but rather are obsessed with collecting art objects or proving (or disproving) various biblical passages. But the times have changed, and we need to realize that many of those scholars are doing state-of-the-art archaeological research. They simply do not call it anthropological archaeology. Furthermore, many of the Third World archaeologists who trained in the United States received their education from those scholars.

Another group of nonanthropological archaeologists includes most European archaeologists. Archaeology in Europe, of course, has followed a completely different development than it has in North America. Many Europeans are much more heavily versed in the natural sciences and consider anthropology as something of an alien field. As the topic of this essay is the Third World, I do not want to dwell on European archaeology, except to note the obvious: European archaeology is alive, well, and active. Furthermore, many European archaeologists are quite active in the Third World, often establishing permanent foreign missions with close ties to local archaeologists and organizations.

A final group to consider is Third World archaeologists. It is here that a tremendous potential exists. Most Third World archaeologists are employed in departments of antiquity, although in many cases, archaeology is considered a valid university offering, and thus the development of archaeology programs in many countries has proliferated.

If we want the impact of anthropological archaeology to truly be felt in the Third World and are serious about abandoning colonial attitudes, we need to start training some of those individuals who ultimately will be in positions of power regarding their country's archaeological resources. If we are convinced, for example, that a American-styled CRM approach is important, then it is incumbent upon us to convince local archaeologists of that importance. And one way to do that is by training many of those persons. We can do it either by having them come to the United States and participate in active research and graduate programs or by our going to their countries on exchange programs, or at least offering "minicourses." The responsibility is on us, and perhaps we can, at last, give something back to those we take from. So we are faced with a diverse group of professionals calling themselves archaeologists. Are we to continue to operate within the narrow confines of disciplinarily defined provincialism? If not, what can be done to improve communication? I would like to close with a few suggestions.

Communication is essential. I occasionally go to the annual meetings of the American Schools of Oriental Research. They are held in conjunction with meetings of the Society of Biblical Literature and the American Association of Religion. Needless to say, there are not too many anthropological archaeologists present. Yet I have heard some excellent papers on *archaeology* at these meetings. We need more cross-fertilization. The First Joint Archaeological Congress held in Baltimore in 1989 was a positive step. There were, indeed, problems with that meeting, but at least there was a huge group of people who call themselves archaeologists present. And not all of them were anthropologists. Cross-disciplinary meetings are one positive way to improve communications.

Archaeology is becoming more and more specialized. It no longer is feasible for one person to be able to do everything. Joint projects with scholars other than Americans, or at least with other than anthropologically trained Americans, are one way to increase awareness of the range of issues that modern archaeology can address.

Our journals also tend to be specialized. Journals such as the *Journal of Field Archaeology (JFA)* are to be encouraged. *JFA* publishes a wide range of articles dealing with archaeology, regardless of what an author's departmental affiliation might be. We need more of that.

Maybe it is time to consider archaeology as its own discipline. I do not want to define archaeology solely as a technique—it is more than that. But we have to realize that there are several ways to do "correct" archaeology. Perhaps the field will best prosper with the development of departments of archaeology. Perhaps archaeology has matured enough to be considered as an independent discipline *not* directly tied to anthropology. That is not to say we should lose the anthropological perspective. We should not—it has provided archaeology with a conceptual framework that has considerable merit. But it is not the only way to do archaeology. Let us not lose sight of what archaeology is supposed to be. We should all be concerned with conducting professionally defensible and responsible archaeology, and only a very narrow mind would still consider the anthropological approach as the *only* way in which to do this.

"Why is the past important?" is a question that also will increasingly be asked of us, and we had better be able to justify what we do. To do that requires a broad view. Examining the past is a difficult task, and we need to be willing to use whatever tools are at our disposal. It will require a tolerant attitude. Why should North Americans even do research in the Third World? One reason is that cultural resources are being destroyed daily. They belong to our worldwide heritage, and the First World has the resources for their protection. Another reason is that by broadening our horizons and dealing on equal levels with other scholars with diverse insights on the record of the past we may be able to more fully understand it. But "why do archaeology" can no longer be answered in purely research frameworks. Archaeology has to be socially responsible, and in order for that to happen, we have to be able to communicate with those outside our own small world. There is absolutely no doubt that the twenty-first century will see a huge impact on the environment and that cultural resources will suffer. We had better start planning for their protection now.

Acknowledgments

Several people read parts or all of the draft of this essay or commented on the ideas presented here. In particular, I would like to thank Bert DeVries and Ruba Kanaan in Amman and Christine Kayden in Los Angeles for reading the entire manuscript and providing me with many useful "nonanthropological" comments.

Notes

1. Many, especially those living there, take offense at the term "Third World"; a more neutral term is "developing countries." I have tried to be sensitive to that throughout this essay. I have, however, retained use of "Third World archaeology" as a less awkward and ambiguous phrase than "developing country archaeology."

2. Although I admit to a certain degree of bias, perhaps an institution such as the one with which I am associated would be an appropriate organization. The Desert Research Institution is part of a university system, but it depends on "sponsored projects" for most of its funding. Thus, we are sensitive to the demands on resources from a variety of perspectives.

References

Black, D.
    1982   Economics, Technology and Rescue Archaeology. In *Rescue Archaeology—Papers from the First New World Conference on Rescue Archaeology*, edited by R. Wilson and G. Loyola, pp. 81–84. The Preservation Press, Washington, D.C.

Cleere, H. F. (editor)
    1984   *Approaches to the Archaeological Heritage*. Cambridge University Press, Cambridge.
    1988   *Archaeological Heritage Management in the Modern World*. Unwin Hyman, Winchester, Massachusetts.

Fitting, J. E.
    1979   Untitled section in Client-Oriented Archaeology: An Exchange of Views (J. E. Fitting and A. C. Goodyear). *Journal of Field Archaeology* 6:351–360.

Goodland, R., and M. Webb
    1987   *The Management of Cultural Property in World-Bank Assisted Projects*. World Bank Technical Paper No. 62, Washington, D.C.

Goodyear, A. C.
    1979   Untitled section in Client-Oriented Archaeology: An Exchange of Views (J. E. Fitting and A. C. Goodyear). *Journal of Field Archaeology* 6:351–360.

Kelley, J. H., and M. P. Hanen
   1988   *Archaeology and the Methodology of Science*. University of New Mexico Press, Albuquerque.

King, T. F.
   1979   The Trouble With Archaeology. *Journal of Field Archaeology* 6:350–351.

Knudson, R.
   1986   Contemporary Cultural Resource Management. In *American Archaeology Past and Future: A Celebration of the Society for American Archaeology 1935–1985*, edited by D. J. Meltzer, D. D. Fowler, and J. A. Sabloff, pp. 395–413. Smithsonian Institution Press, Washington, D.C.

Lipe, W. D., and A. J. Lindsay (editors)
   1974   *Proceedings of the 1974 Cultural Resource Management Conference*. Museum of Northern Arizona Technical Series No. 14. Federal Center, Denver.

MacDonald, W. K. (editor)
   1976   *Digging for Gold: Papers on Archaeology for Profit*. Research Reports in Archaeology: Technical Reports No. 5. Museum of Anthropology, University of Michigan, Ann Arbor.

Mayer-Oakes, W. J., and A. W. Portnoy (editors)
   1984   *Proceedings 1984*. American Society for Conservation Archaeology.

McCreery, D. W., and J. A. Sauer
   1983   *Economic Development and Archaeology in the Middle East*. Department of Antiquities of the Hashemite Kingdom of Jordan and the American Center of Oriental Research, Amman.

Meighan, C. W.
   1986   *Archaeology for Money*. Wormwood Press, Calabasas, California.

National Park Service
   1989   International Perspectives on Cultural Parks. *Proceedings of the First World Conference*, Mesa Verde National Park, Colorado, 1984. U.S. National Park Service and Colorado Historical Society.

Piper, H. M.
   1990   Professional Problem Domains of Consulting Archaeologists: Responsibility Without Authority. *Journal of Field Archaeology* 17:211–214.

Raab, L. M., T. C. Klinger, M. B. Schiffer, and A. C. Goodyear
   1980   Clients, Contracts, and Profits: Conflicts in Public Archaeology. *American Anthropologist* 82:539–551.

Silberman, N.
   1982   *Digging for God and Country: Exploration, Archaeology, and the Secret Struggle for the Holy Land, 1799–1917*. Anchor Books, New York.
   1989   *Between Past and Present: Archaeology, Ideology, and Nationalism in the Modern Middle East*. Henry Holt, New York.

Simmons, A. H.
   1988a   Extinct Pygmy Hippopotamus and Early Man in Cyprus. *Nature* 333:554–557.
   1988b   Test Excavations at Akrotiri-*Aetokremnos* (Site E), an Early Prehistoric Occupation in Cyprus: Preliminary Report. *Reports of the Department of Antiquities of Cyprus, 1988*, pp. 15–24. Department of Antiquities, Nicosia.
   1989   Preliminary Report of the 1988 Season at Akrotiri-*Aetokremnos*, Cyprus.

Reports of the Department of Antiquities of Cyprus, 1989, pp. 1–5. Department of Antiquities, Nicosia.

1991a Humans, Island Colonization and Pleistocene Extinctions in the Mediterranean: The View from Akrotiri-*Aetokremnos*, Cyprus. *Antiquity* 65:857–869.

1991b One Flew over the Hippos' Nest: Extinct Pleistocene Fauna, Early Man, and Conservative Archaeology in Cyprus. In *Perspectives on the Past*, edited by Geoffrey Clark, pp. 282–304. University of Pennsylvania Press, Philadelphia.

Simmons, A. H., I. Kohler-Rollefson, G. O. Rollefson, R. D. Mandel, and Z. Kafafi
    1988   'Ain Ghazal: A Major Neolithic Settlement in Central Jordan. *Science* 240:35–39.

Willey, G. R., and P. Phillips
    1958   *Method and Theory in American Archaeology*. University of Chicago Press, Chicago.

Wilson, R. L. (editor)
    1987   *Rescue Archaeology—Proceedings of the Second New World Conference on Rescue Archaeology*. Southern Methodist University Press, Dallas.

Wilson, R. L., and G. Loyola (editors)
    1982   *Rescue Archaeology—Papers from the First New World Conference on Rescue Archaeology*. The Preservation Press, Washington, D.C.

Woolley, Sir L.
    1952   *Digging Up the Past*. Reprint. Penguin Books, Harmondsworth, Middlesex, England. Originally published 1930.

8. A Feminist Program for Nonsexist Archaeology

Suzanne M. Spencer-Wood

Abstract: This essay advocates a feminist program to correct androcentric biases in archaeology and to develop nonsexist theory and constructions of the past. First, androcentric bias is defined and exemplified. Then feminist critique is briefly defined and differentiated from gender research conducted within male-centered frameworks. Next, androcentric biases are critiqued (1) in particular constructions of the past and (2) in paradigms, including processual, postprocessual, critical, and Marxist archaeology. Then the author's feminist empiricist paradigm is outlined, and a methodology is suggested for developing nonsexist constructions of the past. Finally, five strategies are suggested to facilitate the acceptance of feminist perspectives into mainstream archaeological theory, practice, and discourse.

The Problem: Androcentric Bias

Androcentric bias, most simply defined as sexist prejudice from a male-centered point of view, produces partial, distorted constructions of the past that support the oppression of women in the present. Androcentric archaeology represents male dominance and female subordination as universal, natural, and therefore inevitable and justified (Spencer-Wood 1991a). Sexism is deeply embedded in all aspects of our culture, from language, values, and structures of thought to archaeological research. Thus, most of us have at some point unconsciously produced androcentric archaeology by uncritically using widely accepted but biased paradigms, models, assumptions, or taxonomies.

Androcentric pasts are constructed in the image of current sexist ideals by projecting modern gender stereotypes into the past. Androcentric archaeology considers and represents aspects of culture identified with men as more important than those identified with women (Conkey and Spector 1984:4).

Quandaries and Quests: Visions of Archaeology's Future, edited by LuAnn Wandsnider. Center for Archaeological Investigations, Occasional Paper No. 20. © 1992 by the Board of Trustees, Southern Illinois University. All rights reserved. ISBN 0-88104-075-4.

The following are some sexist prejudices that often bias archaeological theory and research.

> 1. Cultures are represented as ungendered. Gender and sex are equated with women, and all are ignored as insignificant.
> 2. Men's behaviors and viewpoints in the past are generalized to represent those of a whole society, usually masked as cultural norms and purportedly ungendered text.
> 3. Women's behaviors, roles, and viewpoints in the past are either not considered, are considered secondary to men's, are accorded low status, or are treated as deviant from societal (i.e., male) norms (Conkey and Spector 1984:4).
> 4. Women disappear by being subsumed in male-defined units of analysis, such as classes, industries, forms of social organization, or time periods.
> 5. Only men are considered to be agents of social and cultural change.
> 6. Women are portrayed as powerless, passive victims, controlled by men and male-dominated, large-scale, cultural institutions (McGaw 1989; Spencer-Wood 1987, 1991b).
> 7. Modern gender stereotypes are assumed as nonproblematic biological universals, supporting sexist justifications of women's inferior status as natural.
> 8. Evidence of cases in which women and men did not conform to gender stereotypes are considered exceptions that do not invalidate sexist universals.
> 9. Gender is constructed as universal, simplistic dualisms that oppose positively valued, high-status, male attributes versus negatively valued, low-status, female attributes. Sexist male/female dichotomies include dominant/subordinate, active/passive, public/private, culture/nature, sacred/profane, rational/emotional, powerful/powerless, independent/dependent, strong/weak, and clean/unclean.

The primacy and dominance of men over women is linguistically reinforced through the conventions of always listing men and male attributes first and women and female attributes second, as well as the use of male pronouns and nouns to represent both women and men. Thus, women disappear in purportedly ungendered text that subsumes women within male linguistic categories, or women are represented as secondary, and often as opposite, to men (Spencer-Wood 1991a).

Feminist Critiques

Feminism is a theoretical perspective for understanding the ways gender, as a fundamental cultural construct, structures all aspects of culture and conditions the behavior of all members of society, including men and children as well as women. However, feminist and gender research are *not* synonymous. Some attempts at purportedly feminist archaeology involve adding women to male-centered models. While that does make women visible in previously ungendered constructions of the past, simply adding women to androcentric models just further supports and reifies their sexist biases (Conkey and Gero 1988:4).

Feminist archaeology is distinguished from other theoretical approaches not only by its gender consciousness but also by its critique and correction of sexist biases in archaeology. Male-focused models and paradigms must first be rejected in order to create more powerful nonsexist frameworks. This essay argues that feminist perspectives need to be adopted in mainstream archaeological theory and research in order to develop nonsexist constructions of the past. Feminist criticism of the connection between androcentric research biases and sexist disciplinary politics brings to light fundamental flaws in archaeological knowledge, its production, and reproduction (cf. Gero 1991).

Critiques of Androcentric Models

Feminist critiques of androcentric biases in archaeology started in the 1970s with particular models and substantive constructions of the past. The critiques are important not only for particular case studies, but because each biased model supports and reifies deeper biases, such as the dualistic oppositions already mentioned. For instance, although feminists exposed the androcentric biases in the "Man the Hunter" model of early hominid life, the revised version of "Man the Scavenger" perpetuates the same sexist construction of gender roles, with male scavenging becoming the cause of evolution (Conkey and Spector 1984:7; Jolly and Plog 1986:277–279). The search to validate androcentric models has continued to produce biased constructions of the past that are not supported by data.

Feminists have critiqued stereotypic models and constructions of sex roles. They have sought and found evidence of diversity and flexibility in gendered behaviors and of powerful female roles and behaviors, such as leadership. In order to break down archaeologists' monolithic categories of male hunting versus female gathering and childcare, Spector has suggested a corrective "Task Differentiation" framework and methodology for empirically analyzing the multidimensional variability in women's and men's activity patterns (Spector and Whelan 1989:75–77). In primatology, which is used by archaeologists to construct protohominid and early hominid social organization, the androcentric overemphasis on fixed male dominance hierarchies and sexually passive females has been invalidated with empirical observations of male temporary membership in primate social organizations, the cores of which are based on long-term female kinship bonds (Fedigan and Fedigan 1989:41–44).

Some historical archaeologists have also recently critiqued the widespread use of androcentric assumptions, models, and histories (cf. Spencer-Wood 1991a). For instance, the domestic-female versus public-male dichotomy has been corrected with evidence of women's activities in both spheres among contact period Pueblo Indians (Fratt 1991), in an antebellum southern town (Derry 1991), in a nineteenth-century mining town (Hardesty 1989), and in early twentieth-century farms (Stine 1991). Smith (1989) criticized the construction of historic maritime culture as exclusively male and researched gender roles and relationships at sea. Weber (1991) has critiqued historical archaeology's failure to analyze how elite women as well as men expressed social prestige through their gardens.

Thus, feminist archaeology has critiqued the projection of modern sexist stereotypes into the past. Androcentrism has been corrected by empirically testing nonsexist assumptions that females were as important as males and that females also held powerful social positions and controlled critical social relationships and resources. Further, feminists have rejected idealistic constructions to look for evidence of the diversity and flexibility of women's as well as men's roles and relationships.

Critiques of Androcentric Paradigms

This section critiques some androcentric biases in archaeological paradigms and assumptions that support particular models such as those critiqued above. Some of the suggestions grew out of extant feminist critiques of processualism, science, other social sciences, postprocessualism, and philosophical epistemologies related to some archaeological paradigms.

Feminist Critiques of Processualism

In processual archaeology, androcentrism often unconsciously biases inherently subjective aspects of scientific method, including the choice and statement of research framework, problem, and hypotheses; the selection of data considered as evidence relevant to the problem and hypotheses; the categorization and interpretation of those data; and therefore the conclusions drawn (Longino and Doell 1987). Nonprocessual archaeologists generally use but do not explicitly discuss those methodological processes and therefore have even greater potential for unconscious bias.

In processual archaeology the origin of research problems and hypotheses has been considered unimportant, whether from a dream or from inductively analyzed data (Binford 1968:17). The androcentric politics of modern life have often unconsciously limited the kinds of questions that are considered important to answer and support with data. Because archaeology is male-centered, research priorities are set according to male interests and viewpoints. Research problems and hypotheses have focused on men's activities in the past, which have been used as the important identifying characteristics of social forms (e.g., band, tribe, chiefdom, state) and large spatiotemporal periods, as in the Paleoindian Big Game Hunters.

Within processualism the dominant framework is a form of systems theory that does not include gender. Yet cultural constructions of gender ideology, roles, and relationships are fundamental to the construction and operation of social, economic, and political structures that are considered of primary importance, such as form of subsistence, sociopolitical hierarchy, and social stratification. Since there is no gender subsystem in systems theory, gender has not been consciously researched as a cultural construct, but instead has been reduced to sexist, biologically deterministic models that reify beliefs in women's inferiority and dependence on men (cf. Harding 1987a:299). However, cultural constructions of gender vary widely and cannot be reduced to biology or any other variable or more primary cause (Wylie 1991a). The systems framework has also led to the perception that gender and ethnicity are just topics like the economy, inhibiting the development of feminist and ethnic paradigms. Gender needs to be researched not just as a cultural subsystem but as a foundational, all-pervasive cultural construct that structures all social life.

The archaeological emphasis on large-scale theories and constructions of the past can result in sexist bias when specific cases that do not conform to androcentric overgeneralizations are dismissed as exceptions. Conkey and Spector (1984:22–23) have pointed out how the archaeological-systems focus on research questions concerning large processes in functional perspective has resulted in the invisibility of small-group actions, roles, and choices as sources of change. The greater importance accorded large-scale questions, theories, and generalizations is related to the systems idea that large-scale structures are the independent variables that determine internal "microvariables" such as gender and ethnicity, as well as small-scale variations (Binford 1983:221; Wylie 1991b). This apparently scientific justification for the dominance of large-scale causes over small-scale internal causes is actually an arbitrary, empirically untested assumption that supports androcentric bias. In the attempt to support purported cross-cultural universals such as male dominance, those specific contexts in which male dominance cannot be read into the data are dismissed as unimportant anomalous exceptions that are not statistically significant. In a truly scientific methodology, those specific cases would be accorded the greatest significance because they disprove the claimed universality that justifies male dominance and denies the diversity of gendered cultural behavior. Rejecting the deterministic role of large-scale structures, both feminists and the new science of nonlinear systems are demonstrating how small-scale processes can lead to large-scale, context-specific changes (Spencer-Wood 1989a, 1989b, 1990, 1991a, 1991b).

Since prehistoric archaeologists are the reference group for academic historical archaeologists (cf. Yentsch 1991), a Society for Historical Archaeology (SHA) plenary session on "Questions that Count," published in 1988 (*Historical Archaeology* 22[1]:5–42), largely replicated the status hierarchy of research problems in prehistoric processual archaeology. Thus, greater importance was usually accorded to large-scale ungendered questions than to small-scale particularistic research, ignoring the advantages offered by historical archaeology's wealth of context-specific data, both documentary and archaeological, especially on gender and ethnicity. That session also reproduced androcentric bias in prehistoric archaeology, with only one mention of gender as an important topic of archaeological inquiry (Mrozowski 1988). However, the popularity of the first ever feminist session at the SHA meetings in January 1989 (organized by the author) led to gender sessions at the 1990, 1991, and 1992 SHA meetings. But many historical archaeologists do not understand that feminist archaeology is not the same as adding women to sexist models of the past. Feminists need to work to ensure that gender is not treated the same way that ethnicity is treated in historical archaeology, as a topic defined, analyzed, and constructed from a white male point of view.

Feminist critique exposes the inevitable self-referential tautology involved in the way that the scientific method is often used in processual archaeology. The research problem and hypotheses are based on assumed universals, such as a domestic/public sexual division of labor, which are used to classify and interpret the data in ways that support the favored hypothesis, if at all possible. With this method, data can be unconsciously misinterpreted, reifying androcentric assumptions. For instance, Gero (1989) has shown how the sexist assumption that only men made tools (limited by definition to highly retouched standardized forms) for use in male activities leads to the empirically unsupported assumption that flakes with little or no retouch cannot be defined, classified, and interpreted as tools, although women and men used flakes as tools for a variety of tasks. It is one of many instances in which androcentric assumptions lead to a biased classification scheme that results in empirically unwarranted interpretations and research conclusions. With the sexist assumption that women did not make tools, archaeologists exclude women from the very definition of hominids as tool makers and from any significant role in hominid evolution, which purportedly resulted from males' hunting with stone tools (cf. Jolly and Plog 1986:277–279). A completely different construction of human evolution would be created if women were considered as important as men in the creation and use of distinctively hominid tools. Although processualism has advocated overtly stating assumptions, most recently emphasized in building middle-range theory (cf. Binford 1978), many archaeologists have considered androcentric assumptions to be reasonable until their bias is revealed by feminist critique.

Feminist Critiques of Postprocessualism and Critical Archaeology

Postprocessual archaeology and critical archaeology both emphasize that knowledge is socially constituted and context-dependent, opposing the objectivity claims of processualism. A reflexive position is used to deconstruct processual archaeology, but the discourses of postprocessual and critical archaeology are equally unreflexive in their biased use of male perspectives and activities to represent those of the entire species. Englestad (1989:4–5) critiques Shanks and Tilley's books for lamenting the underdevelopment of feminist archaeology and research on "sexual repression and exploitation" (Shanks and Tilley 1987:246) while failing to consider gender as a socially and symbolically constituted structuring principle of societies and agents. Shanks and Tilley (1987:79–81) also unreflexively express a blatantly sexist view of displayed artifacts as "a pornography," "available" for viewing, which is analogous to "rape," and "a violation of the body of the past." In 1986 Hodder (157–161) portrayed archaeological research on women and gender as peripheral and feminist archaeology as outside established discourse in the field, along with a number of other "alternative perspectives," including those of Von Daniken and "indigenous archaeologies." Recently Hodder (1991a) stated that gender is a postprocessual concern. While legitimating gender within the male-dominated theoretical discourse, Hodder subsumed it within an ungendered discourse and reduced feminism to gender as one topic among many in postprocessual archaeology. Although some postprocessual gender research does meet standard criteria for archaeological inference (cf. Biaggi 1989; Gibbs 1987), in other cases that purportedly read the symbolic meanings from data, androcentric dualisms are still often unreflexively applied (cf. Sorensen 1987).

In contrast, feminist anthropologists have reflexively recognized and critiqued their early uncritical use of the purportedly universal sexist dualism of female-domestic-subordinate versus male-public-dominant (Moore 1988:22). Feminists use reflexivity to advance and improve feminist critiques. This creates greater growth in feminist archaeology than in less reflexive theoretical approaches, which tend to stagnate and generate fewer insights over time by repetitively interpreting data to fit idealistic models based on overgeneralizations that are often androcentric, as in simplistic structural dualisms.

Postprocessual archaeology metaphorically considers nonlinear archaeological data as linear text and contends that multiple readings, or interpretations of data, are all equally valid (cf. Hodder 1991b). If interpretation is not limited by data, what purpose do data serve beyond the legitimation of a priori ideas that are read into data? Postprocessualists and critical archaeologists view data as totally subjective and politically theory-laden. That creates a debilitating nihilistic relativism. Mascia-Lees and colleagues (1989) reveal that such relativism is an attempt by the dominant male elite to discredit feminist critique by reducing it from the higher ground of a more complete corrective perspective to simply another point of view that does not invalidate androcentric theory. Englestad (1991) points out that as a result decisions about which constructions of the past are best are based on the power of the male-dominated elite in archaeology, a point with which Hodder (1991a) recently concurred. Thus, relativism supports and validates androcentrism in archaeology. But there is evidence of a contradiction between that theoretical position of extreme subjectivity and Shanks and Tilley's (1987:104) brief vague reference to the network of resistances formed by data to their theoretical appropriation. Furthermore, Hodder recently (1991a, 1991b) backpedaled on his unqualified endorsement of multiple equally valid pasts and addressed the issue of limitations that data place on interpretation.

Critical archaeology emphasizes not only how capitalist political positions affect archaeological interpretation but also how archaeology is used to support and justify social relations in modern capitalism and its politics (Leone et al. 1987). However, the past constructed by critical archaeologists is usually ungendered, although capitalist discrimination against women is a major social problem that exposes the androcentric bias in purportedly gender-neutral capitalist economic theoretical principles, such as the law of supply and demand. Critical theory is concerned with power relationships, but in its application often has been sexist in ignoring gender. Critical archaeology draws heavily on Marxism, which focuses on class and neglects gender and ethnicity as fundamental cultural constructs that structure power in social relationships. Operationally Marxism is sexist in not integrating reproduction and housework as the production of labor. Many Marxists androcentrically overgeneralize in excluding women from the high status of productive members of society because production is defined in male terms (Nye 1988:55–57). In actuality, working women suffer more oppression than their male counterparts, although most critical and Marxist historical archaeologists subsume women within male-defined classes.

A Suggested Feminist Paradigm

This section outlines my feminist paradigm for developing nonsexist constructions of the past. This suggested theoretical perspective combines empiricism, feminist standpoint theory, and some aspects of feminist postmodernism, while rejecting relativism. The paradigm has been developed by examining not only feminist scholarship in archaeology but also the literature on feminist theory and paradigms in other disciplines, especially the sciences and social sciences. Because archaeology has borrowed much of its theory, feminist critiques and paradigms in other disciplines are often relevant to the development of feminist archaeology.

Similar to postmodernism, the suggested paradigm rejects any construction of women as a universal unitary social category. While recognizing sex as a biological category, I contend that women cannot be reduced to their biology any more than can men, because of the variation in women's social conditions and viewpoints. I agree with most feminists that we need to research the multidimensional diversity in historic and prehistoric gender experiences, roles, activities, and relationships, as well as gender concepts, identities, and ideologies. We need to research the relationships between gender norms and ideals and the flexibility in the actual operation of gender systems. All aspects of gender systems vary among individual women and men in different cultures and cultural subgroups such as ethnic groups, classes, age groups, and religions. Because the two genders are defined in relation to each other, I suggest a dialectical approach, analyzing the relationships between women's and men's behaviors and ideologies (Hawkesworth 1989:556–557; cf. Smith-Rosenberg 1986).

My feminist perspective rejects the relativist idea that androcentric and feminist interpretations are equally valid and must both be presented for a balanced perspective. The greater validity of feminist interpretations and critiques results from their use of widely accepted empirical methodology to identify and correct androcentric biases that are easily recognized within conventional standards (Harding 1987b:182–184; Wylie 1991a). For instance, feminist research has revealed how burials have been incorrectly sexed by assuming that males could be identified on the basis of their association with certain artifacts, such as axes or projectile points. The evidence from biological sexing of burials has shown that some women were buried with artifacts, such as axes, that previously had always been assumed to be male funerary objects (cf. Arnold 1991; Fratt 1991). Those studies demonstrate that instead of just presenting androcentric and feminist interpretations side by side we need to empirically invalidate male bias because it results in the construction of an inaccurate past that supports modern sexist beliefs.

Similar to critical archaeology's privileging the viewpoint of the oppressed classes to critique capitalist politics in archaeology, my paradigm privileges a feminist standpoint because it is a more holistic perspective than androcentrism. Feminism is a more powerful framework because it encompasses both the sexist perspectives being analyzed and the critique and correction of them. In male-dominated cultures feminism focuses on women because they have more experience and knowledge of sexism than have men. While the culturally dominant androcentrism is deeply enculturated in women as well as men, only women's experiences and resulting ideologies contradict sexist beliefs and expose the ways that male-dominated cultures have ignored, denied, and masked their oppression of women, using both material culture and words (Harding 1987a:293; Hartstock 1987:159). Thus, I advocate a standpoint that is based on the more complete interpretations of data possible from a feminist point of view, as contrasted to an androcentric point of view. Rejecting sexist representations of women as passive, dependent, and inferior, feminist approaches look instead for evidence of the interdependence between women and men and evidence of women's strengths and empowering behaviors in constructing their own lives.

The suggested paradigm rejects Harding's (1987a:291–293) idea that a subjective standpoint is incompatible with objectivity. Instead, I argue that all research, objective or not, is conducted from a standpoint. Instead of taking one side or the other of the perceived opposition between objectivity and subjectivity, feminist archaeology can offer a middle position that clarifies the dialectical relationship between subject and object. Feminist critique recognizes the unavoidable subjective element in archaeological inference, while at the same time recognizing the limitations that data place on possible interpretation. The complex feedbacks between possible assumptions, alternative interpretations, and objectively measured and described data permit a justifiable decision on which interpretation accounts for archaeological data most completely, logically, and parsimoniously (Harding 1987a:288–292).

Finally, my feminist paradigm is self-critical to continually increase our awareness and rejection of more androcentric biases. This results in the development of less biased models that permit further insight into the past and our construction of it. It is essential for the growth of feminist archaeology. Increasing awareness of the ways that androcentric politics and subjectivity have biased archaeology make feminists more aware of their own unconscious biases, paradoxically resulting in less bias.

The next question is how to implement the feminist theoretical standpoint. First, feminist research questions must be asked if we are to construct nonsexist pasts. Feminist critiques and cultural constructions in anthropology and history suggest feminist viewpoints and questions that can be adapted and expanded for archaeological research. Feminists view women as well as men as powerful agents of culture change, who construct their own gender ideologies, behaviors, and relationships. Rejecting the projection of sexist gender ideals into the past, feminists analyze how women and men in diverse cultural subgroups interacted interdependently and flexibly. Instead of androcentric questions that seek evidence for the ways men have controlled and victimized women, feminists seek evidence of the ways that women controlled their own lives, even in male-dominated societies. Feminists deny that women have been passive victims of male dominance (cf. McGaw 1989; Spencer-Wood 1987, 1991b). While not denying the existence of male dominance, even in that context feminists look for evidence of the ways women empowered themselves. We cannot find evidence of women's power and importance unless we look for it.

My research on domestic reform exemplifies how a feminist paradigm denies the historical reality of modern gender stereotypes and constructs a nonsexist past. Many historical archaeologists have uncritically accepted as historical *reality* a historian's construction of nineteenth-century androcentric *ideals* termed the "Cult of True Womanhood," in which women's important roles are seen as being limited to the home (Welter 1966). In contrast, my feminist research has explored how domestic reformers used women's domesticity as a source of power and dominance not only in the home but also in areas of the male-dominated public sphere that they successfully redefined as parts of the domestic sphere. Domestic reformers raised women's status by bringing public-sphere, scientific-industrial methods to housework and by developing new female "domestic" professions in the public sphere, such as nurses, dieticians, child-care providers, and teachers in kindergartens, kitchen gardens, primary grades, industrial schools for girls, girls' colleges, and home economics classes. It is particularly appropriate for archaeologists to research domestic reform because innovative material culture was used to symbolize and implement the professionalization of women's work (Spencer-Wood 1987, 1989a, 1989c, 1991b).

Recently, feminist historians have analyzed how many historic women developed other positive ideologies, such as the "Cult of Real Womanhood" (Cogan 1989) and the "Cult of Single Blessedness" (Chambers-Schiller 1984). These ideals included beliefs in the positive value of women's work, economic independence, and intellectual, cultural, and physical self-improvement, in contrast to the True Womanhood ideal of the dependent, submissive, weak, decorative female (Welter 1966). Women's positive ideologies were expressed not only in historical documents but also through material culture, such as innovative dress styles and gymnastic equipment, which were designed to eliminate hoopskirts, corsets, and the lack of exercise that made women physically weak and dependent on men. Archaeological data can indicate the extent of material implementation of women's positive ideals and domestic reforms in different classes and ethnic groups (Spencer-Wood 1987, 1989a, 1991a, 1991b).

The suggested paradigm seeks data relevant to questions raised by feminist analyses of historic women's ideals, experiences, and relationships with men, children, and other women. Disciplines such as women's studies, history, and biology, as well as anthropology, offer feminist understandings of women's behaviors that can assist in the development of feminist research questions in both prehistoric and historic archaeology. Feminist analyses raise questions that are not asked or researched within the dominant, androcentric, archaeological discourse.

Promoting Feminist Perspectives in Archaeology

A feminist agenda for developing nonsexist archaeology requires changes in standard androcentric practices of research, publishing, teaching, and tenure. Actions are suggested that address the connection between androcentric bias in archaeological research and the sexist disciplinary politics involved in the production and reproduction of knowledge in the field.

Gero (1991) has researched the connection between high status and male dominance in fieldwork and in creating large-scale, cross-cultural generalizing theories. Conversely, women, shut out of the male networks controlling access to high-status areas, are concentrated in low-status, particularistic, domestic-type lab work and microstudies that produce information often appropriated by men in their purportedly more important large-scale research. Gero predicts that in the future lab analysis will become more important than fieldwork as the avenue to new information. If that happens and women control laboratory archaeology, they might then be accorded higher status. However, as in many types of work, men may use their politically dominant positions to appropriate high-status laboratory positions. Archaeology is male dominated, and men control most leadership positions in the discipline (in academic departments, cultural resource management, the Society for American Archaeology [SAA], and the SHA), the status of *knowledge* produced by archaeologists, its dissemination, and its widespread acceptance in the discipline (through mechanisms including citations and recommendations to colleagues and students).

The following interrelated strategies are suggested in order to generate widespread acceptance of feminist theory and research and to shift the production and reproduction of archaeological knowledge away from androcentric biases and toward nonsexist theories and constructions of the past.

> 1. Increase our use of the enormous, extant, feminist literature in anthropology and in other disciplines to gain greater insight into androcentric biases in archaeology and to develop more feminist archaeological theories, models, and interpretations.
> 2. Increase the number of high-quality feminist articles published in major archaeology journals (cf. Gero 1985) and books by prestigious presses on a range of topics (cf. Gero and Conkey 1991).
> 3. Give more acknowledgment, scholarly citation, and support to feminist scholarship. This is especially needed from leaders in our male-dominated field.

4. Increase the proportion of feminist faculty in order to counteract the dominance of androcentric perspectives in archaeology. Feminist faculty could include some men, though probably most would be women. We must stop the widespread discrimination in hiring women into anthropology faculties and granting them tenure (Levine 1991; Stark 1991). However, while having more women faculty would bring more women's points of view, both feminist and nonfeminist, to the production and reproduction of archaeological knowledge, it seems quite unlikely that men will willingly give up their dominance in archaeology.

5. Therefore, revise textbooks and curricula to increase coverage of feminist corrections to sexist archaeological theory and constructions of the past. This will decrease the widespread acceptance and reproduction of androcentric theory and research by increasing faculty and student awareness of sexist biases in archaeology and nonsexist frameworks developed by feminists. The process has been initiated by Sandra Morgen's Department of Education project, which suggested feminist revisions of five major anthropology textbooks and produced the American Anthropological Association's book, *Gender and Anthropology: Critical Reviews for Research and Teaching* (1989). However, in archaeology, despite corrective feminist reviews, Thomas's (1989) textbook is still androcentrically biased. Feminists have begun and will undoubtedly pursue the process of reducing the numerous androcentric biases in textbooks and curricula that reproduce archaeological knowledge.

Conclusion

This chapter has suggested a feminist paradigm to replace androcentric biases in archaeology with nonsexist constructions of the past. To that end some types of androcentric bias have been identified, and some feminist critiques of archaeological models and paradigms have been outlined. Male-focused paradigms and models must be rejected in order to create more powerful nonsexist frameworks. Finally, strategies have been suggested for shifting the production and reproduction of archaeological knowledge away from androcentric biases and toward nonsexist theories and constructions of the past. As feminist contributions to theory and substantive research are acknowledged by more archaeological researchers and teachers, feminist perspectives increasingly will be adopted by the archaeological mainstream. This is essential if archaeology is to grow out of its deep androcentrism and develop greater understanding of the past through nonsexist perspectives and paradigms. Feminism offers great potential for the future intellectual growth of nonandrocentric archaeological theories and research.

Acknowledgments

My special thanks to Joan Gero, Linda Cordell, LuAnn Wandsnider, and Miriam Stark for their extremely useful comments. Of course, any errors in this essay are my responsibility.

References

Arnold, Bettina
    1991   The Deposed Princess of Vix: The Need for an Engendered European Prehistory. In *The Archaeology of Gender: Proceedings of the 22nd Annual Chacmool Conference*, edited by D. Wade and N. D. Willows, pp. 366–374. University of Calgary Archaeological Association, Calgary.

Biaggi, Cristina
    1989   The Priestess Figure of Malta. In *The Meaning of Things: Material Culture and Symbolic Expression*, edited by Ian Hodder, pp. 103–121. Unwin Hyman, London.

Binford, Lewis R.
    1968   Archaeological Perspectives. In *New Perspectives in Archaeology*, edited by Sally R. Binford and Lewis R. Binford, pp. 5–32. Aldine, Chicago.
    1978   *Nunamiut Ethnoarchaeology*. Academic Press, New York.
    1983   *Working at Archaeology*. Academic Press, New York.

Chambers-Schiller, Lee Virginia
    1984   *Liberty a Better Husband. Single Women in America: The Generations of 1780–1840*. Yale University Press, New Haven.

Cogan, Frances B.
    1989   *All-American Girl: The Ideal of Real Womanhood in Mid-Nineteenth-Century America*. University of Georgia Press, Athens.

Conkey, Margaret W., and Joan Gero
    1988   Building a Feminist Archaeology. Paper presented at the symposium "Theory in Post Processual Archaeology" at the 53d Annual Meeting of the Society for American Archaeology, Phoenix.

Conkey, Margaret W., and Janet D. Spector
    1984   Archaeology and the Study of Gender. *Advances in Archaeological Method and Theory*, vol. 7, edited by Michael B. Schiffer, pp. 1–38. Academic Press, New York.

Derry, Linda
    1991   Daughters and Sons-in-Law of King Cotton: Asymmetry in the Social Structure and Material Culture of Cahawba, an Antebellum Alabama Town. In *The Archaeology of Gender: Proceedings of the 22nd Annual Chacmool Conference*, edited by D. Wade and N. D. Willows, pp. 270–279. University of Calgary Archaeological Association, Calgary.

Englestad, Ericka
    1991   Feminist Theory and Post-Processual Archaeology. In *The Archaeology of Gender: Proceedings of the 22nd Annual Chacmool Conference*, edited by D. Wade and N. D. Willows, pp. 116–120. University of Calgary Archaeological Association, Calgary.

Fedigan, Linda M., and Laurence Fedigan
    1989   Gender and the Study of Primates. In *Gender and Anthropology: Critical*

Reviews for Research and Teaching, edited by Sandra Morgen, pp. 41–64. American Anthropological Association, Washington, D.C.

Fratt, Lee
  1991 A Preliminary Analysis of Gender Bias in the Sixteenth and Seventeenth Century Spanish Colonial Documents of the American Southwest. In *The Archaeology of Gender: Proceedings of the 22nd Annual Chacmool Conference*, edited by D. Wade and N. D. Willows, pp. 245–251. University of Calgary Archaeological Association, Calgary.

Gero, Joan M.
  1985 Socio-Politics and the Woman-at-Home Ideology. *American Antiquity* 50:342–350.
  1989 Women's Roles in Stone Tool Production. Paper presented in the symposium "Women and Production in Prehistory," 54th Annual Meeting of the Society for American Archaeology, Atlanta.
  1991 Gender Divisions of Labor in the Construction of Archaeological Knowledge. In *The Archaeology of Gender: Proceedings of the 22nd Annual Chacmool Conference*, edited by D. Wade and N. D. Willows, pp. 96–102. University of Calgary Archaeological Association, Calgary.

Gero, Joan M., and Margaret W. Conkey (editors)
  1991 *Engendering Archaeology: Women and Prehistory*. Basil Blackwell, Oxford.

Gibbs, Liv
  1987 Identifying Gender Representation in the Archaeological Record: A Contextual Study. In *The Archaeology of Contextual Meanings*, edited by Ian Hodder, pp. 79–89. Cambridge University Press, Cambridge.

Hardesty, Donald L.
  1989 Gender Roles on the American Mining Frontier: Documentary Models and Archaeological Strategies. Paper presented in the session "Gender in Historical Archaeology" at the 22d Annual Chacmool Conference, The Archaeology of Gender, Calgary.

Harding, Sandra
  1987a The Instability of the Analytical Categories of Feminist Theory. In *Sex and Scientific Inquiry*, edited by Sandra Harding and Jean F. O'Barr, pp. 283–302. University of Chicago Press, Chicago.
  1987b Conclusion: Epistemological Questions. In *Feminism and Methodology*, edited by Sandra Harding, pp. 181–190. Indiana University Press, Bloomington.

Hartstock, Nancy C. M.
  1987 The Feminist Standpoint: Developing the Ground for a Specifically Feminist Historical Materialism. In *Feminism and Methodology*, edited by Sandra Harding, pp. 157–180. Indiana University Press, Bloomington.

Hawkesworth, Mary E.
  1989 Knower, Knowing, Known: Feminist Theory and Claims of Truth. *Signs* 14(3):533–557.

Hodder, Ian
  1986 *Reading the Past: Current Approaches to Interpretation in Archaeology*. Cambridge University Press, Cambridge.
  1991a Postprocessual Archaeology and the Current Debate. In *Processual and Postprocessual Archaeologies: Multiple Ways of Knowing the Past*, edited by Robert W. Preucel, pp. 30–41. Center for Archaeological Investigations, Occasional paper No. 10. Southern Illinois University, Carbondale.
  1991b Gender Representation and Social Reality. In *The Archaeology of*

    Gender: Proceedings of the 22nd Annual Chacmool Conference, edited by D. Wade and N. D. Willows, pp. 11–16. University of Calgary Archaeological Association, Calgary.

Jolly, Clifford J., and Fred Plog
    1986 *Physical Anthropology and Archeology*. 4th ed. Alfred A. Knopf, New York.

Leone, Mark P., Parker B. Potter, Jr., and Paul A. Shackel
    1987 Toward a Critical Archaeology. *Current Anthropology* 28(3): 283–302.

Levine, Mary Ann
    1991 An Historical Overview of Research on Women in Anthropology. In *The Archaeology of Gender: Proceedings of the 22nd Annual Chacmool Conference*, edited by D. Wade and N. D. Willows, pp. 117–186. University of Calgary Archaeological Association, Calgary.

Longino, Helen, and Ruth Doell
    1987 Body, Bias, and Behavior: A Comparative Analysis of Reasoning in Two Areas of Biological Science. In *Sex and Scientific Inquiry*, edited by Sandra Harding and Jean F. O'Barr, pp. 165–186. University of Chicago Press, Chicago.

Mascia-Lees, Frances E., Patricia Sharpe, and Colleen Ballerino Cohen
    1989 The Postmodernist Turn in Anthropology: Cautions from a Feminist Perspective. *Signs* 15(1):7–33.

McGaw, Judith A.
    1989 No Passive Victims, No Separate Spheres: A Feminist Perspective on Technology's History. In *In Context: History and the History of Technology. Essays in Honor of Melvin Kranzberg*, edited by S. H. Cutcliffe and R. C. Post, pp. 172–191. Lehigh University Press, Bethlehem, Pennsylvania.

Moore, Henrietta L.
    1988 *Feminism and Anthropology*. University of Minnesota Press, Minneapolis.

Morgen, Sandra
    1989 *Gender and Anthropology: Critical Reviews for Research and Teaching*. American Anthropological Association, Washington, D.C.

Mrozoswki, Stephen A.
    1988 Historical Archaeology as Anthropology. *Historical Archaeology* 22(1):18–24.

Nye, Andrea
    1988 *Feminist Theory and the Philosophies of Man*. Routledge, New York.

Shanks, Michael, and Christopher Tilley
    1987 *Re-Constructing Archaeology: Theory and Practice*. Cambridge University Press, Cambridge.

Smith, Sheli O.
    1989 Women and Seafaring. Paper presented in the session "Gender in Historical Archaeology" at the 22d Annual Chacmool Conference, The Archaeology of Gender, Calgary.

Smith-Rosenberg, Carroll
    1986 Writing History: Language, Class and Gender. In *Feminist Studies/Critical Studies*, edited by Teresa de Lauretis, pp. 31–54. Theories of Contemporary Culture, vol. 8, Kathleen Woodward, general editor. Center for Twentieth Century Studies, University of Wisconsin, Milwaukee.

Sorensen, Marie Louise Stig
    1987 Material Order and Cultural Classification: The Role of Bronze Objects in the Transition from Bronze Age to Iron Age in Scandinavia. In *The Archaeology of Contextual Meanings*, edited by Ian Hodder, pp. 90–101. Cambridge University Press, Cambridge.

Spector, Janet D., and Mary K. Whelan
  1989 Incorporating Gender into Archaeology Courses: A Curriculum Guide for Introductory Human Evolution and Archaeology Classes. In *Gender and Anthropology: Critical Reviews for Research and Teaching*, edited by Sandra Morgen, pp. 65–94. American Anthropological Association, Washington, D.C.

Spencer-Wood, Suzanne M.
  1987 A Survey of Domestic Reform Movement Sites in Boston and Cambridge, ca. 1865–1905. *Historical Archaeology* 21(2):7–36
  1989a Feminist Archaeology and the Pro-active Roles of Women in Transforming Gender Concepts, Roles, and Relationships in 19th Century America. Paper presented at the First Joint Archaeological Congress, Baltimore.
  1989b Culture and the Chaos Paradigm. Paper presented in the session "Current Issues in Archaeological Theory and Method" at the First Joint Archaeological Congress, Baltimore.
  1989c The Community as Household: Domestic Reform, Mid-Range Theory and the Domestication of Public Space. In *Households and Communities: Proceedings of the 21st Annual Chacmool Conference*, edited by S. MacEachern, D. J. W. Archer, and R. D. Garvin. University of Calgary Archaeological Association, Calgary.
  1990 Non-linear Dynamics in Cultural Processes: Implications for Theories of Culture and Cultural Evolution. Paper presented at the Conference on Dynamical Description of Human Systems, University of Cambridge, Cambridge.
  1991a Toward a Feminist Historical Archaeology of the Construction of Gender. In *The Archaeology of Gender: Proceedings of the 22nd Annual Chacmool Conference*, edited by D. Wade and N. D. Willows, pp. 234–244. University of Calgary Archaeological Association, Calgary.
  1991b Toward an Historical Archaeology of Domestic Reform. In *The Archaeology of Inequality*, edited by R. McGuire and R. Paynter, pp. 231–286. Basil Blackwell, Oxford.

Stark, Miriam
  1991 A Perspective on Women's Status in American Archaeology. In *The Archaeology of Gender: Proceedings of the 22nd Annual Chacmool Conference*, edited by D. Wade and N. D. Willows, pp. 187–194. University of Calgary Archaeological Association, Calgary.

Stine, Linda France
  1991 Early 20th Century Gender Roles: Perceptions from the Farm. In *The Archaeology of Gender: Proceedings of the 22nd Annual Chacmool Conference*, edited by D. Wade and N. D. Willows, pp. 496–501. University of Calgary Archaeological Association, Calgary.

Thomas, David H.
  1989 *Archaeology*. 2d ed. Holt, Rinehart and Winston, New York.

Weber, Carmen A.
  1991 The Genius of the Orangery: Women and 18th Century Chesapeake Gardens. In *The Archaeology of Gender: Proceedings of the 22nd Annual Chacmool Conference*, edited by D. Wade and N. D. Willows, pp. 263–269. University of Calgary Archaeological Association, Calgary.

Welter, Barbara
  1966 The Cult of True Womanhood: 1820–1860. *American Quarterly* 18:151–174.

Wylie, Alison
  1991a Feminist Critiques and Archaeological Challenges. In *The Archaeology of*

Gender: Proceedings of the 22nd Annual Chacmool Conference, edited by D. Wade and N. D. Willows, pp. 17–23. University of Calgary Archaeological Association, Calgary.

1991b Gender Theory and the Archaeological Record: Why Is There No Archaeology of Gender? In *Engendering Archaeology: Women and Prehistory*, edited by J. M. Gero and M. W. Conkey, pp. 31–54. Basil Blackwell, Oxford.

Yentsch, Anne

1991 Access to Space, Symbolic and Material, in Historical Archaeology. In *The Archaeology of Gender: Proceedings of the 22nd Annual Chacmool Conference*, edited by D. Wade and N. D. Willows, pp. 252–262. University of Calgary Archaeological Association, Calgary.

9. Archaeology in a Democratic Society: A Critical Theory Perspective

Mark P. Leone and Robert W. Preucel

Abstract: Our aim in this essay is to describe a basis for a rational relationship between archaeological issues and participation in a democratic society. We do this in order to project a condition we suspect will come to characterize the practice of archaeology in the United States and elsewhere in the twenty-first century. This condition is the recognition of multiple interests in the past. We also do this in order to provide some guidance to actions that can be taken once one agrees that the social context of archaeology has an impact on the research process itself. We explore these relationships within the context of the reburial issue.

Introduction

There is a growing recognition within archaeology today that the study of the past is a social and political practice intimately bound to the context within which it is conducted (Gero et al. 1983; Leone 1986; Patterson 1986; Trigger 1989). That recognition has stimulated important research on the effects of gender bias on interpretation (Gero 1985; Gero and Conkey 1991; Gero and Root 1990), the impact of funding institutions on archaeology (Gero 1983; Patterson 1986; Yellen 1983), and the relationships between indigenous peoples and archaeological research (Gathercole and Lowenthal 1990; Layton 1989a, 1989b; Trigger 1980). Our concern in this chapter is specifically with Native Americans and their relationship to the practice of North American archaeology. We begin by describing the social context surrounding the reburial issue and recent legislation.

The new Native American Graves Protection and Repatriation Act (P.L. 101–601) was passed as a result of intense dialogue and discussion between

Quandaries and Quests: Visions of Archaeology's Future, edited by LuAnn Wandsnider. Center for Archaeological Investigations, Occasional Paper No. 20. © 1992 by the Board of Trustees, Southern Illinois University. All rights reserved. ISBN 0-88104-075-4.

Native American and academic and museum interests. It gives Native Americans control over "Federal land that is recognized by the Indian Claims Commission as the aboriginal land of some Indian tribe" and makes them active participants in the arbitration process over the use of those lands. It also sets up a process for repatriating some collections of skeletal materials and grave goods in public and private hands. The social context, however, within which this dialogue is embedded is one that is quite foreign to most archaeologists. It is characterized by a highly charged political atmosphere that calls into question some of the basic tenets of our profession.

This context is full-blown in the following quote from a communique issued by Suzan Harjo, president and director of the Morning Star Foundation.

> THE SITUATION OF AMERICAN INDIAN PEOPLE AT THE BEGINNING OF THE 1990s SUGGESTS THAT THE UNITED STATES HAS YET TO FINALLY DECIDE THE THRESHOLD QUESTIONS of whether or not Native American peoples are human and what rights we may have as human beings with inherent sovereignty and dignity. It is time for these questions to be resolved as we mark the 500-year invasion of Native America and as we approach a new century.
>
> IT IS TIME for the United States and the world community of nations to set policies and engage in practices that deal with all Native peoples as human beings with full self-determination and human rights.
>
> IT IS TIME for the United States to honor, fully enforce and fulfill all treaties and other legally-binding promises and moral duties to assure the survival and future well-being of Native peoples.
>
> IT IS TIME for the United States and Native nations to redefine their status and relationships in light of the history of the past 500 years.
>
> IT IS TIME for Congress to back up policy statements with strong new laws to reverse the disastrous effects of the Indian Claims Commission, and to promote and remove barriers to Indian resource recovery, to due process, to environmental and economic security, to tribal self-determination and to Native peoples' human and sovereign dignity.
>
> IT IS TIME for Congress to protect the free exercise of Native religious prerogatives, to change the laws that classify Indian people as U.S. property, to impose tough penalties at the marketplace for graverobbing, to repatriate Indian national and religious patrimony, to lay to rest all Native human remains and to prevent further desecration of sacred places.
>
> IT IS TIME for the sports world, advertisers and media to stop using mascots, images, team names and terms which dehumanize, cartoon and stereotype Indian people.
>
> IT IS TIME for teachers to stop telling little kids that Columbus discovered this red quarter of Mother Earth. It is time for educators,

anthropologists, historians and archaeologists to stop perpetuating the myths that Native people came from Siberia, Scandinavia, Egypt and anywhere but here to justify past and continuing raids on Native territory.

IT IS TIME for the federal agencies to pursue the anti-Indian racists and hate-groups at least as vigorously as they have hounded Native nations, organizations and people.

IT IS TIME for the U.S. covert and destabilization activities against Native people over the past few decades to be exposed and stopped in the 1990s. It is time for the U.S. to make amends to Native victims of colonization and Indian activists injured in the struggle for survival, and it is time to free Leonard Peltier.

IT IS TIME, while some Native people still have time, for CSCE and other international forums to closely examine the Indian human rights issue within the context of the ongoing pattern of cultural, psychological, economic and physical genocide in America.

The rhetoric of the statement is part of politics and part of the current reburial discourse. In addition, a critical archaeology insists on seeing it as part of a context relevant to science.

In philosophy, both critical theorists and advocates of hermeneutic approaches have argued for the importance of understanding the social context of knowledge production. Both groups have said that knowledge is a function of the interests involved in the context of knowing and that the only way to deal with this inevitable relationship is through an awareness of it. Awareness produces choice, whereas prescribed vision does not. To demonstrate the relationship in Western archaeology, one need simply ask what is the social context of knowledge production underlying the current debate. That question highlights the nonrandom appearance of questions, statements, evaluations, reviews, and so on. A critical archaeology takes the citation of history, tradition, archaeology, folklore, or any part of the past as ideological. That is, when archaeology is cited in a public context, one of its purposes (among other things) is to legitimize a dominant position, and it often requires that the actual conditions of existence be masked or glossed over. This assumption means that archaeological discourse is rarely, if ever, apolitical.

There are two ways archaeologists have reacted to statements like this one. Most commonly, they have exempted themselves and their logical procedures from the criticisms inherent in such assessments. Archaeology and its results are assumed to be of positive benefit to all of society, along with the results of scientific scholarship generally. And the practice of archaeological work, the actual reasoning, is held to be politically neutral because there are no legitimate political goals within scholarly aims and because the self-examining framework of science is constructed to locate bias and to correct for it. Thus, while many archaeologists pay attention to the claims and requests of disenfranchised peoples for greater power and respect, they do so as concerned individuals, not as archaeologists. As archaeologists, they may feel attacked, indifferent, misunderstood, and angry. But they do not feel engaged.

Second, most archaeologists recognize that they are loosely related to over 50 years of effort to formulate federal policy for the protection and management of archaeological remains. Most archaeologists are aware of, if not closely familiar with, the lobbying and government affairs activities that their principal professional society promotes. The Society for American Archaeology (SAA) and, independently, many professionals seek to influence every level of policy making for archaeology. We cannot characterize the degree of knowledge that archaeologists possess on these matters. But we do feel confident in saying that the membership of the SAA fully backs the society's involvement in attempts to formulate and influence public policy. This second way of dealing with the political side of archaeology is institutional, involves delegating the work to professional specialists in government affairs, and does not usually involve most archaeologists directly.

In our opinion, there is an alternative to the first position that is also a complement to the acknowledged success of the second. We propose to use Jürgen Habermas's (1970, 1979, 1984, 1989) theory of communicative action to examine the actual context in which negotiations about the past take place. And we think that the central issue is how archaeologists come to conclusions. With this rhetorical question, we hope to link the scholarly and political thought that most archaeologists are already engaged in so successfully, but that is normally compartmentalized by most professionals. The standard answer, one that we challenge, is that consensus is achieved *solely* through what is usually called analytical or logical reasoning. That form of reasoning is central to scholarly debate and exchange in learned circles. The context for conclusions usually involves—besides data and hypotheses—archaeologists, discussions, written publication, some debate, and a very narrow range of forums. The procedure, long used and long rationalized in scientific archaeology, has been adapted to produce, with various degrees of certainty, knowledge about the past.

We have no investment in criticizing the scientific method. Clearly, it works and it has produced dramatic results in such areas as the study of prehistoric diet, disease, and technology. However, we do not think that the method as currently used by archaeologists is adequately self-referential so as to produce secure knowledge about the past. Instead, we are concerned that whenever archaeological findings are discussed in any public forum, the standard science procedure appears to be incapable of addressing the contexts of knowledge formation and the dynamics of its transmittal. We feel that it is particularly the case in those areas where archaeological findings are a part of political messages about cultural identity, which, as we all know, has been and remains a frequent use of archaeology. In this context, we argue that archaeology is politics: it is not just archaeology and not only political; it is completely both.

Whenever one looks at Colonial Williamsburg, the Fortress at Louisbourg, Masada, the Elgin Marbles, the Pergamon altar in Berlin, or the archaeology of

South African apartheid, the same message is clear again and again: archaeological interpretations are as much a function of the social setting in which they are formulated and presented as they are of the soil matrix from which they are excavated. Thus, we come to the question that is at the heart of our subject. Is there a descriptive scheme that will allow us to expand on the conventional way we conduct our business so that we can be public and political and still remain rational? We believe that Jürgen Habermas's theory of communicative action can be used to provide an answer to this question.

Habermas's Theory of Communicative Action

Habermas's theory of communicative action is a reformulation of traditional critical theory that restates the critique of ideology as a critique of systematically distorted communication. Of particular concern to Habermas is the domination of instrumental reason in subverting the communication process. Instrumental reason is a form of reason that divorces the thinker from the context of thought or consciousness. It refers to the definition of practical problems as technical issues, a tendency that justifies specific class or group interests as general, neutral positions. Habermas's theory of communicative action has recently been effectively applied in such fields as geography (Harley 1988a, 1988b), education (Misgeld 1988; O'Neill 1988), media (Hallin 1988), and public policy (Agger 1988; Fischer 1988; Forester 1988; Kemp 1988). Here we begin with Habermas's conception of rationality, then turn to his discussion of system and lifeworld, and finally conclude with his theory of communicative competence.

Thomas McCarthy (in Habermas 1984), Habermas's translator, has observed that although Habermas has been called the "last great rationalist," he is a rationalist in a very special sense. Habermas incorporates the Kantian critique of rationalism into his own formulation by grounding rationality in its own social context and historical development. In doing that, he moves away from rationality as consciousness (which is how Descartes saw it and how it is embodied in standard scientific scholarship) to rationality as performance. For Habermas, rationality does not have an absolute existence, but rather a conditional one that resides within the workings of the community of practitioners, themselves being subjective and related to context. Because he locates foundations within communities of acting individuals, the problem of knowing and the wisdom of political actions becomes one of reaching consensus through argumentation oriented toward achieving understanding, not argumentation based upon an ultimate foundation for knowledge.

Habermas breaks down rationality into two basic parts. *Instrumental rationality* refers to the acquisition of knowledge necessary to adapt to and manipulate an environment. It is technical, problem-oriented, and directly related to instrumental or strategic action. That form of rationality is what we are familiar with in scientific discourse and in speaking, writing, and reading about archaeology. *Communicative rationality*, in contrast, is based on the social experience of consensus-building. Through it we seek to achieve a shared understanding. Significantly, it has its own kind of discourse, one that is more typical of Native American dialogue or the ideal of the American political process, but it is now foreign to the scholarly or scientific process, as we are used to describing it and living it out. We all know how to use both; however, the two kinds of rationality are not equivalent. For Habermas, communicative rationality is the more general by virtue of its being shared among all the world's peoples.

Parallel with those forms of rationality, Habermas's develops two fundamentally different ways in which humans can view their society. A *systems perspective* requires treating society as a self-regulating system in which social actions are regarded as functionally related to their consequences. Subsystems, such as the economy and the state, are seen as linked together through functional or strategic action that is in turn driven by money and power, or some other motivation that is taken as given. That perspective, according to Habermas, is prevalent within industrial societies where instrumental rationality is dominant. A *lifeworld perspective*, in contrast, involves viewing society as being coordinated by harmonizing actions. The lifeworld serves as the context for the reproduction of culture, society, and personality. That perspective is typical of traditional societies that have not yet been impacted by the West, especially by the West's economic system. The lifeworld perspective is grounded in communicative rationality.

According to Habermas, neither of these theories of society is adequate by itself. A society that sees itself as a system is limited by the focus on regulation and maintenance at the expense of motivation and intentionality. Although the latter categories of reality are acknowledged, they tend to be regarded as irrational, to be suppressed and avoided, and given no descriptive reality. The lifeworld approach, however, is susceptible to the excesses of "hermeneutic idealism," where the causes and consequences of everyday life are ignored and where action is delayed, avoided, or subverted. In order to develop a complete model of society that integrates both theories, Habermas (1989) seeks to combine lifeworld and system in such a way that society is conceived as a "system that has to satisfy the conditions of maintenance of sociocultural lifeworlds." In other words, society should act to preserve the diversity of extant lifeworlds in order to function as a complete system. It goes beyond a claim for tolerance and argues that plurality is required for mutual survival. This plurality is essential because all societies have an inherent right to exist because modern society's instrumental rationality has little inherent capability to examine and restrain its own absorptive qualities, and because a dominating instrumental rationality produces severe pathologies.

In constructing his model of society, Habermas draws attention to those contexts where system and lifeworld perspectives come into contact. The contexts typically represent disequilibrium situations where system impinges on lifeworld in a process Habermas calls the "colonization of the lifeworld." The process threatens the very reproduction of the lifeworld as increasingly complex economic-political systems are introduced into areas where they did not previously exist. This colonization can precipitate a crisis situation that is characterized by loss of meaning, anomie, psychopathologies and often involves the destruction of traditional forms of life and associated communicative ways. According to Habermas, what we need in modern (Western) society is a "decolonization of the lifeworld." He suggests that it is precisely at the interface between system and lifeworld that opportunities for such a reclamation can develop through "resistance and emancipation."

There are two points here that we think are important for our argument. One is resistance and emancipation. Emancipation is a hoped-for end and is an aim focusing on greater participation in democratic society. Resistance constitutes objection to the ways in which the instrumental rationality of modern and early modern societies fragments knowledge, making it and its operation rule-ridden and disciplined. Resistance may take the form of speech or action, does not necessarily mean violence, and is essential to providing alternatives to the homogenization of tasks, routines, and intentions that scholars from Max Weber to Michel Foucault have argued characterizes Western logic since the eighteenth century.

Second, it is necessary to recognize that lifeworld does not only apply to what anthropologists usually think of as distant, isolated, and technologically undeveloped cultures. Lifeworld means people who still live their lives in such a way that emotion, feeling, intention, dreams, fantasies, the supernatural, myths, and traditions govern decisions and daily routines in significant ways. It would include many peoples within Western culture who take their strength from traditional and historically contoured societies. Habermas argues that the West needs to cultivate the existence of such people within our own societies and to realize that they and their opinions provide an essential alternative to our own, largely invisible, and yet newly acquired systems perspective.

In order to describe and thus promote communicative competence, Habermas draws on a form of analysis known as discourse analysis. Discourse in this sense means argument for the sake of reaching rational consensus, not for the sake of obtaining control. For Habermas, such consensus can only be achieved through communicative contexts in which every participant shares roughly equal chances to participate. It is what he calls an "ideal speech situation." At the outset it is important to acknowledge that the concept is a heuristic device that Habermas recognizes can never be fully realized. Therefore, the concept receives its validity as a model for determining the degree to which actual discourse deviates from an ideal situation.

Habermas describes four different speech acts and related validity claims that are necessary for an ideal speech situation. *Communicative* speech acts are those acts that are associated with initiating and furthering discourse. They are related to questions of comprehensibility. Is the speaker clear and understandable? *Representative* speech acts are those that are associated with expressing attitudes, feelings, beliefs and intentions. They are linked to questions of sincerity. Is the speaker trustworthy? *Regulative* speech acts are associated with commanding and opposing, permitting and forbidding speech. They are related to questions of legitimacy. Have all speakers had equal chances to participate? Finally, *constative* speech acts are associated with providing interpretations, offering explanations, and raising criticisms. They are related to questions of truth. Is the speaker believable?

All of these speech acts and validity claims are raised in the course of ordinary speech and in many cases can be more or less immediately substantiated. But when conflicts arise, substantiation must be worked out through discourse. Some of this may seem obvious since in everyday speech we make such judgments and allowances automatically. We do the same in professional contexts. But anyone who has negotiated at the interface between the everyday world in which archaeology may be mentioned and the professional world of archaeologists has experienced the confusion, incomprehensibility, frustration, and defeat that come when one or more of these conditions is absent. How do you explain why things are or are not so deeply buried, when enough digging is enough, why data are or are not valuable, why archaeology takes so long, what the site really contributes to historic preservation, or why you don't popularize this information and let everyone dig too? The meeting of the two worlds that produces these questions is usually quickly avoided by most archaeologists, often by aborting parts of various speech acts of an ideal speech situation.

Communicative Action and the Reburial Issue

In order to place the theory of communicative action within a context that is both archaeological and political, we now turn to a consideration of the discourse and dialogue that characterize the reburial issue. We do this by selectively identifying some examples of the different speech acts associated with the issue and their respective validity claims. Our purpose is to offer some suggestions that may permit an approximation of an ideal speech situation in future dialogues and thus allow for the more rational integration of archaeological knowledge and its political contexts. We feel that this kind of analysis should not only be relevant to the reburial issue but also to any situation in which different worldviews come in conflict.

Communicative speech acts deal with the comprehensibility of statements. To what extent have the participants in the reburial debate been able to raise issues and make their respective positions understood? Even a cursory analysis of the reburial debate is sufficient to demonstrate that there has been considerable variability in the success of the different participants in getting their points across to their intended audiences, including the American public.

Native Americans have been quite effective in this regard because of the power of their arguments and the eloquence and skill of some of their representatives. One powerful argument appeals to the legal double standard that has operated in dealing with burials of peoples of different races. For example, Walter Echo-Hawk, an attorney with the Native American Rights Fund (NARF), in an interview with *People Magazine,* has succinctly placed the debate upon grounds readily understandable to non–Native Americans: "If you desecrate a white grave, you wind up sitting in prison, but desecrate an Indian grave and you get a Ph.D. The time has come for people to decide: Are

Indians part of this country's living culture or are we just here to supply museums with dead bodies?" (cited in Brower and Putnam 1989:43). Most non–Native Americans would easily accept this characterization despite the hyperbole contained within it since they can readily empathize with Native American outrage at having a deceased family member exhumed and subjected to scientific analyses.

By contrast, archaeologists have been markedly less effective in making their professional interests known to the public and to Native Americans. The strongest argument that archaeologists have put forth is that archaeology can potentially contribute to the solution of modern health problems. For example, Douglas Owsley, an associate curator at the Smithsonian Institution, in describing recent advances in the extraction of immunoglobulins from human bones, is quoted as stating that "this technique will help us track the history of human diseases, the antiquity of diseases, even the evolution of diseases. Not only does this promise to revolutionize our understanding of the past, but it might prove a powerful new tool for fighting disease in our time" (Preston 1989:71–72). Many members of the public seem to find that argument unconvincing on two grounds. First, they either do not understand how science works, or, second, they remain skeptical of the ability of archaeology to live up to this promise. After all, they can rightfully ask, What has archaeology contributed to the health sciences up to this point?

Archaeologists have tended to act as though education is the universal answer. They have assumed that everyone, including Native Americans, will support scientific research once it is explained to them. In hindsight, this position can be seen as a naïve misreading of the situation, which displays little sensitivity to alternative lifeworlds. The failure of this approach is described by Larry Zimmerman as follows:

> At the session between Lakota holy men and anthropologists at the 1983 Plains Conference, the audience of anthropologists was asked no less than six times, why they studied skeletons. No answer seemed to satisfy. At the Iowa sessions, the sentiment was the same, and expressed often: "Why do archaeologists study the past? Are they trying to disprove our religion? We do not have to study our origin. I don't question my teachings. I don't need proof in order to have faith" [1989b:212–213].

This example seems to indicate that not only do some Native Americans understand the Popperian basis for the scientific method but that they are concerned that science will be used against them in invalidating religious practices from which they derive their cultural identity. Although that goal is clearly not the intention of most archaeologists, it is quite true that we have not tended to acknowledge the validity of this claim, especially the possibility that others may choose to use the archaeological data we produce in this way.

This analysis allows us to see why the standard strategy of archaeologists in debate has been ineffective. When we defend our field, its procedures and discoveries, our arguments both before Congress and Native Americans have been unsuccessful. We have not always understood whether it was because the defense of our scientific activity was unclear and uncomprehended or because our argument failed to address other concerns. Now we can see that mounting fuller explanations of useful knowledge gained through scientific research is likely to be equally ineffective. Rather than making the education of Native Americans our primary goal, we need to educate ourselves. We need to pay more attention to Native Americans' concerns for their cultural integrity and preservation (Thompson 1991; Vivian and Norcini 1991). We need to consider the effects of our research goals upon the ability of Native Americans to resist the penetration of the system perspective.

Representative speech acts are related to notions of sincerity as expressed by the attitudes, beliefs, and feelings of individuals. They can be seen as an index of one's commitment to a specific cause. As might be expected in a discourse where some Native Americans feel that their way of life is being threatened and some archaeologists feel that their research is being constrained, these speech acts are abundantly exhibited in the reburial debate.

A widely held Native American position is that graves should remain undisturbed in order for society, both theirs and ours, to function properly. That position is particularly well articulated by John Peters (Slow Turtle), a leader of New England tribes:

> We have a spiritual way of life, a cultural thing, part of religion. . . . And we look at the spiritual kind of thing because we're deeply involved in the spirits of all forms of life, not just human life. All forms are equally respected and so, when we have a death the remains are buried in a ceremony. And that ceremony in my area is very intense, because of that spirit and the spirit is continuing on and some of those spirits are not released from the ground. Some of them are kept there because of the failure of that particular person to follow the proper direction. And when people disinter them, remove them from the earth sometimes we feel that the spirit has been released and can cause a lot of harm. A lot of what happens to my people is blamed on our failure to do the right thing in a spiritual way [in Quick 1986:13–14].

Peters's statement is an attempt to relate a deeply meaningful part of his culture to the uninitiated, something that is usually strictly proscribed within most Native American societies. There can be little question of his sincerity, and indeed at one point he found his experience so moving that he felt it necessary to break off his speech prematurely.

Archaeologists, as scientists, are committed to the study of the past for myriad reasons, but for all of us the archaeological record is a source of irreplaceable data that requires management and preservation. One extreme position is reflected in the plea for financial support by the American Committee for the Preservation of Archaeological Collections (ACPAC).

> Archaeologists, your profession is on the line. Now is the time to dig deep and help ACPAC with its expenses for legal fees. Next year or next month will be too late; we have to act immediately to fight this issue. This one will be resolved in court, not by the press. We will be able to

> cross-examine Indians on their tribal affinities, religion, and connection to the archaeological remains they seek to destroy. We will be able to challenge anti-science laws based on race and religion. We can make a strong case, but it takes money [*Newsletter* of the American Committee for the Preservation of Archaeological Collections, November 1986].

Despite certain misrepresentations, the sincerity of that statement lies in the commitment of professional archaeologists to their research. This sentiment is probably not limited to the ACPAC and is likely held by a wider body of archaeologists who simply choose not to enter into debate.

However, not all representative speech acts have been made in good faith, and these thus violate ideal conditions. An example of the consequences of distorted communication can be seen in Zimmerman's experience where people are shown to have misrepresented their attitudes and feelings.

> I was to present the positive aspects of working with Indians and to suggest that the executive committee [of the Society for American Archaeology] postpone any action on an essentially antireburial resolution they were considering. I agreed [to make such a presentation] because the importance of having someone from within the profession to assist in presenting an Indian view seemed clear. . . . The discussion seemed open and friendly, and we left the meeting feeling very positive. The next day was one of the most crushing of my life; I learned about academic racism.
>
> In the morning, I happened to be standing in the lobby near a board member present at the meeting and overheard her discussing the meeting with a colleague. Her words I remember well. She said, "I sure had to swallow a lot of blood last night in the meeting with the Indians." I was somewhat chagrined and commented to [Jan] Hammil that perhaps all had not gone as well as we thought. As late afternoon came I walked back to the hotel and met Hammil and the president of the SAA walking toward me in animated conversation. The latter denounced me as a trouble maker [Zimmerman 1989a:62–63].

Despite the unpleasantness of the face-to-face denunciation of Zimmerman by the SAA's then president, we feel that that speech act was far more representative of the true feelings of the archaeological community than was the discussion at the preceding evening's meeting in which one group had been misled about the sincerity of the other's intentions. It is quite likely that the SAA's executive committee members did not know how each felt until later in their own meeting that evening, and since it is a group that works largely through carefully created consensus, no one might have been able to articulate a representative degree of opposition to the Native American position, including Zimmerman's. Nonetheless, our point here is that the terms of an ideal speech situation were violated substantially in allowing one group to depart with the illusion of sincerity on the part of the dominant group.

Regulative speech acts are associated with controlling the opportunity for speech. They reflect considerations of legitimacy, that is, who may and may not be regarded as having rights to opinions and the opportunity to express them. These speech acts are ultimately grounded in the authority of the individual speaker, authority that is invested by his or her respective interest group. In the reburial case, a number of different interest groups can be identified. These include Native American tribes, pan–Native American support groups, professional anthropological organizations, and professional museum organizations.

Have each of these communities had an equal chance to participate in the reburial debate? Clearly, the professional anthropological and museum concerns have been put forth by organizations such as the SAA, the Society of Professional Archaeologists (SOPA), the Council for Museum Anthropology (CMA), and others. Likewise, pan–Native American interests have been represented by the American Indians Against Desecration (AIAD), the National Congress of American Indians (NCAI), and the NARF. But, it is clear that not all interest groups have been part of the discourse, especially at the national level. Ironically, the groups most commonly absent are the Native American tribes themselves. Relatively few tribal elders and religious leaders appear to have been invited to join in the debate, and among those that have received invitations, very few have acted upon them. Does this mean that the tribes are not interested in the outcome of these issues or, alternatively, that they are satisfied with the current state of affairs? We sincerely doubt this and suggest that we need to examine why it is that tribal leaders have been reluctant to participate.

Although it should be obvious, the point is worth making that the negotiation process is one of our own making. The process involves creating such organizational structures as select committees and special conferences that make policy recommendations to larger legislative bodies. We are privileged in the sense of our being able to restrict and control the timing and content of the debate. We are playing on our own turf, as it were, where the ground rules are known and easily manipulated. Native Americans, in contrast, are immediately disadvantaged, because they are generally less familiar with the procedures and mechanisms of our litigious society (although the success of the NARF clearly shows that this situation is rapidly changing). They have been less able to deal with a foreign instrumental rationality, whereas we, at least, are familiar with aspects of communicative rationality. This results in a fundamental asymmetry of power that contours all aspects of the discourse.

The effects of attempting to participate in a speech situation so heavily dominated by a systems perspective can be traumatic for Native Americans. This point is well evidenced in the following quotation by Weldon Johnson, assistant director of the Colorado Indian Tribal Museum:

> I don't think we should waste a lot of time talking about going to court, because I would like you to really know what it is like to go to court and stand up and speak on cultural resources and religion. It's very rough because you have to pick your words. You have to pick what you can and cannot say, and you have to do a lot of—those lawyers really drill

> you sometimes, on what you know and you don't know. The Mojave for instance. They were told by their creator in the beginning not to have a written language. There are other forms of communications, such as petroglyphs, pictographs, and intaglios, that took this form of communication because they couldn't have a written language form. And also I found myself doing something sacrilegious by writing about religion. In that sense, in the Mojave view, that is wrong. It is wrong to do that. So we're doing these sacrilegious things to try to protect our religious ways. That's the very hard part about going to court. You're doing one thing good for your tribe on one hand, yet on the other hand it's bad [in Quick 1986:146].

Here Johnson is literally caught between system and lifeworld. He must adopt a systems perspective to defend his case in court, yet this very act represents a betrayal of his lifeworld perspective.

There are two points to be made here. The first is that the process itself is in need of revision. We need to explore new ways of establishing communication and dialogue between multiple interest groups. That does not mean that we should throw out conferences or committees, but rather that we pay more attention to how those (and other) processes work. It will require that we pay more attention to how participants are selected, where meetings are held, and the relation of those meetings to the formulation of general policy statements that might be acted upon by other organizations in ways perhaps unintended by the committee. Second, we clearly need to be more sensitive to the difficulties faced by those Native Americans who choose to participate in this dialogue. We cannot expect that every tribe will be willing to send a representative or that each representative will reflect a unified tribal opinion. This obviously makes discourse difficult and time-consuming, but to do otherwise would be to reproduce the historical strategy of the United States government in designating a "favored" representative for a given tribe and then dealing only with that representative.

Constative speech acts involve interpretations and evaluations that attempt to reveal underlying truth in normal discourse. They often seek to locate such interpretations in theoretical structures. Two main explanations, which frame the reburial issue, have been offered. The first, and more particularistic, of these identifies the debate as a conflict between science and Native American belief systems. The second, and more general, of these involves the notion of incommensurable worldviews.

The conflict explanation develops the premise that scientists and Native Americans are fighting against one another for the control of skeletal remains. A brief review of the representation of the debate in popular forum should be sufficient to drive this point home. An article published in *Nation* (10 October 1988) is entitled "Indians Gaining on the U.S. in Battle over Ancestral Bones." A piece in the society section of *Newsweek* (26 June 1989) is entitled "The Plunder of the Past: A Bullish Market for Native American Artifacts Disturbs the Peace of the Dead and Buried." Even an article in the news and comment section of *Science* (245:1184–1186) is entitled "Smithsonian, Indian Leaders Call a Truce." Clearly, the active metaphor here is one of battle, confrontation, and conflict between longtime adversaries. A related notion involves the rightful ownership of the remains. The focus on ownership is a symptom of the commodification of the past and presumes that there can be only one legitimate owner, ignoring the possibility of multiple interests. From our perspective, such metaphors are unfortunate, and indeed damaging, ways of viewing the current discourse since they perpetuate existing stereotypes, false meanings, and racial images that can seriously undermine any consensus-oriented process.

The second explanation is that of irreconcilable worldviews, where mutual understanding is impossible. The article in *Newsweek* cited above characterizes the different claims on the part of scientists and Native Americans as "embod[ying] different attitudes toward the dead. Whereas Western scientists have been matter-of-factly cutting up cadavers since the Renaissance, many tribes believe that disturbing the graves of ancestors will bring a spiritual sickness to the living" (p. 60). Tom Merlan, the New Mexico State Historic Preservation officer, is quoted in the same article as stating that "there is no real possible reconciliation between those views" (p. 60). For us, this statement *must* be wrong if there is any validity in the project of anthropology. We are continually working across cultures trying to explore ways of mutual understanding and cooperation. This *is* possible because there always exists some "background information" that can be exploited in the communication process. It is in this sense that communication is transcendental, part of what Habermas terms "universal pragmatics."

A more comprehensive explanation than either the conflict or worldview metaphors can be offered in terms of Habermas's notions of system and lifeworld. We begin by recognizing the different historical legacies of each of the two perspectives. A systems perspective is the result of the interpenetration of American society by capitalism and is expressed through the segmentation of time, the specialization of labor, and the commodification of objects. Each of these processes can interfere with the ability of lifeworld to reproduce itself since emotions, myths, and harmonizing views are isolated and given secondary status. A lifeworld perspective is the product of generations of oral traditions and myths that give meaning and guidance to everyday life. The myths and traditions are themselves essential to the reproduction of culture, society, and personality and are powerful forces in acts of resistance to a systems perspective. This analysis, linking as it does system and lifeworld, implies that, far from being neutral, archaeology (science), as traditionally practiced, can do and has done unintentional harm to Native American peoples.

The problem then becomes how to redefine the relationship between system and lifeworld so that lifeworld structures can actively participate in the larger social system and yet remain strong enough to resist colonization by the system. Habermas implies several actions for a more rational relationship, most of which are designed to redress the effects of the colonization of lifeworld. Such actions would include reclaiming traditional communicative structures necessary for the material reproduction of social life. These structures are those associated with cultural reproduction, social integration, and the formation of individuals through socialization. In the context of the reburial debate, actions informed by this theory might involve the various interest groups incorporating elements of indigenous decision-making structures to achieve a more democratic result. They might also involve attempts at combating the dehumanizing and decontextualizing effects of the pervasive commodification of skeletal remains and associated burial goods. Vizenor (1986) has even put forth the interesting argument that human remains should be treated "as if" they have legal standing. In that way, archaeology can be seen as playing an active role in the reproduction of lifeworld and thus contributing to cultural diversity.

Toward a Rational Consensus

What does negotiated consensus look like and what does Habermas offer that is any different from what normally occurs in archaeology? The guidance we offer comes from merging the theory of communicative action with the insights of Goldstein and Kintigh, who speak specifically to the reburial issue. In doing this, we hope to contribute to the efforts at implementing the new law and to ways of encouraging the democratic process as it might be described through ideal speech situations.

To answer the second question first, we raise two points to show Habermas's relevance. First, we take Goldstein and Kintigh's (1990) recent *American Antiquity* article. We agree with virtually all they say and acknowledge that their guidelines may even get all parties though the implementation of P.L. 101–601. But we want to generalize their tenets beyond the reburial issue. What happens to archaeologists when some other group demands something with the same kind of powerful arguments Native Americans took to their case? This issue is already at hand as can be seen with the claims being put forward by indigenous groups worldwide (Gathercole and Lowenthal 1990).

Goldstein and Kintigh (1990) and Goldstein (this volume) argue for the value of tolerance grounded in cultural relativism. In order to be achieved, tolerance is guided by compromise and mutual respect. They argue for the ideals of equality and of negotiating in an environment that strives to "achieve equal consideration for all relevant parties" (Goldstein and Kintigh 1990:590). We see this as part of the ideal speech situation and as part of a theory of a democratic society. But Habermas is also dealing with a theory of society as it tries to escape the effects of a largely unanalyzed capitalism and its associated instrumental reason. Goldstein and Kintigh do not address the question of why the reburial issue arose in the first place, and in not providing a theory of action like Habermas's use of language discourse, they cannot generalize beyond this case. Also, they do not deal with the wider pernicious aspects of some of the political uses of archaeology beyond the United States and by non–Native Americans within the United States, such as the promotion of nationalism, racial identity, historical amnesia, fantasy histories, or exaggerated territorial claims.

Second, we take the Native American Grave Protection and Repatriation Act (P.L. 101–601) and ask how it is to be implemented. We can already see two developments. First, the law is very hard to understand: it is difficult to read, complex, hard to fathom in its intentions, and appears to cover areas of already existing law. We say this neutrally, with some experience in reading archaeological legislation. This suggests that there will be ample opportunity for future negotiation and discourse. Second, many key aspects of the new law are to be implemented by the Department of the Interior's Consulting Archaeologist, a relatively small office of eight professional archaeologists. Such an office, and indeed any office in the federal executive apparatus, has a period of consultation and commentary before and after it promulgates regulations and interpretations of laws. But the executive agencies are subject to the lobbying of special-interest groups operating quickly and persistently. The kind of give-and-take behind the dialogue among Native Americans, archaeologists, museum professionals, and Hill staffers that led to the new law is yet to be established in this agency for this law. We cite this context in order to highlight the fact that ideal speech situations are difficult to create, do not necessarily lead to consensus, and take much time.

To return to our first question, we can say that although we do not know what a rational consensus would look like, since we expect it to vary from context to context, we can, however, identify its absence. Keys to identifying less than ideal speech environments include the use of stereotyping, gender-specific language, dialects and mock dialects, oversimplification, demands for entertaining versus instructive prose, scapegoating, and references to mythical groups as strategies in discourse (Agar 1991). We can watch for enemy images, pleas for common sense, mythic responsibilities, and masculine forms and formulas that invite a specific response, which, upon a moment's or a month's reflection, we may choose to reject. We can watch for self-privileging spokesmen and spokeswomen and the representation of ideas so as to distort a lifeworld view for the gain of a systems one.

We do not feel qualified to advise archaeologists on how to work to implement the Native American Graves Protection and Repatriation Act or about other political issues. But we do feel that we can make some general suggestions that, if implemented, may help transform the practice of archaeology into a more self-conscious activity. These suggestions come from looking at the interface of system and lifeworld in archaeological discourse (cf. Forester 1988: Table 5). In our view, archaeologists need to

> 1. educate ourselves about the social context in which archaeology is practiced;
> 2. participate in public debate and discussion about archaeology, rather than depend upon the authority of the written word;
> 3. acknowledge the existence of competing interests concerning archaeology in producing knowledge about the past;
> 4. encourage local community involvement in archaeology;
> 5. organize regular channels of communication and dialogue between interest groups and professional archaeologists; and
> 6. develop skills to work with interest groups so as to anticipate and

address areas of conflict in archaeology, rather than rely upon the expertise of professional negotiators.

Most of the suggestions by themselves are not new to archaeology. In fact, many of them are already firmly established and well implemented. Some archaeological programs routinely involve the local community in pursuing standard archaeological research, usually with the goal of educating the public (e.g., the Jorvik Viking Center [Addyman 1990]). Some archaeologists have been working closely with specific interest groups to address multiple concerns about the past (e.g., Ferguson 1984; Leone et al. 1991; Raharijaona 1989). Some archaeologists have analyzed the uses of archaeological knowledge in particular cultural contexts (e.g., Hall 1990; Knudson 1984; Mangi 1989). But taken together as a coherent program, we believe that the suggestions have the potential to contribute to the process of achieving a more democratic consensus among all interest groups who have a claim on the past in the present. This, then, is the task for archaeology in the twenty-first century, and just how successful we are in accomplishing it will help determine the place of archaeology within modern society.

Conclusion

To conclude, we have attempted only one move here. We are trying to link a theory of a democratic society to archaeological discourse by suggesting that the current debate on the reburial issue can be understood in general terms as well as in its specific context. In making this move, we have relied upon Habermas's theory of communicative action, which focuses on the social use of language. We recognize that the theory is far from complete and is subject to legitimate criticisms (see Roderick 1986), yet we feel that it provides an important starting point for structuring analysis and social action for archaeologists.

We have not aligned ourselves with the predominant theories operating in archaeology, although Habermas's work contains elements of evolutionism, systems theory, and functionalism, as do other critical theorists. We mention these ties briefly because they need to be explored if the intellectual strength of our arguments for archaeology is to be maintained. In general, we think Binford's work in founding and extending a comprehensive way of reconstructing the past by using a systematic method for employing the present offers an important link. And we stand with Hodder in relying heavily on a contextually based understanding of social relations and meanings, but we place a firm base for grounding understanding of the present in the action of modern as well as historical capitalism. In this regard, we feel closest to Shanks and Tilley, both because of their use of critical theory and their use of hermeneutics as a way of seeing that meaning and our understanding of it are unstable and so is their negotiation. These then are our ties to some current theories in which we find important connections by our use of Habermas and critical theory.

Our starting point is to say that the opposition between scientific values and non-Western worldviews, which are often presented as religious beliefs, is one instance of the broader conflict between system and lifeworld, a conflict that is itself driven by the penetration of Western culture, specifically the culture of capitalism, into all aspects of daily life. We have argued that critical theory is a useful complement to traditional theoretical approaches in archaeology since archaeology, science, and politics cannot be separated, using standard theories of knowledge. This is not a radical claim, but the reluctance on the part of much of the archaeological community to recognize this position has had serious consequences for our field. This unreflective mode has sometimes led us to ignore the fact that the divorce between practice and an understanding of our political history is responsible for some of the problems we face now and the problems we will face in the future with native peoples from Africa to Scandinavia to the Northwest Territories.

As advocates of a theory of a democratic society, we have argued that making the past belongs not to scientists, nor to specific ethnic groups, but to all of us by virtue of our common humanity. However, we do not hold with the hyperrelativist view that all positions are equally valid, but rather we argue that all positions deserve a voice *in the context of arriving at archaeological conclusions*. Archaeologists have rarely, if ever, seriously asked what are Native Americans' views of their past. The active engagement of such groups, not their exclusion, may be an effective strategy for democratizing the past. With a general theory of political life and action, such as that provided by Habermas, we may be prepared to negotiate with other groups seeking a voice in the debate. Our advice for archaeologists is that we need to watch and listen to how we talk, including how we are talked to, that we pay attention to what is said, and what it means, and to whom it is directed. This is political discourse, and it may be a practical way of enhancing our work.

Acknowledgments

We are grateful to LuAnn Wandsnider for inviting our contribution and to Linda Cordell for her patience in reading through and critiquing numerous revisions. We also want to thank Keith Kintigh, Lynne Goldstein, Jerry Sabloff, Lane Beck, and Meredith Chesson for their help in interpreting the meaning and intent of the Native American Graves Protection and Repatriation Act.

References

Addyman, Peter V.
   1990   Reconstruction as Interpretation: The Example of the Jorvik Viking Centre, York. In *The Politics of the Past*, edited by Peter Gathercole and David Lowenthal, pp. 257–264. Unwin Hyman, London.

Agar, Michael
  1991 Review of "Language Power and Ideology: Studies in Political Discourse" by Ruth Wodak. *Journal of Pragmatics* 15:195–215.
Agger, Ben
  1988 The Dialectic of Deindustrialization: An Essay on Advanced Capitalism. In *Critical Theory and Public Life*, edited by John Forester, pp. 3–21. MIT Press, Cambridge, Massachusetts.
Brower, Montgomery, and Conan Putnam
  1989 Walter Echo-Hawk Fights for His People's Rights to Rest in Peace—Not in Museums. *People Magazine*. September 32(10).
Ferguson, T. J.
  1984 Archaeological Ethics and Values in a Tribal Cultural Resource Management Program and the Pueblo of Zuni. In *Ethics and Values in Archaeology*, edited by Ernestene L. Green, pp. 224–235. Free Press, New York.
Fischer, Frank
  1988 Critical Evaluation of Public Policy: A Methodological Case Study. In *Critical Theory and Public Life*, edited by John Forester, pp. 231–257. MIT Press, Cambridge, Massachusetts.
Forester, John
  1988 Critical Theory and Planning Practice. In *Critical Theory and Public Life*, edited by John Forester, pp. 202–227. MIT Press, Cambridge, Massachusetts.
Gathercole, Peter, and David Lowenthal (editors)
  1990 *The Politics of the Past*. Unwin Hyman, London.
Gero, Joan
  1983 Gender Bias in Archaeology: A Cross-Cultural Perspective. In *The Socio-Politics of Archaeology*, edited by Joan M. Gero, David M. Lacy, and Michael Blakey, pp. 51–58. Research Report 23, Department of Anthropology, University of Massachusetts, Amherst.
  1985 Socio-Politics of Archaeology and the Woman-at-Home Ideology. *American Antiquity* 50:342–350.
Gero, Joan, and Margaret Conkey (editors)
  1991 *Engendering Archaeology: Women and Prehistory*. Basil Blackwell, Oxford.
Gero, Joan M., David M. Lacy, and Michael Blakey (editors)
  1983 *The Socio-Politics of Archaeology*. Research Report 23, Department of Anthropology, University of Massachusetts, Amherst.
Gero, Joan, and Dolores Root
  1990 Public Presentations and Private Concerns: Archaeology in the Pages of *National Geographic*. In *The Politics of the Past*, edited by Peter Gathercole and David Lowenthal, pp. 19–37. Unwin Hyman, London.
Goldstein, Lynne, and Keith Kintigh
  1990 Ethics and the Reburial Controversy. *American Antiquity* 55:585–591.
Habermas, Jürgen
  1970 Toward a Theory of Communicative Competence. *Inquiry* 13:360–376.
  1979 *Communication and the Evolution of Society*. Beacon Press, Boston.
  1984 *The Theory of Communicative Action. Vol. 1, Reason and the Rationalization of Society*. Beacon Press, Boston.
  1989 *The Theory of Communicative Action. Vol. 2, System and Lifeworld*. Beacon Press, Boston.
Hall, Martin
  1990 "Hidden History": Iron Age Archaeology in Southern Africa. In *The History*

of African Archaeology, edited by Peter Robertshaw, pp. 59–77. James Curry Press, London.

Hallin, Daniel C.
    1988   The American News Media: A Critical Theory Perspective. In *Critical Theory and Public Life*, edited by John Forester, pp. 121–146. MIT Press, Cambridge, Massachusetts.

Harley, J. B.
    1988a   Silences and Secrecy: The Hidden Agenda of Cartography in Early Modern Europe. *Imago Mundi* 40:57–76.
    1988b   Maps, Knowledge and Power. In *Iconography of Landscape: Essays on the Symbolic Representation, Design and Use of Past Environments*, edited by Denis Cosgrove and Stephen Daniels, pp. 277–312. Cambridge University Press, Cambridge.

Kemp, Ray
    1988   Planning, Public Hearings, and the Politics of Discourse. In *Critical Theory and Public Life*, edited by John Forester, pp. 177–201. MIT Press, Cambridge, Massachusetts.

Knudson, Ruthann
    1984   Ethical Decision Making and Participation in the Politics of Archaeology. In *Ethics and Values in Archaeology*, edited by Ernestene L. Green, pp. 243–263. Free Press, New York.

Layton, Robert (editor)
    1989a   *Conflict in the Archaeology of Living Traditions*. Unwin Hyman, London.
    1989b   *Who Needs the Past?: Indigenous Values and Archaeology*. Unwin Hyman, London.

Leone, Mark P.
    1986   Symbolic, Structural, and Critical Archaeology. In *American Archaeology Past and Future: A Celebration of the Society for American Archaeology 1935-1985*, edited by D. Meltzer, D. Fowler, and J. Sabloff, pp. 415–438. Smithsonian Institution Press, Washington, D.C.

Leone, Mark P., Barbara J. Little, Mark S. Warner, Parker B. Potter, Jr., Paul A. Shackel, George C. Logan, Paul R. Mullins, and Julie A. Ernstein
    1991   The Constituencies for an Archaeology of African Americans in Annapolis, Maryland. In *Studies in African American Archaeology*, edited by Theresa Singleton. University Press of Virginia, Charlottesville, in press.

Mangi, Joe
    1989   The Role of Archaeology in Nation Building. In *Conflict in the Archaeology of Living Traditions*, edited by R. Layton, pp. 217–227. Unwin Hyman, London.

Misgeld, Dieter
    1988   Education and Cultural Invasion: Critical Social Theory, Education as Instructing, and the "Pedagogy of the Oppressed." In *Critical Theory and Public Life*, edited by John Forester, pp. 77–118. MIT Press, Cambridge, Massachusetts.

O'Neill, John
    1988   Decolonization and the Ideal Speech Community: Some Issues in the Theory and Practice of Communicative Competence. In *Critical Theory and Public Life*, edited by John Forester, pp. 57–76. MIT Press, Cambridge, Massachusetts.

Patterson, Thomas C.
    1986   The Last Sixty Years: Toward a Social History of Americanist Archaeology in the United States. *American Anthropologist* 88:7–26.

Preston, Douglas J.
  1989 Skeletons in our Museums' Closets: Native Americans Want Their Ancestors' Bones Back. *Harper's Magazine*. February:66–75.
Quick, Polly McW. (editor)
  1986 *Proceedings: Conference on Reburial Issues*. Society for American Archaeology and the Society of Professional Archaeologists, Washington, D.C.
Raharijaona, Victor
  1989 Archaeology and Oral Traditions in the Mitongoa-Andrainjato Area (Betsileo Region of Madagascar). In *Who Needs the Past?: Indigenous Values and Archaeology*, edited by R. Layton, pp. 189–194. Unwin Hyman, London.
Roderick, Rick
  1986 *Habermas and the Foundations of Critical Theory*. St. Martin's Press, New York.
Thompson, Raymond H.
  1991 Looking to the Future. *Museum News* (January/February):36–40.
Trigger, Bruce
  1980 Archaeology and the Image of the American Indian. *American Antiquity* 45:662–76.
  1989 *A History of Archaeological Thought*. Cambridge University Press, Cambridge.
Vivian, Gwinn, and Marilyn Norcini
  1991 Help for the Asking. *Museum News* (January/February):52–53.
Vizenor, Gerald
  1986 Bone Courts: The Rights and Narrative Representation of Tribal Bones. *The American Indian Quarterly: Journal of American Indian Studies* 10:319–331.
Yellen, John
  1983 Women, Archaeology, and the National Science Foundation. In *The Socio-Politics of Archaeology*, edited by Joan M. Gero, David M. Lacy, and Michael L. Blakey, pp. 59–65. Research Report 23, Department of Anthropology, University of Massachusetts, Amherst.
Zimmerman, Larry J.
  1989a Made Radical by My Own: An Archaeologist Learns to Accept Reburial. In *Conflict in the Archaeology of Living Traditions*, edited by R. Layton, pp. 60–67. Unwin Hyman, London.
  1989b Human Bones as Symbols of Power: Aboriginal American Belief Systems Toward Bones and "Grave-Robbing" Archaeologists. In *Conflict in the Archaeology of Living Traditions*, edited by R. Layton, pp. 211–216. Unwin Hyman, London.

10. Conceptual Issues in Americanist Archaeology: A Commentary

Linda S. Cordell

In the preceding chapters, archaeologists who work in a variety of contexts examine conceptual issues that they see facing archaeology today and that they expect to continue into the twenty-first century. The topics addressed and the perspectives taken compose a heterogeneous lot, which may suggest that American archaeology is as intellectually fragmented as claimed in some recent publications (e.g., Earle and Preucel 1987; Leone et al. 1987; Trigger 1989). Yet there are a few general issues of communality that arise when looking both at questions the essays examine and those they entirely ignore. In this discussion, I first very briefly characterize conceptual issues in general and their relation to theory. Then I comment on the individual essays. Finally, I draw attention to some larger issues that seem to underlie the diversity of interests and approaches conveyed by the authors.

Conceptual issues deal with the formation of categories and other mental constructs by combining and integrating characteristics. It is convenient to think about concepts as frameworks or classifications that reflect the particular ways we go about organizing and describing the world around us. Concepts may not be directly theoretical in that theory refers to and implies a coherent set of principles used as *explanation*. Concepts need not be explanatory. Yet the frameworks, the attributes and dimensions we use as archaeologists, versus those we ignore, and the nature of our vocabularies are tied to theoretical positions. They reflect diverse archaeological perspectives: ahistorical, behavioral, cognitive, critical, ecological, empirical, evolutionary, feminist, functional, processual, and postprocessual. Revealing points of conceptual difficulty or disagreement may indicate theoretical issues that should be addressed whether or not they have been explicitly acknowledged. Some of these issues are examined in the chapters discussed here.

Alan Simmons has conducted research in the United States Southwest, in Central Jordan, and on Cyprus. The concerns he examines in his essay relate

Quandaries and Quests: Visions of Archaeology's Future, edited by LuAnn Wandsnider. Center for Archaeological Investigations, Occasional Paper No. 20. © 1992 by the Board of Trustees, Southern Illinois University. All rights reserved. ISBN 0-88104-075-4.

to the development of a global cultural resource archaeology and the possible role American archaeologists may play in global archaeological endeavors. His specific focus is on archaeology in developing countries where financial support for environmental protection and cultural resources programs is extremely limited and where such management programs may not be well understood.

Simmons develops a number of points with which it is difficult to disagree. He cautions United States archaeologists against being arrogant, patronizing, or condescending to colleagues in developing countries. He suggests that United States archaeologists can usefully contribute to others the advances we have made in techniques of analysis, in the findings and ongoing research in ethnoarchaeology, and in developing research designs. He proposes that United States universities provide training programs for archaeologists from developing countries and that, when working in those countries, United States archaeologists work within the structure of joint projects that link foreign and national investigators as equal partners in archaeological work. Simmons also contributes useful insights from his experiences with such joint programs.

There is much valuable, thought-provoking information in Simmons's paper. His discussion about dealing with more than one bureaucracy at a time and fully appreciating that archaeologists in developing countries have priorities that may be completely different from ours is important to take to heart. In some instances, I suspect the pictures Simmons paints are far from worst-case scenarios. For example, national priorities in developing countries may dictate that archaeological projects deal only with restoration, rather than excavation, or that certain culturally sensitive time periods (the Islamic Period in Muslim countries and the post-Neolithic in some communist countries) not be examined by foreign scholars at all. Further, in at least one instance with which I am familiar, engaging the assistance, even if it is only financial, of the U.S. Agency for International Development (USAID) would be a disastrous error of insensitivity. Yet even those who hold a more pessimistic view than Simmons's should find his call for joint projects worth heeding.

Simmons finds that United States anthropological archaeology is anthropocentric. He notes that there are many archaeologists in the United States and in developing countries who were trained in the United States, but who are not trained in anthropology. Many European archaeologists also receive their training outside of anthropology. These scholars may have been trained in classical archaeology, biblical archaeology, the natural sciences, or other fields. As Simmons states, they may be excellent archaeologists with perspectives from which anthropologically trained archaeologists can learn a great deal. Simmons argues that we should not only overcome any of our biased or negative attitudes toward archaeologists trained outside of anthropology but that we ought to give serious consideration to developing departments of archaeology that somehow would not lose the anthropological perspective. I am at somewhat of a loss to understand how the anthropological perspective could be retained within the proposed structure. I also suspect that the specific advances Simmons believes United States archaeologists have to offer archaeologists in developing countries particularly in ethnoarchaeology and in formulating research designs, could not have been attained and cannot be further developed outside of training in anthropology departments. While I agree that anthropologically trained archaeologists should not be arrogant about their perspective, it is predominantly background in anthropology that is their unique contribution to the techniques and methods of archaeology. Ethnoarchaeology is not likely to have developed within the contexts of classical archaeology or the natural sciences.

Suzanne Spencer-Wood has conducted extensive research in historic archaeology. She presents a systematic framework and agenda for the development of a feminist archaeology. Such an archaeology, she argues, is a perspective that seeks to demonstrate that androcentric assumptions, interpretations, and models are not supported by the empirical data available to archaeology and should be exposed and eliminated as biased. The overall goal of feminist archaeology is to eliminate gender-biased, and thus inaccurate, interpretations of the past.

Spencer-Wood's program is developed within the context of empiricism and feminist standpoint theory. She therefore calls for empirical criteria to expose androcentric bias. This is a position comfortable to American archaeologists working with research models that are comparative, processual, and generally scientific. The position is not compatible with the extreme relativism of postprocessualism that considers any possible interpretation as equally valid narrative.

Feminist archaeology is most concerned with the selection of research questions, a key process that I comment on below and that Jeremy Sabloff (this volume) indicates is, unfortunately, of interest to very few professional archaeologists. Spencer-Wood discusses the fact that in order for feminist issues to assume importance as research questions the demography of American archaeology must change. There must be more women engaged in, and adequately rewarded by, professional archaeology. She recognizes that such a demographic change requires political action to overcome problems of recruiting and awarding tenure to women in archaeology. The steps of political action and progress that she outlines are thoughtful and ought to be deeply considered throughout the ranks of professional archaeology.

As with Simmons's chapter, there is little in Spencer-Wood's call for action, or her analysis of the current state of archaeology, with which I would disagree. Here I offer some expansion on a few points toward further clarification of the issues. Spencer-Wood's contention that processual archaeology devoted little attention to the origins of research problems or hypotheses is accurate, yet the reason for that state needs clarification. Within the conventions of traditional philosophy of science, the activities of discovery and those of justification must be kept separate. Most philosophers of science, particularly the positivists, focused on justification and therefore excluded discovery from their consideration (Hempel 1965). Processual archaeology followed that method of inquiry. Other philosophers of science, particularly those such as Kuhn (1970) whose approach is sociological, do consider issues of discovery.

In fact, the interests of American archaeologists have changed over the years as the demography of archaeology has changed. American archaeology has focused more on settlement patterns and subsistence and less on monuments, temples, and elite residences as its membership has increasingly been drawn from the middle rather than the upper classes (cf. Sabloff 1989; this volume). If more women archaeologists are recruited, retained, and rewarded in professional positions, a feminist perspective should contribute to the discovery of gender bias and, one can hope, to its elimination.

On another issue, Spencer-Wood correctly notes that within the hypothesis-testing mode, the data of archaeology have been given interpretive meanings that may be biased by androcentric assumptions. Thus, prior to testing hypotheses, the meaning and functions of artifacts and features are most often *assumed*. Yet the assumed meanings or functions, which are not normally evaluated, may be biased, a situation that Spencer-Wood suggests would be corrected when revealed by feminist critique. While, in my opinion, Spencer-Wood's evaluation of this problem is correct, I suspect that the trouble is not uniquely one of androcentric bias. The meanings and functions of archaeological patterns of artifacts, features, and attributes are virtually always assumed as part of the prior knowledge of archaeology and may be completely wrong. That is why middle-range research, as outlined by Binford (e.g., 1977, 1978), is so important to all archaeology. Middle-range research is not simply making assumptions explicit, which has long been a goal of processual archaeology. Middle-range research addresses itself toward developing methods, based upon theory, for unambiguous determination of function and meaning among the patterns, features, artifacts, and attributes that we study.

Spencer-Wood faults processual archaeology for bias in following the untested assumption that large-scale structures and variables determine smaller-scale variables or that the smaller-scale variations are dismissed as exceptions. In their statement calling for an archaeology of gender, Conkey and Spector (1984) contended that processual archaeology ignores the individual while archaeological data are created within the context of specific individual actions and choices. Their position seems to be that the context of data formation must somehow be relevant to the level of interpretation. On the contrary, virtually all data—for any science—are created by specific small-scale occurrences. Yet such data may not inform at the level of precision within which they were created. The scale of data formation may not be at all appropriate for their interpretation.

What data are not context specific? Radiocarbon dating depends on the actions of very specific individual electrons and equally individual atoms. Geological deposits of sandstone are formed by processes working on individual grains of sand under very specific circumstances. Yet interpretations at the level of precision of the individual electron, or atom, or grain of sand are not informative or appropriate. I suspect the call for the individual in prehistory is a hollow polemic. The importance of Spencer-Wood's critique is that an assumption of the relevance of a particular scale is untested and may be biased. Her program calls for empirical evaluation of such assumptions, which would expose their bias. This, in my view, is a logical and reasoned call for action.

Mark Leone and Robert Preucel work in university-based academic settings, and each conducts research within the United States. In this volume, they focus on a current, highly visible, political topic: the issue of repatriation of Native American remains (see also Goldstein, this volume). Their essay offers ideas derived from the critical theory of Jürgen Habermas as a means to "transform the practice of archaeology into a more self-conscious activity." The goal of this transformed archaeology would be "to contribute to the process of achieving a more democratic consensus among all interest groups who have a claim on the past in the present" (Leone and Preucel, this volume).

Like the other contributors to this section, Leone and Preucel's objective includes opening archaeology to a broader range of social issues and ideas. They also seek to assess the questions and tensions underlying the issue of access to and use of archaeological data. While Leone and Preucel state that they have "no investment in criticizing the scientific method," they also suggest that the methods of science, as practiced by archaeologists, may not be adequate to produce secure knowledge about the past (Leone and Preucel, this volume).

Most archaeologists, I suspect, view the scientific method as a procedure for evaluating ideas about the past in order to contribute to knowledge about the past. Why is that knowledge not secure knowledge? Leone and Preucel seem to argue that secure knowledge would include diverse perspectives, a plurality of points of view. Following Habermas, they suggest that the goal of archaeology is to develop understanding and to actively maintain diverse world views or perspectives of the past. This goal would be furthered, they propose, by consensus-building, which is a political rather than a strictly archaeological activity. But, Leone and Preucel argue that science and politics are inescapably entwined.

Maintaining that archaeology, science, and politics are inseparable (Leone and Preucel, this volume), however, is also a polemic that in no way demonstrates that contributions to politics are also contributions to archaeology, any other science, or knowledge. Politics is part of the cultural context within which we live. It is from the entire context that we derive our inspiration as scientists. The entire context provides the source of the questions we ask. In that sense alone, politics and science are cojoined. Applying concepts derived from the writings of Habermas does not constitute either archaeological research or methods for improving or advancing archaeological research or knowledge. The approach, however, is offered as a programmatic means of democratizing archaeology.

The discourse analysis advocated by Leone and Preucel may help Western-trained white scholars understand the world around them. If so, it would certainly be useful. It seems unlikely to me that that form of analysis will be foremost among the theoretical or philosophical devices Native Americans call upon to understand the same world. It is ironic that one obviously conceptual issue at the core of the controversy examined by Leone and Preucel is not explicitly recognized as a conceptual problem, with the consequence that some aspects of the debate appear to be ignored. Archaeologists clearly *conceive* of human skeletal remains as objects and data. In their published statements, Native Americans state their conception of the same physical remains. They are *conceived* of as ancestors (see Powell and Huffman 1989; Quick 1985). Within the Native American context, there is little value to scientific knowledge. In the absence of a shared cultural system, shared values, and shared ethics, archaeologists and Native Americans will continue to talk past one another.

Archaeologists and Native Americans, in Leone and Preucel's view, each may be seeking to use heritage as part of a power struggle. However, I suggest we must acknowledge that paths to power and power itself, as well as knowledge and paths to knowledge, are culturally defined and therefore may be expected to vary from one cultural setting to another. Archaeology is a product of Western scientific thought. As such, it functions within a particular realm of obtaining confirmation and developing knowledge. That these indeed may not be the only paths to understanding the world is something to which anthropologists, especially, should be sensitive. Perhaps the writings of Habermas may increase that sensitivity.

Clearly, all of the essays in this section are explicit in calling for American archaeology to be more open to and concerned with a broader range of public issues. There is also a pervasive call for American archaeology to respect the training and background of non-American, nonanthropological, and non-Western ways of pursuing knowledge. Yet there is little in the way of explicit direction as to how this openness is to be achieved or what the implications of its pursuit may be for the archaeology of the next century. Leone and Preucel suggest that a more self-conscious archaeology may ask new questions. Simmons and Spencer-Wood go furthest in developing programmatic statements about what American archaeology might have to offer a wider constituency. Simmons suggests the improvement of research designs, technological innovations in the field, and ethnoarchaeology. Spencer-Wood offers a less gender-biased view of the past. Simmons and Spencer-Wood share a concern for integrating archaeology more broadly into public education and for presenting information obtained through archaeology in the educational process.

The discussions of openness and concern for public issues reveal underlying conceptual themes about how American archaeologists think of the archaeological endeavor. There is expressed uncertainty about what the relationship of archaeology to anthropology is and what it should be. Do we conceive of ourselves as anthropologists or archaeologists or both? Are the two compatible or not? Most of the authors of this section work in purely academic and in public archaeological settings. The essays, in turn, reflect positions in which archaeology is conceived of as primarily contributing to the accumulation of knowledge and positions in which it is conceived of as providing a community service. An even more basic conceptual issue is whether or not science and advocacy are conceptually compatible. The dilemma of the role of science in political advocacy, of course, is one that transcends archaeology.

Comparisons among the essays also reveal how American archaeology in the 1990s contrasts with American archaeology of past decades. Unlike the archaeology of the nineteenth century, there are no widely discussed key questions, such as where, when, and how had Native Americans arrived in the Americas or what group of people was responsible for building the mounds of the eastern United States. Unlike the archaeology of the mid-twentieth century, there are no questions about firsts, such as when and where maize was domesticated or what were the oldest civilizations in the Americas. There is also a lack of questions about process that dominated American archaeology in the mid-twentieth century. Thus, there are no questions about the importance of diffusion versus independent invention or about environmental determinism versus environmental possibilism. The explicitly conceptual issues that used to abound in journals are also notably absent. There does not seem to be an equivalent to the questions about whether artifact types are in the eyes of the typologist or are inherent and those of the artifact's maker. There is no discourse on deductive versus inductive reasoning. There is little on the utility or lack thereof of binomial nomenclature for artifact types or of total versus sample surveys or of research designs that do or do not carry multiple working hypotheses.

Perhaps it is a measure of the relative maturity of American archaeology of the 1990s that the key questions and explicitly conceptual issues that dominated the archaeological literature of earlier decades have either been resolved or rephrased. The lack of overriding central questions may, however, be the result of heterogeneity of theoretical positions espoused among archaeologists today (see contributions by Schiffer, Dunnell, and Sabloff, this volume). I suspect that the divergence in theoretical direction is also largely responsible for the lack of focused contrast at the level of concepts, frameworks, and working vocabularies.

It is interesting, though disappointing to me personally, that American archaeologists are not pursuing concepts that developed out of twentieth-century archaeology that may be relevant to the world of A.D. 2010. For example, the concept of the role of population pressure as a prime mover in technological and social change has not been focused on a world in which human populations are being differentially devastated by AIDS. Similarly, the current concern about retaining world biodiversity in general and the rain forest specifically is receiving no attention from students of the collapse of ancient societies from the Maya to the Hohokam. Finally, archaeologists are not sharing their learning about the changing pace of evolutionary change, that is, that change itself is increasingly rapid. Knowing that it took many thousands of years for humans to go from stone tools to steel tools and far fewer to go from cave paintings to computer graphics might indicate how transient both current social and political problems and their solutions might be.

References

Binford, Lewis R.
  1977 General Introduction. In *For Theory Building in Archaeology: Essays on Faunal Remains, Aquatic Resources and Systemic Modeling*, edited by Lewis R. Binford, pp. 1–13. Academic Press, New York.
  1978 *Nunamiut Ethnoarchaeology*. Academic Press, New York.
Conkey, Margaret, and Janet D. Spector
  1984 Archaeology and the Study of Gender. In *Advances in Archaeological Method and Theory*, vol. 7, edited by Michael B. Schiffer, pp. 1–38. Academic Press, New York.
Earle, Timothy K., and Robert W. Preucel
  1987 Processual Archaeology and the Radical Critique. *Current Anthropology* 28:501–538.
Hempel, Karl G.
  1965 *Aspects of Scientific Explanation and Other Essays in the Philosophy of Science*. Free Press, New York.
Kuhn, Thomas J.
  1970 *The Structure of Scientific Revolutions*. University of Chicago Press, Chicago.
Leone, Mark P., Parker B. Potter, Jr., and Paul A. Shakely
  1987 Toward a Critical Archaeology. *Current Anthropology* 28:283–302.
Powell, Shirley, and Jim Huffman
  1989 Objects or Ancestors? A Dialogue for the Society for American Archaeology. Ms. on file, Department of Anthropology, Northern Arizona University, Flagstaff.
Quick, Polly McW. (editor)
  1985 *Proceedings: Conference on Reburial Issues*. Society for American Archaeology, Washington, D.C.
Sabloff, Jeremy A.
  1989 Open Comments about Archaeological Issues Confronting the 1990s. Paper presented at the 54th Annual Meeting of the Society for American Archaeology, Atlanta.
Trigger, Bruce G.
  1989 History and Contemporary American Archaeology: A Critical Analysis. In *Archaeological Thought in America*, edited by C. C. Lamberg-Karlovsky, pp. 19–34. Cambridge University Press, Cambridge.

III. Archaeological Tools and Analysis

11. Future Directions: Management of the Archaeological Data Base

Anne I. Woosley

Abstract: Museum institutions figured prominently over the years as sponsors of archaeological field studies and recipients of the resulting materials and documents. Archaeological collections maintained across the nation number in the millions of objects. Today our museum institutions represent vast storehouses of knowledge with a research potential not yet realized. The present discussion examines trends in archaeology that shaped the historical development of research-oriented museums and attitudes toward the collections amassed. Future directions are explored with specific focus on archaeological collections management issues, changing perceptions of material culture, and research use potential.

The Past—Historical Background

Archaeology is a young discipline. Similarly, the history of research-oriented museums (hereafter simply referred to as museums) in the United States is also recent, perhaps having its beginnings with the founding of the Smithsonian Institution (1846) and the Peabody Museum of Harvard University (1866). The latter half of the nineteenth century into the first decade of the twentieth century was a period of documentation and aggressive, eclectic collecting because both the natural and the cultural histories of enormous geographic expanses of the country were unknown. In the Greater Southwest, Adolf Bandelier began his extensive documentation of the then living peoples and ruins of the region. F. H. Cushing's expedition to the Middle Gila in 1886–1889, J. W. Fewkes's work in Arizona, New Mexico, and Colorado, and G. E. Nordenskiöld's excavations at Mesa Verde all resulted in the accumulation of large amounts of materials, much of which found its way into eastern museums. Passage of the Antiquities Act of 1906 next precipitated a myriad of other data-collecting projects.

Quandaries and Quests: Visions of Archaeology's Future, edited by LuAnn Wandsnider. Center for Archaeological Investigations, Occasional Paper No. 20. © 1992 by the Board of Trustees, Southern Illinois University. All rights reserved. ISBN 0-88104-075-4.

Early archaeological studies demonstrated the regional diversity of prehistoric cultures and material remains throughout North America and set the stage for subsequent efforts directed toward ordering this information in space and time. In the Southwest, N. C. Nelson, N. M. Judd, A. V. Kidder, and H. S. Gladwin were particularly notable in their attempts to determine developmental sequences based on diagnostic ceramics types. Elsewhere, J. A. Ford, Irving Rouse, and W. C. McKern created various ceramic classification schemes for the Southeast, Midwest, and Caribbean.

The shifting emphasis expressed by the young science of archaeology from the nineteenth century focus to record all surviving remains to the chronological ordering of the first half of the twentieth century strongly influenced the composition of material collections accumulating in museums and our attitudes toward them. For example, classification systems in which pottery was considered a temporal and cultural indicator nearly always relied on painted ceramics to designate diagnostic "type." Plainwares, perceived to have no temporal sensitivity and little interpretive value, were usually not kept.

The primacy given diagnostic artifacts is closely linked to what may be termed the "art museum" approach to collecting, which has been a dominant motive in much archaeological data recovery. Basic to the approach is the belief that "showy" or "eccentric" pieces are superior to more modest items. In fact, the underlying criteria initially selected by archaeologists to identify artifacts of interpretive potential derive straight from the long-standing art museum collecting practice in which only the subjectively defined most beautiful object of any material category was of value and the rest were ignored. The consequence of the "diagnostic" artifact doctrine meant that many archaeological collections were biased in favor of specific classes of artifacts (and, therefore, accompanying interpretations) even if they were infrequently represented in the total material assemblage.

At the same time archaeologists were establishing chronological sequences during the 1930s, Works Progress Administration (WPA) projects, including the Tennessee River Surveys (1933–1941) and the later River Basin Surveys (1945–1969), mark another milestone in the development of North American archaeology with the emergence of a conservation ethic. When scheduled inundation predicted a 90% loss of all traces of the prehistoric occupation for 1,000 miles along the main Missouri River Valley, a nationwide response from archaeologists called for the preservation of that intellectual resource. The River Surveys produced quantities of artifacts on a scale seldom previously encountered. But the preservation strategy directed toward data recovery from soon-to-be-destroyed sites did not extend to a concomitant sense of long-term curatorial responsibility. Funding was allocated for fieldwork, but no provisions were made for collections management and many were later lost.

Changing Perspectives, the 1970s and 1980s

The 1970s can be viewed as a time when earlier trends coalesced, challenging archaeologists with new theoretical approaches and methodologies. New archaeology questioned what we might reconstruct from the past and then proposed that almost any dimension of prehistoric society could be determined so long as the relevant tests were applied (Binford 1968:18–27). Advances in analytical techniques opened new avenues in biological (Loy and Wood 1989) and compositional materials studies (Morse and Gordon 1986) and refined chronometric procedures (Hester 1987). The phenomenal growth of Cultural Resource Management (CRM) programs (and associated legislation) generated materials in tremendous quantities (Schiffer and Gumerman 1977). Voices were raised demanding rigor not only during field phases but throughout subsequent stages of collections curation and management. Fresh views on artifacts as documents of culture restored the credibility of material culture studies (Sackett 1977).

For museum institutions and the archaeological collections they contained, the most significant result of recent advances in method and theory was the increased quantity and diversity of data sets. As attitudes toward data recovery changed, so too the composition of collections was altered. If the ordinary collection of the 1920s contained ceramic vessels and painted rim sherds, some stone or bone tools, and human burials, by the mid-1970s literally everything was saved: entire ceramic and lithic assemblages, all manner of complete and fragmentary bone, and any number of organic and inorganic samples. The amounts of the materials increased dramatically as screening of excavation units became standard procedure. The volume of accompanying documentation also exploded. Where once the field director was solely responsible for record keeping, now most crew members maintain notes including site, unit, feature, and specialized sample forms—in addition to photos, topographic, soil, vegetation, or climate maps, and aerial photographs.

Not only are we charged with recovering as much information as possible, but we are required to anticipate intellectual and technological progress. For instance, during the course of the Dolores Archaeological Project in southwestern Colorado, whole stratigraphic columns from an array of site contexts were removed, encased in plaster, and curated for possible future analysis (R. Gwinn Vivian, personal communication 1990). Unlike earlier days when it was customary to discard large portions of the archaeological assemblage once its various components were counted, weighed, and described, today nearly all materials must be conserved. Current archaeological projects also generate materials long after fieldwork is finished. Petrographic thin sections of sherds, vials of pollen residues, computer printouts, and the products of specialized studies are expected to become part of the permanent data base.

Though the data base generated by archaeological projects may be highly informative, its sheer size and diverse composition place serious burdens on institutions and staff responsible for its preservation. Nowhere have the demands for improved collections management been more evident than with the development of CRM programs, the most prolific source of archaeological material remains over the past 20 years.

Elemental to the philosophy of CRM is the importance of "saving the past."

Even so, object curation was, for many years, viewed secondarily to fieldwork and primary laboratory analysis. But the magnitude of materials recovered from CRM-funded projects, the amount of monies expended, combined with a lack of curation facilities, caused archaeologists, institutions, and governmental agencies to actively pursue solutions to inadequate collections management. The creation of regional archaeological repositories represents a recent, federally initiated effort to ameliorate curation problems.

In one such instance, the Portland District of the Army Corps of Engineers established a repository for materials from a historic village visited by Lewis and Clark (National Park Service 1990:1–2). While searching for a satisfactory facility to house the over 500,000 objects recovered, the Corps discovered no regional museum could provide long-term storage. Consequently, a special repository with both environmentally controlled and general storage was constructed to contain the diverse collection and documents associated with the project. In a similar situation, the Dolores Anasazi Heritage Center of Colorado, administered by the Bureau of Land Management and the Bureau of Reclamation, not only serves as a repository but also realized its obligation to public education by establishing an interpretive museum for regional archaeology.

Though repositories represent a much needed attempt to conserve archaeological collections, interestingly, most came about after projects were completed and the truly critical state of archaeological curation needs was recognized. Clearly, curation demands should be anticipated before projects begin so that appropriate management issues can be identified. Federal repositories may well be part of the future answer to the care-in-perpetuity of materials generated by large-scale archaeological studies conducted on state and federal lands, which existing museum institutions are unable to accommodate.

Besides responding to the practical requirements of suitable collections storage, the ability to make use of those archaeological data also became a major topic of discussion. During the 1970s, archaeologists were enthusiastic about the prospect of the enormous volumes of information produced by so many projects and talked in terms of institutional data networks or the consortium approach to assembling and promoting access to the corpus of new data. The GRIPHOS (1971) data base originating at the Arkansas Archaeological Survey, the Arizona State ADAM (1971, Archaeological Data Management) system, and SARG (1971, Southwest Archaeological Research Group) were three early attempts to establish single-source information networks incorporating data gathered from many sites and investigators. Another effort, the San Juan Basin Regional Uranium Study (SJBRUS), initiated under the auspices of the National Park Service, sought to contain several categories of data from some 15,000 sites in a 25,000-square-mile area of the basin (Wait 1982:171–172).

Whatever the actual successes of various ventures to data bank archaeological information, these data bases had several goals. Computerization enabled archaeologists to manipulate large amounts of data either among sites throughout a region or in great detail within a site.

Theoretically, data banks enabled a larger community of researchers to gain access to otherwise dispersed information. Furthermore, because so many sites were being destroyed, either by planned construction or the result of vandalism, there existed a strong belief that data recovered and stored today might well be the sum of information to survive for future problem solving.

During the 1970s and 1980s the recognized importance of material collections to archaeological research was not only measured in terms of incipient improvements in curation practices and data banking, but also in the growth of material culture studies as archaeologists viewed artifacts as expressions of human behavior. Wilmsen's (1970) Paleoindian research, in which he took projectile point interpretations far beyond stylistic attributal analysis into socioeconomic reconstructions, exemplifies this trend. The investigations have continued to accelerate, becoming refined to the point of formulating material culture theory (Conkey 1989:13–31). The awareness of objects as documents of culture spurred organization conferences at the national level to articulate current needs for conserving archaeological (and ethnological) materials (e.g., Cantwell et al. 1981). Though collections were properly viewed as nonrenewable resources worthy of preservation, their research potential as records of human behavior promoted an environment in which improved collections care and use developed.

The Present, the 1990s

Certain developments now evident will continue through the 1990s and beyond, while others just taking shape will gain momentum in the coming years. Archaeologists will routinely be required to deal with many aspects of collections management and will undoubtedly make more frequent use of existing collections. For the first time archaeology is experiencing a level of negativism that seriously questions the most basic strategies for conducting research.

Curation and Conservation

Archaeologists in the United States have been some of the worst offenders in the proper care of collections, though in other countries (e.g., Canada) excavation permits are not granted unless suitable provisions are made for the conservation of artifacts (NIC 1984:15). The lack of concern for the treatment of materials is waning because of the influence of museum professionals knowledgeable in collections management and because stricter legislative collection guidelines demand it. The National Park Service (NPS 1990:1, 3–7) has recommended formalized procedures to manage and preserve archaeological artifacts and collections and has set standards governing repositories with regard to appropriate record keeping, conservation practices, security, staffing, object handling, regular inspections, and periodic inventories, as well as curatorial services regulating access to collections.

The recently initiated multiyear Roosevelt Platform Mound Study (Rice

1990) is a good indication that we are becoming better educated about collections curation and of what is in store for future archaeological projects. At the request of the sponsoring agency, up-front planning included input from museum specialists as well as discussions with the repository personnel responsible for storing the materials recovered. Indeed, besides supervisory archaeologists, a museum collections specialist acts as a project manager for the study. Artifact treatment and conservation in the field and laboratory stages are as much an integral component of research planning strategy as excavation or survey.

Turning to another area of archaeological curation, though we seem to recognize the value of old collections—affirmed by numerous, continual requests for access to them—over the next 20 years we will have to assume responsibility to control their deterioration. Most stone and ceramic objects are relatively stable, but many perishable artifacts and the documentary records that make sense of these material assemblages are disintegrating. Field notes and maps from work conducted even as late as the middle 1950s are brittle and flaking (the result of paper made from acidic pulpwood rather than rag) and will eventually require expensive, time-consuming deacidification to ensure their long-term preservation. Removal of all perishables to stable, acid-free environments will soon be necessary. Obviously, if collections are not conserved, not only will they ultimately not survive, but they will be too fragile to be handled for study purposes. In cooperation with museum professionals, archaeologists will have to turn to conservation project support grants such as the National Science Foundation's systematic anthropological collections program (Greene 1982). In fact, the future may find us submitting proposals involving old collections as frequently as we submit proposals to fund new field research.

Collections Organization

Given an adequate level of conservation, the research potential of any archaeological collection depends on its organization and, by extension, the accessibility of the data it contains. Collections before 1970 often exist in the form of notebooks, photo files, and artifacts shelved in bags and boxes. Going back to those collections means a page-by-page or box-by-box search for information. Apparently overwhelming at first view, in practice the exercise may not be so onerous simply because we did not collect nearly the quantities of materials then. The much larger, later collections (after ca. 1975) consisting of diverse data sets probably pose greater organizational problems. Though some attempts were made to computerize certain classes of information (Wait 1982), most data occur in nonstandardized form. Sheer volume ensures access will be a formidable task, even more than is the case for smaller, older collections.

Computerization may well be the key to enhancing the future use potential of all archaeological collections by helping to resolve access problems. In theory, we are more aware than ever about the benefits of computerization (e.g., Dibble and McPherron 1988). It allows us to assess the range of available data, to select those pertinent to our needs, and to do it without returning to original materials. Though it is applied to many current archaeological projects, computerization has also increased the research potential of older collections. Collections from the Hendricks-Hodge Expedition to Hawikku (1917–1923) were the subject of an organizational study designed to consolidate and cross-reference data, thereby facilitating access (Shears 1989). The present data base consists of five linked files of 8,000 records, which required 700 person-hours of data entry. Once dispersed throughout several locations, 13,000 pages of data are now available for review in the time it takes to call up the information on a screen (Shears 1989). Comparatively little energy was required to computerize the materials, while the return in terms of research potential was enormous.

The movement toward computer management of archaeological collections may actually occur more quickly in CRM projects governed by federal regulations, already encouraging disk storage of all information, than in the research of individual investigators. The previously mentioned Roosevelt Platform Mound study includes an open-ended relational data base. It provides inventories for any provenience, can select analytical units fitting particular criteria (e.g., all room floor strata in a given site), and gives provenience information for specific classes of material. The data base becomes the primary source of all information recovered during the project.

Ultimately, how creative we are in using archaeological information is closely linked to our ability to compare information sets and examine large quantities of information quickly. The National Archaeological Database developed by the National Park Service (Keel et al. 1989:26–29), comprising sites and records from throughout the United States, is a step in this direction. Development of central sources of information is also important if we are not to replicate work already completed needlessly. It would be extremely useful, for instance, to have a single source that inventories existing archaeological data files including those generated by the National Park Service, the National Forest Service, and other agencies, as well as university and museum files.

Future archaeological research and collections management will move, however hesitantly, into the world of digitized information storage. Five- and twelve-inch optical laser disks, capable of holding orders of magnitude more information than either magnetic tape or computer hard disk, can store it in any form—field notes, maps, photographs, slides, or three-dimensional artifacts. The Spanish archives in Seville, Spain, offer a good example of the capabilities of laser disk information storage. Consisting of 80,000,000 documents, the Archivo General de Indias encompasses a city block (Polzer 1989:182). The entire archive can be digitized on 2,000 optical disks housed in a single room; one document is scanned every 15 seconds. Efforts to computerize archaeological data are not new, but as we look ahead, our challenge is to take advantage of the technology available and to create information retrieval systems with standardized finding aids.

Collections Use

Though the utility of collections is variable, some having much better documentation than others, a surprising number are well suited for testing new methods and theories. Increasingly, museum institutions are called upon to provide materials for specialized analyses, often destructive to the objects examined. Stable carbon and nitrogen isotope studies, using tissue in the form of bone collagen, attempt to distinguish cereal grain from legume consumption in paleodiets (Sillen et al. 1989:505–506). Studies involving DNA make use of the tissues of mummies. Advances in skeletal aging and sexing procedures prompted reexamination of Hopewell trophy skulls (Seeman 1988:565–577) and burial populations at Pecos Pueblo (Ruff 1981:147–151). Archaeologists reanalyze collections as they ask new questions of old data as in the possibility of determining craft specialization from microlithics (Yerkes 1983) or tracing prehistoric pottery production and exchange (Bishop et al. 1988). These diverse examples demonstrate that the research potential of archaeological collections is great, limited only by our imagination.

In appraising the value of old archaeological collections, it is worth taking a closer look at the Hendricks-Hodge Hawikku expedition. The materials were principally maintained by the then Museum of the American Indian, Heye Foundation, and consist of 1,000 burials, 1,500 whole ceramic vessels, plus other artifacts numbering about 25,000 objects and documents, including field notes, maps, room floor plans, detailed stratigraphic records, and photographs. In her assessment of the Hawikku collection as a data source for further work, Shears (1989) concluded that it was well suited to biological analysis of human and animal bone, to technological or stylistic ceramic studies, to determining room function, and to demonstrating social organization by employing mortuary data and spatial patterning of architecture. Though not every old collection has the detailed documentation that characterizes the Hawikku material, much useful information begs additional work.

In neglecting extant collections, we are missing significant sources of information. Continued stress on a conservation ethic, which insists we eliminate unnecessary fieldwork, has provoked renewed interest in archaeological collections. Specifically, many archaeologists believe excavation to represent the exploitative or destructive phase of research that should be avoided until all other nondestructive methods of data gathering (e.g., survey or remote sensing) have been explored. Consequently, in a climate emphasizing the preservation of archaeological sites, we will probably make much more frequent use of material collections.

Sociopolitical Attitudes

Attitudes toward archaeology, particularly in the United States, are undergoing a transformation from an almost wholesale acceptance and enthusiasm to a questioning and even a suspicion of its social value. Museums containing the products, that is, material collections, of archaeological studies are feeling keenly the new negativism often expressed as a reservation about the amount of monies expended on federally mandated projects or in terms of the repatriation of the Native American burial remains and grave goods. These are primary concerns to which the profession must respond and which, in the long run, might be a very good thing.

Turning first to the subject of large tax dollar expenditures (the NPS figures are $43.8 million for 1985 and $78.4 million for 1986, Keel et al. 1989:24–25) to support archaeological projects, we face serious interrogation about the actual value of our work. Often abstract statements about the irreplaceable nature of archaeological resources and nebulous prattle that they constitute the only record of our past carry no real meaning for society at large. As interesting as some of our past research has been, with few outstanding exceptions, archaeologists do not have a particularly strong record of promoting public involvement, education, and good will. To some extent, it may be because we are still groping for the theoretical frameworks for doing archaeology. Nevertheless, we must be prepared to foster an interest in archaeology if we expect to revitalize broadly based public support and cooperation.

While the conceptual context of archaeology falls outside the scope of this discussion, tough questions about why, what, and how we do archaeology should cause increased introspection on our part. Our exploitation of archaeological remains deserves self-examination. What, after all, is the use of excavating yet another pithouse? What information are we likely to gain that we do not already have? The growing concerns with the goals of archaeology, perhaps stated in terms of more clearly defined theoretical frameworks, and a reiteration of the conservation ethic that includes realistic uses of nondestructive approaches to data gathering may be in order. Explanations in archaeology may reasonably involve increased use of material collections and decreased field research, at least excavation. A great deal of future archaeology may be conducted within the walls of museums as compared to excavating more archaeological sites.

Any discussion of changing social attitudes toward archaeology must include repatriation, the intent to rebury or return human remains, associated funerary objects, and other sacred objects. The possible implications of related legislation to research and institutions curating archaeological materials need not be repeated here, but repatriation was the principal topic in lead articles of at least five newsletters during the first months of 1990 (e.g., King 1990; Lovis 1990; Lurie 1990). Repatriation will remain sensitive in the foreseeable future. Archaeologists must strive to find compromises between research interests, on the one hand, and the concerns of tribal representatives, on the other (see Goldstein; Leone and Preucel, this volume).

The Future, 2001 and Beyond

Looking ahead to research-oriented museums and their role in archaeological research, seven primary concerns are identified, the foremost of which is funding followed by (in no particular order of priority) management of increasing material collections, construction of storage facilities, creation of material processing/analyzing areas, collection conservation, computerization, and staffing. Though archaeologists must recognize both the social and the economic contexts in which we plan to conduct future work, over the long term, the economic environment may be the single most critical factor influencing archaeological research and museum resources. In assessing our financial health, we must acknowledge the impact of the national debt (in spring 1990, 3 trillion dollars and increasing by $8,000 per second). The Bush administration will probably represent the national leadership through 1996, an indication that present funding strategies will be maintained. A resistance to increased taxes is likely to persist, and what taxes are raised will support social programs; archaeology is not one of these. A shrinking economic base is, therefore, to be expected for collections care and related research, as well as for certain types of new field research.

While we will experience diminished funding in some areas—the National Science Foundation and the National Endowment for the Humanities—CRM projects are likely to proliferate for at least two reasons. Firstly, with persistent population growth in the arid West, more water will be required, resulting in an expansion of existing dams and reservoirs, as well as new construction. The 10-year Roosevelt project, representing an $11 to $12 million Bureau of Reclamation–sponsored archaeological project in conjunction with dam safety programs (Tom Lincoln, personal communication 1990), is an indication of this trend. Secondly, the highway system instigated by the Eisenhower administration during the 1950s is on the brink of ruin, demanding a nationwide improvement program that will include new construction and the widening of many current roadways. Highway construction will impact sites and mandate CRM, especially urban archaeology. Instead of a decrease, dam/reservoir and highway construction will cause a surge of new fieldwork. Meanwhile, field research funded through grant awards will probably decline.

To the accumulated extant collections, CRM projects will add other materials, all of which will require adequate support to curate and maintain and for study purposes. The collections will not only require suitable storage but also space for processing and conducting certain types of analyses. Permanent storage may demand warehouse-size facilities at substantial cost. Archaeologists will have to think in terms of the long-term maintenance costs, not merely the initial fees covering object reception and handling. Perpetual curation and storage costs may come as a surprise to university administrators who have welcomed the revenues of large public projects but are not aware of their continuous responsibilities. Universities and museums have already reached a point where they do not have funding to meet perpetual collections care obligations. The future may find archaeological collections going to federal repositories, the only facilities able to accommodate the quantities of materials produced by CRM projects. Alternatively, we may see an infusion of federal monies into universities and private institutions for repository construction and collections management.

Such cooperative agreements are already emerging as agencies are providing support to bring collections up to acceptable curation standards and to cover annual cost of their maintenance (Fred Wendorf, personal communication 1990).

As we become better educated about collection conservation needs, storage costs will rise concomitantly. A roof, a floor, and four walls will not suffice to contain an entire archaeological collection. Certain artifact classes, documents on paper, and computer disks will require environmentally controlled spaces. Materials including acid-free containers, note paper, and slide frames, along with chemically inert microfoam for packing and shelf lining, will all increase costs.

In managing collections we will make greater use of digitized information. Collections computerization will promote efficient data retrieval and the ability to utilize large quantities of data. Though we are aware that computerization and data banking are essential to maximize the research potential of archaeological collections, here, too, the cost is not negligible. Creating common languages, developing equipment compatibility, and prioritizing projects will all be expensive to achieve.

As we continue to accept our responsibilities in the area of collections care and management, a greater number of trained specialists will be required. Museum-studies students trained in material curation and conservation, together with persons having computer skills, will be frequent contributors to archaeological research. In addition, the museum archaeologist is likely to emerge. As the research potential of collections is recognized, more archaeologists will make use of these data sets than will initiate new fieldwork. The traditional concept of the archaeologist's gaining his or her data primarily from field projects will be transformed to include the archaeologist who mainly turns to museum resources.

Archaeology has always relied on material objects as a significant portion of its data base. Archaeologists will be challenged to better conserve our material collections. While the problems are substantial, we are actively identifying many areas of critical need. Our achievements in the various aspects of collections care and management ensure the preservation of information reflecting past behavior—a past we archaeologists attempt to translate.

References

Binford, L. R.
    1968   Archeological Perspectives. In *New Perspectives in Archeology*, edited by S. R. Binford and L. R. Binford, pp. 5–32. Aldine, Chicago.

Bishop, R. L., V. Canouts, S. P. De Atley, A. Qoyawayma, and C. W. Aikins
    1988   The Formation of Ceramic Analytical Groups: Hopi Pottery Production and Exchange, A.D. 1300–1600. *Journal of Field Archaeology* 15:317–337.

Cantwell, A-M., J. B. Griffin, and N. A. Rothschild (editors)
    1981   *The Research Potential of Anthropological Museum Collections.* Annals of the New York Academy of Sciences, New York.

Conkey, M. W.
   1989   The Place of Material Culture in Contemporary Anthropology. In *Perspectives on Anthropological Collections from the American Southwest*, edited by A. L. Hedlund, pp. 13–31. Anthropological Research Papers No. 40. Arizona State University, Tempe.

Dibble, H. L., and S. P. McPherron
   1988   On the Computerization of Archaeological Projects. *Journal of Field Archaeology* 15:431–440.

Greene, M. W.
   1982   *NSF Anthropology Program: Support for Systematic Anthropology Collections*. National Science Foundation, Washington, D.C.

Hester, J. J.
   1987   The Significance of Accelerator Dating in Archaeological Method and Theory. *Journal of Field Archaeology* 14:445–451.

Keel, B. C., F. P. McManamon, and G. S. Smith (compilers)
   1989   *Federal Archeology: The Current Program*. Department of the Interior, National Park Service, Washington, D.C.

King, J. E.
   1990   Native American Collections Issues. *Science Museum News, Association of Science Museum Directors* 29:1. Carnegie Museum of Natural History, Pittsburgh.

Lovis, W. A.
   1990   How Far Will It Go? A Look at S. 1980 and Other Repatriation Legislation. *Society for American Archaeology Bulletin* 8(2):8–10.

Loy, T. H., and A. R. Wood
   1989   Blood Residue Analysis at Çayönü Tepesi, Turkey. *Journal of Field Archaeology* 16:451–460.

Lurie, N. O.
   1990   Interim Report, AAA Commission on Native American Remains. *Anthropology Newsletter* 31(4):1, 16–18. Washington, D.C.

Morse, B. F., and R. B. Gordon
   1986   Metallographic Examination of Pre-Columbian Mexican Copper and Silver Artifacts from Mitla, Oaxaca (Mexico). *Archeomaterials* 1(1):57–67.

National Institute for the Conservation of Cultural Property (NIC)
   1984   *Ethnographic and Archaeological Conservation in the United States*. Washington, D.C.

National Park Service, U.S. Department of the Interior
   1990   *Federal Archeology Report* 3(1). Archeology Assistance Division, National Park Service, Washington, D.C.

Polzer, C. W.
   1989   The Spanish Colonial Southwest: New Technologies for Old Documents. In *Columbian Consequences: Archaeological and Historical Perspectives on the Spanish Borderlands West*, vol. 1., edited by D. H. Thomas, pp. 179–188. Smithsonian Institution Press, Washington, D.C.

Rice, G. E. (editor)
   1990   *A Design for Salado Research*. Roosevelt Monograph Series No. 1, Anthropological Field Studies No. 22. Arizona State University, Tempe.

Ruff, C. B.
   1981   A Reassessment of Demographic Estimates for Pecos Pueblo. *American Journal of Physical Anthropology* 54:147–151.

Sackett, J. R.
  1977 The Meaning of Style in Archaeology: A General Model. *American Antiquity* 42:369–380.
Schiffer, M. B., and G. J. Gumerman (editors)
  1977 *Conservation Archaeology: A Guide for Cultural Resource Management Studies.* Academic Press, New York.
Seeman, M. F.
  1988 Ohio Hopewell Trophy-Skull Artifacts as Evidence for Competition in Middle Woodland Societies Circa 50 B.C.–A.D. 350. *American Antiquity* 53:565–577.
Shears, B. L.
  1989 *The Hendricks-Hodge Archaeological Expedition Documentation Project: Preparing a Museum Collection for Research.* Master's thesis, Hunter College, New York.
Sillen, A., J. C. Sealy, and N. J. van der Merwe
  1989 Chemistry and Paleodietary Research: No More Easy Answers. *American Antiquity* 54:504–512.
Wait, W. K.
  1982 The Development and Application of a Computerized Data Base for the San Juan Basin, New Mexico. In *The San Juan Tomorrow: Planning for the Conservation of Cultural Resources in the San Juan Basin*, edited by F. Plog and W. K. Wait, pp. 171–218. National Park Service in cooperation with the School of American Research, Santa Fe.
Wilmsen, E. N.
  1970 *Lithic Analysis and Cultural Inference: A Paleo-Indian Case.* Anthropological Papers of the University of Arizona No. 16. University of Arizona, Tucson.
Yerkes, R. W.
  1983 Microwear, Microdrills, and Mississippian Craft Specialization. *American Antiquity* 48:499–518.

12. Instrumentation and the Future of Archaeology

Ronald L. Bishop

Abstract: The development of high-tech instrumentation affords archaeology an opportunity to observe and measure aspects of the archaeological record in a manner that largely outpaces the ability of the involved archaeologists to maximize the interpretative potential of the derived data. Further, archaeological use of technological developments is constrained by the lack of adequate theoretical constructs that permit effective incorporation of the data within a systematized body of archaeological knowledge. Many analytical tools already exist that will permit archaeology to progress in its acquisition of knowledge about the past. It is argued, however, that in the absence of significant changes at the interface between science and archaeology, future instrumentally derived data will contribute negligibly to the resolution of archaeological questions, particularly about the *why* of the observed variation within the archaeological record.

Introduction

The archaeological application of instrumental tools varies dramatically in complexity. Some applications require relatively simple instruments like calipers or a binocular microscope, while other applications use sophisticated instruments like the scanning electronic microscope, mass spectrometer, particle accelerator, or other devices more at home in the hands of physical scientists than archaeologists. It is the archaeologists' relationship with this latter world of highly sophisticated technology, the high-tech world, that is the subject of this brief essay. Let me begin, however, with the following, only marginally overstated, caricature.

Specialists who obtain information from the application of sophisticated instrumentation risk evolving inwardly. Losing their ability to communicate their findings meaningfully to archeological nonspecialists, they constitute a

Quandaries and Quests: Visions of Archaeology's Future, edited by LuAnn Wandsnider. Center for Archaeological Investigations, Occasional Paper No. 20. © 1992 by the Board of Trustees, Southern Illinois University. All rights reserved. ISBN 0-88104-075-4.

pseudopriesthood. An archeologist who accepts the data that has been passed on with scientific blessing feeds these quantified, all equally "good" data into a computer where they are manipulated by black-box, statistical algorithms. Unburdened by lack of familiarity with the assumptions or specifications under which the instrumental findings were obtained and frequently having neglected to work within any theoretical structure that might have guided the problem formulation, sample design, or instrumental selection, the archeologist summarizes the results in the archaeological literature in one of several ways: (1) as a methodological statement, (2) as an interim report with unfulfilled promise of great things to come, or (3) as a cautionary tale. The archaeologist then retires to his or her study to peruse the latest literature, eagerly awaiting the next technological breakthrough that can be used to demonstrate the scientific rigor of the archaeological discipline.

Instrumentation (techniques, technology) is a tool for archaeologists, and as with all tools, certain types of instrumentation are better adapted for some purposes than others. The increasing and uncritical use of instrumental findings found in the literature seems to support the observation made by Gumerman and Phillips over a decade ago that "many practitioners seem to feel that continued improvements in technique will upgrade the quality of archaeological information" (1978:184). And that observation is in agreement with a somewhat more cynical evaluation expressed earlier by the renowned ceramic technologist, Anna O. Shepard, who suggested that "there is an element of exhibitionism in some instrumental analytical work in archaeology" (letter from Anna O. Shepard to Robert H. Brill, February 7, 1968).[1]

I sense that archaeologists tend to ascribe something special to the data produced by instrumentation; data provided through high-tech measurements are viewed as somehow more authoritative, or, as characterized by Shepard, such data give a "frill" of scientific rigor to an otherwise descriptive archaeological report (letter from A. O. Shepard to J. O. Brew, July 21, 1950). If that perception is correct, it would go a long way toward explaining the reason why archaeologists are willing to accept analytical data without understanding the technical details of how they were produced.

Sophisticated techniques, exhibitionism, or scientific flirtation—clearly, there is something about high-tech instrumental analysis in archaeology that demands closer examination. In the following discussion of instrumental analysis in archaeology, I comment generally about certain problem areas and offer suggestions for increasing the efficient use of instrumental analysis through the restructuring of cross-disciplinary interaction.

Traditions of Instrumental Analysis in Archaeology

An appreciation for the place of high-tech instrumental analysis in archaeology can be gained from a review of archaeology's development in the Americas. In the general evolution of the discipline as offered by Trigger (1986, 1989), archaeology's development was closely linked to growth in the natural historic and geologic traditions of the nineteenth century. Most of the archaeologists were trained in the natural sciences. And as archaeologists began to take part in the *scientific* projects being undertaken by newly created organizations such as the American Philosophical Society or through the research programs of the Smithsonian Institution, archaeology as a science received more attention.

At the end of the nineteenth century, the culture area models of the ethnologists were supported by observations of the differential distribution of various items of material culture. Like their sociocultural counterparts, archaeologists described the spatial distribution of material items, and cultural groups were particularized through lists of distinctive traits. Explanations for similarities among cultures were found in such concepts as migration or diffusion. Internal processes that might account for changes within particular cultural groups received virtually no attention because foreshortened chronologies did not provide a period of time sufficient enough to allow for the transformations.

This short chronological perspective changed, however, after the discovery of Paleoindian remains (Willey and Sabloff 1980:121–123). Those finds, combined with the stratigraphic and seriation work of Gamio (1913), Kidder (1962), and others, demonstrated patterns of systematic variation in the archaeological record that could be accounted for through time. Although it was not an instrumental technique, stratigraphy, derived from the *science* of geology, dramatically altered the interpretation of the archaeological record as gradual transformations in the record could now be described.

Technological developments following the conclusion of World War II significantly influenced the way in which archaeology was practiced, particularly through the use of radiocarbon dating. That dating technique permitted the establishment of complete cultural sequences, provided an absolute time-range within which differential rates of change could be assessed, and allowed the comparison of cultures within the same general time period. It made possible the study of the effects of natural and cultural environments on cultural development (Willey and Sabloff 1980:156–157). The development of radiocarbon dating was more pervasive, according to Dunnell, for "it allied archaeology with science and provided a relatively clear means of evaluating archaeological statements" (1986:30). Radiocarbon afforded a means of *empirically* testing statements about the archaeological record.

Perhaps, in fact, radiocarbon dating worked *too well*. The new instrumental techniques made possible the solution of a well-focused question—how old the context of an object was—and it seemingly did so with a single determination! The archaeological utility of radiocarbon dating, combined with its apparent definitiveness involving only a few measurements, raised unrealistic expectations about instrumental techniques that were extended to future technological developments.

Chronometric breakthroughs, including dendrochronology in the American Southwest and other dating techniques (paleomagnetism or archeomagnetism, obsidian hydration, fluorine analysis of bone, etc.), combined to free archaeology from its dominating concern with time. As attention turned from concern with chronology to more contextual issues, new methods derived from the biological as well as the physical sciences provided assistance in the reconstruction of climatic conditions and dietary regimens (Willey and Sabloff 1980:157). Ceramics materials were subjected to petrographic and chemical analysis as "archaeological materials analysis" emerged in Americanist archaeology (e.g., Matson 1967; Shepard 1936, 1956).

Other technical developments, directly derived from World War II research, provided new resolution in the field of aerial photography. Even recently harnessed nuclear power was applied to archaeological materials as the muscle of the physical and chemical sciences began to be felt. These new tools were added to the earlier techniques of the natural sciences with which archaeology had coevolved. In no small measure, the technological developments permitted the formulation of new questions focused on the mechanisms and processes that gave shape to the archaeological record. Technological applications that led to the solution of archaeological problems or that led to the revision of previously held, speculative interpretations demonstrated the value of scientific methods and methodology.

Both instrumental analyses and "the scientific method" became part and parcel of the evolving new archaeology. New techniques were rapidly embraced and applied, leading to a staggering array of data. To cite Patty Jo Watson's succinct statement: "For a while it seemed that with sufficient ingenuity, an emphasis on deductive inference, and the use of new-fangled equipment and techniques . . . wielded by interdisciplinary teams . . . we could say something interesting, significant, and true about any part of the archaeological record" (1986:440). Technology seemed to offer archaeology the scientific means to explore different aspects of cultural remains and the ability to obtain objective data with which to test hypotheses about the past.

Contemporary Instrumental Analysis in Archaeology

Although archaeological questions are being formulated with greater specificity and solutions to some of the questions can be obtained through the informed use of scientific instrumentation, this in no way implies that the understanding of the archaeological record has improved accordingly. And in spite of notable contributions made through instrumental development thus far, the potential benefit has been lessened by four major problems areas: the appropriate choice of instrumentation, the need for specialist information, the lack of a sufficient body of theory for data integration, and the sociocultural context of cross-disciplinary research.

Instrumental Availability

Choices among analytical approaches should be governed with respect to the type of data produced and its adequacy in terms of sensitivity, precision, and accuracy (see Bishop et al. 1990). Cost is yet another concern. In many instances, however, the choice appears to be based on simple availability of a given type of instrumentation. Using what is available represents an operational shortcut that might not be adequate to reach the analytical objects (assuming that they have been defined) but produces data (methodological or descriptive) that nonetheless find their way into publication. Other applications appear to be more of the "what can I do with it next" variety.

Specialist Knowledge

Archaeologists are fragmented along narrow lines of specialization that tend to isolate them from the general discipline, and any attempt to become relatively competent in the concepts, context, and assumptions of some other discipline greatly exacerbates the isolation process. Such subdisciplinary isolation within archaeology, however, is similar to that which may be found to exist in many other disciplines (Denning 1987) and is a normal part of a discipline's evolutionary process.

Whether or not part of a normal process, effective use of instrumentation in archaeology is diminished by persons who are unfamiliar with the nature of the analytical techniques (archaeologists) or the appropriate context for their use (physical scientists). Data generation is far too frequently left to the technician or physical scientist because archaeologists are either unaware of or ignore the parameters used to produced the data.

Attempts to improve cross-disciplinary understanding have considerable time depth but have met with mixed success. For example, since the 1950s certain analytical institutions, for example, the Oxford Laboratory in England, have attempted to develop scientific techniques that could be applied by archaeologists who would be able to produce an adequate number of analyses to solve a particular problem. Unfortunately, it was soon learned that archaeologists preferred to ignore the nuances of specific techniques and await what data might be delivered by their favorite scientist (see De Atley and Bishop 1991; Jope 1990; Warren 1982).

Theoretical Inadequacy

Technological developments notwithstanding, the incorporation of instrumentally acquired data by the archaeological community is not an automatic event. Their acceptance—and significance—depends upon the user's ability to fit the data into some relevant theoretical framework or problem orientation. Several persons, including Dunnell (1982) and Schiffer (1978), have correctly pointed to the absence of a sufficient theoretical framework that would permit the incorporation of data from the physical and natural sciences. Efforts are being expended to develop a middle-range theoretical bridge between observational data and cultural interpretation (e.g., Schiffer and Skibo 1987, 1989), but progress is slow (cf. Dunnell, this volume).

Research objectives respond not only to theoretical structure but also to specific problem domains. For example, in spite of the promising early work by Shepard (1936), extensive analytical investigations dealing with questions of trade had to wait for the broad outlines of culture history to be filled in before attention was given to questions of settlement patterns, social organization, and trade (Cordell 1991). As the research orientation changed, interest turned to promising new techniques in instrumental chemical analysis, while some older techniques, like petrography, gained new prominence (see De Atley and Bishop 1991; Earle and Ericson 1977). The new research directions that were being charted did not simply involve more detailed questions being asked of the archaeological record. Rather, the new directions "were part of a shift from site specific descriptions of archaeological remains and sequences to a broader regional approach, one which led to data interpretation within a more cultural anthropological or an ecological, adaptive framework" (De Atley and Bishop 1991:358–382).

Sociological Organization

Beyond specifics about the nature of archaeological recovery or instrumental development, cross-disciplinary endeavors, like those involving science and archaeology, operate in a social context, and existing weaknesses in how we approach cross-disciplinary activities pose their own special limitations. Physical scientists can become bored with routine data production, preferring instead to refine techniques, to develop new approaches, or to compare results among several techniques (see De Atley and Bishop 1991; van Zelst 1991). The theoretical or methodological perspective guiding their efforts is likely to derive from the natural or physical sciences and correspondence with archaeological interpretation used only as a check on the technique or procedure. If the archaeologist fails to communicate adequately the significant context for particular applications, instrumentation will continue to produce data "in the service" of archaeology, but the findings are unlikely to be an integrated component of the research.

Reorganizing the Context for Instrumentation in Archaeology

Gumerman and Phillips (1978) observed that some of archaeology's notable successes were achieved by using data and models from several disciplines. It would better serve the goals of archaeology, they observed, if archaeology were treated primarily as a body of techniques. Constituted in that manner, archaeology would not be dependent upon models drawn from sociocultural theory and would thus be freer to engage in more effective interdisciplinary communication.

In a somewhat similar vain, Kingery has suggested that our understanding of the past would benefit from a field focused on object interpretation rather than from the discipline of archaeology (Kingery 1987a, 1987b, 1989). Materials selection and processing are viewed as giving rise to structure that determines properties and application (Kingery 1987a:679–680). Structure is conceived at various levels (object, macrostructure, microstructure, crystal-glass, structure, elemental structure), each with appropriate instrumentation for investigation. Object investigation appears to be driven by instrumental analysis, particularly at the microstructural level. One or a few samples for investigation are selected from modal classes, wherein a notion of central tendency, not variation, is the basis of the prevailing model. As a consequence of the modal approach to archaeological materials, the kinds of questions that instrumental data can be used to address are therefore limited to producing functional statements rather than explaining why the archaeological record exists as it does (see Dunnell, this volume).

Explanation of the archaeological record is furthered when an object is viewed as part of a sample whose characteristic parameters have been established and whose relevance to understanding variation and change has been specified. It is the contribution that the sample, not the object, makes to understanding process that is most important. Beyond this, however, characterization beyond the single object forces the investigation to move from a level of objective, scientific empiricism as modified by the rules of probability onto a level where explanation is constrained by theoretical constructs regarding variation.

There presently exist many instrumental techniques that have the requisite sensitivity, accuracy, and precision to contribute substantially to our knowledge about the past. What is lacking is sufficient knowledge of how to maximize our use of them. This ignorance seems to extend from the formulation of a research design through data interpretation, especially in the area of materials characterization. In the absence of adequate theoretical constructs, archaeological interpretations based on materials characterization will seldom move beyond the descriptive level, and attempts to understand the processes responsible for the archaeological record will stay more surficial than substantive. New techniques will offer more data at higher resolution and with a faster turnaround. It is not clear what we will do with these data, and until it is, scientific frill will continue.

In addition to needed theoretical developments, basic management of cross-disciplinary research in archaeology will also need to change. De Atley and I have argued elsewhere that without significant changes at the cooperative interface between science and archaeology, future technological advances will contribute negligibly to the resolution of the archaeological questions, especially to the *why* of the observed variation in the archaeological record (De Atley and Bishop 1991). Archaeologists have the capacity to change the way they use instrumentation and subsequently to derive more interpretive benefits from analytical findings. Yet that will require a change away from archaeology's hierarchically organized flowchart of individual specialists toward an interactive matrix structure.

Organizational matrices must be formed from specialists, archaeologists, natural and physical scientists, and "instrumentalists" who will use their collective expertise and experience to formulate research designs and to decide on appropriate methodologies for a common problem. Participants must meet collectively to evaluate research progress and to modify the design as emerging patterns dictate. During the process, each specialist will learn more about the other's concerns and approaches, about methodological strengths and weaknesses. The traditional role of the "principal investigator" will become more administrative in nature, while the mission of the "grand synthesizer" will move to the collective body.

How will a matrix organization affect the institutional context of archaeology? How will professional advancement be achieved? How will universities cope with multiauthored publications or split grant overhead funds (Sabloff 1991)? Answers to those questions are speculative at present. Subject to less speculation is the assurance that a matrix organization will increase cross-disciplinary communication and will contribute to the more effective use of such scarce resources as instrumental analysis. In the process, a matrix approach to research may even force some people to make a choice between their dedication to personal advancement and their dedication to understanding the past.

Note

1. Letters to and from Anna O. Shepard are part of the Anna O. Shepard Archive curated in the Museum of the University of Colorado, Boulder. A partial synthesis of Shepard's correspondence is found in Bishop (1991).

References

Bishop, Ronald L.
    1991   Anna O. Shepard: A Correspondence Portrait. In *The Ceramic Legacy of Anna O. Shepard*, edited by Ronald L. Bishop and Frederick W. Lange, pp. 42–87. University Press of Colorado, Boulder.
Bishop, Ronald L., Veletta Canouts, Suzanne P. De Atley, and Patricia L. Crown
    1990   Sensitivity, Precision, and Accuracy: Their Roles in Ceramic Compositional Data Bases. *American Antiquity* 55:250–270.
Cordell, Linda S.
    1991   Anna O. Shepard and Southwestern Archaeology: Ignoring a Cautious Heretic. In *The Ceramic Legacy of Anna O. Shepard*, edited by Ronald L. Bishop and Frederick W. Lange, pp. 132–153. University Press of Colorado, Boulder.
De Atley, Suzanne P., and Ronald L. Bishop
    1991   Toward an Integrated Interface for Archaeology and Archaeometry. In *The Ceramic Legacy of Anna O. Shepard*, edited by Ronald L. Bishop and Frederick W. Lange, pp. 358–382. University Press of Colorado, Boulder.
Denning, Peter J.
    1987   The Science of Computing. *American Scientist* 75:572–573.
Dunnell, Robert C.
    1982   Science, Social Science, and Common Sense: The Agonizing Dilemma of Modern Archaeology. *Journal of Anthropological Research* 38:1–26.
    1986   Five Decades of American Archaeology. In *American Archaeology Past and Future: A Celebration of the Society for American Archaeology 1935–1985*, edited by

David J. Meltzer, Don D. Fowler, and Jeremy A. Sabloff, pp. 23–49. Smithsonian Institution Press, Washington, D.C.

Earle, Timothy K., and Jonathan E. Ericson (editors)
   1977   *Exchange Systems in Prehistory*. Academic Press, New York.

Gamio, Manuel
   1913   Arquelogia de Atzcapotzalco, D.F., Mexico. In *Proceedings of the Eighteenth International Congress of Americanists*, pp. 180–187. London.

Gumerman, George J., and David A. Phillips, Jr.
   1978   Archaeology Beyond Anthropology. *American Antiquity* 43:184–185.

Jope, E. M.
   1990   Preface. In *Scientific Analysis in Archaeology*, edited by Julian Henderson, pp. xi-xv. Oxford University Committee for Archaeology, Monograph No. 19, London, and UCLA Institute of Archaeology, Archaeological Research Tools 5, Los Angeles.

Kidder, Alfred V.
   1962   *An Introduction to the Study of Southwestern Archaeology*. Papers of the Phillips Academy Southwestern Expedition 1. Originally published 1924. Yale University Press, New Haven.

Kingery, W. David
   1987a   A Role for Ceramic Materials Science in Art, History, and Archaeology. *Journal of Materials Education* 9:675–718.
   1987b   Microstructure Analysis as Part of a Holistic Interpretation of Ceramic Art and Archaeological Artifacts. *Archaeomaterials* 1(2):91–99.
   1989   Technological Conservatism and Change. Paper presented at the meeting, "History from Things: A Conference on the Use of Objects for Understanding the Past," Smithsonian Institution, Washington, D.C.

Matson, Frederick R.
   1967   Pottery, Appendix A. In *The Younge Site: An Archaeological Record from Michigan*, edited by E. F. Greenman, pp. 99–124. Reprinted. Museum of Anthropology, Occasional Contributions 6. Originally published 1937. University of Michigan, Ann Arbor.

Sabloff, Jeremy A.
   1991   Toward a Future Archaeological Ceramic Science: Brief Observations from a Conference. In *The Ceramic Legacy of Anna O. Shepard*, edited by Ronald L. Bishop and Frederick W. Lange, pp. 394–400. University Press of Colorado, Boulder.

Schiffer, Michael B.
   1978   Taking the Pulse of Method and Theory in American Archaeology. *American Antiquity* 43:153–158.

Schiffer, Michael B., and James M. Skibo
   1987   Theory and Experiment in the Study of Technological Change. *Current Anthropology* 28:595–622.
   1989   A Provisional Theory of Ceramic Abrasion. *American Anthropologist* 91:101–115.

Shepard, Anna O.
   1936   The Technology of Pecos Pottery. In *The Pottery of Pecos*, vol. 2, by Alfred V. Kidder and Anna O. Shepard, pp. 389–587. Papers of the Phillips Academy Southwestern Expedition 7. Yale University Press, New Haven.
   1956   *Ceramics for the Archaeologist*. Publication 609. Carnegie Institution of Washington, Washington, D.C.

Trigger, Bruce G.
  1986 Prehistoric Archaeology and American Society. In *American Archaeology Past and Future: A Celebration of the Society for American Archaeology 1935–1985*, edited by David J. Meltzer, Don D. Fowler, and Jeremy A. Sabloff, pp. 187–216. Smithsonian Institution Press, Washington, D.C.
  1989 *A History of Archaeological Thought*. Cambridge University Press, Cambridge.

van Zelst, Lambertus
  1991 Archaeometry: The Perspective of an Administrator. In *The Ceramic Legacy of Anna O. Shepard*, edited by Ronald L. Bishop and Frederick W. Lange, pp. 346–357. University Press of Colorado, Boulder.

Warren, Stanley E.
  1982 The Education of the Archaeological Scientist. In *Future Directions in Archaeometry: A Round Table*, edited by Jacqueline S. Olin, pp. 36–38. Smithsonian Institution, Washington, D.C.

Watson, Patty Jo
  1986 Archaeological Interpretation, 1985. In *American Archaeology Past and Future: A Celebration of the Society for American Archaeology 1935–1985*, edited by David J. Meltzer, Don D. Fowler, and Jeremy A. Sabloff, pp. 439–457. Smithsonian Institution Press, Washington, D.C.

Willey, Gordon R., and Jeremy A. Sabloff
  1980 *A History of American Archaeology*. 2d ed. W. H. Freeman, San Francisco.

13. Computer Technology, Paradigms, and Quantified Archaeological Analysis

LuAnn Wandsnider and Timothy A. Kohler

Abstract: Quantified archaeological analysis has a long history in Americanist archaeology. A review of archaeological analyses suggests that researcher paradigm is reflected in the content of the analysis, while the nature of computational technology affects analytic form. Given extant and projected innovations in computer technology, the effects upon the form of quantified archaeological analysis are considered here in detail.

Introduction

Archaeological analysis is the manipulation of recorded archaeological variation so as to support some claim to knowledge about the past. Today such analysis often takes a quantitative form and is greatly facilitated by modern computing technology. Throughout the history of archaeology, however, researchers have used quantitative analysis to sustain their interpretations about the archaeological record and about the past. The actual practice of analysis reflects both the paradigm in which researchers operate as well as the technology available. Thus, we follow recent historical and sociological studies of science (e.g., Hull 1988; Rapp 1981) in assuming that both internal (e.g., paradigmatic) and external (e.g., available computing technology) factors shape the practice of archaeological analysis.

Analyses summarized in the first portion of this chapter suggest that the content of archaeological analyses is influenced by the paradigm within which researchers work. The form of analysis, however, is heavily influenced by available computing technology. Whereas other contributions to the volume consider paradigmatic concerns, this chapter focuses on our anticipations for the practice of archaeological analysis as related to technological advances. It

Quandaries and Quests: Visions of Archaeology's Future, edited by LuAnn Wandsnider. Center for Archaeological Investigations, Occasional Paper No. 20. © 1992 by the Board of Trustees, Southern Illinois University. All rights reserved. ISBN 0-88104-075-4.

is our hope that students of archaeology will find this prospectus useful as they make decisions in investing in and refurbishing analytic skills.

Quantitative Archaeological Analysis

A graph of quantification in archaeology, produced by Clark and Stafford (1982) and extended by us through 1989, is presented in Figure 13-1. This graph was constructed by reviewing all *American Antiquity* articles and reports and tallying their use of measurements, tables and charts (simple quantification), simple statistics, or multivariate statistics in presenting and analyzing archaeological data. Several interesting trends evident here deserve mention. First, in the early years of *American Antiquity*, some amount of quantified analysis is represented, with around 5% of all articles making use of tables and graphs. During the 1950s and early 1960s, the relative frequency of quantified analysis appears to fall off but, by the late 1960s, returns to that level seen in the 1930s. The rise continues and peaks in the late 1970s, with more than 20% of all *American Antiquity* articles presenting simple statistics. During the 1980s, tables and graphs continue to be used, appearing in around 25% of all articles, but simple and more complex statistics fall off to about 10%.

Clark and Stafford (1982) interpret the 1970s' peak as a manifestation of the post–World War II trend toward quantification in general, the popularity of the new archaeology, with its emphasis on using archaeological variation to answer any and all questions about the past, and the availability of mainframe computing. Others see the peak as evidence for the unfortunate concern of early new archaeologists with the trappings rather than the substance of archaeological analysis (Aldenderfer 1987:9–11; Thomas 1978). Note that the earlier quantification peak occurred in the absence of high-speed computers. No data were available for Clark and Stafford to recognize the apparent falloff in quantification we see here during the 1980s, when computers became even more accessible given the availability of well-supported statistical software packages. Assuming that *American Antiquity* has remained a constant and reliable monitor of overall trends in Americanist archaeology, then the story of quantification in Americanist archaeology is not a simple story.[1]

We shall consider several of the factors responsible for these trends. Before doing so, however, it is important to recognize the variability in what we term *quantitative archaeological analysis*. Generally, it involves one or more of three strategies. First, it may involve the description or characterization of the observed occurrence of an archaeological entity or relationship. Selection of the entity or relationship for description is either implicitly or explicitly warranted or warrantable. In the formal domain, simple descriptive statistics are frequently used to good effect. In the spatial domain, maps are exceptional communication devices.

Second, quantitative archaeological analysis might entail a targeted search for patterning within some sample of archaeological variation. In that case, the researcher uses exploratory data analysis or dimension reduction techniques

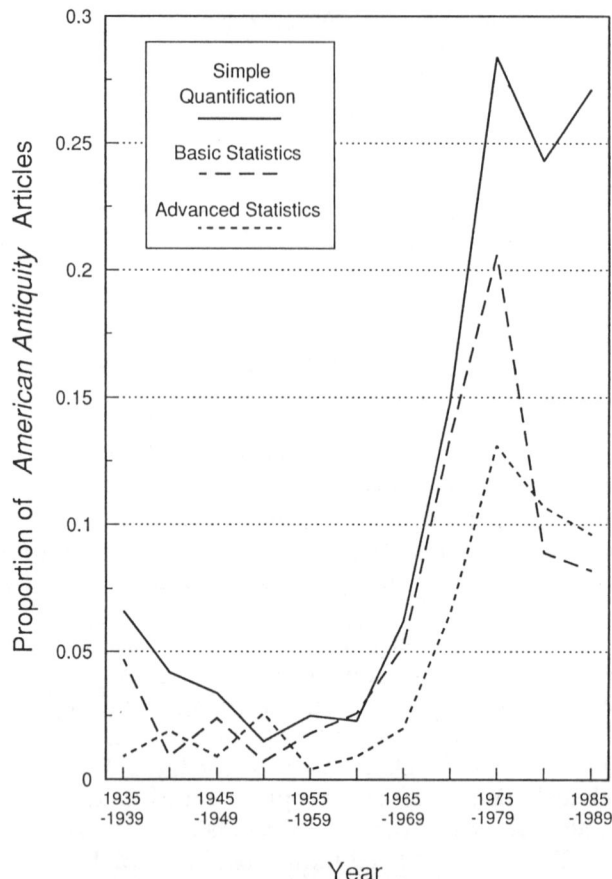

Figure 13-1. *Proportion of* American Antiquity *articles with different levels of quantification (after Clark and Stafford 1982:103).*

to find patterning. Generally, the search is not an unabashed fishing expedition; the general form of the pattern or relationship is anticipated. While described in other terms, Binford and Binford's (1966) inspection of assemblage variability in Middle Paleolithic assemblages using factor analysis of tool type proportions is an example of such a search. They selected entities (tool classes argued to be sensitive to function) that might reflect the different activities responsible for the deposit variability. They also selected a data reduction technique (factor analysis) designed to find structure, should it exist. It was left to them to interpret the identified structure according to the processual paradigm in which they operated.

Finally, archaeological analysis may include the evaluation of fit between archaeologically observed and modeled or expected phenomena. This last activity requires the prior establishment of evaluation criteria; if formally evaluated, then the criteria usually come from probability theory or are, less often, empirically generated. It also requires use of a reference body of knowledge, derived from experience or theory, to which archaeological observations are compared. The referent experience may come from archaeology, ethnography, human ecology; the referent theory, from physics, chemistry, or classical probability theory. For example, through simulation, Thomas (1972, 1973, 1975) generated selected archaeological consequences for long-term land use modeled after Steward's ethnographic experiences in the Great Basin. Using statistical tests based in normal probability theory, he evaluated the degree to which his collected data agreed with the model.

In the following sections, we examine trends in paradigmatic shifts and technological change that are reflected in the *practice* of archaeological analysis, focusing on the last analytic strategy, that incorporating some element of evaluation.

Paradigms and Quantitative Archaeological Analysis

Archaeological variation and its analysis have always played important roles in Americanist archaeology. From the 1910s through the 1940s, archaeologists confronted the problem of chronology and organized their knowledge of archaeological variation by region (Willey and Sabloff 1980). In the following decades, from 1940 to 1960, there was an increased concern with using the form and context of archaeological variation to understand function. Notions of cultural evolution were used to organize recurrent patterning in archaeological variation through time and appeared in the literature of the 1950s. In the 1960s, the emergence of the new archaeology, with its explicit concerns for culture process within an eco-evolutionary context, culture systems, and interpretative procedures, gave a renewed emphasis to the role of archaeological variation in archaeological interpretation. Archaeological variation, especially the genesis of that variation, continued to be a research focus into the 1970s and 1980s, which ethnoarchaeology and other actualistic studies addressed. With the advent of postprocessual and critical archaeologies in the 1980s and 1990s, research into other aspects of archaeological variation has occurred, with interpretations of this patterned variation directed by critical and Marxist thought.

So, the phenomenon of archaeological variation, the stuff of the archaeological record, has received constant attention over the last 70 years, although throughout this time it has been rendered in different entities and manipulated for different ends. Examples from the archaeological analysis of ceramics illustrate these tendencies.

The entities focused upon by 1940s' analyses included cultural traits, that is, artifacts or artifact configurations, artifact types, and archaeological cultures. Thus, Kroeber (1940) compared the inventories of traits documented at several archaeological sites in order to isolate those capable of defining a particular archaeological culture and to locate them in time and space. Kroeber's analysis evaluated the proximity between archaeological deposits measured by the sum of traits that were either present or absent at any pair of sites. In this example, similarity between deposits was relatively, rather than absolutely, determined. Kroeber also recognized that his analytic method was very sensitive to the traits included or excluded from the analysis.

Another example of archaeological analysis comes from the work of James Ford (1952), who focused on the entities of ceramic types and surface sites. His analytic goal was to sequence archaeological deposits using the structured variation manifested by these types. In his analysis, he employed only those ceramic types appearing to be temporally or culturally sensitive. Like Kroeber, he used similarity measures; relatively close deposits with similar proportions of ceramic types were argued to be temporally proximate.

The early 1960s' work of Whallon (1968) focused on explaining temporal trends in ceramic styles from prehistoric New York state. The work is marked by an innovation in the kind of reference knowledge employed. Both Kroeber and Ford worked solely with archaeological variation and, implicitly, with ethnographically informed commonsensical (sensu Dunnell 1982) notions of how that variation related to cultural affinity. Whallon explicitly stated the sociological implications for expected archaeological patternings in stylistic elements, assuming that women were the ceramic artisans and that the residential group was matrilocal. Thus, the reference body of knowledge against which he compared archaeological variation was sociological.

Tilley's (1984) comparative analysis of the Funnel Neck Beaker and Battle-Axe/Corded-Ware traditions in southern Sweden highlights the effects of the reference body of knowledge on interpretative results. In his analysis, Tilley also uses ceramic stylistic elements. The reference body of knowledge employed, however—derived from French Marxist anthropology—links patterning in material culture with the configuration of power within a lineage. Focusing on ceramic stylistic elements as well as architecture, he graphically and statistically evaluates the similarity between archaeological observations and experientially derived expectations.

Schiffer and Skibo's (1987) treatment of ceramic technology provides a last example of archaeological analysis. Their work focuses on building a referent body of knowledge for the functional performance of ceramics having various tempers. With this developed knowledge, they evaluate the transition from fiber- to mineral-tempered ceramics associated with the Archaic-to-Woodland transition in the American Southeast. Quantification plays an important role in this analysis, and, while not stated, the role of the computer in data storage and manipulation and in trend-description would be important. The evaluations of the fit between the archaeologically and actualistically observed are qualitative and graphic rather than statistical. On this basis, Schiffer and Skibo argue for a techno-functional interpretation of the transition.

The five examples illustrate some of the variation seen in archaeological analysis that is related to paradigm and available computer technology. It is likely that another five studies drawn from miscellaneous points in archaeological history would yield similar general insights into the content and form of archaeological analysis. Several analytic trends can be noted. First, the entities involved in analysis differ according to paradigm. Those interested in ordering archaeological cultures in time and space (e.g., Kroeber and Ford) analyzed traits and types; those seeking evidence of process (Whallon) and dominance configurations (Tilley) analyzed stylistic elements; Schiffer and Skibo analyzed the performance qualities of the ceramic attribute of temper. Interestingly, the entity of analysis is more atomic (i.e., cannot be further subdivided) in the later analyses than in the earlier.

Second, in the first two examples, the analysis is solely confined to archaeological variation. In the Whallon and Tilley examples, however, ethnographic experience provides the referent body of knowledge, although the linkages between this experience and the stuff of the archaeological record are not well developed. In the last example, by Schiffer and Skibo, the baseline knowledge against which the archaeological record is compared is derived from actualistic research.

Finally, essentially two kinds of evaluation of the goodness-of-fit between the archaeological and the referent bodies are evidenced in these studies, one statistical and the other diagnostic. The former, used by Kroeber, Whallon, and Tilley, is self-explanatory and has been facilitated by the wide availability of computer hardware and software. The latter depends on establishing a strong relationship between specific configurations of the analyzed entities, on one hand, and specific interpretations, on the other. Because Ford selected only those types known from other studies to be temporally or culturally (in the cultural-historical sense) sensitive, all observed differences and similarities between assemblages in terms of types must be referred, minimally, to these factors. Cultural affinity is thus diagnosed. Similarly, through experimental work, Schiffer and Skibo established the relationship between temper and ceramic performances. Finding that fiber- and mineral-tempered ceramics are temporally disparate, they diagnose the performance qualities of each as responsible for this variation. The existence of a theoretical basis for the entity-interpretation relationship determines the strength of the argument (Dunnell, this volume).

All of the above are examples of archaeological analysis executed from within divergent paradigms; all involve some form of evaluation and interpretation. It is apparent that the strategy of quantified analysis is not tightly coupled to the paradigm within which the analysis rests (Johnston 1986). Variation in the analytic entities, the referent bodies of knowledge, and the goals of the analysis, however, reflect the paradigm within which the researcher is working. As noted below, the junctures at which computational technology most assists archaeological analysis are in description, during evaluation (making both statistical and graphical evaluation easier), and in organizing the observed and referent bodies of knowledge.

Computer Technology and Archaeological Analysis

The definitive history of computer technology, detailing the evolution of the system of computer electronics, computer architecture, software, and educated users, has yet to be written (Mahoney 1988). Suffice it to state that since the 1940s there have been dramatic mutations in the circuitry of computers, from vacuum tubes to transistors and, later, integrated circuits (Williams 1986). Computer architecture, as it changed, did not incorporate these innovations (Smith 1989), responding instead to other demands. In general, the goal of maximizing performance has resulted in increased computation speeds. The goal of minimizing cost has resulted in friendlier and more generalized computers. And software has negotiated the gap between what performs best and is least costly, on one hand, and the user, on the other. We can map changes in quantified archaeological analysis against revolutions in computer technology related to computational speed, memory size, CPU (computer processing unit, the brain of the computer) accessibility, and access to other computers and data bases within a distributed network.

In the 1940s and 1950s, computer technology was primarily a tool of military and atomic research and also was used by government and business with volume accounting needs. By 1960, 5,000 computers were in service in areas of scientific and business computing (Mahoney 1988). During the 1960s, archaeology became one of the many consumers of computer technology. Computer-assisted analysis at that time was done via punched cards using high-level programming languages on single machines that were accessible only to white-clad attendants in a climate-controlled environment (see Evens and Bernard 1987).

During the mid-1970s, statistical packages such as BMDP (formerly Bio-Medical Data Processing), SAS (Statistical Analysis System), and SPSS (Statistical Package for the Social Sciences) became available and supported. These packages effectively made the CPU much more accessible as did the later replacement of the card reader by a command-line (usually a teletype) device. It was at that time that the peak in quantified archaeological analysis was reached. Those software packages and the availability of relatively inexpensive mass storage were used to advantage by major cultural resource management projects that generated and reported on large amounts of archaeological data.

In the mid-1980s to late 1980s, personal computers, with communication between user and CPU by keyboard and bit-mapped graphics, became readily available. The impact of these machines on archaeology until recently has been mostly in the area of manuscript preparation, rather than in analysis (see also Evans and Bernard 1987). The most recent generation of high-end microcomputers, however, are work stations that allow full-scale analysis of large archaeological data bases on the researcher's desk. Statistical and database management packages facilitating this analysis are now widely available. Also available are networks such as BITNET that allow the transmittal of manuscripts and data.

The effect of this technological revolution on archaeological analysis has been variable. Where goodness-of-fit evaluations between observed and expected used to be handled by 10 pencil-pushing graduate students or a desktop calculator, recent and modern computing technology renders it painless to a fault (see Aldenderfer 1987; Thomas 1978). Since the 1960s, computer-assisted evaluation based in classical statistics has played an important role in analysis. Additionally, evaluation that depends on inspection of graphically depicted trends and relationships (Spence and Lewandowsky 1990) is enhanced by available computer technology. This is one aspect of computer-assisted analysis that we see developing further in the near future.

Second, the number-crunching capabilities of mainframe and contemporary desktop computers mean that dimension reduction as part of pattern searching can be executed with relatively little agony. Again, this computational ease has made for past infractions, from which the discipline appears to have recovered.

Third, the reduced cost of data storage that is part of the technological revolution means that large data bases can be accommodated. Through formation process research, researchers recognize that each archaeological deposit is ultimately unique (e.g., Stein 1987). Therefore, comparative analysis to assign and assess levels of similarity and uniqueness (Chippendale 1989) can only proceed if the archaeologist has available multiple cases of an archaeological phenomenon in multiple contexts. The demand for a large number of cases places additional requirements on analytic technology; large storage capacities are necessary as is software to manipulate this bulk. Thus, it is only recently that the computing technology required by archaeological data analysis has appeared.

Computer-Assisted Archaeological Analysis: A Prospectus

While the signs of paradigmatic crisis (Kuhn 1962) are all about us, it is not yet possible to identify the exact direction of the discipline, what the content of archaeological analysis will be, or how long before consensus emerges. Nevertheless, projections about technology availability over the next decade can be made, and they suggest the form that analysis will assume. Here, we identify several technology-based analytic trends and point to issues that bear directly on the power of analysis to inform archaeology.

Again, we refer to computing technology in terms of computational speed, memory capacity, accessibility, and connectivity. The cost for 100 MIPS (million instructions per second) has decreased from about $5,000 in 1980 to $500 in 1990 and is expected to decrease tenfold by 1995 (Campbell 1989). Magnetic and optical storage that is cheaper, has a larger capacity, and is capable of rapid information retrieval, projected a decade ago, is currently available. Under development are communications networks that are fast, handle graphics and voice, and support interactive processing on remote machines as easily as BITNET now handles words (Palca 1990). Translation of voice and handwriting into stored and retrieved characters is likewise in the offing.

The major effects of the innovations have yet to be felt, primarily owing to lags in the development of software that can tap this potential (Allen 1989). Yet there are two analytic areas where the impact can immediately be seen by archaeologists: spatial-formal analysis and empirically generated evaluation criteria.

So-called spatial analysis in archaeology has largely lacked a spatial element. Rather, it has consisted of formal analysis of the elements found in space as partitioned according to some criteria (e.g., Whallon 1984; see Wandsnider 1989:173–216). The expense involved in manipulating spatial data and the lack of software have been primarily responsible for spatially deficient spatial analysis. Geographic Information Systems (GIS) are configurations of hardware and software that allow the user to easily commute between the spatial and the formal domains. Probably there has not been a single meeting of the Society for American Archaeology over the last decade where the imminent arrival of GIS technology, touted as on par with radiocarbon dating, has not been heralded. Yet any impact from this technology has remained perennially on the horizon owing to the costs of purchasing and maintaining the hardware and the costs of generating and inputing the huge amounts of data required for interesting applications. To date, these costs have remained high enough that only organizations with distant time horizons could anticipate a payback on the investment. Consequently, most applications have been oriented more toward agency management of cultural resources than toward interesting research. But initial costs are coming down, as are the costs of storage technology, archival software, and various technologies for data input and display. GIS software for work stations and large PCs is now widely available, and the impact to archaeology is just beginning to be explored (e.g., Allen et al. 1990). We can project that applications of the kind attempted by Binford (1987), that is, deliberately working between the spatial and the formal domains, may follow.

In the area of formal evaluation, of import are the software innovations in bootstrapping. Bootstrapping is a method of empirically generating evaluation criteria from either the data themselves or from a theoretically derived source (Stine 1990). Classical statistical theory was developed to deal with the limitations of technology, which could not support the multiple computations required to determine confidence intervals to evaluate the fit between any and every conceivable body of data and some expected form. With the advent of low-cost computing, the injunction to conserve scarce computing resources is lifted. Thus, assumptions about the normality of the population of phenomena sampled by the archaeologist, which are either skirted by using less robust statistical tests or else violated, become unimportant. In archaeology and in other nonexperimental sciences featuring data with a multivariate nature, large bulk, variable levels of measurement, and indirect interpretation, bootstrap and similar analytic procedures offer much promise (see, for example, contributions to Fox and Long 1990).

Kintigh's (1984) use of such methods to evaluate the diversity of assemblages is one example of the potential of this application.

Two other important areas where archaeology can anticipate change is in educating students in analysis and in the production of analytic procedures tailored to archaeological problems. Both follow from recent software developments that further improve the access of the user to the CPU and that minimize the agonies of software development.

With respect to the user interface, the once more common command-line interface is gradually being supplanted by the Graphic User Interface (GUI), a standard feature on the Apple MacIntosh and now, owing to software enhancements, available in the DOS environment. The GUI is visually oriented and allows communication with the computer via pointers, windows, menus, and dialogues. The advantage of the system is its friendliness, which translates to speed when initially learning a piece of software or procedure and its subsequent use. Where previously archaeological students spent months learning how to communicate with the CPU, the learning curve is reduced to hours per application. Months not spent learning when to type "SAVE" versus "FILE" can be spent learning the art and science of archaeological analysis.

A second major software development is that of Object-Oriented Programming (OOP), first introduced in the late 1970s. An object is a data structure inherent to which are the methods for manipulating those data (Snydam 1990). The user builds procedures by copying an object from a library that contains all commonly used objects, modifying it slightly, and adding it to a sequence of similarly defined objects. The "wheels" needed by the user are already present and need not be reinvented; it is left to the user to modify and assemble the available components to make a bicycle or a roadster. OOP still requires that the user know what he or she is doing. But, by programming with objects, software development time is reduced. Where today individual archaeologists in scattered institutions may redundantly develop software to perform a single task, members of the archaeological community could conceivably contribute to and withdraw from a pool of object-based analytic tools that, through use, could be modified and improved. Thus, OOP should enable the development of software tailored to archaeological needs, which Carr (1985) and Dibble (1990) have identified as desirable and necessary.

One final critical element in archaeological analysis is that of archaeological data. Two issues, their quality and their comparability, deserve comment. Cowgill (1986, 1989) has distinguished archaeological data as being of poor, variable, or unknown quality. Clark (1987:52) suggests that the poor quality of archaeological data is responsible for the limited contribution that quantified archaeological analysis has made to archaeology. By poor quality, Clark alludes to the weak integrity of archaeological deposits, the coarse temporal grain of those deposits, sampling error, and something he calls "incomplete data." From his discussion, it is not clear which agents Clark views as responsible for poor data quality. If by "sampling error" he means that the archaeological record represents a biased sample of prehistoric behavior (see Collins 1975), and if by "incomplete data" he means that not all behaviors are archaeologically preserved, then formation processes are responsible for poor data quality. If that interpretation of Clark is correct, then it appears that Clark is intent on conducting ethnography with the archaeological record. With such a goal, anything that prevents the preservation of materials referable to brief behavioral episodes yields an archaeological record with poor ethnographic data quality. If, however, the archaeological record is viewed as a contemporary phenomenon that represents a variable record of most formation processes (as per Binford's 1975 comments on Collins), then, by definition, poor data quality can only be produced through poor data collection procedures of the archaeologist. It is to this area that Cowgill directs his efforts.

In addition to data quality, the issue of data comparability becomes important in an age of networks when data can easily be shared around the world. The recent experiences of large projects such as the Dolores Archaeological Program in southwest Colorado are pertinent here. Although even this project experienced some minor data comparability problems (Kohler et al. 1988), the most interesting things we have been able to say about the past for this area are derived from having excavated a number of sites using the same protocols and having analyzed the materials in the same way.

To take maximum advantage of the current and arriving computational technology, we must seek greater comparability across projects in data collection, from field techniques to data recording to analysis of recovered materials. No one would argue that all data must be standardized, but entrepreneurs must innovate beyond a core of commonality that is relatively much larger than at present and then convince others to add (rather than substitute) their techniques or variables to the common core.

Of course, deciding how to standardize will require a great deal of reflection. Archaeological typologies typically compress multidimensional information about materials into nominal classes. It is easier to say "Weeden Island Zoned Red" than to specify all of the variable states along the various dimensions of hue and intensity, nature and distribution of stylistic elements, mineral content of paint, and so forth. Typologies are used, however, to communicate more than physical description. By design, they also impart something about analytic domain, be it cultural affinity, time, function, or something else.

Some of the first applications of computing technology to archaeology were in the area of numerical taxonomy and objective typology-building, with disappointing results (see Read 1989). This was clearly an attempt to use the computer to perform traditional tasks more quickly and "objectively" rather than an attempt to rethink our analyses entirely. While the computer as a skeuomorph has let us down in helping to find such typologies, it has the potential to aid in communication using dimensions rather than types. For example, until recently the coding of chipped-stone debitage referenced a typology with flake types classified as primary, secondary, and tertiary. Frequencies of items summarized according to this system communicated consistent information, but only for assemblages from a single project coded by a single analyst. To facilitate interassemblage comparison, reports of reliably measured variable states along specific dimensions, rather than typological states, are required. It requires more space to store data on amount of cortex, number of dorsal scars, number of platform scars, and so forth, but this constraint is becoming increasingly unimportant with decreasing storage costs.

Advances in computer technology have contributed and will continue to contribute in other critical ways to the practice of archaeological analysis. That is, by advancing further the democratization of the field, we see important consequences for the growth and maintenance of paradigms and for the conduct of analysis. Twenty years ago, not all archaeology programs had access to mainframe computing. Further, only the wealthier programs could call upon university support personnel and graduate students to aid in their battle with the mainframe. When it came time for publication, archaeologists in such programs could also count on secretarial assistance to type and retype several drafts of their monographs and could talk their chairs or deans into funds for completing the essential drafting. It should be clear that archaeologists in elite programs enjoyed a huge advantage in the data analysis and publication phases of their projects, as they did in support for fieldwork.

Those advantages have begun to evaporate and will continue to do so over the next ten years. Relatively cheap computers can now do the record shuffling, statistical analysis, and preparation of manuscripts and graphics, formerly the province of graduate students and secretaries (Evans and Bernard 1987). Moreover, dedicated assistance from a central computing center or graduate student wizards in JCL (IBM Job Control Language) and SPSS have become increasingly irrelevant with consistent graphical user interfaces and large, easy-to-use integrated programs for data analysis and graphics running on a desktop. Equal access over broadband networks to the nation's fastest supercomputers will further erode institutional advantages.

Concluding Remarks

To rephrase Thomas (1978:242), computer-assisted archaeological analysis is here to stay. The subject of that analysis is still under debate, as other contributions to this volume attest. With continuing advances in computational systems, especially in software and in the sophistication of the user, the potential contribution of quantified analysis to the entertainment of archaeological questions is great. The mutable nature of the computational resources now available is such that the student of archaeology should be able to construct tools tailored to the needs of archaeological analysis, especially in the areas of evaluation and in spatial-formal analysis. This accommodating nature also invites renewed thought on conceptual, rather than technological, constraints of data acquisition and communication. Beyond merely "riding the data winds" (Martin 1980:34) in a faster, sleeker vehicle, archaeologists armed with these tools now have the opportunity to seize control and pilot the good ship "Archaeological Analysis" to the desired interpretive shore.

Acknowledgments

We thank George Pasdirtz for his insights on computer-assisted quantitative analysis and Peter Bleed and Alan Osborn for comments on an earlier draft.

Note

1. We also assume that our evaluation of more recent *American Antiquity* articles is comparable with that made by Clark and Stafford (1982) for the earlier series. In that we present this information using proportions rather than frequencies, our graph appears different from that of Clark and Stafford in detail but not overall trend.

References

Aldenderfer, Mark S.
    1987   Assessing the Impact of Quantitative Thinking on Archaeological Research: Historical and Evolutionary Insight. In *Quantitative Research in Archaeology*, edited by Mark S. Aldenderfer, pp. 9–29. Sage Publications, Beverly Hills, California.

Allen, Dennis
    1989   The Status of Software Applications: Late. *Byte* 14(11):269.

Allen, K., S. W. Green, and E. B. W. Zubrow (editors)
    1990   *Interpreting Space: GIS in Archaeology*. Taylor and Francis, London.

Binford, Lewis R.
    1975   Sampling, Judgement, and the Archaeological Record. In *Sampling in Archaeology*, edited by James W. Mueller, pp. 251–257. University of Arizona Press, Tucson.
    1987   Researching Ambiguity: Frames of Reference and Site Structure. In *Method and Theory for Activity Area Research*, edited by Susan Kent, pp. 449–512. Columbia University Press, New York.

Binford, Lewis R., and Sally R. Binford
    1966   A Preliminary Analysis of Functional Variability in the Mousterian of Levallois Facies. *American Anthropologist* 68:238–295.

Campbell, Gordon A.
    1989   Inventing the PC's Future. *Byte* 14(11):229.

Carr, Christopher
    1985   Perspective and Basic Definitions. In *For Concordance in Archaeological Analysis*, edited by Christopher Carr, pp. 1–17. Waveland Press, Prospect Heights, Illinois.

Chippendale, Christopher
    1989   Philosophical Lessons from the History of Stonehenge Studies. In *Critical*

Traditions in Contemporary Archaeology, edited by Valerie Pinsky and Alison Wylie, pp. 68–79. Cambridge University Press, Cambridge.

Clark, G. A.
1987 Paradigms and Paradoxes in Contemporary Archaeology. In *Quantitative Research in Archaeology*, edited by Mark S. Aldenderfer, pp. 30–60. Sage Publications, Beverly Hills, California.

Clark, G. A., and C. R. Stafford
1982 Quantification in American Archaeology: Historical Perspective. *World Archaeology* 14:98–119.

Collins, Michael B.
1975 Sources of Bias in Processual Data: An Appraisal. In *Sampling in Archaeology*, edited by James W. Mueller, pp. 26–32. University of Arizona Press, Tucson.

Cowgill, George L.
1986 Archaeological Application of Mathematical and Formal Methods. In *American Archaeology Past and Future: A Celebration of the Society for American Archaeology 1935–1985*, edited by David J. Meltzer, Don D. Fowler, and Jeremy A. Sabloff, pp. 369–394. Smithsonian Institution Press, Washington, D.C.
1989 Formal Approaches in Archaeology. In *Archaeological Thought in America*, edited by C. C. Lamberg-Karlovsky, pp. 74–88. Cambridge University Press, Cambridge.

Dibble, Harold L.
1990 A Personal Perspective on the Computerization of Archaeology. *Bulletin of the Society for American Archaeology* 8(5):9–10.

Dunnell, Robert C.
1982 Science, Social Science, and Common Sense: The Agonizing Dilemma of Modern Archaeology. *Journal of Anthropological Research* 38:1–25.

Evans, Michael, and H. Russell Bernard
1987 Word Processing, Office Drudgery, and the Microcomputer Revolution. In *Technology and Social Change*, 2d ed., edited by H. Russell Bernard and Pertti Pelto, pp. 359–376. Waveland Press, Prospect Heights, Illinois.

Ford, James A.
1952 Measurements of Some Prehistoric Design Developments in the Southeastern States. *Anthropological Papers of the American Museum of Natural History* 44.

Fox, John, and J. Scott Long (editors)
1990 *Modern Methods of Data Analysis*. Sage Publications, Newbury Park, California.

Hull, David
1988 *The Process of Science*. University of Chicago Press, Chicago.

Johnston, R. J.
1986 *On Human Geography*. Basil Blackwell, Oxford.

Kintigh, Keith
1984 Measuring Archaeological Diversity by Comparison with Simulated Assemblages. *American Antiquity* 49:44–54.

Kohler, Timothy A., Carl J. Phagan, and Eric Blinman
1988 Sources of Confounding Variability in Archaeological Collections. In *Dolores Archaeological Program: Supporting Studies: Additive and Reductive Technologies*, compiled by Eric Blinman, Carl J. Phagan, and Richard H.

Wilshusen, pp. 487–499. U.S. Department of the Interior, Bureau of Reclamation, Denver.

Kroeber, A. L.
    1940   Statistical Classification. *American Antiquity* 6(1):29–44.

Kuhn, Thomas S.
    1962   *The Structure of Scientific Revolutions.* University of Chicago Press, Chicago.

Mahoney, Michael S.
    1988   The History of Computing in the History of Technology. *Annals of the History of Computing* 10:113–125.

Martin, George R. R.
    1980 Nightflyers. *Analog* 50(4):5–105.

Palca, Joseph
    1990   Getting Together Bit by Bit. *Science* 248:160–162.

Rapp, Friedrich
    1981   *Analytical Philosophy of Technology.* Boston Studies in the Philosophy of Science, vol. 63. D. Reidel, Dordrecht, Holland.

Read, Dwight W.
    1989   Statistical Methods and Reasoning in Archaeological Research: A Review of Praxis and Promise. *Journal of Quantitative Anthropology* 1(1/2):5–78.

Schiffer, Michael B., and James M. Skibo
    1987   Theory and Experiment in the Study of Technological Change. *Current Anthropology* 28(5):595–622.

Smith, Richard E.
    1989   A Historical Overview of Computer Architecture. *Annals of the History of Computing* 16:277–303.

Snydam, Bill
    1990   Smalltalk as a Programming Environment. *Computer Language* 7(4):34–40.

Spence, Ian, and Stephan Lewandowsky
    1990   Graphical Perception. In *Modern Methods of Data Analysis*, edited by J. Fox and J. S. Long, pp. 13–57. Sage Publications, Newbury Park, California.

Stein, Julie K.
    1987   Deposits for Archaeologists. In *Advances in Archaeological Method and Theory*, vol. 11, edited by Michael B. Schiffer, pp. 337–395. Academic Press, New York.

Stine, Robert
    1990   An Introduction to Bootstrap Methods: Examples and Ideas. In *Modern Methods of Data Analysis*, edited by J. Fox and J. S. Long, pp. 325–373. Sage Publications, Newbury Park, California.

Thomas, David Hurst
    1972   A Computer Simulation Model of Great Basin Shoshonean Settlement Patterns. In *Models in Archaeology*, edited by David L. Clarke, pp. 671–704. Methuen, London.
    1973   An Empirical Test of Steward's Model of Great Basin Settlement Patterns. *American Antiquity* 38:155–176.
    1975   Nonsite Sampling in Archaeology: Up the Creek Without a Site? In *Sampling in Archaeology*, edited by James W. Mueller, pp. 61–81. University of Arizona Press, Tucson.

1978 The Awful Truth about Statistics in Archaeology. *American Antiquity* 43:231–244.

Tilley, Christopher
   1984 Ideology and Legitimation of Power in the Middle Neolithic of Southern Sweden. In *Ideology, Power and Prehistory*, edited by Daniel Miller and Christopher Tilley, pp. 111–146. Cambridge University Press, Cambridge.

Wandsnider, LuAnn
   1989 *Long-term Land Use, Formation Processes, and the Structure of the Archaeological Landscape: A Case Study from Southwestern Wyoming*. Ph.D. Dissertation, University of New Mexico. University Microfilms, Ann Arbor.

Whallon, Robert, Jr.
   1968 Investigations of Late Prehistoric Social Organization in New York State. In *New Perspectives in Archaeology*, edited by Sally R. Binford and Lewis R. Binford, pp. 223–244. Aldine, Chicago.
   1984 Unconstrained Clustering for the Analysis of Spatial Distributions in Archaeology. In *Intrasite Spatial Analysis in Archaeology*, edited by Harold Hietala, pp. 242–277. Cambridge University Press, Cambridge.

Willey, Gordon R., and Jeremy A. Sabloff
   1980 *History of American Archaeology*. 2d ed. W. H. Freeman, San Francisco.

Williams, M.
   1986 *A History of Computing Technology*. Prentice-Hall, Englewood Cliffs, New Jersey.

14. Ethnoarchaeology: Obnoxious Spectator, Trivial Pursuit, or the Keys to a Time Machine?

Steven R. Simms

Abstract: Prospecting a future for ethnoarchaeology will require attention to at least three issues. Ethnoarchaeology tends to employ a style of discourse that limits itself to cautionary tales. Most ethnoarchaeology fails to employ the techniques of typology and analyses common to field archaeology, especially in increasingly standardized CRM contexts, and that lack of operationalization also limits its contribution. Ethnoarchaeology can correct some of the problems with minor adjustments, but the pioneering research will come from an explicit attempt to go beyond consideration of middle-range issues and incorporate general theory into ethnoarchaeological research strategies. In this way, ethnoarchaeology can help explain behavioral systems in addition to furthering a descriptive decoding of the past.

Introduction

Predicting the future is treacherous, but since the future of scientific disciplines can be created, it may be more useful to anticipate, or prospect. The "history" of ethnoarchaeology has left some marks, and I identify some of them, not to review the literature or even to evaluate our progress so far, but as points of departure for anticipating a future. I speak to three points selected from a broad array of ethnoarchaeology:

1. Ethnoarchaeology is well known for its ability to evaluate assumptions used by archaeologists. While serving as useful correctives, the evaluations have most frequently been presented in a style of argumentation that has come to be known as "cautionary tales." With the passage of time, that practice has put ethnoarchaeology in the unflattering role of obnoxious spectator. In the future, practitioners may transcend that limited role.

Quandaries and Quests: Visions of Archaeology's Future, edited by LuAnn Wandsnider. Center for Archaeological Investigations, Occasional Paper No. 20. © 1992 by the Board of Trustees, Southern Illinois University. All rights reserved. ISBN 0-88104-075-4.

2. Numerous ethnographic analogies have been produced under the rubric of ethnoarchaeology. This combines with a high frequency of poor linkage to practical archaeology and leads to a trivial pursuit. I explore this phenomenon as evident in the cultural resource management (CRM) literature and suggest a need for better operationalization of the ethnographic with the archaeological in the course of ethnoarchaeological research. In this way, ethnoarchaeology can realize its potential to redirect archaeological research.

3. I conclude with a perhaps naive vision of a time machine, but, after all, the future of science demands a certain optimism. Besides, pessimism, like a cautionary tale, is easy. I briefly discuss the prospects for linkages between the mundane of the middle range that preoccupies ethnoarchaeology with the excitement of the exploration of ultimate causation found only in general theory. General theory is not offered as a panacea. However, attention to the higher levels could help mitigate the negative effects of the obnoxious spectator. It could do the same for the trivial pursuit of an ethnoarchaeology spawning schools of ethnographic analogies with unstated relevance for practical archaeology.

A Boundless Ethnoarchaeology

Ethnoarchaeology was one of those terms engendered during the sixties, a time of reflection, upheaval, and idealism in archaeology. In the wake of debate over whether anything new was actually happening, whether it was simply ethnography or whether it was an invention of burgeoning numbers of archaeologists hungry to carve an intellectual niche, there is now clear recognition of the term *ethnoarchaeology* in the professional lexicon. For most, ethnoarchaeology is here to stay as a category to help explore something very old in archaeology—the means of inference (Grayson 1986). On this level there is nothing new. On the other hand, the concerns and some of the failures of the new archaeology of the 1960s attuned us to the importance of an explicit concern with middle-range issues to help "decode" a difficult and misleading archaeological record (Binford 1983b).

Ethnoarchaeology has typically been seen as one facet of middle-range research or theory. Whether ethnoarchaeologists tend toward the optimistic positivism of Schiffer (e.g., 1976), the methodological processualism (in practice) of Binford (e.g., 1983a), the more explicitly hierarchical view of Raab and Goodyear (1984), or all of the above, understanding the middle range is important.

A less bounded ethnoarchaeology is advocated here so I employ a definition that displays, but is not limited to, a concern with the middle range. Ethnoarchaeology is research attempting to bond the patterned relationships between the static material remains that constitute the archaeological record and some of the corresponding but dynamic behaviors responsible for the creation of that record. This definition is pliable enough to allow for ethnoarchaeology to grade into other named realms such as historic archaeology (Schiffer 1978) and experimental archaeology (Ingersoll et al.

1978). It is also open enough to accommodate study of the systemic causes of behavioral form that subsequently shape the material record. As we look to the future, it may be useful to question the limitation of ethnoarchaeology to the middle range. Ethnoarchaeology should be just as useful in general theory building. The potential becomes clearer and more urgent as we examine some of the characteristics of ethnoarchaeology.

Ethnoarchaeology as an Obnoxious Spectator

Prior to the crystallization of an ethnoarchaeology, the new archaeology pursued an ambitious "decoding" of the archaeological record. But many of the early (and decidedly nonethnographic) studies of middle-range issues prompted easy critiques. In general, ethnoarchaeology opened the eyes of a discipline whose ambition to be prehistoric ethnography often outstripped the potential of available data (e.g., Bonnichsen 1973; David 1971; Donnan and Clewlow 1974; Gould 1971; Longacre and Ayres 1968; O'Connell 1974). At the same time, critiques of analogy as a general philosophical issue flowed anew, and cautions were plentiful.

In the mid-1970s Diane Gifford made an observation about ethnoarchaeology that could apply today. Soon after participating in the seminar that led to the volume *Explorations in Ethnoarchaeology* (Gould 1978), she spoke of the dangers of ethnoarchaeology's negative commentary, an ethnoarchaeology that can only correct, or define, the limits of archaeology but that is less than explicit in directing *practical* archaeology.

Indeed, correctives are still needed, and the remedy need not be so extreme as Bambi's admonition to Thumper, "If you can't say something nice, don't say anything at all." But even in cases where ethnoarchaeological research actually includes an archaeological component potentially applicable to the realities of surveys and excavations, it is common to see only vague generalizations based more on ethnography than archaeology. I submit that the lack of clear linkage often stems from the cautionary style of the "suggestions," testifying to the lack of operationalization typical in ethnoarchaeological comment. I do not offer these observations for historical purposes—the trend continues.

Ethnoarchaeology's Trivial Pursuit and the Redirection of Archaeological Research

Ethnoarchaeology and middle-range research highlight the role of analogy in scientific reasoning. The important consideration is how analogy is employed, and a constructive reading of the cautionary literature shows that progress has been made. For instance, there is less ambition toward reconstructing past social systems as conceptualized by ethnographers and more emphasis on identifying behavioral realities such as group size, mobility, and gender (see, for instance, Whitelaw 1989).

This trend suggests that ethnoarchaeology is aware that analogies will always be produced and employed but cannot be employed well in the absence of a consideration of the archaeological. However, I see a huge gulf between the analogies generated by ethnoarchaeologists and their employment by practical field archaeologists. As long as ethnoarchaeology remains happy with the generation of vast numbers of possible analogies, leaving the archaeologists to figure out what to do with them, ethnoarchaeology will risk the label of a trivial pursuit.

One place to really see the effects of ethnoarchaeological effort is in the everyday technical reports produced in archaeology, especially the CRM literature. This literature is the modern engine of archaeological knowledge on an international scale (see Simmons, this volume), and it increasingly reflects interaction with ethnoarchaeology.

When the results of ethnoarchaeology are presented as cautions or vague implications to the practical archaeologist operating under ever-expanding constraints and standards, the problems associated with the abuse of analogy are exacerbated. The technical literature in CRM indicates this. One need not cite the extreme abuses of analogy in often regionally potent CRM reports because they are probably the exception. However, consider the potential for abuses of analogy by noting how many prehistoric cases in North America are interpreted with reference to the Nunamiut (especially Binford 1978), the !Kung (especially Yellen 1977), a few comparative treatises (*especially* Binford 1980), and an overlay of whatever direct historical analogs are available.[1]

It is easy to lay the blame on field archaeologists' continuing to practice the traditional ex post facto and intuitive means of interpretation, with an overlay of ethnoarchaeologically generated analogs. However, it is arguable that ethnoarchaeology has with few exceptions gone the easy route—failing to make full linkage with archaeology in shaping *how* analogs are applied and how ethnoarchaeological research affects day-to-day field practices, typologies, analyses, and interpretation. The amount of ethnoarchaeology *that involves no archaeology at all* testifies to this. By archaeology, I mean the application of procedures, categorizations, and especially analyses that are becoming increasingly standardized in cultural resource bureaucracies. How often do we see the use of flotation for botanical or microrefuse analysis, plant phytolith analysis, lithic use wear analysis, or geomorphology in ethnoarchaeological settings? This degree of linkage represents the minority of ethnoarchaeology.

As an example of the potential for ethnoarchaeology to redirect archaeology, even CRM policy, I refer to my own experiences in archaeological and ethnoarchaeological studies of perishable housing in the Great Basin (Simms 1989; Simms and Heath 1990) and portable housing in Arabia (Russell and Simms 1991; Simms 1988). A study of protohistoric and historic wickiups compares the location of structures to various types and patterns of debris (Simms 1989). The goal is to improve the means of inference for cases deeper in prehistory where the temporary houses have vanished from easy detection at the surface and may be difficult to directly recognize through subsurface investigation.

Without getting too involved here, one of the messages of that study for policy is that current criteria for defining and recording sites in the Great Basin, and especially criteria for test excavation, exacerbate the problem. We are left with potentially misleading interpretations about the function of sites based on negative evidence (i.e., there are no residential structures here so this must be a ———) spawned by years of routine practice that out of sheer tradition have evolved into agency policy. Furthermore, the apparent paucity of debris in and immediately around many such structures has led to the attitude that little can be learned.

If my study of the debris and structures in the preserved cases, a de facto form of ethnoarchaeology, had only played the role of obnoxious spectator and pointed out how misleading lithic scatters can be, the negative attitude toward the sites would only be strengthened. The work would have exemplified a trivial pursuit. Therefore, it became imperative for the "ethnoarchaeology" to spell out what could be done in such cases. This was attempted in an application of ethnoarchaeology to improve the interpretation of a fifteenth-century camp, a purely archaeological case (Simms and Heath 1990). Our ethnoarchaeological studies of portable bedouin housing in Jordan (Russell and Simms 1991; Simms 1988) brings this thinking to another region and may improve our ability to recognize early phases of pastoral nomadism.

An ethnoarchaeology that practices archaeology is in a position to redirect the lines of archaeological investigation toward the issues and questions that can be addressed in the mundane world of real archaeology. Despite the value of ethnoarchaeology for correcting interpretation, improving the means of inference, and shaping archaeological research or perhaps even policy, none of the studies cited in the above example evaluates or influences general theory. This is perhaps the most unrealized potential of ethnoarchaeology.

Ethnoarchaeology and Theory: Another Level

In 1982 Barbara Price wrote,

> What is surprising, however, is that the "new archaeology" begins its downward deductions at so resolutely middle a level, precluding significant generalization and producing a corpus of work remarkable (at least in retrospect and given its initially revolutionary program) for its intellectual conservatism. Interest in the higher levels has, if anything, dwindled. Despite the early focus on the discovery of laws there remains a sense of trivialization. . . . The results "float," unanchored at the top (1982:714).

Operating in the wake of the new archaeology, ethnoarchaeology takes much of its character from the habits of the former, including what may be termed a preoccupation with the middle range. To be sure, concern with middle-range research is of great importance, but explanation of archaeological data may still not be at hand simply by the piecemeal addition of bridging arguments to everyday archaeological data. There remains the role of general theory, not as something rarified and "unanchored" to the empirical world, but as the very glass we use to perceive *both* the middle range and our explanation of the past.

David Thomas's (1983a, 1983b, 1988) study in Monitor Valley provides an example of the need for this link. A study of changing subsistence and settlement over several millennia, this work has been deservedly complimented as an example (as one reviewer put it, the *best* example) of the application of ethnoarchaeology and the middle range to a substantive problem in prehistory.

Thomas attempted to operationalize ethnoarchaeology and other middle-range research to distinguish up to five contrasting adaptive strategies. The project was a model of modern research design and linkage between fieldwork and middle-range research but remained chained to Great Basin ethnographic analogy, especially the work of Julian Steward. Thomas tapped into everything ethnoarchaeology had to offer to try and operationalize middle-range knowledge (much of it ethnoarchaeological) in a specific case, but there was nothing in the middle-range work that helped him to break the confines of the historical analogies he employed and nothing to indicate how and why these systems evolved. In the end, the conclusions were limited to empirical generalizations.

The fault does not lie in Thomas's choosing to use the historical analogs, nor is something wrong with empirical generalization. The problem is that middle-range research based on cross-cultural comparisons (analogies) *by itself* cannot lead to an explanation of the system. Such knowledge would enable predictions beyond those analogs provided by history or modern experience. The study suffers from a lack of general theory.

For the purposes of argumentation I offer the challenge that archaeology must be able to identify past behavioral systems with no modern systemic analogy. Portions of such past systems (individual sites, site types, site formation processes, etc.) may be found in modern analogs—hence, the importance of middle-range research—but the systemic consequence of those analogies could conceivably be systems previously unknown, unimagined, and even "counter-intuitive" (intuition being a culture-bound concept). If we really want to step into our time machine, into prehistory, this is appropriate, at least as a guiding goal. As with all lofty goals, complete realization of the above challenge may be impossible. But let's not throw the ethnoarchaeological baby out with the bath of impracticality.

In order to approach this challenge, explorations of the middle range will have to co-occur with the application of models about the expected shape of the world generated from *general theories of behavior*. Some of the postprocessualists may be talking about this (Hodder 1982; but more explicitly, Kobylinski 1989), but I suspect that the paradigm(s) of this group will prevent any work along these lines from going beyond more cautions. Gould (1985) realizes the need to go beyond analogy but seems to see the different approaches as just different kinds of ethnoarchaeology, a matter of "themes." Binford (1977, 1985) is closer to the mark in seeing the different lines of questioning in ethnoarchaeology as stemming from fundamental differences in paradigms. He has long argued for more explicit attention to higher level constructs, but in practice he remains decidedly middle range. Nevertheless, much recent thinking sets the stage for a move to an ethnoarchaeological-archaeological research program that integrates what is currently isolated as middle- and high-level theory under the tacit assumption that theory is the simple sum of empirical generalizations decoded from the archaeological record.

Maybe Price was right when she accused the new archaeology of "intellectual conservatism" and "a sense of trivialization." The label may in fact be appropriate for the humanist and social science enterprise in general (see Dunnell, this volume). We often seem preoccupied with validating the complexity we can all readily acknowledge rather than finding ways through it. Historians of archaeology continue to juxtapose complexity with determinism (Trigger 1989:367), wrongly assuming that we can only have one of the two and ensuring that explanation will never amount to more than some agreed-upon increase in descriptive "understanding." We can hope to transcend the knee-jerk denunciations of the determinism and the reductionism common to disciplines such as evolutionary biology (see Dunnell, this volume, for some reasons why this may not happen).

Behavioral ecology, for one, seems more comfortable in braving the dangerous waters of reductionism, realizing that models must begin simple and reduced in order to evaluate the role(s) of different variables in shaping the consequent complex system (humans do not corner the market on learned behavioral and social complexity). By making simple and expectedly inadequate predictions, the amount of variation that can be explained by a simple model can be compared to that which cannot be explained. Additional variables can then be brought into play, building a more comprehensive model. In that way, alternative models predicting what the organism should be doing as circumstances vary can be offered and then compared with ethnoarchaeologically documented behaviors, other middle-range studies, and the bridges they build to the actual material record.

The additional ingredient in a theory that can model the historically unknown is some knowledge of and assumptions about the fundamental processes of the system. Middle-range research, with the analogs we have at hand in the modern world provides this, but the critique of Raab and Goodyear (1984) still stands—the practice of middle-range research is decidedly methodological. Archaeologists have remained reluctant to employ general evolutionary theory, especially that occurring under the rubric of behavioral ecology (note the absence of references in this vein even in Dunnell's advocacy for evolutionary thinking, this volume).

In essence, what I have advocated here is the use of general theory to generate hypotheses that are tested ethnoarchaeologically prior to archaeological application. The hypotheses for testing would be the same as those we would want to test archaeologically but would allow us to evaluate the proposition more expeditiously than if forced to rely only upon the difficult and fragmentary archaeological record.

All theories employ assumptions, and in the case of behavioral ecology, the theory of natural selection is the driving force to develop models based on "selection thinking" (e.g., Blurton-Jones 1976; Foley 1987; Krebs and Davies 1984; Standen and Foley 1989; Stephens and Krebs 1986).[2]

Recognizing the work is nascent, I offer some examples of studies stimulated by general evolutionary theory as it might be applied to ethnoarchaeology and archaeology. I offer behavioral ecology as one example of general theory capable of directing ethnoarchaeological inquiry; anthropology still holds the potential to generate its own.

Ethnoarchaeological Explorations and General Theory

Kelly and Todd (1988) developed a model of North American Paleoindian hunting and mobility behavior different from any single modern systemic analog. To model the character of adaptive strategies during the initial wave of New World colonization, they meshed various analogs from around the world with ecological studies (from highly general theory) of foraging, risk, and the like in a general but unstated context of selection thinking to envision an ecological niche and an adaptive strategy that no longer exists anywhere.

Even their implicit appeal to general principles informed their model beyond what could be expected of a strict use of ethnographic analogy and an understanding of middle-range processes. Furthermore, they were able to present a model that could potentially explain *why* Paleoindian adaptive strategies should be as they described, in addition to merely describing the prehistoric behavior.

An appropriate topic for the application of ethnoarchaeology to situations likely divergent from modern analogies is early hominid behavior. Gould (1980) has advocated the use of analogs from both human and carnivore behavior to help model early hominid systems, and this has been pursued. More analogies and empirical generalizations are always helpful, but higher-level theory will not to be reached by simply adding more of them while acknowledging that cultural systems are evolutionary. "Any evolutionary scheme presented must be consistent with our current understanding of how natural selection operates" (Hill 1982). Yet the employment of the theory of natural selection, *as currently understood*, has been rare in archaeology—ethno or otherwise.

Recent ethnographic work among the Hadza in Tanzania (O'Connell et al. 1988, 1990) is important here. It explicitly employs "selection thinking" that documents the workings of the contemporary system (hunting, butchering, and bone transport among others), identifying the contexts in which certain behaviors obtain. The studies show how general features of systems can be examined from an empirical standpoint via the integration of middle-range and general theory. Take the case of Hadza scavenging, a kind of behavior suspected of early hominids based on archaeological finds. Ethnographic observations of Hadza scavenging from carnivore kills and knowledge of the role of scavenging in the larger system, coupled with assumptions stemming from "selection thinking," led to several propositions about the characteristics of early hominid scavenging (O'Connell et al. 1988). The arena of early hominid behavior is sure to generate additional ethnoarchaeology and perhaps applications of general theory in the coming years.

The deep past is not the only place where behaviors different from the present may be expected. Ethnographic and archaeological observations can be guided by the theory of natural selection to offer general propositions. This approach has been widely employed and successful in nonhuman evolutionary ecology. It has been employed in the analysis of existing ethnographic, archaeological, and ethnoarchaeological data in studies of hunter-gatherer foraging (O'Connell and Hawkes 1984), mobility (Kelly 1983), resource transport (Jones and Madsen 1989a), transport and diet choice (Jones and Madsen 1989b), and bone transport (Metcalfe 1989), to name a few.

These and other studies suggest the goal is not only to evaluate and interpret the archaeological record, the typical end point for archaeology, but also to evaluate explanations of human behavior over time spans that transcend the lives of individuals. Of course, the benefit is the potential for the work to contribute to the general theory that informed the research. Could there be such a future for ethnoarchaeology?

Program for Ethnoarchaeology

Looking to advocate more than anticipate, I present the following prospectus for the future of ethnoarchaeology. Ethnoarchaeology will go beyond an exposé of archaeological naiveté; empty "conclusions" about the multivariate nature of cultural causality; or the truism, "we need more research," along yet more and more lines of, yes, you guessed it, middle-range investigation. Ethnoarchaeological conclusions will not stop at the cautionary but will elicit the expected character of the material record under various archaeological conditions, enabling application and test. Pursuant to this prospectus, one way for ethnoarchaeology to stretch itself is to explicitly redirect archaeological research—a goal that would force the operationalization I advocate.

Some work will continue along the lines of the recent past, including studies of the relationships between material culture and the symbolic realm. While it is conceivable that such work can be linked to larger theory and the past, I suspect it will remain divergent. The direct historical analogies that have been archaeology's bread and butter will continue to be used, carefully, as they should. There will be increasing realization that all analogy extracted from a dynamic world carries problems and that the key is not to be found in the location of the Perfect Analogy. Some of this realization will stem from the beating the Direct Historical Approach in the New World has taken from evidence for disease-induced upheaval long before Europeans could make the observations we use for many of our analogs.

Middle-range ethnoarchaeological research will continue, but there will be a greater consciousness about including an archaeological component in research claiming to be ethnoarchaeology. The most pioneering ethnoarchaeology will be that which escapes the trivial by becoming explicitly but not exclusively concerned with general theory. Fewer ethnoarchaeologists will resist the temptation to isolate the middle range, a habit that tacitly assumes explanation will be an intrinsic outcome of merely "decoding" the record. Since general theory guides the development of the middle-range questions, the two are essentially coterminous. General theory does not wait for the middle-range research to be "done." The reward of these efforts will be an improved position from which to enter the archaeological record and understand a past that may have been far different from our present. That would be the closest thing to a time machine.

Acknowledgments

Thanks to LuAnn Wandsnider for the opportunity to participate in the conference and for her comments on the manuscript and the philosophy of archaeology that went well beyond editorial advice. Questions and comments raised at the conference influenced my thinking, and I thank the other participants. Others who, over the years, have shaped ideas submitted here include Kristen Hawkes, Kevin Jones, Duncan Metcalfe, James O'Connell, and Ken Russell.

Notes

1. This is based on an informal survey of CRM bibliographies for the western United States, showing that these references are the all-time favorites. The use of favorites has to do with a variety of things ranging from the quality of a study to publishing inertia, exposure, and academic bloodlines favoring the easy location of a few studies by a hard-pressed group of "consumers" making their living in CRM.

2. These references reflect a range of descriptions of behavioral-evolutionary ecology, a range of applications from nonhumans to humans, and a responsible comparison between evolutionary biology and anthropology. Far from exhaustive, it stresses the need for anthropologists to comprehend behavioral ecology through interdisciplinary links rather than the interpretive writings on contemporary evolution found in some recent treatises by archaeologists.

References

Binford, L. R. (editor)
   1977 *For Theory Building in Archaeology: Essays on Faunal Remains, Aquatic Resources and Systemic Modeling.* Academic Press, New York.
Binford, L. R.
   1978 *Nunamiut Ethnoarchaeology.* Academic Press, New York.
   1980 Willow Smoke and Dogs' Tails: Hunter-Gatherer Settlement Systems and Archaeological Site Formation. *American Antiquity* 45:4–20.
   1983a *Working at Archaeology.* Academic Press, New York.

1983b *In Pursuit of the Past: Decoding the Archaeological Record.* Thames and Hudson, New York.

1985 Brand X Versus the Recommended Product. *American Antiquity* 50:580–590.

Blurton-Jones, N.
1976 Growing Points in Human Ethology: Another Link Between Ethology and the Social Sciences? In *Growing Points in Ethology,* edited by P. P. G. Bateson and R. A. Hinde, pp. 427–449. Cambridge University Press, Cambridge.

Bonnichsen, R.
1973 Millie's Camp: An Experiment in Archaeology. *World Archaeology* 4:277–291.

David, N.
1971 The Fulani Compound and the Archaeologist. *World Archaeology* 3:111–131.

Donnan, C. B., and C. W. Clewlow, Jr. (editors)
1974 *Ethnoarchaeology.* Institute of Archaeology, Monograph 4. University of California, Los Angeles.

Foley, R.
1987 *Another Unique Species: Patterns in Human Evolutionary Ecology.* Longman Scientific and Technical, Essex, England.

Gould, R. A.
1971 The Archaeologist as Ethnographer: A Case from the Western Desert of Australia. *World Archaeology* 3:143–177.

1980 *Living Archaeology.* Cambridge University Press, Cambridge.

1985 The Empiricist Strikes Back: Reply to Binford. *American Antiquity* 50:638–644.

Gould, R. A. (editor)
1978 *Explorations in Ethnoarchaeology.* University of New Mexico Press, Albuquerque.

Grayson, D. K.
1986 Eoliths, Archaeological Ambiguity, and the Generation of "Middle-range" Research. In *American Archaeology Past and Future: A Celebration of the Society for American Archaeology 1935–1985,* edited by D. J. Meltzer, D. D. Fowler, and J. A. Sabloff, pp. 77–133. Smithsonian Institution Press, Washington, D.C.

Hill, K.
1982 Hunting and Human Evolution. *Journal of Human Evolution* 11:521–544.

Hodder, I.
1982 *Symbols in Action: Ethnoarchaeological Studies of Material Culture.* Cambridge University Press, Cambridge.

Ingersoll, D., J. E. Yellen, and W. MacDonald (editors)
1978 *Experimental Archaeology.* Columbia University Press, New York.

Jones, K. T., and D. B. Madsen
1989a Calculating the Cost of Resource Transportation: A Great Basin Example. *Current Anthropology* 30:529–534.

1989b Transportation Cost and Diet Choice in the Great Basin. Paper presented at the 54th Annual Meeting of the Society for American Archaeology, Atlanta.

Kelly, R. L.
1983 Hunter-Gatherer Mobility Strategies. *Journal of Anthropological Research* 39:277–306.

Kelly, R. L., and L. C. Todd
1988 Coming into the Country: Early Paleoindian Hunting and Mobility. *American Antiquity* 53:231–244.

Kobylinski, Z.
1989 Ethno-archaeological Cognition and Cognitive Ethno-archaeology. In *The*

Meaning of Things: Material Culture and Symbolic Expression, edited by I. Hodder, pp. 122–129. Unwin Hyman, London.

Krebs J. and N. B. Davies
   1984 *Behavioral Ecology*. 2d ed. Blackwell, Oxford.

Longacre, W. A., and J. E. Ayres
   1968 Archaeological Lessons from an Apache Wickiup. In *New Perspectives in Archaeology*, edited by S. R. Binford and L. R. Binford, pp. 151–159. Aldine, Chicago.

Metcalfe, D.
   1989 A General Cost/Benefit Model of the Tradeoff Between Transport and Field Processing. Paper presented at the 54th Annual Meeting of the Society for American Archaeology, Atlanta.

O'Connell, J. F.
   1974 Spoons, Knives and Scrapers: The Function of Yilugwa in Central Australia. *Mankind* 9:189–194.

O'Connell, J. F., and K. Hawkes
   1984 Food Choice and Foraging Sites among the Alyawara. *Journal of Anthropological Research* 40:504–535.

O'Connell, J. F., K. Hawkes, and N. Blurton-Jones
   1988 Hadza Scavenging: Implications for Plio/Pleistocene Hominid Subsistence. *Current Anthropology* 29:356–363.
   1990 Reanalysis of Large Mammal Body Part Transport among the Hadza. *Journal of Archaeological Science* 17:301–316.

Price, B.
   1982 Cultural Materialism: A Theoretical Review. *American Antiquity* 47:709–741.

Raab, L. M., and A. C. Goodyear
   1984 Middle-range Theory in Archaeology: A Critical Review of Origins and Applications. *American Antiquity* 49:255–268.

Russell, K. W., and S. R. Simms
   1992 *The Bidul Bedouin of Petra: Studies in the Ethnoarchaeology of a Pastoral-Agricultural People in the Near East*. Submitted to the Registration Center, Department of Antiquities, Jordan.

Schiffer, M. B.
   1976 *Behavioral Archaeology*. Academic Press, New York.
   1978 Methodological Issues in Ethnoarchaeology. In *Explorations in Ethnoarchaeology*, edited by R. A. Gould, pp. 229–247. University of New Mexico Press, Albuquerque.

Simms, S. R.
   1988 The Archaeological Structure of a Bedouin Camp. *Journal of Archaeological Science* 15:197–211.
   1989 The Structure of the Bustos Wickiup Site, Eastern Nevada. *Journal of California and Great Basin Anthropology* 11:2–34.

Simms, S. R., and K. M. Heath
   1990 Site Structure of the Orbit Inn: An Application of Ethnoarchaeology. *American Antiquity* 55:797–812.

Standen, V., and R. A. Foley (editors)
   1989 *Comparative Socioecology: The Behavioral Ecology of Humans and Other*

Mammals. Special Publication No. 8 of the British Ecological Society. Blackwell Scientific Publications, Oxford.

Stephens, D. W., and J. R. Krebs
   1986 *Foraging Theory*. Princeton University Press, Princeton.

Thomas, D. H.
   1983a *The Archaeology of Monitor Valley 1: Epistemology*. Anthropological Papers 58: Part 1. American Museum of Natural History, New York.
   1983b *The Archaeology of Monitor Valley 2: Gatecliff Shelter*. Anthropological Papers 59: Part 1. American Museum of Natural History, New York.
   1988 *The Archaeology of Monitor Valley 3: Survey and Additional Excavations*. Anthropological Papers 66: Part 2. American Museum of Natural History, New York.

Trigger, B. G.
   1989 *A History of Archaeological Thought*. Cambridge University Press, Cambridge.

Whitelaw, T. M.
   1989 *The Social Organization of Space in Hunter-Gatherer Communities: Some Implications for Social Inference in Archaeology*. Ph.D. dissertation, Faculty of Archaeology and Anthropology, University of Cambridge, Cambridge.

Yellen, J. E.
   1977 *Archaeological Approaches to the Present: Models for Reconstructing the Past*. Academic Press, New York.

15. Directions in Archaeological Analysis: A Commentary

Nan A. Rothschild

> Predicting has always been difficult with regard to the future.
> —General Colin Powell

The examination of the current state of a discipline by its members is usually done with several goals in mind. One is to understand the historical process by which the discipline has developed, and the other, whether explicit or not, is to see whether a trajectory can be identified that will allow some understanding of the future, even though we realize that long-term predictions of the future are probably best saved for science-fiction writers or other visionaries. As archaeologists we are familiar with using the past to understand the present and to suggest timeless processes that may illuminate any period, including the future; this is an important use of the past.

The four chapters in this portion of the volume are in an excellent position to generate a retrospective analysis and perhaps a vision of the near future, or at least a set of wish lists for it. Their focus is primarily pragmatic; they offer relatively little discussion of theoretical conflict or paradigms appropriate to the archaeological future. They form an interesting, albeit somewhat disparate, group. The Bishop and Wandsnider-Kohler chapters are similar in their methodological-technical approach, and since one application of ethnoarchaeology is that of interpretive technique, we might say that they share that perspective with Simms's contribution. I see the Woosley chapter as quite different from the others, focusing on archaeologically important institutions (i.e., museums) and data sources (i.e., collections), rather than on analytic methods and techniques. I will discuss each article separately, pointing to commonalties as I find them, and then I will summarize them as a group.

Woosley shares a historical perspective with the other authors in this section, applying it to her discussion of museums and collections, but she

Quandaries and Quests: Visions of Archaeology's Future, edited by LuAnn Wandsnider. Center for Archaeological Investigations, Occasional Paper No. 20. © 1992 by the Board of Trustees, Southern Illinois University. All rights reserved. ISBN 0-88104-075-4.

concentrates primarily on current and future issues related to the storage and maintenance of collections, the provision of access to them, and their use for research. While she addresses archaeological collections in particular, most of what is discussed pertains to ethnographic collections as well.

She documents thoroughly the reasons for overcrowding of existing repositories: new ideas about what data are important, the explosive growth in archaeological projects conducted under CRM legislation, and the recognition that the range of variation expressed in an object is more important than a normative type. These factors have greatly increased the quantity of objects requiring storage and care in repositories throughout the United States. Many archaeologists, notably those in urban areas, have faced the problem of finding repositories for collections, especially if they are large ones that do not include many "display-quality" objects.

Add to those problems the increased sense of awareness in museums of the need for conservation and electronic inventories, and you can see how museums, notoriously underfunded, are in real trouble, even without Republican economic priorities and a national recession. One positive benefit of federal involvement in cultural resource protection has been the creation of federal repositories and the development of programs such as that sponsored by the National Science Foundation to fund improved treatment for extant systematic collections. But the staff time required to sort and assess holdings can be a problem, and most museums have at least some unsystematic collections.

Almost ten years ago Bert Salwen suggested that we should think about ways to sample large, seemingly redundant collections (Salwen 1981). The obvious problem here is deciding how many apparently similar Levanna points or pieces of hand-painted pearlware constitute an adequate sample. For the most part, I do not think we fully understand yet all the dimensions of similarity or difference, so I am not comfortable with the idea of discarding many kinds of objects, unless they are machine-made and are true duplicates of other objects. However, we can and should create hierarchical storage facilities, with less frequently used things stored in old warehouses or fallout shelters, away from urban centers where land is less costly. We could then reserve museum space for type collections or a sample of an assemblage. Scholars could travel to the storage area to study the rest of a collection. For some kinds of objects, documentation on tape or by computer imaging might provide adequate recording, allowing the objects to be discarded.

If overcrowding is on one side of the coin, on the other is the pressure to empty museums of great quantities of prehistoric Native American objects and skeletal material. The issues of repatriation and reburial are difficult ones, as Goldstein (this volume) has discussed (also see Goldstein and Kintigh 1990). We are in the early stages of coping with these issues, and it is not yet clear to what degree they will affect the quantities of artifacts stored in museums.

The bottom line for us is the research significance of the collections. Patty Jo Watson suggested a few years ago that much of the prehistoric past in the United States will be gone in the near future (Watson 1986:453) because of the destruction of sites. The fact that some collections will be repatriated and that there is increasing difficulty in doing fieldwork in some parts of the world will exacerbate the problem. Those remaining collections will thus become even more important. In order to make use of them, they must be conserved, cataloged, and stored so that they are accessible. They can be used in many types of research as innovative techniques or new research questions are developed; even objects without good provenience information can be useful for some investigations (Conkey 1981; Kintigh 1981).

While the archaeological community may appreciate the value of extant collections, unfortunately, we have not been effective in explaining to the public why our collections (and archaeology itself) are so important. The Society for American Archaeology has been trying to remedy the situation, with its lobbying efforts and its attempts to bring avocational archaeologists into the organization. Many professional archaeologists interact with avocational groups and the public at large in a variety of ways. For example, in New York City we have a symposium each spring that presents recent local excavations and analyses to the public. Many nonarchaeologists retain a sense of awe and excitement about our profession, which takes real skill to preserve, presenting (in jargon-free language) our results in a meaningful way. I think we are not always successful at doing that, but it is self-evident that if we want funding maintained we all have to become public relations experts.

The second chapter in this section, authored by Wandsnider and Kohler, begins with a brief history of computer technology and quantitative applications. They make the interesting point that while there was an initial burst in the use of computer-facilitated quantitative methods in the late sixties and seventies, the absolute use of the technology has slowed down since then. Is this due to something as trivial as the loss of novelty, or have archaeologists as a group realized that complex techniques are often inappropriate for many of our data sets (Cowgill 1986; Thomas 1978)? The authors also note the persistence of similar analytic strategies used by archaeologists in spite of the fact that both content and form (the former related to paradigm and the latter to available technology) have changed. Again, one wonders whether this derives from the weight of tradition, the constraints of our data, or some other factor.

Quantitative applications employing computers have been successful in several areas of archaeology, including data collection and description, and the development of inferences and interpretations from data. However, a great deal of time, money, and energy have been wasted on inappropriate applications. This chapter notes another significant problem in the area of sophisticated analytical methodologies and computer technology, namely, the time needed to learn their use, their strengths, and their requirements. And, as noted by the authors, there are inherent limitations on the use of these tools because of the nature (and poor quality, in statistical terms) of the archaeological data themselves. The limitations are particularly frustrating since our goals are not just description but explanation.

Wandsnider and Kohler's suggestions for improvements to the practice of archaeology are very concrete and will appeal to anyone who has tried to use field data (or other sorts of information) collected by other archaeologists. They would allow for the creation of large data sets suitable for addressing certain types of research questions. They would facilitate the experimentation with scale that these authors suggest, which, I agree, is essential to the interpretation of data. We *are* in urgent need of some form of standardized (in the sense of meeting minimum criteria) and consistent data collection and recording (difficult though it may be), especially if we want to tackle problems requiring information beyond the level of a single site or survey area. If standardization existed, data could be shared, as could the expense of data entry for Geographic Information Systems and similar applications requiring large data sets.

As the potential technical capabilities of the microcomputer increase, it will be important to rely, to some degree, on specialists, comparable to archaeologist-technicians in other areas—archaeologists who focus on these applications, but who understand the unique problems of archaeological data. There are some individuals who fill this need at present, but they will be even more critical in the future.

The vision of technical specialists is shared by Bishop, who believes that they must bridge archaeology and the technical applications of instrumental analysis if they are to be truly reliable interpreters, aware of the limitations of both types of scientific endeavor. That is one of several similarities in approach shared by the two presentations. The authors all believe that the techniques under discussion are to be handmaidens (or manservants) to research questions for archaeologists. They also recognize that there are limitations on our objectivity, as well as in our data.

As archaeology has developed an enhanced "sciency" identity because of increasingly sophisticated analytic techniques, it has become more urgent to place the analysis in meaningful context through the construction of appropriate research designs. I agree with Bishop that the most difficult part of the process is linking the very detailed information that technical reports generate with culture and behavior. The greatest successes in this area seem to have occurred in the areas of subsistence and paleoenvironmental reconstruction, long-distance trade, and details of ancient technology (Trigger 1984:277).

The question is, Will we be able in the near future to go beyond those aspects of culture that are most closely tied to the material world? Some of the recent work in symbolic archaeology attempts to do just that, but thus far it is rather "low-tech" (or "anti-tech") in approach. However, I think there can be a useful fusion of symbolic and high-tech approaches. For example, postprocessual archaeology is often critical of the processual approach for its neglect of the individual. And yet there are technical skills available by which individual potters or lithic toolmakers might be recognized, allowing a new dimension to the analysis of craft production and the significance of stylistic expression.

The most thought-provoking aspect of Bishop's paper for me is his reference to the need for archaeologists to draw on other disciplines for several kinds of help, including theoretical interpretations. I agree with

Gumerman and Phillips (1978) that archaeology consists mostly of techniques and methods, and for me, that is not a negative statement. In one sense, we might say that the only genuine *archaeological* contribution to scientific endeavor is that of stratigraphic excavation (and even that has roots in geology). We use our techniques to gather information about a specific segment of human behavior, namely, that from the past. Salwen has described our method as that of archaeography, the collection of descriptive information about behavior patterns of no-longer-living sociocultural groups (1988:4). The models with which we interpret our data derive primarily from cultural anthropology but also from other fields: cultural geography, history, ecology, and others. It is the unique combination of the source and type of information we collect and our research problems that makes archaeology distinctive within the social sciences. I agree with Bishop about the importance of interdisciplinary cooperation and think we will need to consider his "matrix structure" seriously.

I also share his concern with the sterility of research focused on objects that is sometimes associated with materials analysis such as that advocated by Kingery, however sophisticated and hierarchically nested in a discussion of structure and sampling it may be. Historical archaeology has had a longstanding interest in objects, derived from its early antiquarian perspective, making it difficult for this subdiscipline to consider processual questions. There are important research issues involving objects, but they must be seen, as Bishop notes, as elements of a sample, not as the universe.

It is interesting that he thinks that the significant developments of the short-range future will not be in the area of new technological embellishments but in the development of ways to incorporate information generated from existing technology. That slightly pessimistic view ties into the last chapter of this section, by Steven Simms. Bishop ends his paper with a call for the continued development of middle-range theory in order to avoid "scientific frill," or semimindless applications of new methods of analysis acquired from the technical "priesthood."

Simms's paper explicitly considers middle-range theory as one of the applications of ethnoarchaeology. He sees ethnoarchaeology as a many-headed beast that offers cautionary comments; testable middle-range propositions, some of which may provide practical assistance for field archaeologists and possibly for cultural resource managers, particularly if issues of analogy can be worked out; and, most important, a means by which we may decode the past, examining the relationship between symbols, social issues, and material things in the present day while developing broader, more general theory.

Although Simms seems to envision the future importance of ethnoarchaeology as leading to the development of general theory, he also values the way in which it has become important to Binford and others as a middle-range testing ground. In this regard he alludes to an interesting question: How can we go beyond analogy to model systems of the past for which there are no living analogs? Simms links this problem to the lack of an overarching theory of human behavior and culture, but I see them as separate issues to be solved in different ways, without resort to "deterministic or reductionist" explanations. In the first place, I doubt that there were past societies for which we do not have at least partial analogs. And the current emphasis on the middle range, in my opinion, is a dialectical reaction to monolithic theories based mostly on ideas of cultural evolution that are no longer generating creative thought.

There is often a tension between different levels of theory and analysis. Proponents of higher-order versus middle-range theoretical levels, theory versus testable applications, and analysis at different scales create a zigzag pattern of progress rather than a straight line. At the moment the profession seems to be in a stage of looking at things with a hand glass (midway between a telescope and a microscope) on a scale that allows us to examine the actual observable interaction between a behavior and the physical manifestation of that behavior. Undoubtedly we will move to other scales of investigation, as the dialectical process continues. We may see a pendulum swing back toward higher-order theories again, perhaps incorporating recent thought in the area of natural selection (Dunnell 1980; Rindos 1984). It is hoped that we will be able to integrate these levels to some extent, so that ground truth, middle-range, and higher-order theory can flow smoothly and enrich each other.

Simms, in common with Bishop, Kohler, and Wandsnider, stresses the importance of a multilevel evaluation of archaeological information and suggests that ethnoarchaeology may be useful (and able to redirect research) at several levels: in defining archaeological categories, in delineating important lines of questioning, or even in structuring research designs, with the overall goal being that of decoding the record. I agree with him that they are the areas in which ethnoarchaeology's contribution can be the most significant. Cautionary tales are interesting (and I am guilty of producing some myself) but will not be productive unless they pertain to systemic factors rather than individual cases.

In terms of the goal of the volume, I think we have been successful in both assessing the state and visualizing a future of Americanist archaeology. Our review of the past has led to a clearer idea of important future developments in archaeology. Of course, thoughts about the future are always structured by what we know in the present, perhaps because, for most of us, our imaginations are constrained by the known. The easiest type of prediction, for example, is a limited one that merely combines an old tool with a new component, such as a laser dental drill or levitating trains and cars. What the four authors in this section have done quite successfully is look at where we are, using the historical perspective that we as archaeologists are so comfortable with, and then suggest where we might like to be, or in which direction we would like to be moving, in 10 years.

However, the use of historical trend to approach the future implies that there will be no major changes in trajectory. Some improvements in technology are inevitable; most mentioned here would result in access to new and larger data sets, and it is clear that that is a minimal goal. The group of archaeologists contributing to the volume will have some ability to strongly affect future directions for the discipline. There are, of course, external forces beyond our control, as the development of equipment and software, for example, is more likely to be directed by the wishes of the corporate power structure than by our needs. Happily, I think, there are also unknowable and therefore unpredictable aspects of the future, both in technology and in paradigm, that may make the next generation of archaeology rather different from our imagination of it. We will certainly continue to try to understand the often elusive past, both the details of people's lives and the larger-scale processes of human history, being as creative as we can with the technology and the resources at our disposal.

References

Conkey, Margaret W.
   1981   What Can We Do with Broken Bones? Paleolithic Design Structure, Archaeological Research, and the Potential of Museum Collections. In *The Research Potential of Anthropological Museum Collections*, edited by A-M. Cantwell, J. B. Griffin, and N. A. Rothschild, pp. 35–52. Annals of the New York Academy of Sciences, New York.

Cowgill, George L.
   1986   Archaeological Applications of Mathematical and Formal Models. In *American Archaeology Past and Future: A Celebration of the Society for American Archaeology 1935–1985*, edited by D. J. Meltzer, D. D. Fowler, and J. A. Sabloff, pp. 369–393. Smithsonian Institution Press, Washington, D.C.

Dunnell, Robert C.
   1980   Evolutionary Theory and Archaeology. In *Advances in Archaeological Method and Theory*, vol. 3, edited by Michael B. Schiffer, pp. 35–99. Academic Press, New York.

Goldstein, Lynne, and Keith Kintigh
   1990   Ethics and the Reburial Controversy. *American Antiquity* 55:585–591.

Gumerman, George J., and David A. Phillips, Jr.
   1978   Archaeology Beyond Anthropology. *American Antiquity* 43:184–191.

Kintigh, Keith W.
   1981   An Outline for a Chronology of Zuni Ruins, Revisited: Sixty-five Years of Repeated Analysis and Collection. In *The Research Potential of Anthropological Museum Collections*, edited by A-M. Cantwell, J. B. Griffin, and N. A. Rothschild, pp. 467–488. Annals of the New York Academy of Sciences, New York.

Rindos, David J.
   1984   *The Origins of Agriculture: An Evolutionary Perspective*. Academic Press, New York.

Salwen, Bert
   1981   Collecting Now for Future Research. In *The Research Potential of Anthropological Museum Collections*, edited by A-M. Cantwell, J. B. Griffin, and N. A. Rothschild, pp. 567–574. Annals of the New York Academy of Sciences, New York.
   1988   Archaeography, Archaeology, Anthropology, and History. Paper presented at the Annual Meeting of the Society for Historical Archaeology, Reno, Nevada.

Thomas, David H.
   1978   The Awful Truth about Statistics in Archaeology. *American Antiquity* 43:231–244.

Trigger, Bruce G.
    1984   Archaeology at the Crossroads: What's New? *Annual Review of Anthropology* 13:275–300.

Watson, Patty Jo
    1986   Archaeological Interpretation, 1985. In *American Archaeology Past and Future: A Celebration of the Society for American Archaeology 1935–1985*, edited by D. J. Meltzer, D. D. Fowler, and J. A. Sabloff, pp. 439–458. Smithsonian Institution Press, Washington, D.C.

IV. Archaeological Programs and Goals

16. Archaeology and Evolutionary Science

Robert C. Dunnell

Abstract: The history of archaeology is a succession of different interpretative algorithms, variously denominated approaches, theories, and most recently paradigms. The inability of any particular algorithm to gain discipline-wide consensus is a consequence of the absence of an agreed epistemological standard: we have no definitive way to distinguish answerable from unanswerable questions or a correct answer from an incorrect one. The traditional goal of archaeology becoming science entails the adoption of an empirical epistemological standard. This action alone would rectify much of the current disciplinary malaise. Given that archaeological interest is focused on change, archaeological theory must be evolutionary theory. Thus, a more detailed development of the nature of evolutionary theory in an archaeological context occupies the essay.

Introduction

Archaeology has a long history of competing approaches (Dunnell 1986; cf. Willey and Sabloff 1980), a feature of the discipline that, if anything, is more exaggerated today than it has been at any other time. Although different positions are always argued with self-righteous conviction, the fact remains that no single view has come to dominate the field. As a consequence, our history is one of changing interpretations, or changing justifications for the same interpretations, coupled only loosely with an increase in "data" and technical improvements. One approach does not build upon or expand upon its predecessor; there is no cumulative increase in knowledge beyond the simple accumulation of "facts" about the archaeological record. William Henry Holmes decried this very situation 100 years ago as "a war of words [that] has been kept up for generations and the battle still goes on without being won or lost" (1892:240). Albert Spaulding criticized the discipline in

Quandaries and Quests: Visions of Archaeology's Future, edited by LuAnn Wandsnider. Center for Archaeological Investigations, Occasional Paper No. 20. © 1992 by the Board of Trustees, Southern Illinois University. All rights reserved. ISBN 0-88104-075-4.

similar terms in his famous critique of Ford more than a half century later: "Truth is to be determined by some polling of archaeologists, that productivity is doing what other archaeologists do, and that the only purpose of archaeology is to make archaeologists happy. This is simply a specialized version of the 'life is just a game' constellation of ideas, a philosophical position which cannot be tolerated in a scientific context" (1953:590). The same sentiments underlay the new archaeology (Binford 1968; Watson et al. 1971). No doubt Holmes would be embarrassed by the passage of a century without any material progress on what he considered a central issue to the health and development of the discipline.

The advocacy of a particular kind of archaeology is rather pointless unless the problem raised by those authors is addressed. Why should one kind of archaeology be preferred over another? In large measure, the issue is epistemological (e.g., Trigger 1985:118): How can we tell a correct answer from an incorrect one? For over a century (e.g, Holmes 1892; Parker 1935; Thomas 1898; Watson et al. 1971), the solution that archaeologists have pursued explicitly, however unsuccessfully, has been to adopt scientific standards. In recent years, some archaeologists have argued for the abandonment of both the goal and the concern for epistemological justification as a whole (e.g., Hodder 1986; Shanks and Tilley 1987; cf. Trigger 1985:119). Consequently, not only how a scientific standard might be implemented in archaeology but also the choice of science as a standard needs to be considered. It is in this context that I argue for an archaeology founded in evolutionary theory. *If* scientific knowledge is accepted as a goal, I attempt to show, through a consideration of the nature of our interest in the archaeological record and examinations of both causal and observational languages, that an evolutionary archaeology offers a way out of the disciplinary crisis in which we find ourselves. In short, there are reasons to prefer it over all other disciplinary strategies.

Archaeology as Science

As I have argued ad nauseam (e.g., Dunnell 1982, 1986), a major reason why archaeology has failed to become science after a century of effort is a deep confusion about what science itself is. In recent years this has been compounded by intentional ambiguity, redefining science to suit the state of the field or disallowing the distinctiveness of science as an explanatory system (e.g., Christensen 1989). Much of the concern over whether archaeology is science is a misdirected assertion of the legitimacy of archaeology as an academic field on the post-Sputnik assumption that being science is a sufficient, if unnecessary, warrant for academic legitimacy. Of course, not all legitimate academic fields are science or even pretend to be. That supplies a second reason to consider the choice of the scientific framework as well as the means by which such a framework might be implemented.

It is essential to be clear about what is meant by science. It is not necessary, however, to become bogged down in the century-old philosophic debates on the issue. A highly restrictive definition is not essential. Two elements suffice to delineate the critical features of science as an explanatory system; neither is particularly controversial. First, science as an explanatory system is a two-part construction—it uses theory to explain phenomena. Cause is theoretical, not empirical (e.g., Lewontin 1974; Popper 1974; Sellars 1962; Willer and Willer 1973). Beyond this, there is no noncontroversial characterization of science as a logical system. Second, science employs a uniform epistemological standard, an empirical (e.g., Hesse 1978) or a performance standard (Dunnell 1978a).

Much has been said about the development of archaeological theory even if there is little or nothing to show for the discussion. The critical issue is not the theory itself, but the framework that determines the character of the theory, in this case, science. Even Karl Popper, no friend of evolutionary theory, admits that once one settles upon the combination of historical questions and science, evolution is the only theoretical choice possible (Popper 1974:134).

Epistemological Standards

The empirical epistemological standard is a useful place to start. Entailed are two analytically distinct but nonetheless related considerations: the nature of the epistemological standard characteristic of science; and its application in the peculiar circumstances necessitated by archaeology's distinctive context. Resolution of those two issues both justifies the choice of science and scientific standards of truth in archaeology and provides a context for the development of an evolutionary archaeology.

The key word is empirical. Ultimately, a proposed explanation is accepted or rejected on the basis of its performance in the empirical world, period. The structure of science, scientific methodology, is expressly designed to allow its proposed explanations, hypotheses, to be tested in this manner. Propositions that are incapable of empirical testing—generically, speculations—are rejected as explanations, however important they may be in the creative side of science.

Testing is a matter of comparing a forecasted outcome with an empirical realization under a specified set of tolerance limits. Positive and negative outcomes are not symmetrical. A positive match between prediction and outcome, while elevating the hypothesis to an explanation, makes no ultimate claim to truth. Different accounts may work as well. However, failure to match the empirical realization, barring technical errors, forever eliminates the hypothesis as an explanation. Hence, scientific strategies are falsification strategies, not confirmation strategies, however pleasing the latter may be psychologically. Despite the new archaeology's commitment to confirmation strategies (e.g., Watson et al. 1971, 1984), a confirmation strategy is really only appropriate to plausible argument (Polya 1954). What archaeologists have routinely failed to appreciate from their nineteenth-century beginnings to the new archaeology's call to science is that becoming scientific means acquiring *the ability to be wrong*, not just unpopular. Even the idea of being genuinely wrong is foreign to archaeological training where a humanistic tradition emphasizes cleverness and debating skills.

The empirical standard is also responsible for the cumulative nature of scientific knowledge, particularly its ability to accumulate even across paradigm or theoretical boundaries. So long as a single standard is used to accept or reject conclusions, the conclusions will stand regardless of the particulars of their explanation.

Alternative epistemological standards have not been in force in archaeology; on the contrary, the pattern of unresolved differences that characterizes our history arises from the *lack* of epistemological standards. That results in a condition that I have characterized as the "Merlin syndrome" (Dunnell 1988). As you may recall from *A Connecticut Yankee in King Arthur's Court* (Clemens 1982:132–133), Merlin was a great magician of tyrannical power who was held in awe by King Arthur and his court. Merlin's power rested on his ability to tell the court what the Emperor of China was doing at that very moment halfway round the world, a truly impressive ability, it must be conceded. Twain, however, as the Connecticut Yankee, brought this house of cards to ruin by asking the great magician to tell the court what the Connecticut Yankee had concealed in his hip pocket! The "success" of archaeology, like that of Merlin, rests on the tactic of making claims that cannot be subjected to empirical testing. Of course, archaeologists talk about "testing" all the time, but it almost never amounts to anything more than an assessment of plausibility. Archaeology's continued existence rests only in the uncritical faith of a gullible audience. It is only a matter of time before a Connecticut Yankee appears in our midst, a good reason both to embrace an empirical standard of truth and science as a methodology. The Merlin syndrome, our inability to assess the correctness of our conclusions, is at the root of the great diversity of approaches and many of our current problems.

Archaeology Is Historical

Archaeological efforts to become scientific (when not simply rhetorical claims, redefinitions of "science" to include the current passion, or "ritualistic" [Dunnell 1978a:193]) have been derailed by attempting to model archaeology on the structure of physics. Not only has it been partly responsible for our failure to become scientific, but it has also dissuaded not a few archaeologists from the scientific objective itself. A sterile physics of the archaeological record is not something that intuitively appeals to a broad audience (e.g., DeBoer and Lathrap 1979), even if most archaeologists might agree that the physics of artifacts has some role to play in archaeology as a whole. The inappropriate model, coupled with the new archaeology's open hostility to history and historical explanation (e.g., Spaulding 1968), in part a polemical necessity to break the stranglehold of Culture History on the discipline, obscured a fundamental issue.

The archaeological record is generated continuously. In this regard, it constitutes a body of phenomena not different in any significant way from that studied by the hard sciences. Indeed, if our *interests* were really those of the ahistorical sciences, upon which we have attempted to model our discipline unsuccessfully, a concern for the preservation of the record would

Archaeology and Evolutionary Science | 213

be nonsense. If our goal really were timeless/spaceless laws of artifacts, people, or whatever, then one piece of the record would serve just as well as another. The costly, controversial conservation of archaeological resources would be entirely unnecessary. In spite of the superficial commitment to physicslike models of scientific archaeology and the unrelenting search for "laws," archaeologists have not embraced *this* logical consequence of the commitment to laws and science as physics.

The archaeological record is a nonrenewable resource *only* because our interest in that record is historical, that is, archaeologists are committed to ultimate causation, why human history unfolded in the way in which it did. To answer why-questions, each bit of data makes a unique contribution; no data are redundant. Indeed, the archaeological record is the only body of *phenomena* that bears on how and why human beings are the way they are. A scientific archaeology requires phenomena; a historical science requires exhaustive rather than sample data. Other kinds of archaeology, while they may use data, do not *require* an empirical data base of any specific sort. In many, the archaeological record frequently serves only as an inspiration for telling stories, a nonessential function and weak justification for conserving archaeological materials at best.

Until the last couple of decades, physics served as everyone's model of SCIENCE. The persistent difficulties that biology, particularly evolutionary biology, posed for that view (e.g., Popper 1963) led to the gradual recognition that there are two broadly different kinds of science (e.g., Dunnell 1980; Gould 1986; cf. Neiman 1990; Sober 1980). One, representing the classic sciences like physics and chemistry, conceives of the empirical world as a finite series of discrete things or kinds, variation within which is noise and between which is significant. The set of empirical kinds thus posited provides the terms with which to write laws of universal application. These sciences, termed essentialist, are able to *predict* because their terms are timeless. They are limited, however, to functionalist statements of causation (i.e., they explain how systems work, not why they are).

The other kind of science, termed materialistic, takes the view that the empirical world is always in a state of becoming. Kinds are a consequence of observation, not inherent in the phenomenological world itself. Variation is causally significant. One consequence of this position on the significance of variation is that there are no empirical constants to which laws can refer; laws in the physics sense of the term cannot exist. This observation alone goes a long way toward explaining why archaeologists, for all of their commitment to the search for laws of human behavior or cultural change, have no archaeological laws to show for their efforts. They never will; such laws are structurally impossible because "human" is continuously changing. The materialistic sciences are unable to predict, for want of the timeless/spaceless terms and laws; but unlike the essentialist sciences, they provide ultimate cause. Explanation in this framework is a recitation of the history of the operation of physical laws on the phenomenon in question, not simply its subsumption under laws. For that reason evolutionary theory has the potential to unite the otherwise competitive historical and functionalist interests that have characterized all of anthropology over the past century and a half. It does not mean that specific historical and functional approaches can be salvaged—as will be addressed momentarily—but that those kinds of questions and interests are not only accommodated but required in evolutionary theory.

Evolutionary theory is a materialistic theory, one that is designed to explain *why* organismic history has taken the course it has. Evolutionary theory was developed in the nineteenth century in the context of nonhuman organisms (Darwin 1859). The extension of evolutionary theory to cultural phenomena has taken one of three broad courses: (1) the "classical" sociobiological position in which, to variable degrees (cf. Alexander 1979; Lumsden and Wilson 1981; Wilson 1975), cultural phenomena are treated as epiphenomena that can be explained with reference to biological evolution and genetics à la the "new synthesis"; (2) the social scientific position in which an effort is made to construct a "separate but equal" cultural evolution more or less analogous to biological (genetic) evolution (e.g., Boyd and Richerson 1985; Durham 1976); and (3) an attempt to generalize evolutionary theory as used in biology by removing the accidental historical constraints that have arisen in the context of nonhuman organisms so that it applies to all living things (e.g., Bonner 1980, 1988; Dunnell 1978b, 1980, 1989; O'Brien and Holland 1990).

While it would be interesting to explore the virtues and liabilities of the three tacks on extending evolution to the cultural realm, this is not the place to do so. Suffice it to say that the sociobiological approach has generally been rejected on empirical grounds (i.e., genetics controls too little of the behavioral phenotype to generate detailed causal statements) and that the social scientific approach seems to be a theory in search of an application (i.e., it has yet to be shown that a separate theory is required). Consequently, in the remainder of the essay I sketch some of the main features of an evolutionary theory of the third sort. None of the approaches should be confused with "cultural evolution" as developed in anthropology (Blute 1979; Dunnell 1980) and which is irrelevant here.

Evolutionary Theory

Causal Language

Certainly, one of the greatest barriers to the understanding and acceptance of evolutionary theory in archaeology is the failure to distinguish different systems of causation or different causal languages. Two grand causal systems, the "manifest" and scientific systems of Sellars (1962), or reason-giving and cause-giving (Dunnell 1980), are usefully distinguished. In the manifest or reason-giving language, cause is attributed to the actors, to the data. In the case of people, the actors' *intentions* are regarded as causal. Human intentions thus are substituted for theory. Sellars, in fact, regards intention as the central feature of the manifest causal system (1962:78). All teleological explanations are, however, of this general sort. In the scientific or cause-giving system, cause is attributed to theoretical propositions. For this reason such explanations are often termed *mechanistic* because the cause is seen as a mechanism external to the phenomena being explained. The idea of theoretical cause is just as much a universal characteristic of science as the empirical epistemological standard. Any explanatory system with pretense to science must be of this sort.

It is crucial to recognize that the difference between the two explanatory "agents" is *not* empirical. One cannot "prove" that thus and such is due to intention *or* to the operation of a law. One *chooses* to explain a given phenomenon in one fashion or another. It is the consequences of that choice that need to be considered. Reason-giving rests upon cultural convention and, in the human case, *both* theirs and ours. Cultural conventions are transitory. It is for this reason that we study cultural change. In turn, cultural change is the only reason why the archaeological record need be preserved and investigated; were it not for change, everything of interest would be observable in the present. Reason-giving, the causation of common sense, does not admit falsification. Consequently, reason-giving does not produce cumulative knowledge.

There can be no doubt that archaeology is committed to reason-giving. For example, Rindos's (1980) evolutionary account of the origin and spread of agriculture was reviewed in *Current Anthropology*. Not many reviews were enthusiastic; however, it is interesting that none of those objecting did so because Rindos failed to explain some facet of the origin or spread of agriculture, but *because human intention had been omitted* (e.g., Ceci 1980; Shaffer 1980)! This is tantamount to an assertion that no explanation of cultural phenomena can ever be scientific, let alone evolutionary! Precisely the same criticism was made of his (Rindos 1984) book-length treatment five years later (e.g., Blumler and Byrne 1991; Yarnell 1985).

It has been easy for archaeology to ignore the nature of its explanations. Archaeology has the decided advantage that no actions are taken on the basis of archaeological "knowledge." Archaeology is not an engineering discipline. Nobody dies because archaeological "knowledge" is just opinion without empirical import. On the other hand, now that society at large has to pay a high price for archaeological "knowledge" (not just the cost of doing archaeology, but the cost associated with conservation of the archaeological record), we are playing a new game. How long will society pay for self-righteous opinion when it can get the same stuff from Jean Auel or the local Boy Scout master free? Because the manifest system, reason-giving, is the causal language of common sense, it is easy to overlook the fundamentally different kind of causation entailed in scientific explanation, but without general recognition of this difference, there is little reason to be hopeful about the future of archaeology as science.

Observational Language

The language of observation, the "things" that are explained, constitutes the second major ingredient of an explanatory system. The only requirement that stems directly from science is that the subject matter must be empirical. Without an empirical subject matter, the empirical epistemological standard cannot be applied; "testing" would be ritualistic or euphemistic.

The traditional observational language of archaeology is strongly behavioral and has mostly been borrowed from common sense or sociocultural anthropology: that is, we describe the archaeological record the way in which we describe ourselves or strangers in the here and now. It is not surprising in that the commitment to reason-giving explanation entails the use of commonsense categories. The most immediate consequence of this commitment is that archaeologists do not attempt to explain phenomena. The archaeological record is "reconstructed" and the *reconstruction*, not the record, is the subject of explanation. In essence, reconstruction is simply a transformation that converts the phenomena of the archaeological record into English so that common sense, reason-giving, can explain it. The problem thus posed is obvious. Since no phenomena are directly involved, no empirical testing is possible. Archaeology as currently constituted lacks empirical sufficiency (Lewontin 1974:8).

The so-called middle-range theory (e.g., Raab and Goodyear 1984; Schiffer 1988) in most of its guises is an oblique recognition of the problem. It is an effort to secure the relation between the archaeological record and the reconstruction that is the subject of explanation. While much of value has come from this general approach, most notably knowledge about formation processes, middle-range theory is itself a worthless effort (cf. Neiman 1990). There is no deterministic relation between the behavioral terms of reconstruction and the debris of the archaeological record. Such a relationship would have to be founded in laws, and behavioral laws, as just noted, cannot exist because behavior changes. Without a deterministic relation between the two, behavioral explanations are untestable in the archaeological record. Indeed, many archaeologists as much as admit this general contention. Ethnographic analogy, in one or another guise, is deemed by most archaeologists as indispensable and unavoidable to reconstruction and thus archaeological explanation as a whole (Watson et al. 1971). Yet even the strongest advocates of the use of analogy quickly admit that such arguments are ampliative and thus not determinant (e.g., Watson 1982; Wylie 1982, 1985). Archaeologists use analogy, even though it is admittedly defective in the role in which it is cast (e.g., Longacre 1970), because (1) they do not see any other alternative methods for reconstruction and (2) they regard reconstruction as an essential methodological element (Watson 1982).

The argument might well be taken to preclude any further discussion of a scientific archaeology or an evolutionary archaeology; indeed, were the two contentions true, it would. But neither is true. Reconstruction is necessitated only by the commitment to a behavioral data language and the manifest causal language, not by any intrinsic property of the archaeological record. Furthermore, analogy is wholly unnecessary, and the defects thus introduced in archaeological methodologies are wholly avoidable. As Richard Gould (1980) appreciated, the need for analogy would be mitigated if we had access to laws. He also appreciated that those laws could not be laws of human behavior. In the last analysis, however, he was unable to realize his insight

(Wylie 1982). His "laws" were empirical ecological generalizations, and his arguments by anomaly thinly disguised analogies. Nonetheless, his methodological argument was perfectly sound: laws, as timeless/spaceless propositions, apply to the past and the future (hence prediction) just as readily as they do in the present.

An apparent paradox is generated. Laws do away with the need for analogy, but laws cannot exist in materialist science, the kind of science already identified as appropriate to evolution and underlying archaeology. There are no constants of human behavior when the subject of investigation is the process by which the beasts now called human beings became the way they are. However, once shed of the notion that reconstruction is required for explanation and that explanation must take the form of reason-giving, it is apparent that we do have a time machine, the laws of physics and chemistry. While it may be relatively obvious, an often overlooked consequence is that the physical and chemical laws necessarily *determine the data language,* how we describe the archaeological record. If we persist in treating object function, for example, with terms like chopping, then the only way to falsify such statements is to transport the observer (i.e., the manifest causal system) back in time. If, on the other hand, we deal with the same problem in terms of friction, fracture mechanics, and other physical forces, we can say how an object interacted with its environment with exactly the same certainty as if it were moving in front of us. Fracture mechanics, by definition, are true, then and now. Physical theories, our only time machine, fix, absolutely, the terms with which we can describe the archaeological record so that it is susceptible to explanation. Recognizing this distinction goes a long way to explain the lapsed communication between physicists and other scientists and archaeologists who seek their help (e.g., Schiffer 1979:138).

To paraphrase Lewontin (1974:8), we cannot go out and describe the world any old way we please and expect to be able to generate testable explanations. The way in which we conceive the archaeological record is dictated not by some intuitive behavioral constructs borrowed from everyday life or the current "theoretical" fad in the social sciences but by the terms that occur in the theories of physics and chemistry. Much in the way of basic research remains to be done simply because the scale at which archaeological interest lies is usually larger than that which occupies the focus of physicists and chemists. Regardless of the resolution of these details, it is clear that empirical sufficiency can be achieved for archaeology only if archaeologists employ a descriptive language founded in the essentialist sciences.

The role of evolutionary theory is to organize the functional meaning thus created into a historical account that explains why those functions occur where and when they do and in what forms (Gould 1986; Wassermann 1981). Exactly how to model the logical structure of evolutionary theory is not a settled matter (e.g., Sober 1984; Wassermann 1981). Wassermann, for example, characterizes it as a "hypertheory" because it incorporates all of the laws of the physical sciences in its lower-level structure and thus avoids modeling any evolutionary concept as a law. Alternatively, as suggested by the limited successes of culture history, I have supposed that it may be modeled more nearly like other scientific theories if its units are "hyperunits," formulations with variable content but constant meaning. Such units, and archaeologists have already manufactured some units of this sort, are the product of a universal method of classification rather than a universal classification per se (Dunnell 1986). This is the kind of difference that obtains between the Linnean hierarchy operationalized with the concept species and the periodic table of elements. Perhaps both models will have to be combined to account for evolutionary theory adequately.

There is a second feature of the language of observation that requires comment, a feature that is specifically linked to evolutionary theory. As noted earlier, in materialist science variation is causal. Traditional archaeological description, on the other hand, has been modal. If construed as empirical, types and other kinds suppress variation. Units like phases, foci, and cultures come to acquire unitary properties: for example, Culture X has thus and such subsistence or settlement systems. Even in modern "quantitative" archaeology, the focus is modal (e.g., quantitative methods to find and manipulate "real" types [Luedtke 1986]). Under these conditions, evolutionary explanations are not possible because, first and foremost, evolution explains why frequencies change and why particular variants expand at the expense of others (Sober 1984). Advances in computer technology (Wandsnider and Kohler, this volume) now make it practical to document and manipulate variation rather than being forced to lump variation into a small number of general-purpose "types."

The requirement for variation is responsible for much frustration. As when any new approach is introduced, there is always a call, a seemingly reasonable call, for demonstrations of its applicability (Sabloff 1989). For the various interpretive algorithms, characteristic of archaeology's past and protected from empirical contradiction by Merlin's syndrome, that poses no problem. A new story can be spun using the new rules on the same old stuff almost immediately. Indeed, not a few "new approaches" probably arose as rationalizations for new stories! But as Mayr (1959) noted long ago, evolutionary theory is a *different kind of theory*. As a different kind of theory it *requires a different kind of data*. The best one can do with traditional data is supply an explanatory sketch not really different than the other just-so stories already available (Dunnell 1987; cf. Kirch and Green 1987). Pragmatically, this constitutes the strongest barrier to adoption of evolutionary theory in archaeology. Archaeological data have not been, for the most part, generated in forms that can be explained by evolutionary theory; traditional archaeological data are the product of the essentialist perspective of common sense. Before any major gains will be made by evolutionary theory, large bodies of new data that incorporate, rather than suppress, variation are essential. In turn, these demands imply major changes in the character of fieldwork, sampling, and research design generally.

Summary and Conclusions

The changes required in archaeology for evolutionary theory to have a serious impact are fundamental. Some of the changes, like that from reason-giving to cause-giving explanations, are required of any scientific approach. The key point about this particular change is that it represents a choice, our choice, not some inherent property of the world. Because it is a choice, it is not impossible to imagine such a change actually taking place in spite of the commonsensical barriers against such a shift. The key is simply recognizing that there is a choice. The other general requirement of any scientific approach is an empirical subject matter. Our data language, taken from common sense and ethnography, is heavily behavioral. Behavior is, however, empirical only in the present. Consequently, our uncritical appropriation of that sort of conception of our subject deprives us of an empirical subject matter and compels us to engage in reconstruction, a process that is otherwise unnecessary. Initially, a new and different kind of data language may be a little difficult to visualize (cf. Sullivan, this volume), but there are good models in the existing sciences that actually will determine the descriptive requirements. While more complicated to effect for the discipline as a whole because it necessitates a redescription of existing data, it is also easy to see such a change taking place, at least conceptually.

Other changes are specific to an evolutionary archaeology. The need to focus on variation rather than kind is the principal requirement of this sort. Having been generated from an essentialist perspective, traditional archaeological data are modal, are focused on central tendencies. Their modal character precludes the application of evolutionary theory in any nontrivial way. While reanalysis can convert some existing data to an appropriate form, by and large, the problem is more severe; often we have not collected the necessary information in the first instance. The longer we delay the development and implementation of materialist research designs, the greater the damage done to the record by archaeologists themselves and the greater the difficulty in making a shift to an evolutionary archaeology. An ancillary consequence of this requirement is that it is not possible to provide quick-fix demonstrations of the applicability of evolutionary theory, so it is always at a disadvantage in relation to simple interpretive algorithms.

Given the disadvantages, why should anyone bother? Why not business as usual with one fad replacing another in endless succession, especially if we as a profession attempt to peddle our products to the public through "education," which seems to be the main thrust of the Society for American Archaeology currently (Sabloff 1990), or, as has been recently suggested, as recreation (McGowan 1989)! The answer partly arises from the characteristics of science and partly from the peculiar features of evolutionary theory. There is a variety of ways in which the justification of scientific knowledge might be pursued (e.g., Jarvie 1985; Popper 1974; Sellars 1962), but I think it is sufficient for an archaeological audience to note that once we agree that the archaeological record is a nonrenewable resource, we commit ourselves to cumulative knowledge as a goal. We really cannot have it both ways—on the one hand, claim protection for the record by virtue of historical value and, on the other, deliver a product that is nothing more than contemporary opinion.

If we have learned nothing else from the new archaeology, it is that the intellectual posture we assume today determines the physical character of the archaeological record of tomorrow. It is impossible to justify the cost of archaeology and the protection of the archaeological resource with dated stories that are no different in kind than those told by nonarchaeologists without the slightest benefit of record. We have been shielded from accountability by Merlin's ability to awe the masses. The current structure of the discipline is a weak basis for a discipline and offers poor prospects for those just now training for a career. It is well to remember that once a piece of the record is gone, it is gone forever and no amount of regret can bring it back. The record is disappearing rapidly enough while we posture and debate and generally engage in the "war of words" that so distressed Holmes a hundred years ago. Even more important, by not producing a product of lasting value we also risk the hard-won protection of the record and thus jeopardize the whole discipline. While we may not have our act together, we can say one thing with certainty: the archaeological record is the *only* empirical record that we have pertaining to why we are the way we are, and all scientific inquiries into our history must use it.

Archaeologists, in spite of their superficial involvement with essentialist models of science, have not really evinced much interest in a physics of artifacts or the archaeological record. Again, so long as we are committed to the historical dimension of the record, the only kind of scientific theory developed to explain data so conceived is evolution. If we want archaeology to be science, it will be an evolutionary science. There is nothing radical in this particular conclusion. After all, Binford (1965) recognized this very point, albeit conflating scientific and cultural evolution, in his initial formulations of the new archaeology. What no one imagined then, and what continues to plague the discipline, is exactly how fundamental the changes are that those lofty goals presuppose. I, at least, believe those initial visions are realizable; what is not clear is whether we will quit playing academic games before time and the archaeological record run out.

Acknowledgments

Fraser Neiman, LuAnn Wandsnider, and Robert J. Wenke read this essay in draft and made many useful suggestions. Mary D. Dunnell made major editorial contributions. I am most grateful for their assistance.

References

Alexander, R. D.
  1979 *Darwinism and Human Affairs*. University of Washington Press, Seattle.
Binford, L. R.
  1965 Archaeological Systematics and the Study of Process. *American Antiquity* 31:203–210.

    1968   Archeological Perspectives. In *New Perspectives in Archeology*, edited by S. R. Binford and L. R. Binford, pp. 5–32. Aldine, Chicago.
Blumler, M. A., and R. Byrne
    1991   The Ecological Genetics of Domestication and the Origins of Agriculture. *Current Anthropology* 32:23–54.
Blute, M.
    1979   Sociocultural Evolutionism: An Untried Theory. *Behavioral Science* 24:46–59.
Bonner, J. T.
    1980   *The Evolution of Culture in Animals*. Princeton University Press, Princeton.
    1988   *The Evolution of Complexity by Means of Natural Selection*. Princeton University Press, Princeton.
Boyd, R., and P. J. Richerson
    1985   *Culture and Evolutionary Process*. University of Chicago Press, Chicago.
Ceci, L.
    1980   Comment on "Symbiosis, Instability, and the Origins and Spread of Agriculture (Rindos)." *Current Anthropology* 21:766.
Christensen, A. L.
    1989   Preface. In *Tracing Archaeology's Past: The Historiography of Archaeology*, edited by A. L. Christensen, pp. ix–xi. Southern Illinois University Press, Carbondale.
Clemens, S. L.
    1982   *A Connecticut Yankee in King Arthur's Court*, edited by A. R. Ensor. Norton, New York. Originally published 1889.
Darwin, C.
    1859   *The Origin of Species*. John Murray, London.
DeBoer, W. R., and D. W. Lathrap
    1979   The Making and Breaking of Shipibo-Conibo Ceramics. In *Ethnoarchaeology: Implications of Ethnography for Archaeology*, edited by C. Kramer, pp. 102–138. Columbia University Press, New York.
Dunnell, R. C.
    1978a   Style and Function: A Fundamental Dichotomy. *American Antiquity* 43:192–202.
    1978b   Natural Selection, Scale, and Cultural Evolution: Some Preliminary Considerations. Paper presented at the 77th Annual Meeting of the American Anthropological Association, Los Angeles.
    1980   Evolutionary Theory and Archaeology. In *Advances in Archaeological Method and Theory*, vol. 3, edited by Michael B. Schiffer, pp. 35–99. Academic Press, New York.
    1982   Science, Social Science, and Common Sense: The Agonizing Dilemma of Modern Archaeology. *Journal of Anthropological Research* 38:1–25.
    1986   Five Decades of American Archaeology. In *American Archaeology Past and Future: A Celebration of the Society for American Archaeology 1935–1985*, edited by D. J. Meltzer, D. D. Fowler, and J. A. Sabloff, pp. 23–49. Smithsonian Institution Press, Washington, D.C.
    1987   Comment on "History, Phylogeny, and Evolution in Polynesia" (R. V. Kirch and R. C. Green). *Current Anthropology* 28:444–445.
    1988 Archaeology and Evolutionary Theory. Paper presented at the University of Missouri, Columbia.
    1989   Aspects of the Application of Evolutionary Theory in Archaeology. In *Archaeological Thought in America*, edited by C. C. Lamberg-Karlovsky, pp. 35–49. Cambridge University Press, Cambridge.

Durham, W. H.
    1976   The Adaptive Significances of Cultural Behavior. *Human Ecology* 4:89–121.
Gould, R. A.
    1980   *Living Archaeology*. Cambridge University Press, Cambridge.
Gould, S. J.
    1986   Evolution and the Triumph of Homology, or Why History Matters. *American Scientist* 74:60–69.
Hesse, M.
    1978   Theory and Value in the Social Sciences. In *Action and Interpretation: Studies in the Philosophy of the Social Sciences*, edited by C. Hookway and P. Pettit, pp. 1–16. Cambridge University Press, Cambridge.
Hodder, I.
    1986   *Reading the Past: Current Approaches to Interpretation in Archaeology*. Cambridge University Press, Cambridge.
Holmes, W. H.
    1892   Evolution of the Aesthetic. *Proceedings of the American Association for the Advancement of Science for the Forty-First Meeting Held at Rochester, N. Y., August 1892*, edited by F. W. Putnam, pp. 239–255. Salem, Massachusetts.
Jarvie, I. C.
    1985   Anthropology as Science and the Anthropology of Science and of Anthropology, or Understanding and Explanation in the Social Sciences, Part II. In *PSA 1984*, vol. 2, edited by P. D. Asquith and P. Kitcher, pp. 745–763. Philosophy of Science Association, East Lansing, Michigan.
Kirch, P. V., and R. C. Green
    1987   History, Phylogeny and Evolution in Polynesia. *Current Anthropology* 28:431–456.
Leudtke, B. E.
    1986   Flexible Tools for Constructing the Past. *Man in the Northeast* 31:89–98.
Lewontin, R. C.
    1974   *The Genetic Basis of Evolutionary Change*. Columbia University Press, New York.
Longacre, W. A.
    1970   Current Thinking in American Archeology. In *Current Directions in Anthropology*, edited by A. Fischer, pp. 126–138. Bulletin of the American Anthropological Association 3 (Part 2). Washington, D.C.
Lumsden, C., and E. O. Wilson
    1981 *Genes, Mind, and Culture*. Harvard University Press, Cambridge.
Mayr, E.
    1959   Typological Thinking Versus Population Thinking. In *Evolution and Anthropology: A Centennial Appraisal*, edited by B. J. Meggars, pp. 409–412. Washington Anthropological Society, Washington, D.C.
McGowan, K. P.
    1989   Archaeology as Recreation: An Alternative Approach to the Public. *ASCA Report* 16(2):11–20.
Neiman, F. D.
    1990   *An Evolutionary Approach to Archaeological Inference: Aspects of Architectural Variation in the 17th Century Chesapeake*. Ph.D. dissertation, Yale University. University Microfilms, Ann Arbor.
O'Brien, M. J., and T. D. Holland
    1990   Variation, Selection, and the Archaeological Record. *Archaeological Method*

and Theory, vol. 2, edited by Michael B. Schiffer, pp. 31–79. University of Arizona Press, Tucson.

Parker, A. C.
   1935   Editorial. *American Antiquity* 1:2–3.

Polya, G.
   1954   *Mathematics and Plausible Reasoning*. 2 vols. Princeton University Press, Princeton.

Popper, K.
   1963   *The Poverty of Historicism*. Routledge and Kegan Paul, London.
   1974   Autobiography of Karl Popper. In *The Philosophy of Karl Popper*, edited by P. A. Schilpp, pp. 2–181. Open Court, LaSalle, Illinois.

Raab, L. M., and A. C. Goodyear
   1984   Middle Range Theory in Archaeology: A Critical Review of Origins and Applications. *American Antiquity* 49:255–268.

Rindos, D. J.
   1980   Symbiosis, Instability, and the Origins and Spread of Agriculture. *Current Anthropology* 21:751–772.
   1984   *The Origins of Agriculture: An Evolutionary Perspective*. Academic Press, New York.

Sabloff, J. A.
   1989   Analyzing Recent Trends in American Archaeology from a Historical Perspective. In *Tracing Archaeology's Past: The Historiography of Archaeology*, edited by A. L. Christensen, pp. 34–40. Southern Illinois University Press, Carbondale.
   1990   Surveying the Field. *SAA Bulletin* 8(2):2.

Schiffer, M. B.
   1979   Discussion: Fractures and Angles. In *Lithic Use-Wear Analysis*, edited by B. Hayden, pp. 137–141. Academic Press, New York.
   1988   The Structure of Archaeological Theory. *American Antiquity* 53:461–485.

Sellars, W.
   1962   Philosophy and the Scientific Image of Man. In *Frontiers of Science and Philosophy*, edited by R. G. Colodny, pp. 5–78. University of Pittsburgh Press, Pittsburgh.

Shaffer, J. G.
   1980   Comment on "Symbiosis, Instability, and the Origins and Spread of Agriculture (Rindos)." *Current Anthropology* 21:768.

Shanks, M., and C. Y. Tilley
   1987   *Re-Constructing Archaeology: Theory and Practice*. Cambridge University Press, Cambridge.

Sober, E.
   1980   Evolution, Population Thinking, and Essentialism. *Philosophy of Science* 47:350–399.
   1984   *The Nature of Selection*. MIT Press, Cambridge, Massachusetts.

Spaulding, A. C.
   1953   Review of *Measurements of Some Prehistoric Design Developments in the Southeastern States* (J. A. Ford). *American Anthropologist* 55:588–593.

    1968   Explanation in Archeology. In *New Perspectives in Archeology,* edited by S. R. Binford and L. R. Binford, pp. 33–40. Aldine, Chicago.

Thomas, C.
    1898   *Introduction to the Study of North American Archaeology.* Robert Clarke, Cincinnati.

Trigger, B. G.
    1985   Marxism in Archaeology? Real or Spurious. *Reviews in Anthropology* 12:114–123.

Wassermann, G. D.
    1981   On the Nature of the Theory of Evolution. *Philosophy of Science* 48:416–437.

Watson, P. J.
    1982   Untitled section in A Dialogue on the Meaning and Use of Analogy in Ethnoarchaeological Reasoning (R. A. Gould and P. J. Watson). *Journal of Anthropological Archaeology* 1:355–381.

Watson, P. J., S. A. LeBlanc, and C. L. Redman
    1971   *Explanation in Archeology: An Explicitly Scientific Approach.* Columbia University Press, New York.
    1984   *Archeological Explanation. The Scientific Method in Archeology.* Columbia University Press, New York.

Willer, D., and J. Willer
    1973   *Systematic Empiricism: A Critique of a Pseudoscience.* Prentice-Hall, Englewood Cliffs, New Jersey.

Willey, G. R., and J. A. Sabloff
    1980   *A History of American Archaeology.* 2d ed. W. H. Freeman, San Francisco.

Wilson, E. O.
    1975   *Sociobiology: The New Synthesis.* Harvard University Press, Cambridge.

Wylie, A.
    1982   An Analogy by Any Other Name Is Just as Analogical: A Commentary on the Gould-Watson Dialogue. *Journal of Anthropological Archaeology* 1:382–401.
    1985   The Reaction Against Analogy. In *Advances in Archaeological Method and Theory,* vol. 8, edited by Michael B. Schiffer, pp. 63–111. Academic Press, New York.

Yarnell, R.
    1985   Review of *The Origins of Agriculture: An Evolutionary Perspective* (D. Rindos). *American Antiquity* 50:698–699.

17. Archaeology and Behavioral Science: Manifesto for an Imperial Archaeology

Michael Brian Schiffer

Abstract: This essay argues that archaeologists need to be more aggressive in applying their conceptual framework to problems traditionally attacked by the other social and behavioral sciences. As behavioral archaeologists have noted, the archaeological perspective is based on an appreciation for the multifarious relationships between people and their things, which are at the core of human behavior. This polemic is illustrated by a case study from the history of twentieth-century electronics. Recent assertions by political scientists, economists, and others about the early history of U.S.-Japanese competition in consumer electronics are shown to be erroneous on the basis of an archaeological analysis of the problem.

Today archaeologists passively consume the theoretical products of other disciplines, from Darwinian selectionism to critical theory. Tomorrow we must spread among other disciplines—and society at large—a new view of human behavior founded upon an archaeological perspective. To promote such developments, this essay furnishes the mandate for—and an example of—an imperial archaeology.

Toward a New Behavioral Science

A number of years ago, behavioral archaeologists began to advocate a new definition for the discipline, one that could integrate the disparate research interests sired by the new archaeology. Archaeology's irreducible core, according to the behavioral archaeologists, is the study of relationships between human behavior and material culture in all times and

Quandaries and Quests: Visions of Archaeology's Future, edited by LuAnn Wandsnider. Center for Archaeological Investigations, Occasional Paper No. 20. © 1992 by the Board of Trustees, Southern Illinois University. All rights reserved. ISBN 0-88104-075-4.

all places (Rathje 1979; Rathje and Schiffer 1982; Reid et al. 1975; Schiffer 1976). Whether this definition is accepted, it must be granted that the study of artifacts makes archaeology a unique intellectual enterprise among the social and behavioral sciences. Only in archaeology are the ordinary and extraordinary things of daily life of central concern.

What the other social and behavioral sciences are missing is nothing less than the essence of human behavior. Indeed, what gives human behavior its distinctive character is an uncompromising, pervasive reliance on artifacts. To be human, then, is to manipulate matter and energy—and, as post-processualists stress (e.g., Hodder 1982), other people—with things. That becomes evident if we regard human behavior, as an archaeologist must, as concrete activities embedded in ever larger aggregates of activities (Rathje and Schiffer 1982; Schiffer 1992). Because activities at all scales involve artifacts, no serious study of human behavior can proceed without a thoroughgoing treatment of artifacts.

Social and behavioral sciences that build their foundations on artifactless conceptions of behavior—as all but archaeology do—have no hope of illuminating the principles of human behavior. Their rarefied conceptions float too far above the incessant behavioral-material transactions that are the stuff of life. Perhaps in this world of their own creation, social and behavioral scientists can escape the material reality in which people ply their existence. It is a curious intellectual tradition, perhaps traceable to the philosophers of ancient Greece and Rome (who held technology in low regard), that defines away the heart of human behavior.

Archaeologists cannot afford the luxury of ignoring artifacts or their centrality in human life. The past exists today only in artifacts, as we are painfully aware. Yet it is not a cup half empty, as some would maintain, but a cup nearly full. As Binford (1962) has reminded us, those artifacts played a part in diverse activities—technological, social, and ideological—and so their study can tell us much about what life in the past was really like. To extract behavioral information from things, archaeologists have developed a surprising variety of theories and lower-level principles, many of which treat behavioral-material interactions (Schiffer 1988). Though the building of such theories, through experimental archaeology, ethnoarchaeology, comparative ethnography, and so forth, is far from complete, archaeology alone among the mainline social and behavioral sciences is forging the conceptual tools for creating a sound understanding of human behavior. Archaeology's main advantage is that its conceptual framework accords artifacts a place of prominence in human affairs; artifact-behavior relationships are at the core rather than at the periphery of theory-building.

If archaeology's way of looking at human behavior has no counterparts among the other social and behavioral sciences, as behavioral archaeologists maintain (cf. Schiffer 1992), then we should be able to provide fresh insights into long-standing problems. This can come about through the reformulation of questions to include behavior-artifact interactions and, especially, the gathering of new behavior-artifact data. In addition, issues of public policy should benefit from archaeological scrutiny (Rathje 1979; Rathje and Schiffer

1982). To date, we have as a group been reluctant to apply our conceptual scheme beyond the discipline's borders. That will slowly change in the years ahead as archaeologists begin to explore the dimensions of an imperial archaeology. I am optimistic that, by the turn of the millennium, Rathje will no longer be alone in demonstrating the power and relevance of archaeological principles beyond archaeology.

The case study that I shall employ to underscore the plausibility of an imperial archaeology is based on my recent research into the history of consumer electronic technology. What follows is condensed from the last three chapters of *The Portable Radio in American Life* (Schiffer 1991).

An Archaeological Look at U.S. Competitiveness

During the 1950s, approximately half the U.S. workforce was engaged in manufacturing; today it is around 20% (cf. Cohen and Zysman 1987). Since 1980, an endless stream of weighty tomes, written by think tanks, industrial consultants, and professors (some commissioned by the president and the national academies), has examined America's industrial decline. Often, the investigators carrying out the studies have been economists and political scientists. For the most part, they have diagnosed the problem as a failure of U.S. industries to compete successfully in the new global economy (e.g., Kotler et al. 1985; Lodge and Scott 1985). Case studies have chronicled the demise of one American industry after another—steel, textiles, automobiles, consumer electronics, and so on—with the express purpose of galvanizing policymakers to provide a more favorable environment for industrial investment at home. The recommendations advanced range from a needs-based Social Security system to a value-added tax on all consumer goods. While some of these "remedies" may have merit, they all rest in part on the lessons allegedly taught by the historical cases.

On the basis of macroeconomic statistics, such as balance of payments, most investigators have concluded that problems in the consumer electronics industry began in the 1970s (cf. Lodge and Scott 1985), though a few put the origin in the mid-sixties. Thus, the alleged experts usually confine detailed analysis to the last two decades and concentrate on color TV (e.g., Baranson 1981; Millstein 1983; Office of Technology Assessment 1983), although it was one of the last U.S. products to give way to foreign competition. Reliance on macrostatistics has, I suggest, prevented recognition of the crucial first stages of the process. For example, I place the beginnings of the consumer electronics industry's woes in the late fifties.

Although recent studies fail to treat in detail the early history of U.S.-Japanese competition in consumer electronics, analysts do not hesitate to generalize about the beginnings of the process. In one of the earliest and most influential books on the problems faced by the U.S. industry, Baranson made the following assertions:

> In the early 1950s, U.S. component makers were moving into a limited production of transistor radios, built as electronic curiosities. The major

U.S. radio manufacturers had traditionally built large console and tube radios, had major investments in tube radio production facilities, and in most cases were also major producers of tubes. Thus they saw little incentive for pursuing the new technology extensively. The Japanese government and its fledgling electronics industry, however, saw the small transistor radio as a unique opportunity to enter the world market and earn badly needed foreign exchange. . . . A key ingredient in these early Japanese successes was the lack of competition from the major U.S. consumer electronic companies [1981:41–42].

In a more recent work, Sanderson constructs the following scenario:

U.S. firms willingly licensed their technology to Japanese firms that improved on the basic designs, and commercialized these "seed technologies." Using adaptive research, development, and engineering, Japanese firms made many product and process improvements. . . . Increasingly, U.S. firms lagged behind in developing and refining designs and production processes [1989:8–9].

The clear implication of this quote is that American electronics companies lost out because they fell behind technologically. This assessment is perhaps accurate for the 1980s, but it may not fit the earliest stages of the process. Probably following Baranson (1981), Sanderson also implies that American firms were simply unable and unwilling to respond to serious competitive pressure; they turned tail and ran.

Another rather widely held assumption is that Japanese firms developed unique products unavailable from American companies (cf. Baranson 1981; Kotler et al. 1985; Millstein 1983; Office of Technology Assessment 1983). This is what I call the "open niche hypothesis." It assumes that American consumers were poised at the docks, checkbook in hand, waiting for wonderful new products from abroad. The open niche hypothesis is irresistible from a macroeconomic perspective because it can allow the investigator to avoid dealing altogether with the consumer and the place of the product in the consumer's life.

In addition, those who accept the open niche hypothesis seemingly are forced to ignore or distort data not to their liking. For example, Kotler and others (1985:192) claim that in 1957 "the Japanese exported about one hundred thousand small, three-transistor radios to the United States, priced at $14, when U.S. firms were marketing six-transistor radios for $60." The material reality is somewhat different. Only one Japanese transistor radio was imported in 1957; it had six transistors and sold for $39.95. Small American-made transistor radios of 1957 were competitively priced at $30–45 (*Consumer Bulletin*, January 1958; *Consumer Reports*, November 1957). Ironically, the cheap Japanese import portables of 1957 contained tubes.

Where did these investigators obtain their ideas about what happened in the late fifties and early sixties? I suggest that there are two main sources. The first is the extrapolation of recent trends into the past, which assumes that the processes operating over more than two decades were unchanged. Second, investigators could have been taken in by what I call "cryptohistory": history-like statements that companies use to garner favor with consumers, investors, and the media (Schiffer 1991). Recently, cryptohistory about transistor radios, created by Japanese firms, including SONY, has been widely disseminated by the U.S. media. Regardless of their sources, ideas about what took place at the outset of U.S.-Japanese competition in consumer electronics can be treated as historical hypotheses and tested on relevant evidence.

Testing such hypotheses requires the examination of lines of historical evidence—artifacts all—ordinarily ignored by political scientists, economists, and others who do not deign to inspect real objects or the primary literature pertaining to real objects. Obviously, examples of radios made in the fifties and sixties survive in systemic context and can be scrutinized closely; I have examined an assemblage of more than 200 sets from that time period. The assemblage undoubtedly has its biases, and so one must consult additional information.

An especially valuable written source is *Howard W. Sams Photofacts*. These are service bulletins issued to subscribers (like radio-TV repair shops) after the appearance of a new model. For each model, *Photofacts* contains a parts list, a circuit diagram, and photos of the chassis. Because Japanese firms did not always supply the requisite technical information, *Photofacts* coverage of early Japanese transistor sets is spotty.

Another important source is *TV Digest*, a trade newsletter of the radio-TV manufacturing industry. This weekly publication documented the inroads made by Japanese radios in the U.S. market as well as the responses of U.S. firms—as they took place.

Advertisements in magazines and newspapers, articles in technical journals, and reports in consumer magazines help to flesh out the story. Information on the place of the radios in peoples' lives also derives from diverse sources (primary and secondary) of that time period, including magazine articles, social histories, and informants (including the author).

In short, this is a motley corpus of data, the sort of historical leavings that political scientists and economists apparently avoid. Yet an archaeologist is at home trying to integrate such diverse evidence into a coherent picture of past processes. Ironically, the most serious obstacle encountered during the study was the recent literature: many of its conclusions about early U.S.-Japanese competition are fictional. It was also comforting to discover that the important features of the process stand out clearly in the radios themselves. Doubtless a latter-day Rathje, excavating twentieth-century landfills, would be able generally to figure out what happened to the U.S. consumer electronics industry.

The first electronic product to be overwhelmed by Japanese competition was the portable radio; in particular, the shirt-pocket radio. Already in 1960, more than half the portables sold in the United States were made in Japan. Did Japanese companies, as some modern observers believe, see the transistor's potential for building portable radios before U.S. companies? Did they rush to fill a large niche left empty because U.S. firms were slow to see the transistor's potential for consumer products? Did U.S. firms quickly fall behind in technology? Let us see what really happened.

The transistor was invented in 1947 by AT&T, which launched it in 1948 with a public show-and-tell (Braun and MacDonald 1978). The demonstration included the playing of an all-transistor portable radio. The transistor's greatest advantage over tubes then was in much lower power consumption; everyone in the U.S. industry appreciated that the transistor would make possible portable radios that could be operated much more economically than their tube counterparts.

Transistors, however, were at first very difficult to mass produce (Braun and MacDonald 1978). In 1951, for example, a few companies were selling them commercially for about $18 each—compared to less than $1 for a tube. From 1951 to 1954, as the price of transistors descended, radio companies began planning for the manufacture of transistor portables. RCA, for example, issued to its licensees a circuit diagram for such a radio in 1953 and exhibited a demonstration set to the media along with other transistor products (*Radio and Television News*, January 1953). It was about the size of a small lunchbox, with a large enough speaker to sound decent. Much smaller radios were also on the drawing boards, though few were shirt-pocket size.

The major companies believed there was little market for a radio that small because it could not reproduce music well. A few shirt-pocket radios with tubes actually were marketed between 1945 and 1954, but consumer response was minimal. To most people a radio that small was a novelty item or toy.

At the same time that miniaturization in home radios was being widely eschewed, U.S. electronics companies—sometimes the same ones that made consumer products—were developing technologies of solid-state miniaturization on cost-plus contracts for the U.S. military (cf. Gilbert 1961), then engaged in the missile race. Transistor-making companies were heavily subsidized by military purchases, and the manufacture of miniature parts and assemblies of all kinds was promoted vigorously. As a result of that process, the trajectories of military and consumer electronic technologies diverged during the fifties, one hell-bent on miniaturization of components and apparatus at any cost, the other cranking out effective products of ordinary size using larger and cheaper components.

One transistor-making company, Texas Instruments (TI), decided in 1954 that a commercial transistor radio could serve its purposes. An outsider in the electronic components industry, TI was especially eager to showcase its ability to mass-produce high-quality transistors (Wolff 1985). TI engineers designed a shirt-pocket portable radio and shopped around for a company to make it using TI transistors. They got no takers among the established radio firms; after all, most were planning their own transistor sets, and many were also making transistors. Moreover, they were not interested in a shirt-pocket design. TI finally found a small but reputable Indiana company, I.D.E.A., to build its set. The president of I.D.E.A.—which made sundry electronic devices but no other radios—was convinced that Americans would buy 20 million of their Lilliputian sets to use for civil defense (*Los Angeles Mirror*, October 19, 1954). Portable radios, after all, were a necessity for the home bomb shelter.

And so, in time for Christmas 1954, appeared the Regency TR-1, the world's first commercial transistor radio.

More than 100,000 Regency TR-1 sets were sold in the first year at $49.95 (Wolff 1985), but not many more were bought afterward—even at $39 and $29, despite national advertising. Apparently, the shirt-pocket radio market was saturated. I.D.E.A. and TI made no money on the TR-1—development costs had exceeded $1 million (Wolff 1985)—and in some quarters it is considered a commercial failure.

Although the Regency TR-1 was not a money-maker, other American transistor radios soon were. With transistor prices at around $3 each in early 1955, other radio companies soon brought their first solid-state sets to market. They were more than double the price of tube portables but had marvelous battery economy and, especially, that high-tech cachet, the transistor. Few companies besides I.D.E.A. brought out a shirt-pocket set per se, but there were some rather small U.S.-made transistor radios in 1955–57.

The larger transistor radios sold quite well. By the time SONY sent its first set to the United States in 1957, dozens of American transistor models were already available, and some played pretty well. Indeed, *Consumer Reports* (July 1958) gave check-ratings to many transistor sets. The end of the tube portable was in sight.

SONY's TR-63—a shirt-pocket set—was the first imported transistor radio to enter the U.S. market. SONY was followed in 1958 and 1959 by scores of other Japanese brands of shirt-pocket radios. Though they had built-in speakers, none reproduced music well. As a group the shirt-pocket radios were a runaway success, with millions selling annually by 1960.

Why did the Japanese sets have such robust sales? To answer that question, one has to look at the role of these tinny, tiny radios in the lives of Americans. Superior technology, it turns out, had nothing to do with the triumph of Japan's shirt-pocket portables.

In 1954, when the Regency TR-1 was introduced, Elvis Aron Presley still made his living driving a truck (Hammontree 1985). Rock and roll was not yet a national phenomenon, much less big business. By 1957 and 1958, however, rock was on a roll, and the musical tastes of generations had diverged. To serve these differing interests, popular-music radio stations began to specialize, some playing old favorites to adults, others playing only rock to American youth. Increasingly, the transistor radio, particularly the shirt-pocket portable, was adopted as an adult solution to the rock-and-roll problem. Teenagers equipped with the sets (usually as gifts), which included earplugs, had an unprecedented mobility while listening to their music. In the late fifties, these miniature radios became the symbol of rock and roll's first generation of listeners.

The Japanese, pure and simple, lucked out. The entry of their transistor radios into the U.S. market coincided perfectly with the growth of rock-only radio stations. In 1959, Japan produced a total of about 12 million radios, of which more than 5 million were transistor portables—mostly shirt-pocket size—exported to the United States (M.I.T.I. 1960). Clearly, the musical tastes of America teenagers had everything to do with the success of the Japanese radio makers in the U.S. market. (For themselves, adults bought the larger, American-made transistor sets.) The shirt-pocket radio, then, was at the beginning of two interrelated technological processes: the rise of Japanese consumer electronics in the world market and the decline of the U.S. consumer electronics industry.

Having laid this foundation, let us return to the hypotheses about the process. Did the Japanese enter an open product niche? The answer is, only in part. American companies in 1957 already offered a wide range of transistor portables that had been well received by both consumers and consumer magazines. However, in 1957 only a very few sets were being produced in the shirt-pocket format. Major American companies were confident, based on experience, that American adults—traditionally the buyers of consumer electronic products—would not want shirt-pocket radios. Even after the Regency TR-1's modest showing, American firms did not immediately jump in with copies. That narrow niche was surely open, but U.S. radio makers believed, on the basis of previous experience, that it was small. Neither they nor the Japanese foresaw that rock and roll would vastly expand this niche. Yet, when it did expand, the Japanese were there with transistor shirt-pocket radios by the millions.

In meeting the demands of the U.S. teenage market, the Japanese turned out radios that were judged as good quality by American industry observers (cf. *TV Digest*, February 15, 1958) and consumer magazines (*Consumer Bulletin*, November 1959). What had facilitated Japan's incipient solid-state revolution? Was it cheap labor and American technology, as American observers in the late fifties believed, or was it an American technology highly perfected, as many of today's analysts contend? Let us address those interesting questions before we turn to the American response to the Japanese imports.

Japanese labor rates in fact were much lower than those in the United States in the late fifties. For example, assembly line workers at Hitachi, mostly young women, made about $10/week, plus benefits (Leary 1960)—about one-seventh the pay of U.S. workers.

Insofar as technology is concerned, the radios themselves tell an interesting story. The SONY TR-63, which opened the floodgates for Japanese shirt-pocket sets, contains a printed circuit board, a technology already widely used in U.S. portables. Not only was SONY a latecomer to printed circuits, but the company had not yet mastered them. The less-than-optimum design of the TR-63's circuit board necessitated several labor-intensive fixes, including a number of traditional wire connections and the soldering of six components on the bottom of the board. By this time, Motorola in the United States had refined the use of printed circuits to the point where soldering could be done mechanically in a dipping process. In the SONY set, however, all parts were soldered individually by hand. The indisputable evidence of the radio itself indicates a labor-intensive manufacturing technology.

In the fifties, Motorola was moving ahead briskly on process technology, attempting to squeeze out as much labor as possible from radio (and TV) assembly lines (*Business Week*, April 27, 1957). Consumer electronics was an unusually competitive American business (*contra* Borrus et al. 1983:148) long before the Japanese arrived. For example, in what Robert Galvin (personal communication, 1989), a former president of Motorola, calls a "reverse auction," large retailers would take bids from manufacturers on a specific number of units—say 5,000 table radios—and accept the lowest bid. Needless to say, profits were slim. Indeed, in the late fifties, the industry was undergoing another of its periodic shakeouts, with many companies forced to merge or drop unprofitable products. Among the survivors were several companies that, like Motorola, had made extensive use of printed circuit boards. Motorola and other firms also employed early integrated circuits in which a dozen or so components were made on a single ceramic substrate. Though costing more than the set of individual components that were replaced, integrated circuits also reduced assembly costs (*TV Digest*, January 5, 1957). These technological innovations were being widely adopted in the fifties by many companies to save labor. Although Japanese firms eventually mastered printed circuits and dip soldering, almost none made use of integrated circuits; it is clear from the sets themselves that labor-saving innovations were of secondary concern.

What distinguishes the early Japanese radios technologically is their size. Beginning with the SONY TR-63, the Japanese pursued miniaturization in portable radios with unprecedented vigor. Miniaturization was achieved in two ways. First, components were crowded together on the circuit board to an extreme degree. This strategy meant higher labor input because of the tight spaces in which parts had to be manipulated by hand. Second, components themselves were miniaturized. It is evident that Japanese firms were trying to scale down all components more or less to transistor size. They were remarkably successful. Using miniature components, Toshiba in 1959 made a shirt-pocket radio that was only 2–15/16 inches tall.

To American radio makers, the shrinking derby made no sense for consumer products; smaller radios would simply produce a tinnier sound—it was technological virtuosity for its own sake. Radios with tubes had already reached the limits of miniaturization that would be judged by adults as acceptable performers. The Japanese, however, apparently took their cue from American military electronics, where ultraminiaturization was the highest priority. To the Japanese it was obvious that a world-class electronics industry for the transistor age would require miniature components. Unlike the miniature components produced by American companies for military equipment, Japanese parts were sold at low prices.

The rapid and thorough move to miniature components put Japanese consumer electronics on a trajectory far different from that of U.S. firms. By 1960, although the United States was the world's leader in miniaturization— an entire radio circuit could be made the size of a thimble—the technologies were still prohibitively expensive. Japanese companies, who had no significant military markets, pursued miniaturization of components relentlessly, even though further miniaturization of the products themselves did not appear to be needed. The result was the creation of a huge capacity to make transistors and transistor-compatible, miniature components that were cheap and of good quality. Those parts served as the foundation of Japan's entire consumer electronics industry as it converted from tubes to transistors.

Having established the basic differences in technology between American and Japanese consumer electronics companies in the late fifties, we can now examine how American companies coped with the new foreign competition.

Beginning in 1959 and 1960, all U.S. companies began to sell shirt-pocket portables to counter the growing presence of Japanese imports. Although the youth market was vast, profit margins were apt to be small because of Japanese price-cutting and the entry of so many American companies. U.S. firms differed in the ways they coped with the anticipated low profit margins; these varied responses and their ultimate outcomes tell us much about how the United States began the retreat from consumer electronics more than three decades ago.

In 1959, several companies immediately turned to Japanese firms to supply complete shirt-pocket radios that carried the American brand names. (Usually the made-in-Japan radios were not conspicuously identified as such.) The big surprise was that among the companies making this move was Motorola (*TV Digest*, July 13, 1959), industry leader in integration and process technology. Motorola had apparently concluded that, even with their technological lead, making shirt-pocket radios in the United States was not a winning proposition. A second response was to make shirt-pocket radios in the United States that included some Japanese parts.

A third and final response, *adopted by most of the major companies*, was to compete with an all-American shirt-pocket radio (*TV Digest*, July 13, 1959). Although U.S.-made parts were not as small as Japanese equivalents, they were adequately miniaturized for shirt-pocket radios.

How did the U.S. companies fare? Although in 1960 some companies were selling all-American shirt-pocket sets for $29.95 (*TV Digest*, January 11, 1960), a few Japanese sets were now at $20. The price pressure was so intense that many more American companies switched to Japanese parts or Japanese manufacture of their sets. By 1962, only three companies were still making all-American shirt-pocket portables (*TV Digest*, February 5, 1962). Surprisingly, in the spring of 1962, a few U.S.-made sets, which contained many Japanese parts, dropped to the $15 level to match the imports (*TV Digest*, April 9, 1962). Yet it was clearly a losing battle, especially when Japanese companies or their affiliates in Hong Kong and other East Asian nations began to flood the market with even cheaper radios (*TV Digest*, February 11, 1963). By the end of 1963, there were no all-American sets (cf. *TV Digest*, April 1, 1963). Just a few years later, in 1967, no company was making a shirt-pocket radio in the United States. At the end of the decade, only 10% of all portable radios sold in the United States were made here (E.I.A. 1970).

Clearly, U.S. companies did not roll over and play dead in the face of foreign competition, as many observers today believe (e.g., Baranson 1981; Borrus et al. 1983; Kotler et al. 1985). They did mount a diversified challenge to the imports, and many important companies—for example, RCA, Zenith, and General Electric—took the Japanese head-on with all-American radios. Yet, in the end, all abandoned U.S. production, regardless of which strategy they had initially pursued. Even companies that used mostly Japanese parts were driven out of the shirt-pocket radio market. It would appear that cheaper labor—not superior technology—explains much about why the Japanese were able to prevail.

Although cheap labor was the critical factor in Japan's domination of the shirt-pocket radio market, a significant role was also played by Japanese innovations in marketing strategies. In the late 1950s, Japanese companies distributed their radios through unconventional channels for electronic products, for example, relying on distributors of novelty items (*TV Digest*, July 13, 1959). As a result, Japanese shirt-pocket radios were presented to the consumer on almost every front: drugstores, jewelry stores, department stores, discount stores, even hardware stores (Baranson 1981:42). In countless retail outlets, inexpensive Japanese shirt-pocket portables were very visible indeed to the product's ultimate consumer—American teenagers.

The Japanese were also able to capture a large market share because they had so many brands (about 75) and models (more than 200). Some of them, of course, were the exact same radio with a different name or number, probably sold through different distributors. American adults, who bought many of the shirt-pocket sets as gifts for their teenagers, had at that time strong loyalty to American-made products; however, few probably suspected that radios named "Americana," "Hudson," and "Marvel" were made in Japan. Most Japanese companies used American-sounding brand names. Even when Japanese origins were clear, the sheer numbers of sets available in so many outlets was a significant marketing asset, for many consumers would doubtless buy the first or cheapest set they encountered. In contrast, the number of all-American radio brands—major and minor—had dropped below 20 by 1960. The probabilities were clearly in favor of the Japanese. And, of course, teenagers themselves did not feel compelled to buy American.

It should also be noted that many people in the United States electronics industry did not regard loss of the shirt-pocket radio as calamitous or as a taste of things to come. After all, it was a child's radio that, at best, yielded low profits. U.S. companies were confident that the Japanese, still technological imitators, would not quickly master TV (cf. *TV Digest*, July 13, 1959). This was clearly wishful thinking. But it was also believed that, because the market for TVs in Japan was almost totally untouched in the late fifties, Japanese companies would first concentrate on the home market (*TV Digest*, March 22, 1958). American companies also thought that their lead in technology could be maintained (cf. *TV Digest*, January 11, 1960), which would compensate—especially in more expensive products—for low wages in Japan. Moreover, color TV was finally beginning to interest consumers, and so companies expected to reap huge profits from this high-ticket item (and they did).

Though generally upbeat about the future of consumer electronics, a few American companies did sound the alarm, beginning in the late fifties, trying to convince federal officials and Congress that Japanese shirt-pocket radios represented a threat to the industry—even to national security (cf. *TV Digest*, October 12, 1959). Aside from being ludicrous at face value, the claims fell on deaf ears at the time. Macroeconomic indicators, upon which policymakers relied, simply did not register any ominous trends. Sales and profits in the electronics industry as a whole, pumped by military spending, were at historic highs in the late fifties and sixties (*Electronics*, January 5, 1962). Even consumer electronics—portable radios in particular—were profitable. The Japanese were simply taking a small nibble from a rapidly enlarging electronic pie. In addition, statistics showed that the United States still retained a trade surplus with Japan. Not until the 1970s would the macroeconomic statistics turn uniformly unfavorable, stimulating calls for action across a broad front. However, those calls came long after the decline of the consumer electronics industry had become critical.

Loss of the shirt-pocket portable was the beginning of the end for U.S. consumer electronics. This stage of the process was, for all practical purposes, complete by the early sixties. The first of many high-tech U.S. products had been completely overwhelmed by foreign competition. An entire industry had begun a retreat that, decades later, would culminate in the near-total abandonment of consumer electronics by American companies.

Conclusion

The preceding analysis has shown that an archaeological perspective has much to contribute to discussions of contemporary issues, particularly when material-culture processes provide important reference points. Many of today's policy statements on America's industrial decline are flawed—some fatally—by the backward projection of trends and patterns seen during the last 15 years.

Using the demise of the consumer electronics industry as an example, I have shown that the crucial first stage of the process, from which manufacturers learned the lessons they would apply later, occurred more than 25 years ago. Contemporary analysts, using a macroeconomic perspective, have misrepresented the early stage of the process. Although they have written about artifacts and technology at a high level of abstraction, they have not intensively *examined* artifacts and technology, nor have they investigated the relevant behaviors involved in the life histories of those artifacts.

Let me conclude by expressing the hope that the preceding example has at least raised the possibility that archaeology can make unique contributions to the study of human behavior. It is time, I submit, to build an imperial archaeology. In my view, an imperial archaeology is one that regards its focus on artifacts as a strength not a weakness, does not apologize for the incompleteness of the archaeological record, refuses to accept inferior status within the social and behavioral sciences, seeks to play a meaningful role in public policy, takes pride in its theory-building accomplishments, and strives constantly to find new applications for its principles.

Acknowledgments

I thank Zenith Electronics for allowing me to use their run of *TV Digest*. The Department of Anthropology, University of Arizona, and Lee Sigelman, dean of Social and Behavioral Sciences, granted me travel funds to visit various archives. James M. Skibo, LuAnn Wandsnider, and Teresita Majewski gave me helpful comments on an earlier draft of the essay. (More complete acknowledgments are furnished in Schiffer 1991.)

References

Baranson, Jack
   1981   *The Japanese Challenge to U.S. Industry*. Lexington Books, Lexington, Massachusetts.

Binford, Lewis R.
   1962   Archaeology as Anthropology. *American Antiquity* 28:217–225.

Borrus, Michael, James E. Millstein, and John Zysman
   1983   Trade and Development in the Semiconductor Industry: Japanese Challenge and American Response. In *American Industry in International Competition: Government Policies and Corporate Strategies*, edited by John Zysman and Laura Tyson, pp. 142–248. Cornell University Press, Ithaca, New York.

Braun, Ernest, and Stuart MacDonald
   1978   *Revolution in Miniature: The History and Impact of Semiconductor Electronics*. Cambridge University Press, Cambridge.

Cohen, Stephen S., and John Zysman
   1987   *Manufacturing Matters: The Myth of the Post-Industrial Economy*. Basic Books, New York.

Electronics Industries Association (EIA)
   1970   *Electronic Market Data Book, 1970*. Marketing Services Department, EIA, Washington, D.C.

Gilbert, Horace D. (editor)
   1961   *Miniaturization*. Reinhold, New York.

Hammontree, Patsy Guy
   1985   *Elvis Presley, a Bio-Bibliography*. Greenwood Press, Connecticut.

Hodder, Ian
   1982   *Symbols in Action*. Cambridge University Press, Cambridge.

Kotler, Philip, Liam Fahey, and Somkid Jatusripitak
   1985   *The New Competition*. Prentice-Hall, Englewood Cliffs, New Jersey.

Leary, Frank
   1960   Japanese Production Workers: A Close-up. *Electronics*, April 1, pp. 36–37.

Lodge, George C., and Bruce R. Scott (editors)
   1985   *U.S. Competitiveness in the World Economy*. Harvard Business School Press, Boston.

Millstein, James E.
   1983   Decline in an Expanding Industry: Japanese Competition in Color Television. In *American Industry in International Competition: Government Policies and Corporate Strategies*, edited by John Zysman and Laura Tyson, pp. 106–141. Cornell University Press, Ithaca, New York.

Ministry of International Trade and Industry (MITI)
   1960   *Transistor Radio Industry in Japan.* MITI, Tokyo.
Office of Technology Assessment
   1983   *International Competitiveness in Electronics.* U.S. Congress, Office of Technology Assessment, Washington, D.C.
Rathje, William L.
   1979   Modern Material Culture Studies. In *Advances in Archaeological Method and Theory,* vol. 2, edited by M. B. Schiffer, pp. 1–37. Academic Press, New York.
Rathje, William L., and Michael B. Schiffer
   1982   *Archaeology.* Harcourt Brace Jovanovich, New York.
Reid, J. Jefferson, Michael B. Schiffer, and William L. Rathje
   1975   Behavioral Archaeology: Four Strategies. *American Anthropologist* 77:864–869.
Sanderson, Susan Walsh
   1989   *The Consumer Electronics Industry and the Future of American Manufacturing. How the U.S. Lost the Lead and Why We Must Get Back in the Game.* Economic Policy Institute, Washington, D.C.
Schiffer, Michael B.
   1976   *Behavioral Archeology.* Academic Press, New York.
   1988   The Structure of Archaeological Theory. *American Antiquity* 53:461–485.
   1991   *The Portable Radio in American Life.* University of Arizona Press, Tucson.
   1992   *Technological Perspectives on Behavioral Change.* University of Arizona Press, Tucson.
Wolff, Michael F.
   1985   The Secret Six-Month Project. *IEEE Spectrum,* December.

18. The Role of Theory in Solving Enduring Archaeological Problems

Alan P. Sullivan III

Abstract: Archaeologists are generally aware that equifinality and the use of interpretive conventions attenuate their efforts to acquire knowledge of the past. These perennial problems affect the conduct of archaeological research, yet archaeologists reluctantly, if rarely, address them directly. The implications of the two enduring problems are explored and illustrated with examples drawn from the American Southwest. To resolve these problems and reduce their debilitating effects on the interpretation of archaeological variability, the role of theory in archaeological research is reexamined. Additional examples show that the development and use of interpretation-neutral units of observation and analysis, when coupled with hypothesis testing, facilitate an understanding of the origins of archaeological data. Such a strategy effectively dilutes the effects of equifinality and reduces dependence on interpretive conventions.

> Some pranksters at an end-of-the term dance released into the hall a piglet which had been smeared with grease. It squirmed between legs, evaded capture, squealed a lot. People fell over trying to grasp it, and were made to look ridiculous in the process. The past often seems to behave like that piglet.
> —Julian Barnes, *Flaubert's Parrot*

Introduction

While getting a firm grasp on the past is analogous to corralling a rambunctious, greased piglet, Julian Barnes's lucid observation, nevertheless, understates the dimensions of the problem. If anything, attempting to acquire secure knowledge of the past is a lot like choreographing a barnyard of wallowing, half-ton hogs for Swan (Swine?) Lake. The past *is* as unruly and uncooperative as a herd of pigs *en point*, and there are few of us who can deny

Quandaries and Quests: Visions of Archaeology's Future, edited by LuAnn Wandsnider. Center for Archaeological Investigations, Occasional Paper No. 20. © 1992 by the Board of Trustees, Southern Illinois University. All rights reserved. ISBN 0-88104-075-4.

that we occasionally find ourselves wondering whether its pursuit is commensurate with the effort.

Furthermore, it seems that not only can archaeologists not agree on what the past was like (e.g., O'Brien et al. 1989; Reid et al. 1989), but they likewise are seldom capable of settling on accords for bringing the beast under control (e.g., Binford 1981; Schiffer 1985). Regrettably, the current situation can be summed up as follows: "Particular interpretations can be more or less popular, but there is no definitive way to show that one is better than another" (Dunnell 1989:37).

Despite the occasionally strident rhetoric (e.g., Graves 1987; Upham and Plog 1986), these disputes do highlight some perennial epistemological issues that afflict archaeological inquiry (Clarke 1973:7; Schoenwetter 1990). Assuming that archaeologists seek to know the past or at least ascertain aspects of it, the nature of the task is little different from that faced by geomorphologists or astrophysicists. That is, as scientists, we seek information about phenomena that are not directly observable (Fritz 1972). The principal difficulty, of course, is that we must rely on observations of another phenomenon, the contemporary character of the archaeological record, to develop and test inferences about the nature of the past (Sullivan 1978). Hence, on what basis can archaeologists have any confidence whatsoever that they have acquired knowledge of the past? Although deliberately overstated, the question exemplifies the long-standing concern among archaeologists for inference justification (e.g., Guthe 1939:528; Schiffer 1976:11–18), assuming that we are all interested in objective, ideologically noncontingent knowledge of the past (Watson and Fotiadis 1990; Wylie 1989).

Although the philosopher Lester Embree (1987) contends that archaeology is an elementary science, two enduring problems hobble our ability to acquire basic information about the cultural past: (1) the equifinal origins of the archaeological record and (2) the use of interpretive conventions in assigning meaning to archaeological variability. Failure to address those problems has adversely affected the development of the discipline (e.g., Thomas 1983:8–9). Indeed, until archaeologists assail equifinality and eschew interpretive conventions, inference justification is likely to remain a popularity contest. If the problems persist, then we may become victims of the hubris that seduces us into assuming that such frivolity will be tolerated indefinitely by even the staunchest supporters of archaeological research (see also Dunnell, this volume).

To resolve this lamentable situation, I explore ways in which an archaeological theory might be constructed to overcome equifinality and reduce or eliminate the use of interpretive conventions, thereby enhancing inference validation and securing knowledge of the past. In executing this general strategy, I will describe briefly the nature of each problem and, using examples from some recent excavations near the Grand Canyon, highlight the consequences of each before proposing solutions to them.

Enduring Problem #1: Equifinality

Archaeologists have flirted with equifinality indirectly by focusing on the deleterious effects of ambiguity and strategies for its control (e.g., Binford 1983:21; Grayson 1986; Lamberg-Karlovsky 1970:113). Ambiguity is a complication because it creates, ironically, an abundance of riches in the form of multiple interpretations for a given body of archaeological data—hence, the current contentious nature of our discipline. Yet ambiguity is merely a symptom of equifinal systemic processes. For instance, featureless artifact scatters, which are a poorly understood class of archaeological sites, may originate through a variety of activities. Asserting merely that artifact scatters arose as a result of "limited activities" (e.g, Upham 1984) hardly accounts for the extensive differences in size and artifact density among them (Sullivan 1987a).

As an example, Figure 18-1 displays the distribution of artifact density classes for a portion of a large artifact scatter (AZ I:1:20[ASM]) near the Grand Canyon (Density Class I = 1–34 artifacts per $16m^2$; Density Class II = 37–73 artifacts per $16m^2$; Density Class III = 83–137 artifacts per $16m^2$). The subsite areas noted in Figure 18-1 were defined on the basis of discontinuities in the clinal variation of the density classes. Those areas are units of analysis, comparable to Carr's (1984:117) "anthropic depositional units," that were designed to explore possible sources of variation that contributed to the site's character. Areas 2 and 3—the only subsite areas with high-density artifact concentrations (Density Class III) and adequate samples of ceramics (23 and 67 sherds, respectively)—differ negligibly with respect to the composition of their debitage assemblages (Figure 18-2). It is difficult to argue, therefore, that lithic technology alone could account for the formation of the two subsite areas.

However, Areas 2 and 3 do differ substantially with respect to plainware assemblage composition (Figure 18-3). It seems more likely, then, that Site AZ I:1:20(ASM) is the equifinal result of at least two separate, though functionally similar, occupations. Although the interpretation of artifact density clinal variation is not unequivocal (Camilli 1989; Wandsnider and Ebert 1988), the example does illustrate the necessity for considering the origins of archaeological data and evaluating competing explanations for the same set of observations (cf. Binford 1977:7). Identifying and controlling for the effects of equifinality are considerable tasks, but making the effort clearly does not guarantee the eradication of equifinality. Perhaps, as Aberle (1987:556) remarked recently, "the past can be reconstructed, but not perfectly."

Enduring Problem #2: Interpretive Conventions

Interpretive conventions are assertions about the meaning of archaeological variability. Their use denies archaeologists access to variability that is critical to the investigation of many problems (Clay 1976:311; Reid et al. 1989). In the American Southwest, for instance, it has not been uncommon for

242 | A. P. Sullivan III

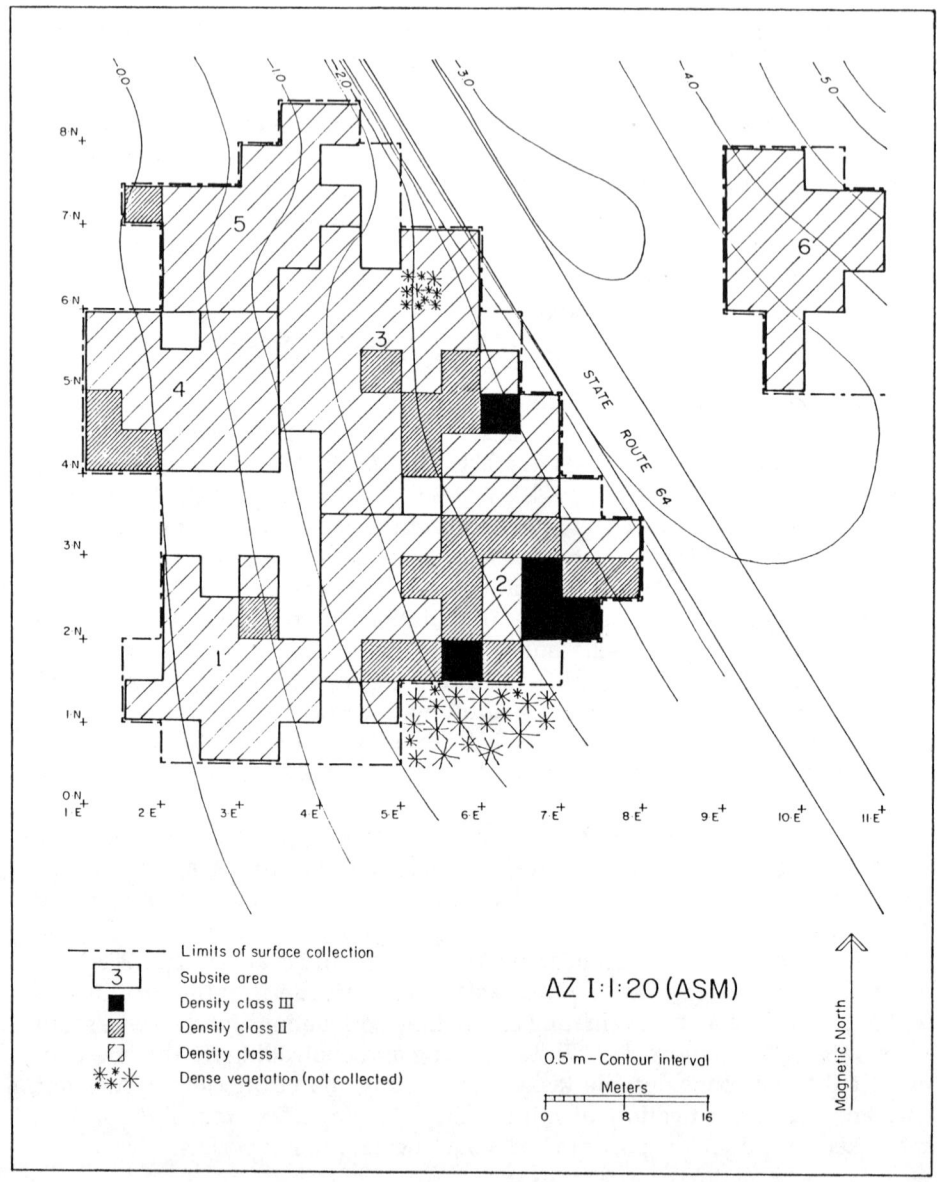

Figure 18-1. *Map of Site AZ I:1:20(ASM) showing the distribution of artifact density classes and the spatial extent of subsite areas defined on the basis of artifact density clinal variation.*

Theory and Archaeological Problems | 243

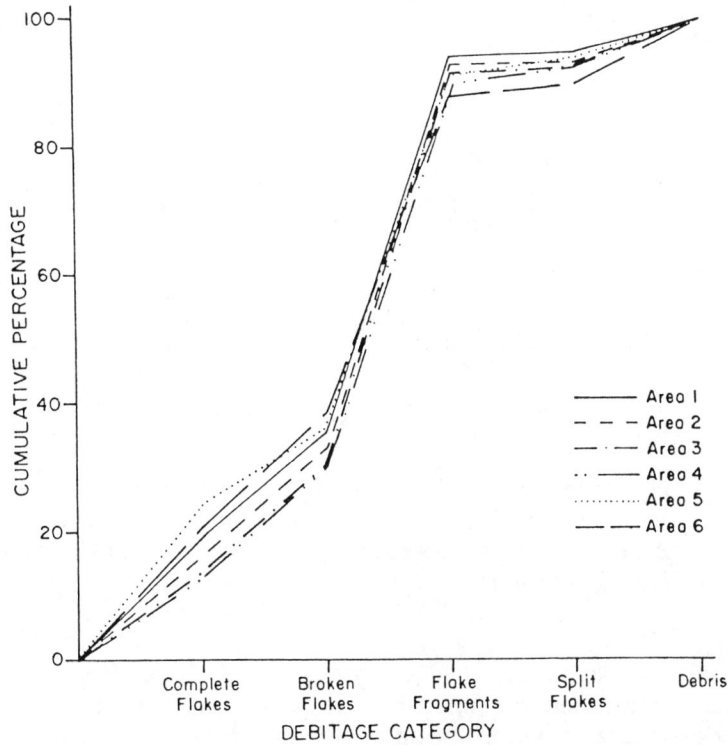

Figure 18-2. *Cumulative percentage graph of debitage assemblage variation between the six subsite areas at Site AZ I:1:20(ASM). Note the minimal differences between the subsite areas with respect to debitage category percentages.*

archaeologists to equate agricultural production with the occurrence of ground-stone artifacts (e.g., McGregor 1951:93; Wills 1989:149). The fallaciousness of this interpretive convention is easily demonstrated (see also Adams 1988).

With one possible exception, all floor-contact manos from Site AZ I:1:17(ASM), which was a burned Pueblo II Kayenta Anasazi site occupied between A.D. 1049 and 1064, were found on the floor of one structure (Sullivan 1986:129–133). Yet systematic sampling did not produce a single grain of domesticate pollen (Davis 1986:335), and domesticate macrobotanical remains of any sort were rare (0.5% [$n = 1,160+$]; Scott 1986). Despite preexcavation predictions that the site represented the remains of what traditionally would have been called an agricultural "fieldhouse" (based on an architectural interpretive convention; cf. Wilcox 1978), archaeobotanical evidence indicated that the settlement's occupants subsisted predominantly on wild seeds and

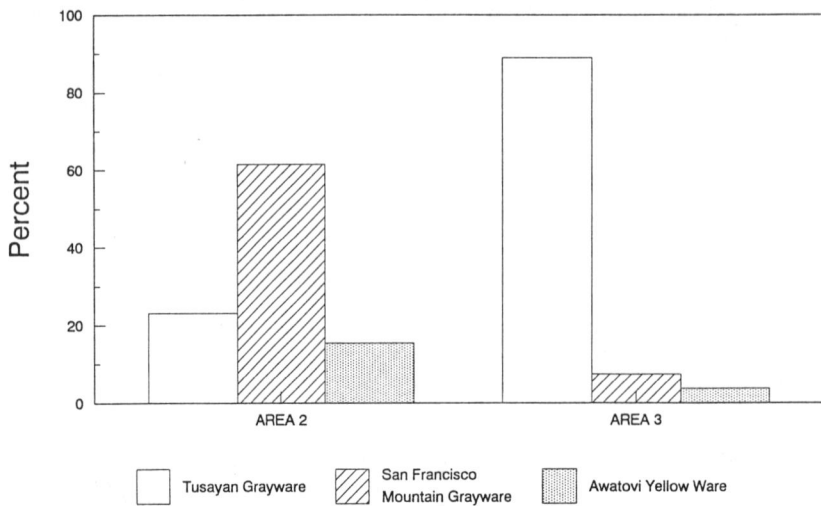

Figure 18-3. *Bar chart of plainware percentages for subsite Areas 2 and 3 at Site AZ I:1:20(ASM). Note the substantial differences between subsite Areas 2 and 3 with respect to percentages of Tusayan Grayware and San Francisco Mountain Grayware ceramics.*

nuts (Sullivan 1987b). Also, had a dense cluster of sherds from the same site not been refitted and examined for use-alteration traces, the remains of a pottery-making and pottery-firing area would have been misinterpreted as "trash" (Sullivan 1988). That error would have been particularly unfortunate because unambiguous examples of spaces dedicated to ceramic production are rare finds in Southwestern archaeology (Ambler and Olson 1977:28–29). Quite simply, the use of interpretive conventions misdirects our efforts to know the past because they insidiously perpetuate the notion that inferences based on them are self-justified, thereby relieving archaeologists of the burden of testing them with independent data.

The Role of Theory in Solving Enduring Problems

In framing an approach to deal effectively with equifinality and interpretive conventions, I urge that we reexamine the theoretical foundations of our discipline—a totally unoriginal suggestion (e.g., Chang 1967:4; Dunnell 1989:45; Lowther 1962). A reexamination is especially critical at this time, however, because our views of how information about the past is acquired affect the conduct of archaeological research, which may, after all, be the flashpoint for the exchanges enumerated above. If "everything archaeologists do is infused with theory" (Schiffer 1988:461; also Spaulding 1988:264), then at least a brief assessment of theory in archaeology seems appropriate (cf. Kluckhohn 1939:344).

Structurally, theories are composed of primitive or irreducible terms and of rules that stipulate relations among the terms (Blalock 1969; Dunnell 1982:5, 1989:36), which together become basic building blocks of larger systems of description and explanation (Achinstein 1968; Salmon 1988). Krause and Thorne (1971:247–248), for example, defined an *enactment* as a primitive term and then specified whether the linkages among enactments were commutative (interchangeable) or noncommutative (noninterchangeable) in order to develop inferences of varying specificity about prehistoric behavioral sequences. Their strategy is exemplified in the archaeological situation depicted in Figure 18-4, where a consideration of the contacts between architectural elements (primitive terms)—horizontal logs (wall logs), daub facing (wall daub), and horizontal plastered surface (floor plaster)—leads to an unambiguous reconstruction of the time-dependent relations between them, that is, the order in which the architectural elements were installed in the past (logs > floor plaster > [logs and floor plaster] > wall daub). Similarly, Wilcox (1982:20–23) has used the *building episode* as a primitive term and examined bonding and abutting relations between building episodes to derive construction histories of masonry pueblos. From those kinds of elementary descriptions, strong inferences can be developed regarding settlement history, occupational dynamics, and intrasettlement variation in activity locations (Wilcox 1975). Each of the inferences, in turn, contributes to an understanding of how the archaeological record assumed the properties that it expresses currently.

A commonality of theme and purpose among these and other studies (e.g., Harris 1979) suggests that, recent proclamations to the contrary (Dunnell 1989:44), archaeology *does* have its own theory, albeit embryonic. Indeed, theory in archaeology focuses on understanding our usufruct—the archaeological record (Bettinger 1987:128; Binford and Binford 1968:2; also Schiffer 1988:469–474; cf. Watson 1973:119).

Equifinality and Hypothesis Testing

Kelley and Hanen (1988:356) have recommended that archaeologists "must look to discover the processes that have resulted in the phenomena we observe." An archaeological theory that focuses on understanding the origins of the archaeological record compels us to consider its sources of variability. Interestingly, archaeologists initially concentrated on assessing the effects of functional variability alone (e.g., Binford and Binford 1966). Since then, several other sources of variability have been enumerated, including organizational variability (e.g., Binford 1979), occupational variability (Schlanger 1990; Yellen 1977), cultural variability (Bordes and De Sonneville-Bordes 1970), and stylistic variability (Plog 1983) among others (Mellars 1970; Wilmsen 1974:88–94). In the past few decades alone, methods have been advanced that are intended to identify which sources may have been responsible for contributing to intersite assemblage and nonassemblage differences (e.g., Dunnell 1989:45; Sullivan 1987c). These considerations are

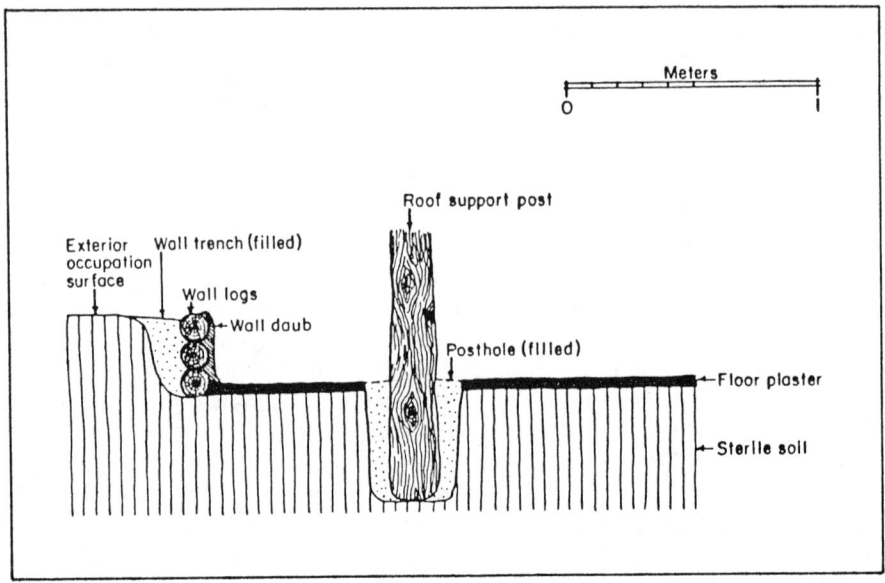

Figure 18-4. *Profile illustrating architectural elements at Site AZ I:1:17(ASM). Analysis of the contacts between the wall logs, floor plaster, and wall daub indicates an invariant (noncommutative) construction sequence.*

important because the ambiguity surrounding the origins of archaeological phenomena is inversely proportional to the number of sources of variability inferred to have been involved in the origins of those phenomena.

The testing of multiple hypotheses that stipulate different sources of systemic variation provides an analytic entry point for investigating ambiguous archaeological phenomena (Cahen and Van Noten 1971:212). Consider the following example. Thirty percent of all sherds recovered from the complete excavation of Site AZ I:1:17(ASM) were found in architectural debris (Sullivan 1989). By examining the properties and contexts of reconstructed vessel fragments and cross-testing them with other data, a number of alternative hypotheses, such as that the sherds represented once-intact vessels stored on structure roofs or scavenged refuse used as construction material, were evaluated. All but one of the hypotheses—that the sherds were part of the architecture—was rejected. This simple example illustrates how an understanding of the origins of archaeological deposits facilitates the elimination of initially equally probable inferences, promoting, in the process, an assessment of the effects of equifinality.

Interpretive Conventions and Hypothesis Testing

Hypothesis testing also allows us to make inroads against the use of interpretive conventions. That is, in trying to understand the origins of our data—in moving from "present to past"—archaeologists, like evolutionary ecologists, struggle with the "problem of evaluating nonexperimental evidence" (Connor and Simberloff 1986:155). Because we cannot study directly the causal processes (Kelley and Hanen 1988:355) that we think gave rise to observed variability, the selection and use of interpretive conventions seem eminently reasonable because they represent such appealing explanatory proxies, especially if they are core interpretive concepts of regional archaeological traditions (e.g., Lekson 1988).

In a provocative study that employed ethnographic and archaeological information pertaining to a range of Southwestern subsistence economies, Hard (1990:147) concluded that "the mean length of a representative sample of manos from an archaeological assemblage can be used as an approximate relative index of the use [sic] of agricultural (maize) dependence." Figure 18-5 is a bar chart of the lengths of 14 manos recovered from Site AZ I:1:17(ASM) (Sullivan 1986:135–137,147,150); the sample size meets Hard's (1990:148) recommended minimum requirements. Depending on whether the mean lengths of all manos (mean = 21.3 cm), all the manos from Structure 4 ($n = 11$, mean = 19.9 cm), or only those manos from Structure 4 that were not recycled ($n = 9$, mean = 19.8 cm) are considered, Hard's (1990:148) scale of agricultural dependence compels the conclusion that the occupants of the site were highly dependent on maize agriculture. As noted above, however, no domesticate pollen whatsoever was found, and maize accounted for only 0.5% of all archaeobotanical remains from AZ I:1:17(ASM) (Sullivan 1987b:144).

The discrepancies between Hard's model and the subsistence remains from Site AZ I:1:17(ASM) illustrate two general difficulties that are associated with interpretive conventions. First, in their application, it is difficult to avoid the fallacy of affirming the consequent (Salmon 1973:27–28). Second, it is difficult to specify the nature of the problem: "Does a lack of isomorphism between model and description arise because the model is incorrect or the reconstruction constituting the description is incorrect?" (Dunnell 1989:43; see especially Blurton Jones 1986:155–156; also Reid et al. 1989:803–804). In the case of Site AZ I:1:17(ASM), the latter possibility can be excluded because the site, which was destroyed catastrophically by fire, was excavated completely and sampled extensively for botanical remains (Sullivan 1987b). It is difficult to escape the conclusion that interpretive conventions—be they simple assertions or elaborate cross-cultural models (such as Hard's)—actually promote the advancement of unreliable inferences about archaeological variability, especially if such conventions are applied blindly or are not tested with independent data.

Concluding Thoughts on the Future of Archaeological Research

Building on the arguments presented above, I close with some programmatic comments that are intended to reflect future prospects for the conduct of archaeological research. Geoffrey Clark (1987:31) recently pointed

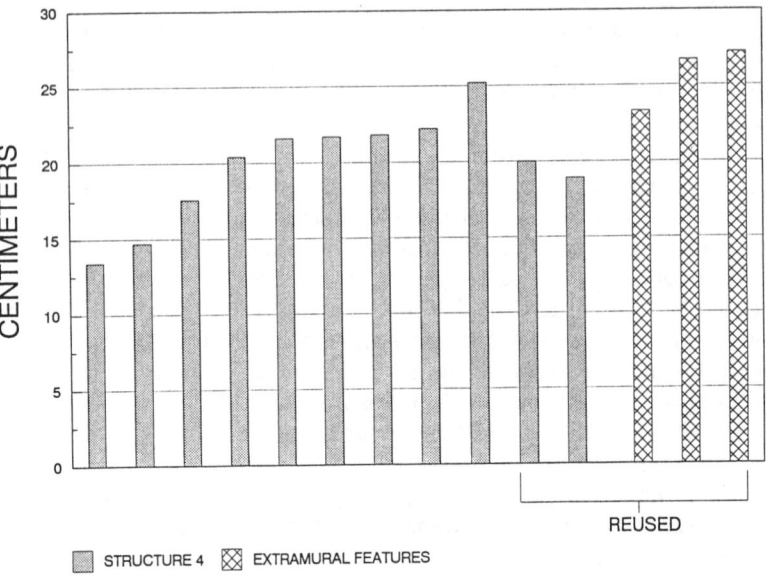

Figure 18-5. *Bar chart of the lengths of 14 manos recovered from Site AZ I:1:17(ASM).*

out that "what we have now, and have always had in place of archaeological theory, is a partial and eclectic, at times even idiosyncratic dependence, upon selected aspects of social anthropology." This dependence has necessitated that analogical arguments be used almost exclusively to interpret archaeological variability described in ethnological terms—a procedure that has always bothered archaeologists (e.g., Fritz 1975; Gould 1978; Schoenwetter 1981).

Thus, we might consider developing an independent archaeological theory. At the very least, this suggestion seems warranted because of the considerable gap between archaeological data and the descriptive lexicons of archaeology and sociocultural anthropology (Lamberg-Karlovsky 1970:111; Meltzer 1979:654), even though evolutionary or processual problems are shared (Bailey 1981:4). An independent archaeological theory composed of interpretation-neutral units of observation and analysis may provide a way to decouple our descriptions of archaeological phenomena from our meaning-laden inferences about the processes we think were responsible for those phenomena (Dancey 1988:16; Klejn 1977:11). If we advance the discipline along these lines, then our theories will entail methods for pinpointing and eliminating errors, rather than assumptions and procedures that perpetuate them.

Acknowledgments

I thank Robert Connolly, Rebecca A. Hawkins, and LuAnn Wandsnider for their comments on earlier drafts of this essay. Also, thanks are extended to Charles Sternberg and Anthony Tolonen for their artwork.

References

Aberle, David F.
 1987 What Kind of Science Is Anthropology? *American Anthropologist* 89:551–565.
Achinstein, Peter
 1968 *Concepts of Science: A Philosophical Analysis*. Johns Hopkins Press, Baltimore.
Adams, Jenny L.
 1988 Use-Wear Analyses on Manos and Hide-Processing Stones. *Journal of Field Archaeology* 15:307–315.
Ambler, J. Richard, and Alan P. Olson
 1977 *Salvage Archaeology in the Cow Springs Area*. Technical Series No. 15. Museum of Northern Arizona, Flagstaff.
Bailey, G. N.
 1981 Concepts of Resource Exploitation: Continuity and Discontinuity in Paleoeconomy. *World Archaeology* 13:1–15.
Bettinger, Robert L.
 1987 Archaeological Approaches to Hunter-Gatherers. In *Annual Review of Anthropology*, vol. 16, edited by Bernard J. Siegel, Alan R. Beals, and Stephen A. Tyler, pp. 121–142. Annual Reviews, Palo Alto.
Binford, Lewis R.
 1977 General Introduction. In *For Theory Building in Archaeology: Essays on Faunal Remains, Aquatic Resources, Spatial Analysis, and Systemic Modeling*, edited by Lewis R. Binford, pp. 1–10. Academic Press, New York.
 1979 Organization and Formation Processes: Looking at Curated Technologies. *Journal of Anthropological Research* 35:255–273.
 1981 Behavioral Archaeology and the "Pompeii Premise." *Journal of Anthropological Research* 37:195–208.
 1983 *In Pursuit of the Past: Decoding the Archaeological Record*. Thames and Hudson, New York.
Binford, Lewis R., and Sally R. Binford
 1966 A Preliminary Analysis of Functional Variability in the Mousterian of Levallois Facies. *American Anthropologist* 68 (No. 2, Part 2):238–295.
Binford, Sally R., and Lewis R. Binford
 1968 Archeological Theory and Method. In *New Perspectives in Archeology*, edited by Sally R. Binford and Lewis R. Binford, pp. 1–3. Aldine, Chicago.
Blalock, Hubert M., Jr.
 1969 *Theory Construction*. Prentice-Hall, Englewood Cliffs, New Jersey.
Blurton Jones, Nicholas G.
 1986 Towards Hypothetico-Deductive Anthropology? *Reviews in Anthropology* 13:151–160.
Bordes, F., and D. De Sonneville-Bordes
 1970 The Significance of Variability in Paleolithic Assemblages. *World Archaeology* 2:61–73.

Cahen, D., and F. Van Noten
  1971   Stone Age Typology: Another Approach. *Current Anthropology* 12:211–215.
Camilli, Eileen L.
  1989   The Occupational History of Sites and the Interpretation of Prehistoric Technological Systems: An Example from Cedar Mesa, Utah. In *Time, Energy, and Stone Tools*, edited by Robin Torrence, pp. 17–26. Cambridge University Press, Cambridge.
Carr, Christopher
  1984   The Nature of Organization of Intrasite Archaeological Records and Spatial Analytic Approaches to Their Investigation. In *Advances in Archaeological Method and Theory*, vol. 7, edited by Michael B. Schiffer, pp. 103–222. Academic Press, New York.
Chang, K. C.
  1967   *Rethinking Archaeology*. Random House, New York.
Clark, Geoffrey A.
  1987   Paradigms and Paradoxes in Contemporary Archaeology. In *Quantitative Research in Archaeology: Progress and Prospects*, edited by Mark S. Aldenderfer, pp. 30–60. Sage Publications, Newbury Park, California.
Clarke, David L.
  1973   Archaeology: The Loss of Innocence. *Antiquity* 47:6–18.
Clay, R. Berle
  1976   Typological Classification, Attribute Analysis, and Lithic Variability. *Journal of Field Archaeology* 3:303–311.
Connor, Edward F., and Daniel Simberloff
  1986   Competition, Scientific Method, and Null Models in Ecology. *American Scientist* 74:155–162.
Dancey, William S.
  1988   Archaeological Survey in Central Ohio: The 1970s. *American Archaeology* 7:13–17.
Davis, Owen K.
  1986   Pollen Analysis from AZ I:1:17(ASM). In *Prehistory of the Upper Basin, Coconino County, Arizona*, edited by Alan P. Sullivan III, pp. 333–338. Arizona State Museum Archaeological Series No. 167. University of Arizona, Tucson.
Dunnell, Robert C.
  1982   Science, Social Science, and Common Sense: The Agonizing Dilemma of Modern Archaeology. *Journal of Anthropological Research* 38:1–25.
  1989   Aspects of the Application of Evolutionary Theory in Archaeology. In *Archaeological Thought in America*, edited by C. C. Lamberg-Karlovsky, pp. 35–49. Cambridge University Press, Cambridge.
Embree, Lester
  1987   Archaeology: The Most Basic Science of All. *Antiquity* 61:75–78.
Fritz, John M.
  1972   Archaeological Systems for Indirect Observation of the Past. In *Contemporary Archaeology: A Guide to Theory and Contributions*, edited by Mark P. Leone, pp.135–157. Southern Illinois University Press, Carbondale.
  1975   Review of *A History of American Archaeology* by Gordon R. Willey and Jeremy A. Sabloff. *Science* 187:425–426.
Gould, Richard A.
  1978   Beyond Analogy in Ethnoarchaeology. In *Explorations in Ethnoarchaeology*, edited by Richard A. Gould, pp. 249–293. University of New Mexico Press, Albuquerque.

Graves, Michael W.
  1987 Rending Reality in Archaeological Analyses: A Reply to Upham and Plog. *Journal of Field Archaeology* 14:243–249.
Grayson, Donald K.
  1986 Eoliths, Archaeological Ambiguity, and the Generation of "Middle-Range" Research. In *American Archaeology Past and Future: A Celebration of the Society for American Archaeology 1935–1985*, edited by David J. Meltzer, Don D. Fowler, and Jeremy A. Sabloff, pp. 77–119. Smithsonian Institution Press, Washington, D.C.
Guthe, Carl E.
  1939 The Basic Needs of American Archaeology. *Science* 90:528–530.
Hard, Robert J.
  1990 Agricultural Dependence in the Mountain Mogollon. In *Perspectives on Southwestern Prehistory*, edited by Paul E. Minnis and Charles L. Redman, pp. 135–149. Westview Press, Boulder.
Harris, Edward C.
  1979 *Principles of Archaeological Stratigraphy*. Academic Press, London.
Kelley, Jane H., and Marsha P. Hanen
  1988 *Archaeology and the Methodology of Science*. University of New Mexico Press, Albuquerque.
Klejn, Leo S.
  1977 A Panorama of Theoretical Archaeology. *Current Anthropology* 18:1–42.
Kluckhohn, Clyde
  1939 The Place of Theory in Anthropological Studies. *Philosophy of Science* 6:328–344.
Krause, Richard A., and Robert N. Thorne
  1971 Toward a Theory of Archaeological Things. *Plains Anthropologist* 16:245–257.
Lamberg-Karlovsky, C. C.
  1970 Operations Problems in Archaeology. In *Current Directions in Anthropology*, edited by Ann Fischer, pp. 110–114. Bulletins of the American Anthropological Association 3(3), Part 2. Washington, D.C.
Lekson, Stephen H.
  1988 The Idea of the Kiva in Anasazi Archaeology. *The Kiva* 53:213–234.
Lowther, Gordon R.
  1962 Epistemology and Archaeological Theory. *Current Anthropology* 3:495–509.
McGregor, John C.
  1951 *The Cohonina Culture of Northwestern Arizona*. University of Illinois Press, Urbana.
Mellars, Paul R.
  1970 Some Comments on the Notion of "Functional Variability" in Stone-Tool Assemblages. *World Archaeology* 2:74–89.
Meltzer, David J.
  1979 Paradigms and the Nature of Change in American Archaeology. *American Antiquity* 44:644–657.
O'Brien, Michael J., Jacqueline A. Ferguson, Thomas D. Holland, and Dennis E. Lewarch
  1989 On Interpretive Competition in the Absence of Appropriate Data: Monte Alban Revisited. *Current Anthropology* 30:191–200.
Plog, Stephen
  1983 Analysis of Style in Artifacts. In *Annual Review of Anthropology*, vol. 12,

edited by Bernard J. Siegel, Alan R. Beals, and Stephen A. Tyler, pp. 125–142. Annual Reviews, Palo Alto.

Reid, J. Jefferson, Michael B. Schiffer, Stephanie M. Whittlesey, Madeleine J. Hinkes, Alan P. Sullivan, Christian E. Downum, William A. Longacre, and H. David Tuggle
   1989   Perception and Interpretation in Contemporary Southwestern Archaeology: Comments on Upham, Cordell, and Brock. *American Antiquity* 54:802–814.

Salmon, Wesley C.
   1973   *Logic*. 2d ed. Prentice-Hall, Englewood Cliffs, New Jersey.
   1988   Introduction. In *The Limitations of Deductivism*, edited by Adolf Grunbaum and Wesley C. Salmon, pp. 1–18. University of California Press, Berkeley.

Schiffer, Michael B.
   1976   *Behavioral Archeology*. Academic Press, New York.
   1985   Is There a "Pompeii Premise" in Archaeology? *Journal of Anthropological Research* 41:18–41.
   1988   The Structure of Archaeological Theory. *American Antiquity* 53:461–485.

Schlanger, Sarah H.
   1990   Artifact Assemblage Composition and Site Occupation Duration. In *Perspectives on Southwestern Prehistory*, edited by Paul E. Minnis and Charles L. Redman, pp. 103–121. Westview Press, Boulder.

Schoenwetter, James
   1981   Prologue to a Contextual Archaeology. *Journal of Archaeological Science* 8:367–379.
   1990   Lessons from an Alternative View. In *Powers of Observation: Alternative Views in Archaeology*, edited by Sarah M. Nelson and Alice B. Kehoe, pp. 103–112. Archeological Papers of the American Anthropological Association No. 2. Washington, D.C.

Scott, Linda J.
   1986   Analysis of Selected Macrofloral Samples from AZ I:1:17(ASM). In *Prehistory of the Upper Basin, Coconino County, Arizona*, edited by Alan P. Sullivan III, pp. 339–346. Arizona State Museum Archaeological Series No. 167. University of Arizona, Tucson.

Spaulding, Albert C.
   1988   Archeology and Anthropology. *American Anthropologist* 90:263–271.

Sullivan, Alan P., III
   1978   Inference and Evidence in Archaeology: A Discussion of the Conceptual Problems. In *Advances in Archaeological Method and Theory*, vol. 1, edited by Michael B. Schiffer, pp. 183–222. Academic Press, New York.
   1986   Occupational Dynamics of a Small Kayenta Anasazi Settlement. In *Prehistory of the Upper Basin, Coconino County, Arizona*, edited by Alan P. Sullivan III, pp. 47–190. Arizona State Museum Archaeological Series No. 167. University of Arizona, Tucson.
   1987a   Artifact Scatters, Adaptive Diversity, and Southwestern Abandonment: The Upham Hypothesis Reconsidered. *Journal of Anthropological Research* 43:345–360.
   1987b   Seeds of Discontent: Implications of a "Pompeii" Botanical Assemblage for Grand Canyon Anasazi Subsistence Models. *Journal of Ethnobiology* 7:137–153.
   1987c   Probing the Sources of Lithic Assemblage Variability: A Regional Case Study near the Homolovi Ruins, Arizona. *North American Archaeologist* 8:41–71.
   1988   Prehistoric Southwestern Ceramic Manufacture: The Limitations of Current Evidence. *American Antiquity* 53:23–35.

1989 The Technology of Ceramic Reuse: Formation Processes and Archaeological Evidence. *World Archaeology* 21:101–114.

Thomas, David H.
1983 *The Archaeology of Monitor Valley 1. Epistemology.* Anthropological Papers of the American Museum of Natural History, vol. 58, Part 1. New York.

Upham, Steadman
1984 Adaptive Diversity and Southwestern Abandonment. *Journal of Anthropological Research* 40:235–256.

Upham, Steadman, and Fred Plog
1986 The Interpretation of Prehistoric Political Complexity in the Central and Northern Southwest: Toward a Mending of the Models. *Journal of Field Archaeology* 13:223–238.

Wandsnider, LuAnn, and James I. Ebert
1988 Issues in Archaeological Surface Survey: Meshing Method and Theory. *American Archaeology* 7:2.

Watson, Patty Jo
1973 The Future of Archeology in Anthropology: Culture History and Social Science. In *Research and Theory in Current Archeology*, edited by Charles L. Redman, pp. 113–124. John Wiley and Sons, New York.

Watson, Patty Jo, and Michael Fotiadis
1990 The Razor's Edge: Symbolic-Structuralist Archeology and the Expansion of Archeological Inference. *American Anthropologist* 92:613–629.

Wilcox, David R.
1975 A Strategy for Perceiving Social Groups in Puebloan Sites. In *Chapters in the Prehistory of Eastern Arizona IV*, edited by Paul S. Martin, Ezra B. W. Zubrow, Daniel C. Bowman, David A. Gregory, John A. Hanson, Michael B. Schiffer, and David R. Wilcox, pp. 120–159. Fieldiana:Anthropology 65.
1978 The Theoretical Significance of Fieldhouses. In *Limited Activity and Occupation Sites*, edited by Albert E. Ward, pp. 25–32. Center for Anthropological Studies, Albuquerque.
1982 A Set-Theory Approach to Sampling Pueblos: The Implications of Room-Set Additions at Grasshopper Pueblo. In *Multidisciplinary Research at Grasshopper Pueblo, Arizona*, edited by William A. Longacre, Sally J. Holbrook, and Michael W. Graves, pp. 19–27. Anthropological Papers of the University of Arizona No. 40. University of Arizona Press, Tucson.

Wills, W. H.
1989 Patterns of Prehistoric Food Production in West-Central New Mexico. *Journal of Anthropological Research* 45:139–157.

Wilmsen, Edwin N.
1974 *Lindenmeier: A Pleistocene Hunting Society.* Harper and Row, New York.

Wylie, Alison
1989 The Interpretive Dilemma. In *Critical Traditions in Contemporary Archaeology*, edited by Valerie Pinsky and Alison Wylie, pp. 18–27. Cambridge University Press, Cambridge.

Yellen, John E.
1977 *Archaeological Approaches to the Present: Models for Reconstructing the Past.* Academic Press, New York.

19. Toward a Reconciliation of Processual and Postprocessual Archaeology

Robert L. Kelly

Abstract: Postprocessualism challenges archaeology with the claim that interpretations of the past are only impositions of the present social order on the past and can therefore only be judged in political terms. This criticism has its merits; however, its solution lies not in declaring the search for the past quixotic, but in constructing more accurate methods, in encouraging the diversity of thought in archaeology, and in paying more attention to the application of archaeological knowledge to modern issues, as well as encouraging critical self-reflection. Archaeology's strengths lie in its ability to study both long-term processes and the histories of all the world's peoples. By focusing on those strengths and building stronger methods, archaeology can be made more useful to society.

> Before I built a wall I'd ask to know
> What I was walling in or walling out,
> And to whom I was like to give offence.
> Something there is that doesn't love a wall.
> —Robert Frost, "Mending Wall"

Let me make clear at the outset that I am an unabashed processual archaeologist guided by a theoretical paradigm, at times more poorly implemented than at others, that is grounded in evolutionary theory. But my intent in this essay is not to praise processual archaeology, nor is it to bury postprocessualism; instead, I wish to examine the wall between the two. Like Robert Frost, I question whether walls make good neighbors, and I also question whether they make good science. In many ways, processual and

Quandaries and Quests: Visions of Archaeology's Future, edited by LuAnn Wandsnider. Center for Archaeological Investigations, Occasional Paper No. 20. © 1992 by the Board of Trustees, Southern Illinois University. All rights reserved. ISBN 0-88104-075-4.

postprocessual archaeology are not reconcilable; nonetheless, a common ground lies in a shared purpose of archaeology—to learn about humanity for the sake of humanity. I am concerned with the role archaeology plays in helping to restructure our world and the observation that archaeological interpretations are a product of archaeologists' cultural environments.

It would be nice if archaeology were easy, but it is not. Fieldwork is hard enough, but interpreting data derived from buried remains is even more difficult. Our data sets are plagued by postdepositional processes, and the relationships between human behavior, system organization, and the deposition of material remains are bewildering, to say the least. Methods come under ever-increasing scrutiny and criticism as we discover the plethora of factors affecting material remains both before and after deposition. In brief, archaeologists have had to come to grips with the realization that we cannot know everything about the past and that what we can recover will not come easily. But many postprocessualists see such issues as secondary, for they question whether *any* reconstruction of the past is ever possible.

Postprocessual archaeology includes many different—sometimes overlapping, sometimes contradictory—perspectives. Some postprocessual approaches focus on the role of individuals actively negotiating their own culture and on interpreting artifacts within their now extinct context of meaning (Hodder 1985, 1986). Other postprocessual writings are grounded in Marxism (primarily the structural variety), using it to understand both prehistory and the creation of archaeological knowledge (e.g., papers in Miller and Tilley 1984). Still others advocate the importance of a self-conscious reflection and evaluation of archaeology's claims (Leone 1986; Leone et al. 1987), that is, an understanding of the context within which archaeological knowledge is generated. I will not review the various positions here (see Hodder 1985; Leone 1986; P. Watson 1991; R. Watson 1990). Instead, I deal with one of the criticisms leveled at processual archaeology that I take to be critical.

Postprocessualists—and many processualists as well—note that archaeologists do not "study the past." In fact, they study broken bits of rock, bone, and pottery, and create a past through their interpretation of those objects. The interpretations are made within a theoretical paradigm, and whether the archaeologist is aware of it or not, that theoretical paradigm is strongly affected by its sociopolitical environment (which for Western archaeologists is largely capitalism). Consequently, the methods we select, the problems we focus on, the interpretations we draw, and the conclusions we come to in trying to reconstruct the past are strongly affected by the present, by our cultural, social, and political matrix. Postprocessualists, however, take this claim further. Archaeologists, they say, do not reconstruct the past. Instead, they *impose* modern capitalist, imperialist, racist, or sexist society onto the past and, in so doing, legitimate that society for the present (see Trigger 1989 for examples). Depending on whom one reads, processual archaeologists appear as either the scientific *collaborateurs* or the willing dupes of an evil agenda.

The essence of the postprocessual critique can be accepted without hesitation. There can be little doubt that the way we view the past is affected and perhaps even dictated by our modern sociocultural context (Leone 1986; Trigger 1986). Richard Wilk (1985) provides an excellent example by demonstrating a correlation between published discussions of the Maya Collapse and the American sociopolitical scene. During the Vietnam War era, warfare was the favored explanation for the Maya Collapse. During the ecology movement of the 1970s, theories of self-inflicted ecological disaster gained popularity. During the Watergate era, collapse was attributed to infighting and abuse of authority by political elites. Wilk's detailed argument could be representative of other "big" issues in American archaeology. It is easy to see, for example, the shadow of capitalist thought in evolutionary ecology or a parallel between the concern with risk minimization in anthropology and Americans' concern with skyrocketing health insurance costs. And it is clear that male bias has affected archaeological interpretations for many years (Conkey and Spector 1984). We could cite many more instances (e.g., Dennell 1990). Archaeologists must agree that there is a relationship between the times we live in and the way we perceive and understand the world.

For many this is a depressing revelation. Trained to believe that an archaeological science was capable of seeing the past directly, many of us became frustrated at the realization (of the anthropological truism!) that we are cultural beings, that we see the world through cultural filters. For some, abandoning the fantasy of objective science meant abandoning the scientific effort. Space was made for a swing to the opposite pole, an assertion that our understanding of the past can be nothing more than an imposition of the present on that past, as expressed by Arthur Keene's fear that we cannot "hope to do anything but create a reflection of the current dominant political and economic structure in our reconstructions of the past" (Keene 1983:148). In this essay, I wish to explore what we might accomplish by accepting the postprocessualist critique of processual archaeology without abandoning the intellectual gains of our processualist past.

Can We Know the Past?

I see no way around our being cultural animals. We always have been and always will be products of our time: our interpretations of the past will always be based on reigning cultural values. Given that, can we ever learn anything true about the past? Can we evaluate different interpretations of archaeological data independent of the sociopolitical environment within which they are generated?

To the last question, two of the main proponents of postprocessualism, Michael Shanks and Christopher Tilley (1987a, 1987b) say no. They claim that there

> is no way of choosing between alternative pasts except on essentially political grounds, in terms of a definite value system, a morality. So criteria for truth and falsity are not to be understood purely in terms of

the logic and rationality, or otherwise, of discourses *but require judgement in terms of the practical consequences of archaeological theory and practice for contemporary social change* [Shanks and Tilley 1987b:195, emphasis added].

Excavation to them "has a unique role to play as a theatre where people may be able to produce their own pasts, pasts which are meaningful to them" (Tilley 1989:280). Thus, they argue that there are "multiple" pasts, one of which is better not because it is more correct but because it serves modern political agendas of the archaeologist: "The point of archaeology is not merely to interpret the past but to change the manner in which the past is interpreted in the service of social reconstruction in the present" (Shanks and Tilley 1987b:195).

According to Shanks and Tilley, then, the purpose of archaeology is to alter modern society. But postprocessual archaeology as envisioned by Shanks and Tilley cannot do this. They (1987b:213) state: "We do not argue for truths about the past but argue through the medium of the past to detach the power of truth from the present social order." But if reconstructions of the past cannot be judged true or false on some basis other than whether we *want* them to be true or false, how long-lasting can the change they might engender be? What is the power of interpretation based on falsehoods, or on (mis)interpretations fostered by political expediency, current or transient visions, or, especially, on the claim that the past cannot truly be known?

Consider, for example, perhaps the best instance of archaeology actually shaping social-political reality: Native American land rights litigation. Archaeology has long been and continues to be used on behalf of Native Americans to support their land and water rights claims. But imagine what could happen if the opposing attorneys do their homework and read the postprocessualist literature? When a tribe's expert witness is on the stand, couldn't the opposing attorney ask why it is that some archaeologists say we can never really know the past but only impose our political values onto it? Regardless of the accuracy of the archaeological data, what will the jury think?[1] It is disturbing that an esoteric debate in archaeological theory could do damage to those who play no role in it and whom we claim to assist. Nothing good comes from falsehoods, even if they are unintentional or proposed for good reasons. There is a fundamental contradiction between the desire to use the past to effect social change and the assumption that the past cannot be known. While I am sympathetic to the postprocessualists' desire to confront and challenge political doctrine and cultural values, doesn't allowing people "to produce their own pasts" also allow racist arguments that justify looting? (More than one American pothunter has responded to my antilooting pleas with the dismissive "they're only Indians," a view of the past, and present, that is meaningful to them.) The extreme postprocessual position is indeed an "extraordinary abdication of academic and intellectual responsibility" (Mithen 1989:490) that leads to legitimate fears of political litmus tests (Schiffer 1988) and that contains internal contradictions that prevent it from achieving its professed goals (R. Watson 1990).

But this is a wall-building that Robert Frost would disapprove of. There are grounds on which the wall can and should be dismantled. While I disagree with the methodology of the postprocessualists and their extreme relativism, I certainly agree with the sentiment behind their position—that archaeology can be more than it is today. We often justify the meager funds spent on archaeology in this country by claiming that those who forget the mistakes of the past are doomed to repeat them or by arguing that we have lost some quality that prehistoric peoples had in abundance, such as respect for nature. Such justifications emerge as self-defensive platitudes and carry little conviction.

What underlies the position of many postprocessualists is a desire to do more than that, to use the past to effect real social change. Postprocessual criticism springs from a sincere desire to see archaeology as an active agent in making the world more just. Who could not admire this goal? But it can be reached in archaeology *only* by searching for the past, not by declaring the search quixotic, *only* by making archaeology a better science, not by declaring it a purely political exercise. To achieve an archaeology that is both scientifically valid and socially responsible, we must reconsider two elements of archaeology: its science and its goals.

Archaeological Science

As we noted above, there are many instances in which archaeology's theoretical paradigm or sociopolitical context dictates its conclusions. In rebuttal, processual archaeologists claim that we can break out of our culture-bound theories through scientific testing of our ideas. If an idea is an erroneous product of our cultural matrix, then a scientific test will prove the idea wrong. To refer to Wilk's example, just because the ecology crisis of the 1970s made some think that ecological disaster caused the Maya Collapse does not mean that it was *not* a causal factor. Yet some postprocessualists (e.g., Shanks and Tilley 1987a, 1987b) deny the validity of scientific testing as being constrained by Western notions of objectivity.[2] They insist that it results in little more than the *imposition* of ideas on the past. Is this true?

Archaeology is not the only science that can fall prey to imposing ideas onto data. Indeed, any intellectual endeavor can do so. At the same time, anyone who has had a penicillin shot, driven a car, or seen Voyager's photos of Jupiter knows that the physical and biological sciences learn things that are true, that are not simply the product of a scientist's imposing ideas on data. Yet those sciences seem less troubled by the issue—Steven Jay Gould's many writings on the history of biology and paleontology notwithstanding. The reason those scientific endeavors succeed, if I may be pretentious for a moment, is that other sciences deal with simpler phenomena and have more definite feedback as to whether their ideas are correct or not: the vaccine makes the patient well or it does not, the gears turn or they do not, the telescope gives a clear image or it does not. Without belittling other sciences, we must admit that archaeology—the study not only of human society, the most complex system on earth, but also of the material remnants of *past* human society—is extraordinarily difficult. Methods to do archaeology will not come easily (and we must construct them on far less funding than that of the physical or biological sciences).

Binford has pointed out repeatedly that the reason archaeologists continue to impose theoretical paradigms onto archaeological data (what Binford calls arguments of accommodation) is that archaeologists lack the methods—middle-range theory—to test our ideas (Binford 1986). To test ideas about the relationship between population growth and agriculture, for example, entails methods to "measure" changes in population size and ways to recognize domesticated plants. The current paucity or weakness of archaeological methods (and the structure of testing in archaeology—see Sullivan, this volume) makes us highly susceptible to the impulse to impose our models onto the past. If those models are drawn from our experience, and I see no other source for them, then there is a high probability that we will impose the present on the past.

In contrast to the historical sciences, experimental sciences have more definite feedback as to the predictive capacity of their ideas. Consequently, they seem to realize that paradigms are tools, not God's truth. Take, for example, arguments over the nature of the atom. Like archaeologists, atomic physicists cannot directly see or measure what they study. When Neils Bohr first devised his model of the atom, he needed a way to communicate what he thought were essential properties of the atom, a nucleus surrounded by electrons. The solar system was the closest analogy he could come up with. Later, physicists learned that electrons do not circle the nucleus like planets. Instead, they portrayed the atom as a nucleus surrounded by an electron "cloud"; the electrons were no longer seen as planets, but as balls attached to the nucleus by springs of various lengths, vibrating at various frequencies. Does that mean the knowledge gained from the atom-as-universe model is incorrect, that atomic bombs really do not explode? Of course not. It simply means that the ability of the atom-as-universe model to inform us about essential properties of the atom had been exhausted.

Archaeologists, in contrast, continue to argue over the shape of the "atom" when we ought to be concerned with understanding and testing ideas of culture's essential properties and processes—we argue over the implications of Marxist, feminist, evolutionary, humanist, or symbolic paradigms rather than test the utility of each perspective on a particular problem or issue. For all the discussion of science in archaeology, therefore, there are actually few instances of genuine hypothesis-testing or efforts to falsify proposed ideas. Much of the problem is a lack of methods: it's hard to take a patient's temperature if you don't have a thermometer. Consequently, we are rewarded instead for proposing paradigms, new ways of viewing the past, or for making arguments of accommodation. We are rewarded for convincing others that we are right, not that we are wrong, yet science is mostly about falsification, not verification—it's about being wrong, not right. One way out of this is to focus attention in the next decade on the development of more accurate archaeological methods (see Dunnell, this volume)—and to encourage this research with funding and departmental support (see Stark, this volume).

But methods are only part of the answer. Ideas are tested in relation to one another. If we only have one idea with which to work or one frame of reference for viewing the world, there is also an increased likelihood that we will simply impose our view of the world onto the prehistoric case. Binford has also repeatedly pointed out that we cannot think with thoughts we do not have. Accepting this, we must maximize the thoughts we do have. That means maximizing the diversity of ideas in our discipline (see Goldstein, this volume, on the importance of a Native American "voice" in American archaeology), and it can be accomplished in part by increasing the diversity of our own field. Look around at a Society for American Archaeology meeting, and you will see few people of color and virtually no Native Americans. American archaeology has slowly diversified itself over the decades, but intellectually it is still dominated by white, male members of the middle class. That limits the ideas we have to work with as well as our ability to define our paradigms and see where they may be (mis)leading us. To make archaeology a better science, explicit attention will have to be given to diversification in the future. (The Society for American Archaeology is moving toward that goal by trying to encourage more interaction between Native Americans and archaeologists and by establishing a Native American scholarship fund.)

The Goals of Archaeology

Methods, however, are developed to fulfill particular goals. What should the general goals of archaeology be? Cordell (this volume) notes with dismay that archaeologists do not debate "big"' questions anymore, that after the heated culture history/culture process debates of the 1960s and 1970s, archaeologists no longer seem to have a consensus as to what we even should be arguing about. Paradoxically, the nature of archaeology's goals lies within the culture history/culture process debate, for that debate pointed to the two major strengths of archaeology: First, archaeology has the ability to observe and study long-term processes of change on wide spatial scales. No other discipline can do it on the scale that we can, for we have the entire world and its entire (pre)history at our disposal.[3] Second, archaeology is the only means whereby the history of all the world's peoples can be reconstructed—Native American history, for example, or the early Black experience in the United States. The culture history/culture process debate was so heated because both sides were right!

Keeping those proposed strengths of archaeology in mind, I ask if it might be profitable—for archaeology as a science and the public that supports it—to approach the future goals of archaeology in terms of what it is we want to teach and in terms of specific modern problems that need resolution or that could benefit from an understanding of specific prehistories or long-term cultural processes.[4] There should be a constant dialogue between what we learn from archaeological data and what we teach (see Hodder 1991), not so that archaeological results can be judged in terms of political doctrine, but so that archaeology plays an active role in social change by helping students (and their instructors) understand long-term cultural processes as well as the histories of specific societies, especially those often left out of traditional history courses. This is not a gimmick to sell archaeology as "relevant" but is a way to actually improve the scientific validity of knowledge received from archaeology by bringing it into a larger intellectual sphere for critique, thus making it more accurate, valuable, *and* useful (Hodder 1991). In this way, archaeology is improved in the same way that vaccines are improved when they are injected into a patient and the results monitored. A few major research areas in cultural process are (*a*) the contexts that promote cooperation versus competition, hierarchy versus egalitarianism, (*b*) the formation and maintenance of "ethnic" groups, (*c*) the conditions for war and for peace, (*d*) the long-term effects of population increase and migration under different environmental and economic conditions, and (*e*) the long-term, stable strategies of tropical forest use.

Archaeologists could also undertake research designed to answer specific legal or economic issues. The use of archaeology in Native American land and water rights cases is fairly well known. Prehistory is of direct legal relevance in those cases; could archaeological data also be used in understanding other current problems? For example, could archaeology be used to inform southwestern cities of the specific long-term consequences of population growth and ever-increasing water use? Research in the Southwest (e.g., Dean et al. 1985) suggests that regional abandonments may be related to changes in the spatial correlation of rainfall and the degree of annual variance in precipitation. Can we predict how future climate change will affect modern cities and thus help plan water policies?

Many will say that most of these have long been the big questions and objectives of prehistoric archaeology. But, honestly, have they? Most have been little more that throwaway lines at the ends of papers, proposals, and PBS specials. The use of archaeology in commenting on specific issues of the day is often seen as a lagniappe of research, not its focus. (In fact, it is often avoided since as soon as research becomes legally or economically relevant it also becomes a political lightning rod.) In our conclusions we often say that our particular research can help us understand the effects of X on Y, but we do not go on to say exactly *how* it helps us understand—and others are not trained to take up the task. I am not suggesting that archaeologists become legal or economic consultants but only that they know where their research fits into the "big picture" and devise their research accordingly.

In the area of culture history, we could also undertake research that explicitly sets out to answer specific historical questions raised by indigenous peoples (which may also have legal, political, or economic ramifications). In my own, admittedly limited, experience with archaeology outside the United States, I find that few people are interested in "scientific" questions about cultural change but are intensely interested in specific historical questions (When did we come here? Who built those ruins?). In other words, we need to also ask how we can be of service to other people rather than to ask only how other people's past can serve our goals (e.g., Anyon 1990; Creamer 1990; Layton 1989; Meehan 1990).

We also need to take a more active role in the presentation of the past to the public—especially culture-historical "stories." We must remember that our research will ultimately reach the public—and not always in a form we will appreciate if we take a laissez-faire attitude toward that public. The presentation of archaeology is often the purview of educators, historical societies, or government employees. Many of them are well intentioned, but untrained, and can mislead the public. Until recently, slavery went unmentioned at visits to some historic plantation homes in the Southeast because it did not fit with the vision of the past that historic societies tried to construct. Or take Anasazi sites in the American Southwest. Visit places such as Mesa Verde and you will learn about the Lost Anasazi, a people who, according to the guides I've listened to, built a remarkable civilization and then mysteriously vanished. A mystery makes good copy, but in this case it is simply wrong, and it leaves the living descendants of Mesa Verde, the modern Puebloan peoples, hanging in time. With no connection between them and the prehistoric ruins, modern Native Americans are seen as imitations of the romantic real thing, like Taiwanese kachina dolls. People perceived as "without history," in Eric Wolf's apt ironic phrase, are people who don't count. In other words, archaeology affects the public perception and, consequently, the political empowerment of Native Americans—and others as well—for all peoples have history, and for much of the world, archaeology is the only means to recover it. In doing culture-historical research, therefore, we help grant respect and dignity to all peoples. But by giving in to the difficulty of archaeology and claiming that the past cannot be known at all, we defeat this worthwhile task.

Conclusions

Postprocessualists rightly admonish all of us to keep in mind that we are cultural, that we view the world in a particular perspective, and that we should be as fully aware of that perspective as possible. Postprocessualists rightly point out that archaeological theory and method are linked. We have no direct access to the past. However, if we impose the present on the past, it is not because that is an intrinsic element of the archaeological endeavor but because it is a product of the paucity of accurate methods for squeezing information from archaeological remains. Better methods will give us more accurate and unambiguous checks on whether our ideas are correct or not.

By increasing the diversity of our own field and through critical self-reflection, we also decrease the probability of simply imposing the present onto the past. While self-reflection is scientifically productive, even critical, it is not useful if taken to an extreme. It is harmful to turn to a form of scientific McCarthyism, to flagellate ourselves for being trapped in our culture, or to deny that anything true can ever be learned about the past. There is a set of values behind everything we have done, do now, and will do in the future.

We cannot hope for a value-free archaeology, although we can and must remind ourselves of why we study and teach about the past at all. Postprocessualism will not replace processual archaeology, but it will make it better.

It is in the area of archaeological practice that I also see a reconciliation between processual and postprocessual archaeology. If we want archaeology to involve "a reading of the past [that] invites us to shape a different future" (Shanks and Tilley 1987b:196), then we should focus on how archaeology's unique knowledge of long-term processes and its ability to study the histories of all people can contribute to understanding the problems facing the world. But we should not forget that "a commitment to improving the world is no substitute for understanding it" (Hastrup and Elsass 1990:307). We cannot build a better tomorrow on fictions of yesterday.

Patty Jo Watson recently asked, "What legitimates the critical theorists' authority as analysts and arbiters of archaeological (or any other) praxis?" (P. Watson 1990:221). The answer is *nothing*. Even the observation that we see the world through cultural filters is a product of this time. It does no good to spend *all* our time arguing about whose perception of the "atom," or human society, is absolutely better, though such arguments are necessary for the progress of the field. Models are tools, "necessary fictions"; when they are useful, use them, when they are not, discard them (see Feinman 1990). Our ways of thinking are like snakeskin: without them we perish, yet we must continue to shed them in order to grow. As we do so, we will discover with the hindsight that comes with time that many previous interpretations were incorrect, but we will penetrate new layers of understanding, and in replacing knowledge, we will build upon it. This is the most we can hope for, since no one can step completely outside their culture.

If the structure of archaeology as a discipline is affected by our sociopolitical context, then the future of archaeology is promising. Walls are coming down around the world in many places; the recognition that diversity is necessary and cooperation valuable is emerging in many contexts. That recognition needs to appear in archaeology. And that's not just good politics—it's also good science.

Notes

1. We could enumerate other cases, e.g., the 1976 Mashpee trial in Massachusetts in which Morton Fried's concept of "tribe" was on trial (Clifford 1988).

2. At other times, many postprocessualists express a concern with verification, although it does not entail a typical scientific strategy but one borrowed from literary analysis, i.e., a procedure concerned with meaning or interpretation rather than causality (Hodder 1991). I do not reject such approaches, but they should be cast as a complement to, and not a substitute for, a scientific approach.

3. I agree with Dunnell (this volume) that evolutionary theory is our best candidate for a framework to understanding long-term historical processes, though the nature of cultural (as opposed to biological) transmission of information means that evolutionary theory to date is not complete and will benefit from the insights of other paradigms.

4. This is not to undermine the utility of applying archaeological methods to modern problems (e.g., William Rathje's analyses of modern landfills) or of applying an archaeological perspective to modern social change (see Schiffer, this volume).

References

Anyon, R.
  1991 Protecting the Past, Protecting the Present: Cultural Resources and American Indians. In *Protecting the Past: Readings in Archaeological Resource Protection*, edited by G. S. Smith and J. E. Ehrenhard, pp. 215–222. CRC Press, Boca Raton, Florida.
Binford, L. R.
  1986 In Pursuit of the Future. In *American Archaeology Past and Future: A Celebration of the Society for American Archaeology 1935–1985*, edited by D. J. Meltzer, D. D. Fowler, and J. A. Sabloff, pp. 459–479. Smithsonian Institution Press, Washington, D.C.
Clifford, J.
  1988 *The Predicament of Culture: Twentieth-Century Ethnography, Literature, and Art*. Harvard University Press, Cambridge, Massachusetts.
Conkey, M., and J. D. Spector
  1984 Archaeology and the Study of Gender. In *Advances in Archaeological Method and Theory*, vol. 7, edited by Michael B. Schiffer, pp. 1–38. Academic Press, New York.
Creamer, W.
  1990 Archeological Research in the Northern Rio Grande: Keeping in Touch with the Pueblos. Paper presented at the 89th Annual Meeting of the American Anthropological Association, New Orleans.
Dean, J. S., R. C. Euler, G. J. Gumerman, F. Plog, R. H. Hevly, and T. N. V. Karlstrom
  1985 Human Behavior, Demography, and Paleoenvironment on the Colorado Plateaus. *American Antiquity* 50:537–554.
Dennell, R.
  1990 Progressive Gradualism, Imperialism and Academic Fashion: Lower Paleolithic Archaeology in the 20th Century. *Antiquity* 64:549–558.
Feinman, G.
  1990 Archaeology Without a Capital "D." Paper presented at the 85th Annual Meeting of the Society for American Archaeology, Las Vegas.
Hastrup, K., and P. Elsass
  1990 Anthropological Advocacy: A Contradiction in Terms? *Current Anthropology* 31:301–311.
Hodder, I.
  1985 Postprocessual Archaeology. In *Advances in Archaeological Method and Theory*, vol. 8, edited by M. Schiffer, pp. 1–26. Academic Press, New York.
  1986 *Reading the Past: Current Approaches to Interpretation in Archaeology*. Cambridge University Press, Cambridge.
  1991 Interpretive Archaeology and Its Role. *American Antiquity* 56:7–18.
Keene, A.
  1983 Biology, Behavior, and Borrowing: A Critical Examination of Optimal Foraging Theory in Archaeology. In *Archaeological Hammers and Theories*, edited by J. A. Moore and A. S. Keene, pp. 137–155. Academic Press, New York.

Layton, R. (editor)
  1989   *Conflict in the Archaeology of Living Traditions.* Unwin Hyman, London.
Leone, M. P.
  1986   Symbolic, Structural and Critical Archaeology. In *American Archaeology Past and Future: A Celebration of the Society for American Archaeology 1935–1985,* edited by D. J. Meltzer, D. D. Fowler, and J. A. Sabloff, pp. 415–438. Smithsonian Institution Press, Washington, D.C.
Leone, M. P., P. B. Potter, Jr., and P. A. Shackel
  1987   Toward a Critical Archaeology. *Current Anthropology* 28:283–302.
Meehan, B.
  1990   The Long and Winding Road: A Personal Trek Through Antipodean Anthropology. Distinguished Address at the 6th International Conference of Hunting and Gathering Societies, Fairbanks, Alaska.
Miller, D., and C. Tilley (editors)
  1984   *Ideology, Power, and Prehistory.* Cambridge University Press, Cambridge.
Mithen, S.
  1989   Evolutionary Theory and Post-Processual Archaeology. *Antiquity* 63:483–494.
Schiffer, M.
  1988   The Structure of Archaeological Theory. *American Antiquity* 53:461–485.
Shanks, M., and C. Tilley
  1987a   *Re-Constructing Archaeology: Theory and Practice.* Cambridge University Press, Cambridge.
  1987b   *Social Theory and Archaeology.* Polity Press, Cambridge.
Tilley, C.
  1989   Excavation as Theatre. *Antiquity* 63:275–280.
Trigger, B.
  1986   Prehistoric Archaeology and American Society. In *American Archaeology Past and Future: A Celebration of the Society for American Archaeology 1935–1985,* edited by D. J. Meltzer, D. D. Fowler, and J. A. Sabloff, pp. 187–215. Smithsonian Institution Press, Washington, D.C.
  1989   *A History of Archaeological Thought.* Cambridge University Press, Cambridge.
Watson, P. J.
  1990   Review of *Re-Constructing Archaeology* and *Social Archaeology. Journal of Field Archaeology* 17:219–221.
  1991   A Parochial Primer: The New Dissonance As Seen from the Midcontinental United States. In *Processual and Postprocessual Archaeologies: Multiple Ways of Knowing the Past,* edited by R. W. Preucel, pp. 265–274. Center for Archaeological Investigations, Occasional Paper No. 10. Southern Illinois University, Carbondale.
Watson, R.
  1990   Ozymandias, King of Kings: Postprocessual Radical Archaeology as Critique. *American Antiquity* 55:673–689.
Wilk, R. R.
  1985   The Ancient Maya and the Political Present. *Journal of Anthropological Research* 41:307–326.

20. Visions of Archaeology's Future: Some Comments

Jeremy A. Sabloff

> "Why should society pay to be told people don't mean what they say or say what they mean?"
>
> "Because it's true."
>
> "I thought there was no such thing as truth, in the absolute sense."
>
> —David Lodge, *Nice Work*

There is an old story about a physicist and an archaeologist who are both on a small plane flying to an out-of-the-way campus to give lectures. In the midst of the flight, one of the airplane's engines catches fire, and the pilot tells the scholars to put on parachutes and bail out while he tries to save the plane. After jumping out, the physicist pulls his rip cord and his parachute opens. The archaeologist plummets by with his parachute unopened. "Pull your rip cord," yells the physicist. A few moments later he yells, "Pull your rip cord, you have only 1,000 feet to go." "You have only 500 . . . 100 . . . oh, you're only 20 feet above the ground and you're going to die," screams the physicist. "No, it's OK," yells the archaeologist, "I can jump from this height."

I am concerned that the field as a whole is in a situation like that of the archaeologist in the story. We all may be in deeper trouble than we realize unless we develop a more productive theoretical approach, which—despite all the rhetoric, polemic, and intellectual excitement of the new archaeology, postprocessual archaeology, critical archaeology, and so forth—we have still not achieved. Thus, if I were asked what emotions I have when contemplating the current state of the archaeological enterprise, I would have to reply: a mixture of guarded concern and optimism, with the emphasis on the latter.

It would be reasonable to inquire if archaeology is facing a situation in the coming decade that is analogous to that of geography in the 1970s, when

Quandaries and Quests: Visions of Archaeology's Future, edited by LuAnn Wandsnider. Center for Archaeological Investigations, Occasional Paper No. 20. © 1992 by the Board of Trustees, Southern Illinois University. All rights reserved. ISBN 0-88104-075-4.

many departments in the United States were disbanded. The discipline of geography at that time was accused—unfairly in my view—of being descriptively oriented and lacking any theory of its own. It could best be taught, it was argued by some university administrators, in descriptive introductory courses, while its more intellectual concerns could be absorbed by departments of history, anthropology, economics, and sociology.

My answer to such an inquiry would be no. Given the growing student interest on both the undergraduate and graduate levels, the relatively strong availability of funds for field research and analysis, the ever-growing number of professional publications, the broad evidence of huge public interest, as evinced by regular newspaper and magazine articles, television shows, and wide-selling popular books, and the liveliness and vitality of the current theoretical and methodological debates in the discipline, archaeology in the Americas seems to be alive and well.

However, there is no cause for complacency either. Clearly, serious problems face the field, as is revealed in the essays in this volume. While there is nothing inherently wrong with the pluralism of approaches in archaeology today, the gaps appear so great that it may seem as if the field has lost its way. The lack of clear theoretical focus is particularly evident in the teaching and training of introductory graduate students today. It is difficult indeed to point to one or two publications that students can read in order to obtain a grasp of the current intellectual controversies or to understand where the field might be heading in contrast to where it has been or where it stands today.

Given this situation, the four essays that I have been asked to discuss and comment on are especially exciting because they offer four different visions of how archaeology can extricate itself from its apparent anomie. Before turning to the essays, however, let me make two related observations that will provide a partial context for my remarks and give some indication of my personal biases.

First, it is my impression—based on conversations with a wide variety of North American and Latin American scholars, travels throughout the country, and readings of a number of different publications in the academic and cultural resource management arenas—that a number of archaeologists today are still practicing what is in essence a preprocessual archaeology that has only been mildly influenced by new archaeological tenets such as problem orientation. They are undertaking productive fieldwork and laboratory analyses, they apparently assume chronology building as their principal goal, they have a normative view of culture, and they are not deeply concerned with controlling or understanding variability. Presumably, many of them would agree with Courbin (1989) that much of the theoretical writings of the past thirty years can and should be ignored, although none of them have been untouched by processual archaeology.

Second, I find it difficult to consider a postprocessual archaeology when a full-blown processual archaeology has yet to come into being. Although the initial "call to arms" by Lewis Binford and David Clarke garnered great attention, there subsequently has been all too much rhetoric and all too little practice. I believe that the field has been sidetracked from the paths outlined by Binford (see Binford 1972) and Clarke (see D. Clarke 1968) and that much of the early promise has yet to be fulfilled not because processual archaeology has failed, as writers like Courbin (1989), Hodder (1986), and Shanks and Tilley (1987) have argued, but because some of the best methodological, theoretical, and substantive suggestions of the 1960s and early 1970s have not been sufficiently followed. For example, following Clarke (1977), and as recently argued by Richard Hodges (1987), I believe that one of archaeology's greatest strengths—as we are often reminded—is not just time but space as well. Many of the leads of Spatial Archaeology, for instance, cry out for examination but have been largely ignored in recent years as the pendulum of intellectual attention has shifted away from such concerns. I clearly am sympathetic with the argument that it is taking the field longer to develop the tools and methods to reach the goals outlined in the 1960s than the impatient polemicists of that time realized or allowed for and that we should not permit that impatience to dictate the time period needed before processual archaeology is declared a success or failure. At the same time, we must be careful not to confuse the means—the development of the tools and methods—with the larger goals of understanding culture change. Thus, it is my belief that as we enter the 1990s much of the exciting promise of the 1960s remains unfulfilled yet still appears reachable.

With that brief background, let me now turn to the papers by Dunnell, Schiffer, Sullivan, and Kelly. I was momentarily tempted by the thought that I might play a "Great Synthesizer" role and try to combine all four discussions into one tour de force argument, but I was neither sure that it could be done nor that I could do it. However, it is fair to say that a few aspects of the four essays are compatible, although, by and large, this is not the case. I should further note that if my remarks on these essays sound positive or negative, it does not mean that I believe that Dunnell is "right" or Schiffer is "wrong," but that of the legitimate visions of future directions in the field, I find x to have more productive potential than y or that x is closer to my own views.

"Uncertain, indecisive, irresolute, unsettled, inconclusive, unsure, infirm of purpose, doubtful, dubious, hesitant, hesitating, faltering, at loose ends, of two minds, fluctuating, vacillating"—these are all terms that The Synonym Finder (Rodale 1978) lists as synonyms for "ambivalent," which perhaps best defines the emotion I felt after first reading the essays in this section. While I found myself agreeing with many of the arguments being made and seeing considerable merit in the impressive visions of the next decade presented by Dunnell, Schiffer, Sullivan, and Kelly, nevertheless, I frequently found myself muttering, "Yes, but. . . ." It probably would be grossly unfair to expect any one of these scholars to be able to present a completely satisfying program in their relatively short essays. Moreover, it would be unprofitable for me to critically discuss important differences that I might have with the authors on philosophical issues such as my disagreement with Dunnell on whether or not falsification is really the only viable means of explanatory confirmation. So in the space that I have, I thought it might be useful to offer my opinion on the strengths of the programs these scholars have outlined for the 1990s, as well as some of the gaps or problems I perceive.

Turning first to Robert Dunnell's essay, I find much merit in his argument, even though I have a number of questions about its specifics. Dunnell has long been interested in archaeological theory and method in general and evolutionary approaches in particular (see, for instance, Dunnell 1980 or 1989). However, for the first time I believe that I really understand what he means by evolutionary theory in archaeology. Despite some quibbles, he makes a strong case. In fact, although Dunnell would certainly disagree, I believe that he is actually calling for the rigorous application of middle-range theory with the bridging arguments being borne by established laws from the hard sciences rather than by analogies from ethnography or history.

But I find his view—at least as expressed in this volume—too narrow. I wonder whether the kinds of information that will be derived from applying physical laws to aspects of the archaeological record will prove to be relatively trivial. Moreover, there are a number of critical questions about his evolutionary archaeology that Dunnell still has not tackled in an unambiguous fashion. For example, he does not clearly indicate what he considers either the archaeological units of selection or the agents of selection to be. Nor does he go beyond the persuasive case he makes for the application of physical laws to the analysis of the archaeological record to make a link between such applications and the explanation of evolutionary change, if analogs to biological evolution are avoided.

In addition, I have great doubts that Dunnell's vision is one that many archaeologists will find supportable because it is so much at variance with what they consider the subject matter and nature of archaeological research. Moreover, I find it hard to foresee much public support for Dunnell's program. I bring this point up because he frets that the public will soon lose patience with contemporary archaeology's lack of explanatory advance. I fear that the public that supports archaeology would see Dunnell's brand of evolutionary archaeology as much too esoteric and different from what they have been led to believe archaeology is all about—and not very appealing, to boot. However, he might be able to convince a growing number of adherents of its viability through the building piece by piece of a successful series of explanations, particularly if Dunnell can reconcile his more traditional goal of explaining human nature while eschewing interest in "intentional behavior." I can only say to Dunnell, "Go for it."

Turning to the essay by Michael Schiffer, a widely recognized pioneer in modern material culture studies and behavioral archaeology, my general reaction is that he has provided an exciting vision of a new kind of approach to social scientific problems. However, I have the kind of doubt that he must be very tired of hearing, but is nevertheless, I believe, a legitimate reservation. Is this approach really an archaeological one? If so, I found much of it, no matter how stimulating and intriguing, very reminiscent of an archaeological "just-so" story. Like such stories, it may well be right, but to echo Dunnell, how do we know? What differentiates Schiffer's approach from that which business or economic historians might utilize? Presumably, it is more than just an interest in material culture?

We also might ask of Schiffer why his perspective hasn't won more advocates, although he has been a forceful and skilled proponent since the early 1970s. If he labeled this type of research "behavioral anthropology," would it more readily gain adherents? In relation to one of Schiffer's more specific pleas, I do find the one for a relevant archaeology very well taken and appealing. It should also be pointed out that the Dunnell and Schiffer views are really not reconcilable. It will be interesting to see how these opposing visions fare in the coming years.

We next move on to the paper by Alan Sullivan, who has published extensively on site formation processes and Southwestern United States prehistory. Sullivan's arguments for archaeological theory, null hypotheses, and neutral observational language all are well taken. If combined with Dunnell's program, it would provide a broader, more appealing vision, although there appear to be important philosophical differences between the two, particularly as regards Sullivan's interest in behavior. The major problem I see here has to do with observational language. Even if one accepted the philosophical possibility of neutral terms, the task of inventing such a neutral language would be formidable at best, particularly in light of the difficulty of rooting out covert analogies upon which archaeologists have come to rely.

The sentiments expressed by Robert Kelly, an insightful thinker on the changing lifeways of ancient hunter-gatherers, would be hard to disagree with. I am particularly supportive of Kelly's call for archaeologists to recognize the relevancy of their discussions of the past to what is happening today (see, for example, Sabloff 1990:chap. 6). Moreover, I am sympathetic with his argument that there are some compatible elements in the so-called processual and postprocessual approaches, although I strongly feel that the fundamental intellectual thrusts of the two are diametrically opposed. But Kelly does not really make clear how his ecumenical approach, no matter how appealing, would succeed where neither opposing one has succeeded separately to date.

So where can archaeology go from here? If it is going to receive continuing support and have broad appeal, that is, have the relevance that Michael Schiffer so convincingly calls for, as an unrepentant "child" of the 1960s, I would argue that the field must go back to one of the earliest and most central of the new archaeology's tenets: namely, the nature of the human adaptation to the environment and how the human-environmental interaction is systemically related to culture change. Concern with the environment and the need to better understand its use and abuse through space and time will grow in importance in the post–Cold War world of the 1990s. Thus, to my mind, an evolutionary archaeology that broadens its focus to concentrate on exploitation of and adaptation to changing environments will have the greatest chance of success.

While it can be argued that my approach is yet another example of modern political concerns influencing the nature of archaeological thought, I believe that it is not an example of a passing intellectual fancy. Unless global ecological dangers are successfully solved in the next few decades, we will not have to worry about the future of archaeology. It would be ludicrous to argue that archaeology can solve modern ecological problems, but it can feasibly provide a crucial intellectual context to such problem-solving.

When I was younger, I thought that it was useless to plan far ahead because the world might be blown up at any moment. While I am pleased and relieved to find us still here and find myself able to look a little further than I used to, the vision of the globe slowly strangling to death rather than disappearing in one big bang is in many ways even more appalling than earlier fears. I strongly feel that archaeologists can use their research to help the modern world grapple with its ecological distress. Archaeological concern with understanding human-environmental interactions through space and time has been around for many years. It is not trendy, although its significance has increased rapidly in recent years.

If some few colleagues see such interest in an evolutionary archaeology focused in part on human ecology as the result of the capitalistic, colonialist United States's attempt to make up for its past mistakes or as a new attempt to limit freedom of development in the Third World, they would be incorrect, but so be it. I have no apologies in this regard. I believe that an evolutionary ecological archaeology can be justified as an ethical enterprise just as much as any critical archaeological agenda that has been put forward to date.

Robert Dunnell has indicated a possible way to make this approach work, and if his view, as outlined in his essay, is expanded to include some of the ecological insights of recent years—including contributions of evolutionary ecology (see Simms, this volume)—I am guardedly hopeful about its chances of success in the future. However, it may be too optimistic to envision this program's spreading beyond a small group of theoretically oriented archaeologists to the field at large. But so much of what has seemed science fiction at one point in time has more rapidly than anyone ever dreamed possible become science fact. As Arthur C. Clarke (1968) states in the "Foreword" of his classic book *2001: A Space Odyssey*, "Please remember: this is only a work of fiction. The truth, as always, will be far stranger." Perhaps it is not too much to hope that the optimistic programs presented in the four very stimulating essays in this section, in particular, and by many authors throughout this volume, in general, will come to pass within our lifetimes.

Acknowledgments

I am especially grateful to Merrilee Salmon, LuAnn Wandsnider, and Alan Sullivan for their very helpful comments on an earlier draft of this essay and for their suggestions for improving and clarifying the text. In addition, I wish to thank my daughter Saralinda for telling me a version of the story that I recount at the beginning of my discussion. I also wish to thank LuAnn for her kind invitation to participate in the conference and for her skillful organization of the two-day event and of this volume. The stimulating nature of the presentations and discussions helped make the conference one of the most interesting I have ever been privileged to attend.

References

Binford, Lewis R.
    1972   *An Archaeological Perspective*. Seminar Press, New York.
Clarke, Arthur C.
    1968   *2001: A Space Odyssey*. Signet, New York.
Clarke, David L.
    1968   *Analytical Archaeology*. Methuen, London.
Clarke, David L. (editor)
    1977   *Spatial Archaeology*. Academic Press, New York.
Courbin, P.
    1989   *What is Archaeology?* University of Chicago Press, Chicago.
Dunnell, Robert C.
    1980   Evolutionary Theory and Archaeology. In *Advances in Archaeological Method and Theory*, vol. 3, edited by Michael B. Schiffer, pp. 35–99. Academic Press, New York.
    1989   Aspects of the Application of Evolutionary Theory Archaeology. In *Archaeological Thought in America*, edited by C. C. Lamberg-Karlovsky, pp. 35–49. Cambridge University Press, Cambridge.
Hodder, Ian
    1986   *Reading the Past: Current Approaches to Interpretation in Archaeology*. Cambridge University Press, Cambridge.
Hodges, Richard
    1987   Spatial Models, Anthropology and Archaeology. In *Landscape and Culture: Geographical and Archaeological Perspectives*, edited by J. M. Wagstaff, pp. 118–133. Basil Blackwell, Oxford.
Rodale, J. I.
    1978   *The Synonym Finder*. Rodale Press, Emmaus, Pennsylvania.
Sabloff, Jeremy A.
    1990   *The New Archaeology and the Ancient Maya*. A *Scientific American* Library Book. W. H. Freeman, New York.
Shanks, Michael, and Christopher Tilley
    1987   *Re-Constructing Archaeology: Theory and Practice*. Cambridge University Press, Cambridge.

Contributors

Ronald L. Bishop, senior research archaeologist, Conservation Analytical Laboratory, Smithsonian Institution, Washington, D.C.

Linda S. Cordell, Irvine Curator and chairperson, Department of Anthropology, California Academy of Sciences, San Francisco, California.

Robert C. Dunnell, professor, Department of Anthropology, University of Washington, Seattle, Washington.

Lynne Goldstein, associate professor, Department of Anthropology, University of Wisconsin-Milwaukee, Milwaukee, Wisconsin.

Robert L. Kelly, assistant professor, Department of Anthropology, University of Louisville, Louisville, Kentucky.

Timothy A. Kohler, associate professor, Department of Anthropology, Washington State University, Pullman, Washington.

Mark P. Leone, professor, Department of Anthropology, University of Maryland, College Park, Maryland.

Francis P. McManamon, Departmental Consulting Archaeologist, National Park Service, U.S. Department of the Interior, Washington, D.C.

Robert W. Preucel, assistant professor, Department of Anthropology, Harvard University, Cambridge, Massachusetts.

Nan A. Rothschild, associate professor, Department of Anthropology, Barnard College, Columbia University, New York, New York.

Jeremy A. Sabloff, University Professor in Anthropology and the History and Philosophy of Science, Department of Anthropology, University of Pittsburgh, Pittsburgh, Pennsylvania.

Michael Brian Schiffer, professor, Department of Anthropology, University of Arizona, Tucson, Arizona.

Michael J. Shott, assistant professor, Department of Sociology and Anthropology, University of Northern Iowa, Cedar Falls, Iowa.

Alan H. Simmons, associate research professor, Quaternary Sciences Center, Desert Research Institute (University of Nevada System), Reno, Nevada.

Steven R. Simms, associate professor, Department of Sociology, Social Work, and Anthropology, Utah State University, Logan, Utah.

Suzanne M. Spencer-Wood, Schlesinger Library Honorary Visiting Scholar, Radcliffe College, Cambridge, Massachusetts.

Miriam T. Stark, doctoral candidate, Department of Anthropology, University of Arizona, Tucson, Arizona.

Alan P. Sullivan III, assistant professor, Department of Anthropology, University of Cincinnati, Cincinnati, Ohio.

LuAnn Wandsnider, assistant professor, Department of Anthropology, University of Nebraska-Lincoln, Lincoln, Nebraska.

Anne I. Woosley, director, Amerind Foundation, Dragoon, Arizona.

DATE DUE